Green Energy and Technology

Climate change, environmental impact and the limited natural resources urge scientific research and novel technical solutions. The monograph series Green Energy and Technology serves as a publishing platform for scientific and technological approaches to "green"—i.e. environmentally friendly and sustainable—technologies. While a focus lies on energy and power supply, it also covers "green" solutions in industrial engineering and engineering design. Green Energy and Technology addresses researchers, advanced students, technical consultants as well as decision makers in industries and politics. Hence, the level of presentation spans from instructional to highly technical.

Indexed in Scopus.

Indexed in Ei Compendex.

Muhammad Hussain · Tieling Zhang · Uzma Nazir

Hydrogen Pipeline Integrity

Inspection, Risk Assessment, and Mitigation for Future Energy Infrastructure

Springer

Muhammad Hussain
Faculty of Engineering and Information Sciences
University of Wollongong
Wollongong, NSW, Australia

Tieling Zhang
Faculty of Engineering and Information Sciences
University of Wollongong
Wollongong, NSW, Australia

Uzma Nazir
AMCO Reliability Pty Ltd.
Waterford West, QLD, Australia

ISSN 1865-3529 ISSN 1865-3537 (electronic)
Green Energy and Technology
ISBN 978-981-95-5608-3 ISBN 978-981-95-5609-0 (eBook)
https://doi.org/10.1007/978-981-95-5609-0

This Springer imprint is published by the registered company Springer Nature Singapore Pte Ltd.
The registered company address is: 152 Beach Road, #21-01/04 Gateway East, Singapore 189721, Singapore

Preface

As the world undergoes a profound transformation in its pursuit of sustainable and low-carbon energy systems, hydrogen has emerged as a cornerstone of the future energy landscape. Among the many technical, environmental, and logistical challenges accompanying this transition, the integrity and reliability of hydrogen pipeline infrastructure stand out as critical to the success of large-scale hydrogen adoption.

This book, *Hydrogen Pipeline Integrity: Inspection, Risk Assessment, and Mitigation for Future Energy Infrastructure*, offers an authoritative and deeply technical exploration of the challenges and solutions involved in building and maintaining safe, efficient, and robust hydrogen pipelines. It is both timely and essential, providing comprehensive guidance on materials science, inspection methodologies, corrosion mechanisms, quantitative risk assessment, and integrity management strategies tailored to hydrogen's unique properties.

The scope of this work reflects the urgency and complexity of the task at hand. With chapters dedicated to emerging technologies, digital twins, regulatory frameworks, and real-time monitoring systems, the book addresses not only current best practices but also future-proofing strategies that will support the evolution of hydrogen infrastructure across global markets. Equally important are the discussions on environmental, societal, and economic dimensions, highlighting that pipeline integrity is not merely a technical issue, but a multifaceted pillar of energy transition success.

What distinguishes this volume is its systematic structure and multidisciplinary perspective. It balances engineering rigor with practical implementation, making it an indispensable resource for engineers, infrastructure planners, regulators, policymakers, and investors alike. Whether exploring the physics of hydrogen embrittlement or the financial implications of infrastructure retrofitting, the book equips its readers with the tools to make informed, strategic decisions in a rapidly evolving sector.

As we accelerate toward a cleaner energy future, hydrogen pipelines will be the arteries of a new global energy system. Ensuring their integrity is not just a technical imperative—it is a societal obligation. This book rises to meet that challenge, serving as both a technical manual and a strategic guidebook for stakeholders committed to enabling a safe, resilient, and sustainable hydrogen economy.

Wollongong, Australia Muhammad Hussain
Wollongong, Australia Tieling Zhang
Waterford West, Australia Uzma Nazir

Acknowledgments

The development of this book has been both a technical journey and a collaborative endeavor. This work is made possible by the contributions, insights, and encouragement of many individuals and organizations committed to advancing the hydrogen economy.

First and foremost, we extend our deepest gratitude to the researchers, engineers, and practitioners across academia, industry, and government whose groundbreaking work has informed the knowledge presented in this book. Their ongoing efforts to explore hydrogen compatibility, pipeline materials, digital inspection technologies, and risk mitigation strategies have laid the foundation for a safer and more sustainable hydrogen infrastructure.

We are especially thankful to the subject matter experts who generously shared their time, critical feedback, and case study insights throughout the writing process. Their input has been invaluable in ensuring that the content reflects both scientific rigor and practical relevance.

Our appreciation also goes to the organizations and regulatory bodies pioneering hydrogen infrastructure development and setting new benchmarks in safety, innovation, and performance. Their policy papers, technical standards, and public reports have been essential reference points in shaping the scope and direction of this work.

We acknowledge the editorial and production teams who brought clarity and coherence to this complex subject, as well as the support staff and research assistants whose diligent background work helped maintain accuracy and completeness across all chapters.

Finally, we are grateful to our families, colleagues, and professional communities for their unwavering support throughout this endeavor. Their patience and encouragement sustained us during the long hours of research, writing, and review.

To everyone who believes in the promise of hydrogen and is working to make it a safe, scalable, and sustainable energy solution—this book is for you.

Muhammad Hussain
Tieling Zhang
Uzma Nazir

Contents

List of Figures

List of Tables

Chapter 1
Introduction to Hydrogen in the Energy Transition

1.1 Introduction

Hydrogen is increasingly recognized as a crucial component in the transition toward sustainable energy systems [1, 2]. As the world seeks to reduce carbon emissions and shift to cleaner energy sources, hydrogen, as a clean energy carrier, offers significant potential to decarbonize in various sectors, particularly when integrated into existing natural gas infrastructure [3]. Global hydrogen demand exceeded 97 Mt in 2023 and could approach 100 Mt in 2024. This growth, however, reflects broader economic trends rather than effective policy implementation [4]. However, the integrity management of hydrogen pipelines presents unique challenges that must be systematically reviewed to ensure safe and efficient operations [5]. The transportation of hydrogen, whether in pure form or blended with natural gas, necessitates a thorough understanding of material compatibility, risk factors, and maintenance strategies involved in pipeline systems [6–8].

Hydrogen's integration into energy systems is a growing trend, supported by a surge in government policies, industrial initiatives, and international collaborations [9]. For instance, the European Union's Green Deal and Hydrogen Strategy, Japan's Basic Hydrogen Strategy, and South Korea's Hydrogen Economy Roadmap have set ambitious targets for hydrogen adoption, including the development of extensive pipeline networks [10, 11]. These initiatives reflect a global consensus that hydrogen can play a pivotal role in achieving net-zero carbon emissions by 2050. Yet, despite the enthusiasm, there is a critical need to address the challenges associated with transporting hydrogen safely and efficiently through pipelines, which serve as the backbone of any large-scale hydrogen economy [12–14].

The regional distribution of hydrogen demand showed minimal variation from 2022, with China leading as the largest consumer, representing nearly one-third of global demand (exceeding 29 Mt), almost twice the usage of North America, the second-largest consumer at around 16 Mt (16% of global demand). While hydrogen demand experienced moderate growth across major regions, the Middle East recorded

M. Hussain et al., *Hydrogen Pipeline Integrity*, Green Energy and Technology,
https://doi.org/10.1007/978-981-95-5609-0_1

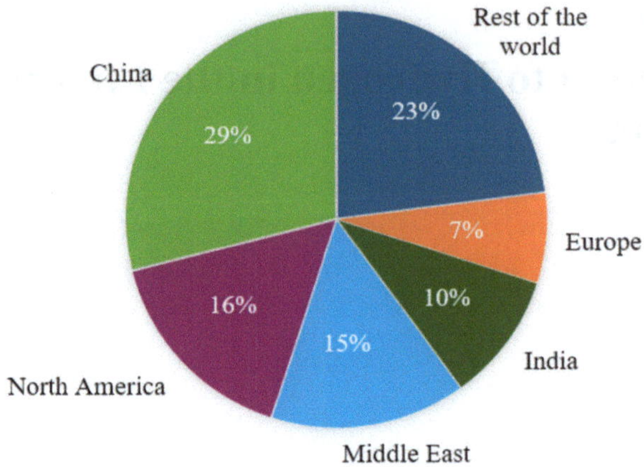

Fig. 1.1 Hydrogen use by region, 2024

a more pronounced increase (almost 6% year-on-year), driven by rising requirements in refining and methanol production, and India recorded a growth of over 4% year-on-year, attributed to higher demand in refining and steel industries, see Fig. 1.1 [4].

Approximately 130 export-oriented projects for low-emissions hydrogen production have been identified, with capacities ranging from a few kilotonnes to 3.6 Mtpa for the largest project. Five major projects alone represent 8.3 Mtpa, or half of the total planned export-oriented production of 16 Mtpa by 2030. However, none of these projects has reached a final investment decision (FID); one is in the feasibility study phase, and four are in very early development stages. Consequently, the actual volume of low-emissions hydrogen traded by 2030 could vary considerably based on the advancement of these large projects. Figure 1.2 shows the total pipeline length for hydrogen around the Globe.

Recent studies have highlighted the importance of adapting existing natural gas pipelines for hydrogen transport, emphasizing the need for robust integrity management frameworks that incorporate advanced monitoring and maintenance practices [7, 15, 16]. The integration of data-driven methodologies, such as risk-based inspection and predictive maintenance, can enhance the reliability of hydrogen pipeline systems [15, 17, 18]. Furthermore, the establishment of regulatory standards and guidelines specific to hydrogen transport is essential to ensure safety and operational efficiency [8, 19].

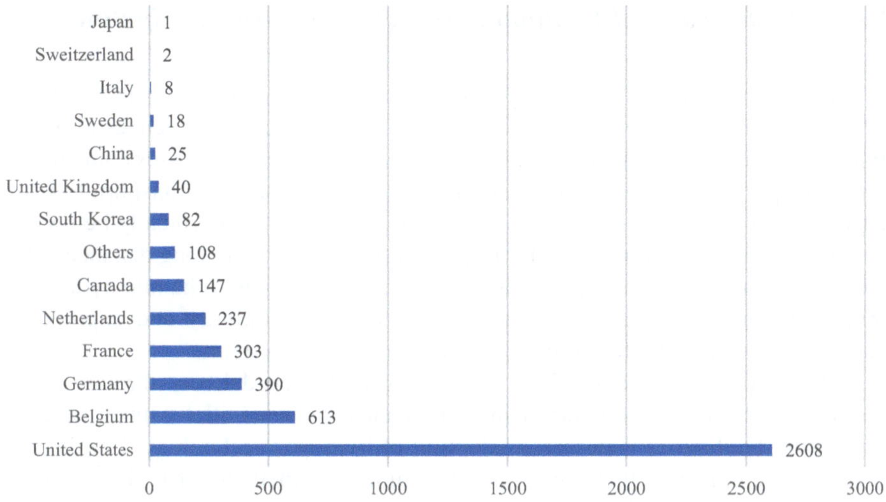

Fig. 1.2 Length of hydrogen pipelines worldwide

1.1.1 The Importance of Hydrogen as an Energy Carrier

Hydrogen demonstrates significant promise as a clean energy carrier, particularly when produced via renewable energy sources, known as green hydrogen. The adoption of green hydrogen aligns with global efforts to combat climate change by reducing greenhouse gas emissions. The International Energy Agency (IEA) suggests that integrating hydrogen into the energy mix can yield substantial environmental benefits, especially in hard-to-decarbonize sectors such as heavy industry, shipping, and aviation [20]. Through well-designed hydrogen networks, renewable energy can be harnessed efficiently and stored for various applications, thereby addressing the intermittency of renewable sources like solar and wind power.

Hydrogen pipelines facilitate large-scale transport over long distances and provide a practical solution for overcoming logistical challenges associated with hydrogen delivery. According to Zhang et al. [8] existing natural gas pipelines can be repurposed for hydrogen transport through blending hydrogen with natural gas, thereby utilizing advanced technologies to ensure efficient and safe delivery. This method not only capitalizes on established infrastructure but also minimizes the costs and complexities of building entirely new systems. The strategic blending of hydrogen with natural gas can represent a significant transitional step toward a fully hydrogen-based infrastructure while maintaining energy security.

1.1.2 Technical and Economic Aspects of Hydrogen Pipelines

The reliance on pipelines for hydrogen transport offers several technical advantages, including efficient delivery mechanisms and cost-effectiveness. Pipelines allow the transportation of large quantities of hydrogen with lower energy losses compared to other transport methods, such as tanker trucks or compressed gas transport. Pipeline networks can efficiently handle gaseous hydrogen at pressures typically below 100 bars, which facilitates economical transport over both short and long distances [21]. While challenges remain in adapting existing pipe materials to handle hydrogen's unique properties and associated risks, advances in metallurgy and engineering continue to enhance the feasibility of hydrogen pipeline systems.

In terms of economic viability, integrating hydrogen delivery through repurposed natural gas infrastructure can significantly reduce initial capital expenditures while facilitating widespread adoption of hydrogen technology. Cerniauskas et al. [22] demonstrate that transitioning natural gas pipelines for hydrogen transport can achieve cost reductions exceeding 60%, aligning expenditures with current infrastructural capabilities and ongoing energy demands. Furthermore, reducing hydrogen's transportation costs is pivotal in making it competitive against more conventional fossil fuel resources, facilitating its adoption as a mainstream energy source [23].

1.1.3 Regulatory Framework and Global Policies

The ambitious vision of a hydrogen-based economy requires robust policy frameworks that incentivize investment and facilitate the safe integration of hydrogen technologies into the existing energy landscape. Regulatory standards must evolve to address the specific challenges posed by hydrogen, particularly concerning safety, transport, and production technologies. Chen et al. [24] note that many countries have begun developing guidelines and best practices for hydrogen pipeline systems, resulting in comprehensive standards that enable safe and efficient hydrogen transport mechanisms. As nations strive to standardize practices, ensuring compliance with safety regulations will be paramount to mitigate risks associated with hydrogen transport and enhance public trust in hydrogen technologies.

In the context of international collaboration, substantial momentum exists to create a global hydrogen market where countries can trade hydrogen based on their production capabilities. The establishment of hydrogen corridors across borders will streamline trade, improve energy security, and incentivize innovation in hydrogen technologies. The G20 nations play a significant role in promoting these global strategic collaborations, focusing on geopolitical strategies that support the development of clean hydrogen technologies [25].

1.2 Background and Importance

An overview of the hydrogen industry chain is shown in Fig. 1.3 [8]. Unlike conventional natural gas, hydrogen presents unique challenges due to its small molecular size, high diffusivity, and propensity to cause material degradation, often leading to potential risks such as leaks, embrittlement, and cracking [26]. Hydrogen contains more energy per unit of mass than natural gas or gasoline, making it attractive as a transport fuel [27]. These properties necessitate specialized considerations in pipeline design, material selection, and maintenance practices.

The potential for hydrogen embrittlement, increased permeability, and material fatigue presents a considerable concern for the safe and efficient transport of hydrogen [26, 28, 29]. As a result, ensuring the integrity of hydrogen pipelines is not only a matter of engineering but also a critical issue for the large-scale adoption of hydrogen as a clean energy solution [30, 31]. Understanding these challenges is paramount for developing effective inspection, monitoring, and maintenance strategies that will enable the safe and sustainable use of hydrogen pipelines [32–34].

The growth in investments has been accompanied by a substantial increase in the number of announced hydrogen projects, reflecting the sector's global expansion. The number of projects in the pipeline has surged from 228 in December 2020 to 1,572 in May 2024, with a notable rise in projects reaching the committed stage, increasing from 102 to 434 over the same period. Since 2020, the clean hydrogen supply capacity past Final Investment Decision (FID) for 2030 has expanded significantly, growing from 716 tonnes per annum (kt p.a.) dominated by low-carbon hydrogen to 4.6 million tonnes per annum (Mt p.a.), with a more balanced split between low-carbon and renewable hydrogen sources.

Between 2020 and 2024, the planned clean hydrogen supply capacity through 2030 has risen dramatically from approximately 7 to 48 Mt p.a., consistent with the growth in the number of projects. This trend suggests that the average project size has remained relatively constant, likely influenced by the prevalence of large-scale

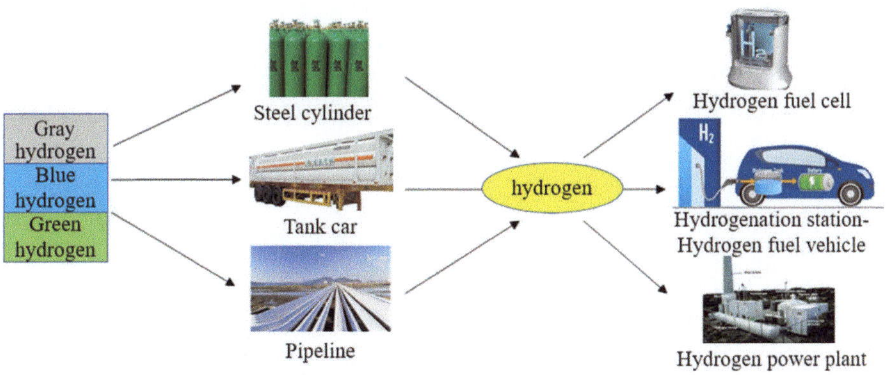

Fig. 1.3 Overview of the hydrogen industry chain [8]

low-carbon projects deployed before 2020, particularly in conjunction with carbon capture and storage (CCS) technologies. Furthermore, the current project pipeline includes nearly 200 giga-scale projects, which represent approximately two-thirds of the total announced supply capacity through 2030.

Concurrently, the composition of hydrogen supply has shifted. In 2020, renewable hydrogen accounted for about 60% of the total supply, a figure that has increased to approximately 75% by 2024. This shift reflects the growing number of announced projects in regions rich in renewable energy resources, such as Latin America, Australia, Africa, and the Middle East, see Fig. 1.4 for an overview of hydrogen projects between 2020 and 2024 [35].

In 2020, Europe dominated the development of hydrogen projects, accounting for 55% of the global project pipeline by the number of projects. However, recent years have seen a notable geographical shift, with the Global South taking on an increasingly prominent role in the hydrogen project landscape. Europe's share of projects within the global pipeline has decreased to 40%, despite an increase in the absolute number of projects from 125 in 2020 to over 600 by 2024. North America has emerged as the second-largest region, now accounting for 20% of the global pipeline, followed by China and Latin America, each contributing 10%.

Notably, North America has experienced the most significant relative growth in projects that have reached the committed stage. The number of projects past Final Investment Decision (FID) in North America has surged from fewer than 10 in 2020 to nearly 100 by 2024. As a result, North America's share of projects past FID has increased substantially, rising to more than 20% of the global total, compared to less

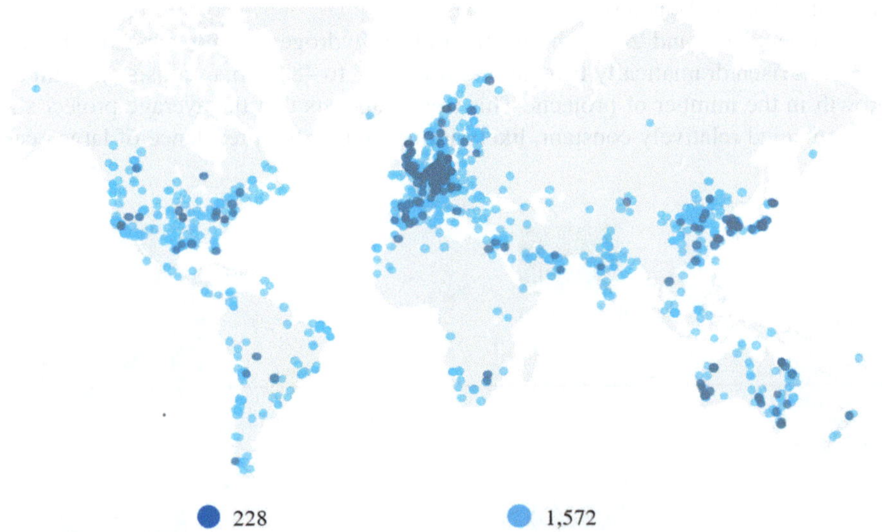

Fig. 1.4 Project overview for December 2020 versus May 2024 [35]

than 10% in 2020. This reflects a broader trend of increasing hydrogen development activity in North America.

1.3 The Role of Hydrogen in Global Decarbonization

Hydrogen has emerged as a critical player in the pursuit of global decarbonization, serving as a versatile energy carrier that can facilitate the transition to cleaner energy systems while addressing pressing climate challenges. The transition away from fossil fuels is underscored by hydrogen's potential to decarbonize various sectors, including transportation, industry, and power generation. As emphasized by Andrews and Shabani [36], renewable energy sources play a decisive role in pre-empting catastrophic climate change, with hydrogen fueling various transport modes as a key component of a sustainable energy strategy.

Substantial research has demonstrated that hydrogen derived from renewable sources, known as green hydrogen, provides an effective means to mitigate greenhouse gas emissions. In particular, the work of Zhong and Wu [37] highlights the importance of cohesive strategies for deploying distributed green hydrogen systems, especially in urban communities across North America. By analyzing deployment strategies across a broader range of future climate conditions, they establish that green hydrogen systems can significantly enhance energy sustainability in line with evolving climate conditions.

The benefits of hydrogen extend beyond mere emission reductions; they encompass economic and societal dimensions as well. The establishment of a green hydrogen economy is pivotal for rapidly delivering low-carbon energy solutions that can meet ambitious decarbonization targets [38]. Investments in hydrogen infrastructure can stimulate local economies, create job opportunities, and lead to innovations in sustainable technology. Despite existing challenges regarding the high cost of hydrogen production and the readiness of distribution infrastructures, strategic advancements can drive the adoption of green hydrogen solutions [39]. Moreover, as hydrogen's role expands, it is essential to consider its environmental impacts closely. Current research underscores both the short- and long-term climate implications of hydrogen emissions. Ocko and Hamburg [40] argue that hydrogen can lead to warming effects in the near term, which must be considered alongside its long-term benefits. Understanding these dynamics is critical for policymakers when assessing hydrogen deployment alongside other clean technologies, ensuring that such strategies do not inadvertently exacerbate climate issues. Indeed, the interplay between immediate climate impacts and long-term benefits poses a nuanced challenge for the integration of hydrogen into existing systems.

One promising development in hydrogen usage is the creation of Hydrogen Valleys—localized ecosystems that showcase the production, distribution, and use of hydrogen. According to Bekele et al. [38], these Hydrogen Valleys have significant potential to accelerate local energy system decarbonization, provided that technological advancements and adequate infrastructure can support their implementation. By fostering localized hydrogen integration, these initiatives become instrumental not only in reducing carbon footprints but also in catalyzing community involvement in sustainable energy transitions. The implications of hydrogen on a global scale also extend to international energy markets. Hydrogen can facilitate the trade of energy between countries, enriching energy security by diversifying energy sources and routes. As more nations commit to hydrogen as part of their energy strategy, the potential for cross-border hydrogen trade becomes increasingly apparent.

Despite its promise, the deployment of hydrogen is accompanied by several challenges. For instance, significant investment is needed in both production technologies and transport infrastructure to make green hydrogen accessible and economical. Initiatives such as the industrialization of electrolysis technology are vital for scaling up hydrogen production capacity efficiently and sustainably [39]. Strategic policies that incentivize research and development, coupled with international collaborations, are essential for overcoming the logistical hurdles associated with hydrogen logistics and distribution. Moreover, societal aspects related to the deployment of hydrogen technology cannot be overlooked. Zhong and Wu [37] emphasize that increasing discussions on social justice and ethical concerns are essential for ensuring diverse communities can benefit from energy transition decisions. Energy policies must be inclusive, addressing existing inequalities while maximizing access to the advantages of hydrogen technologies. Engaging communities in the development and deployment phases can enhance acceptance and promote widespread adoption of hydrogen systems.

1.4 Evolution and Overview of Hydrogen Infrastructure

The evolution of hydrogen infrastructure has been shaped by a confluence of technological, economic, and policy factors that reflect hydrogen's growing prominence in the global energy landscape. This section reviews the development of infrastructure critical for the production, transport, storage, and utilization of hydrogen, with a focus on pipeline systems, which are essential for enabling the widespread adoption of hydrogen energy.

Historically, pipeline transportation has been recognized as one of the most efficient methods for conveying hydrogen, given its capacity to move significant volumes over long distances at reduced costs compared to other transport methods such as truck or rail transport [23]. The establishment of hydrogen pipelines has accelerated since the early 2000s, driven by increasing demand for cleaner energy sources and the need to transition away from fossil fuels. As highlighted by Chen et al. [24], the development of standards and guidelines for hydrogen pipeline systems is critical, as they facilitate safe and efficient operations across various scales and regions. Countries like China have initiated comprehensive standards for hydrogen pipeline transportation, aiming to build a robust infrastructure that can support growing hydrogen sectors.

In Europe and North America, established natural gas pipeline networks present potential pathways for hydrogen integration, with many studies advocating for the repurposing of existing resources for hydrogen transport. For example, Cerniauskas et al. [22] demonstrate through a German case study that adapting natural gas pipelines for hydrogen use is economically advantageous, allowing for continuity in infrastructure investment while transitioning to cleaner energy. The practice of blending hydrogen with natural gas in existing pipelines presents a viable transitional strategy, enabling the gradual incorporation of hydrogen without necessitating the immediate construction of dedicated hydrogen pipelines [41].

Recent advancements have also focused on ensuring the integrity and safety of hydrogen transport, particularly in light of unique challenges posed by hydrogen's properties, such as its low molecular weight, high diffusivity, and potential for embrittlement of pipeline materials [42]. Research by Capelle et al. [42] underscores the importance of selecting appropriate materials and ensuring robust design to mitigate risks related to hydrogen transport, particularly in higher concentrations. As a result, ongoing investigations into suitable alloy formulations and pipeline configurations have gained traction to enhance performance and longevity in hydrogen service.

To facilitate the economic viability of hydrogen delivery, various technologies are being explored, including advanced compressors and hydrogen-specific pipeline materials that withstand the effects of hydrogen embrittlement [43]. This focus on innovation has spurred investments in hydrogen hub networks that integrate production, storage, and transportation within localized systems, which can transition into larger-scale infrastructure over time. Several regions are implementing hydrogen hubs, emphasizing local production linked to existing natural gas networks, thereby enhancing regional energy resilience and sustainability.

Globally, the perspective on hydrogen infrastructure is also evolving to incorporate environmental and geopolitical considerations. As emphasized by Noussan et al. [44], hydrogen plays a significant role in energy transition strategies, particularly in decarbonizing sectors traditionally dependent on fossil fuels. The integration of hydrogen into national energy portfolios is often accompanied by strategic roadmaps and policies that aim to align infrastructure development with sustainability goals. For instance, significant investments in public–private partnerships are essential for building robust value chains that cover all aspects of hydrogen utilization, from generation to end-use applications.

A notable aspect of the hydrogen infrastructure evolution is the increasing importance of regulatory and policy frameworks that govern the development of hydrogen supply chains. These frameworks tend to encourage technological innovation and provide clarity for investors looking to finance hydrogen infrastructure projects. According to Zhang et al. [8], clear guidelines and incentives for hydrogen infrastructure can lead to accelerated deployment of hydrogen technologies, making them more accessible to end users. This trend is also evident in the establishment of dedicated hydrogen corridors, such as those being developed in Europe and Asia, which facilitate the cross-border transport of hydrogen and promote international cooperation in energy transition strategies [45].

An essential consideration in hydrogen infrastructure development is the role of cities and urban environments, where hydrogen use can complement broader sustainable urban strategies. The integration of hydrogen-based systems for heating, transportation, and power generation within urban contexts allows for more efficient urban energy ecosystems and attractive solutions to local energy challenges.

1.5 Overview of Pipeline Systems for Hydrogen

Understanding the infrastructure necessary for hydrogen delivery involves examining various aspects of pipeline systems, including design and construction standards, material selection, operational safety, and the key differences between hydrogen and natural gas pipelines.

1.5.1 Design and Construction Standards

The design and construction standards for hydrogen pipeline systems are essential to achieve safe, efficient, and reliable hydrogen transport. This section examines the key standards currently guiding the design and construction of hydrogen pipelines, focusing on the technical requirements, material choices, safety measures, and regulatory frameworks that govern these activities.

1.5.1.1 Technical Standards for Hydrogen Pipelines

The development of specific technical standards for hydrogen pipelines has become increasingly vital as the hydrogen economy matures. Hydrogen transports via pipelines entail unique challenges due to the gas's physical properties, including high diffusivity, low density, and the propensity for embrittlement in metallic materials. To address these challenges, several relevant standards have been established or are in development.

One of the primary design standards applicable to hydrogen pipelines is the ASME B31.12, which provides guidelines for hydrogen piping systems, including the materials, design, construction, and operation aspects unique to hydrogen infrastructure [46]. This standard aims to enhance safety and performance while addressing hydrogen-specific risks. As volatility in hydrogen can pose significant risks, compliance with ASME B31.12 ensures that pipeline systems are designed with adequate provisions for pressures, material compatibility, and installation practices. In addition to ASME B31.12, other standards such as the ISO/TS 19880-1 offer guidance on hydrogen fuel quality and safety requirements for hydrogen refueling stations, which also apply to hydrogen pipelines. This standard is significant as it defines the parameters that ensure compatibility between the pipeline materials and the transported hydrogen, aiming for a reliable infrastructure.

1.5.1.2 Material Selection and Quality Assurance

Selecting appropriate materials for hydrogen pipelines is paramount, given the risks posed by hydrogen embrittlement, which can significantly reduce material toughness and fatigue resistance. Research has shown that different steel alloys exhibit varying degrees of resistance to hydrogen-induced degradation. Therefore, materials such as high-strength steels with careful alloy compositions have been recommended.

The European standard EN 1594 outlines pipelines for the transport of gases, including natural gas and hydrogen, emphasizing the need for quality assurance and rigorous testing [47]. Following this standard ensures that the materials used in the construction of hydrogen pipelines maintain integrity throughout their operational life. Implementing a framework for quality assurance additionally ensures compliance with technical specifications, which govern material performance under pressurized conditions.

The need for regular monitoring and inspection of hydrogen pipelines cannot be overstated. The standards advocate for the integration of asset management protocols, predictive maintenance practices, and real-time monitoring systems to detect early signs of degradation or failure. By employing advanced inspection techniques, including ultrasonic testing and fiber-optic sensors, operators can ensure that pipeline integrity is maintained and safety is prioritized.

1.5.1.3 Safety and Environmental Considerations

Safety is a critical consideration in the design and construction of hydrogen pipelines. Comprehensive risk assessments must be conducted to evaluate potential hazards, ensure proper emergency response mechanisms, and implement safety management systems. The NFPA 2 standard, promulgated by the National Fire Protection Association, covers the safety aspects of hydrogen systems, including those related to fire and explosive hazards [48]. Operators must adhere to these safety regulations throughout the pipeline's lifecycle, from design to decommissioning.

Environmental considerations also play a significant role in shaping the design and construction standards for hydrogen pipelines. Environmental impact assessments (EIA) are required to evaluate the potential effects of constructing and operating hydrogen pipelines on ecosystems and surrounding communities [49]. These assessments should identify risks such as soil contamination, disturbance of habitats, and potential emissions during construction activities. Regulations concerning land use, restoration, and mitigation strategies must be incorporated into pipeline planning and execution to minimize ecological footprints.

1.5.1.4 Regulatory Framework and Compliance

A well-defined regulatory framework is essential to facilitate the safe and effective development of hydrogen infrastructure. In many regions, hydrogen pipeline construction is regulated by existing gas pipeline regulations; however, adapting and updating these to consider hydrogen-specific properties and risks is necessary. For instance, European Union member states are gradually aligning national regulations with the overarching EU Hydrogen Strategy, mandating clear pathways for constructing hydrogen infrastructure and ensuring compliance with international safety protocols.

Collaboration among industry stakeholders, regulators, and researchers is critical to developing coherent regulations that can foster innovation while prioritizing public safety and the environment. Regulatory bodies need to promote dialogue among stakeholders to refine standards continually and incorporate cutting-edge technologies into hydrogen pipeline design and construction practices.

1.5.2 Differences Between Hydrogen and Natural Gas Pipelines

The differences between hydrogen and natural gas pipelines significantly influence their design, construction, operation, and safety. As the energy landscape shifts towards greater use of hydrogen as a clean energy carrier, understanding these distinctions is crucial for developing effective and efficient pipeline infrastructure. This section delves into the key differences, focusing on material properties, operational conditions, safety considerations, and economic aspects.

1.5.2.1 Material Properties and Design Considerations

One of the most significant differences lies in the materials used for pipeline construction. Hydrogen, with its small molecular size and low viscosity, poses unique challenges as it can cause embrittlement in many metals, particularly in common piping materials used for natural gas, such as carbon steel. Research indicates that hydrogen embrittlement can lead to a significant loss of ductility and tensile strength in pipeline steels, necessitating the use of specialized materials that can withstand these effects. In contrast, natural gas pipelines can effectively utilize standard carbon steel due to the gas's larger molecular structure and the resulting lack of interaction with the material.

The design standards applicable to hydrogen pipelines, such as ASME B31.12, specifically address unique challenges posed by hydrogen transport, including the risk of embrittlement and the need for higher-quality materials [50]. These considerations differ from those used in natural gas pipeline design, where the primary focus is on ensuring durability and safety under relatively stable pressure regimes.

In the context of pipeline construction, appropriate welding techniques must be employed to minimize the potential for defects that could exacerbate the risk of hydrogen permeation and embrittlement. Research shows that the welding methods used in hydrogen systems must account for the risk of hydrogen-induced cracking and be tailored to the specific materials chosen for hydrogen service.

1.5.2.2 Operational Conditions

Operational conditions, such as pressure and temperature requirements, also differ markedly between hydrogen and natural gas pipelines. Hydrogen pipelines typically operate at higher pressures—often exceeding 100 bar—to deliver significant quantities of gas while maintaining efficiency. This pressure range can induce different mechanical stresses than those experienced in natural gas pipelines, which often operate at lower pressures. Higher operational pressures necessitate stringent safety measures, including robust monitoring systems, to ensure pipeline integrity [51].

The Joule-Thomson effect also exhibits differences between hydrogen and natural gas, impacting how each gas behaves under pressure within pipelines. For instance, hydrogen expands and cools more rapidly than natural gas, leading to different thermal management requirements in pipeline systems [52]. This factor must be taken into account during the design and operation of hydrogen pipelines, as inadequate thermal management could create conditions favorable for condensation or other operational risks.

1.5.2.3 Safety Considerations

Safety considerations represent a crucial area where hydrogen and natural gas pipelines diverge. Hydrogen, being flammable and having a wider range of flammability, poses different safety risks compared to natural gas. Studies have shown that hydrogen flames are less visible and have a higher diffusivity, complicating leak detection and emergency response [53]. Hydrogen's potential to accumulate in confined spaces increases the risk of explosions, making the safety protocols for hydrogen pipelines markedly different from those applicable to natural gas pipelines.

Natural gas pipeline networks have established decades of operational history, while hydrogen pipelines are still emerging, leading many safety standards to adapt from natural gas regulations without fully addressing hydrogen-specific risks. Regulatory measures must evolve to encompass the unique hazards associated with hydrogen, necessitating specialized training for personnel involved in the operation and maintenance of hydrogen pipeline systems.

Proper risk assessment methodologies are necessary to evaluate pipeline integrity, and specialized technologies, such as fiber-optic sensing and advanced monitoring techniques, are employed to enhance safety. The potential for leakage in hydrogen pipelines also necessitates comprehensive emergency response plans that exceed those traditionally used in natural gas systems.

1.5.2.4 Economic Aspects

From an economic perspective, constructing hydrogen pipelines tends to be more expensive than natural gas pipelines. The material and construction costs associated with pipelines designed to handle hydrogen's unique properties can be substantial, often estimated to be 30–50% higher than those for natural gas pipelines [54]. An analysis of repurposing existing natural gas infrastructure for hydrogen transport has been proposed as a cost-effective intermediate solution to mitigate initial investment costs while facilitating the transition to a hydrogen economy.

The ongoing development of regulatory frameworks and standards specific to hydrogen pipelines will continue to define the economic landscape as the hydrogen market grows. The integration of effective blending methods for hydrogen in natural gas pipelines represents a potential economic strategy that enables operators to utilize existing assets while gradually introducing hydrogen into the energy mix. However, achieving optimal operational efficiency in hydrogen transport through natural gas pipelines remains contingent upon understanding the limitations in blending ratios and operational risks associated with varying gas compositions [54].

1.6 Advantages of Hydrogen Pipelines

The development of a reliable and efficient hydrogen infrastructure is a cornerstone for the successful transition to a low-carbon energy system. Among various hydrogen transportation methods, pipelines represent one of the most promising options for moving large volumes of hydrogen over both short and long distances. Unlike road or sea transport, pipelines offer a dedicated, continuous channel that can deliver hydrogen in a controlled and cost-efficient manner. As hydrogen production scales up, especially from renewable sources such as electrolysis powered by wind or solar energy, the ability to transport this energy carrier safely and economically becomes increasingly critical.

Hydrogen pipelines offer a range of advantages spanning technical, economic, environmental, and operational domains. These include enhanced safety due to reduced handling and transport risks, lower operational costs over extended distances, and the potential for integration with existing natural gas pipeline infrastructure. Additionally, pipelines enable steady and high-capacity transport, supporting the growing demand for hydrogen in industrial applications, fuel cell vehicles, and power generation. Understanding these advantages is essential for policymakers, industry stakeholders, and engineers tasked with designing hydrogen delivery systems that are scalable, sustainable, and resilient.

1.6.1 Enhanced Safety and Reliability

Hydrogen pipelines are engineered to stringent safety standards that minimize leakage and rupture risks. Compared to trucking compressed hydrogen gas or liquid hydrogen, pipelines provide a continuous and controlled environment for hydrogen transport, significantly reducing the risk of accidents as briefly discussed in Table 1.1.

1.6.1.1 Cost Efficiency Over Long Distances

While initial capital costs for hydrogen pipelines are significant, the operational expenditure (OPEX) tends to be lower than other transport methods over long distances, refer to Table 1.2. Pipelines avoid recurring fuel costs associated with trucks or ships and benefit from economies of scale.

1.6.1.2 Environmental Benefits

Hydrogen pipelines contribute to reducing greenhouse gas emissions by lowering the energy intensity associated with transport [55]. Unlike trucking, which relies on fossil fuel-powered vehicles, pipeline operation can be powered by renewable energy sources, especially when employing electrically driven compressors.

Table 1.1 Comparative safety metrics of hydrogen transport methods

Parameter	Hydrogen pipelines	Truck transport	Liquefied hydrogen shipping
Leak probability	Very low	Moderate	Moderate to high
Accident rate (per km) (%)	0.01	0.1	0.05
Pressure regulation	Automated, continuous	Manual/periodic	Manual/periodic
Safety incidents impact	Contained	Potentially severe	Potentially severe

Table 1.2 Cost and energy efficiency comparison of hydrogen transport methods

Cost component	Pipelines	Trucking	Liquefied hydrogen shipping
Capital cost (USD/km)	High (e.g., $1–3 million)	Moderate (per vehicle)	High (port + ship infrastructure)
Operating cost (USD/MWh)	Low ($1–3)	High ($10–20)	Moderate ($5–10)
Energy loss (%)	~10–15% (compression)	~20–30% (fuel)	~20% (liquefaction & boil-off)

Table 1.3 Infrastructure adaptability and scalability metrics

Feature	Hydrogen pipelines	Dedicated hydrogen trucks	Adaptability
Integration with natural gas network	Possible (up to 20%)	Not applicable	High
Capacity scalability	High (thousands of tons/day)	Low (tons per truckload)	Moderate
Continuous flow	Yes	No	Yes

1.6.1.3 Scalability and Integration with Existing Infrastructure

Hydrogen pipelines can be integrated with existing natural gas pipelines (blending hydrogen up to certain percentages), reducing infrastructure costs and accelerating deployment as shown in Table 1.3. This scalability supports gradual market expansion from localized production to widespread hydrogen distribution networks.

1.7 Technical and Economic Benefits of Hydrogen Pipelines

The development and deployment of hydrogen pipelines present significant technical and economic advantages that are pivotal for the transition towards a sustainable energy landscape. As the world increasingly recognizes the critical role of hydrogen in decarbonization, hydrogen pipelines become essential for facilitating the large-scale transport of hydrogen from production sites to end-users.

1.7.1 Technical Benefits of Hydrogen Pipelines

One of the foremost technical advantages of hydrogen pipelines is their ability to efficiently transport large volumes of hydrogen over long distances. As articulated by Fekete et al. [56], pipelines are particularly effective at conveying hydrogen due to their lower friction losses and capability to handle high pressure compared to other transport modes like trucking or rail. Utilizing pipelines minimizes logistical complexities and reduces delivery timeframes, thus ensuring a more reliable supply of hydrogen to various sectors. This efficiency is demonstrated across existing natural gas pipeline networks, where repurposing for hydrogen transport has been proven technically feasible [7].

Safety remains a paramount consideration in hydrogen pipeline technology. Hydrogen's unique characteristics—its light molecular weight, diffusivity, and propensity for embrittlement—pose challenges to pipeline integrity. As identified by Capelle et al., extensive research into materials suited for hydrogen transport is ongoing to mitigate risks of hydrogen embrittlement and maintain pipeline durability

[42]. The development of specialized materials and advanced monitoring technologies will enhance the resilience of hydrogen pipelines, ensuring long-term safety and operational efficiency.

The integration of existing natural gas infrastructure presents an opportunity to leverage established networks for hydrogen distribution. This not only accelerates the speed of hydrogen deployment but also reduces the capital costs associated with building new pipeline systems [22]. A case study in Germany estimates that reassignment of natural gas pipelines for hydrogen can cut transmission costs by over 60%, greatly enhancing economic feasibility [22]. These synergies make hydrogen pipelines a pragmatic choice for communities transitioning to hydrogen energy systems.

1.7.2 Economic Benefits of Hydrogen Pipelines

The economic case for hydrogen pipelines is supported by several factors that underscore the cost-effectiveness of this transportation mode. According to Fekete et al., pipeline delivery of hydrogen is particularly advantageous in densely populated areas, where demand is highest, as it reduces costs associated with transportation logistics while promptly meeting energy needs [56]. The scalability of pipeline systems means that they can be adapted to accommodate increasing hydrogen demand as market conditions evolve.

The construction of dedicated hydrogen pipelines carries significant upfront costs, which must be justified through long-term operational savings and enhanced reliability [24]. However, current analogous systems are increasingly demonstrating that the cost of establishing hydrogen pipelines can become competitive over time, especially as technologies mature and production costs reduce. Zhang et al. [8] posit that a comprehensive analysis of hydrogen blending within natural gas infrastructure reveals positive economic ramifications, especially in operational cost reduction through infrastructure retrofitting.

The economic benefits of hydrogen pipelines also extend to job creation and local economic stimulation. With the establishment of hydrogen networks, local economies can experience growth through the development of new markets for hydrogen technology, including production facilities and maintenance services for pipeline systems. This local focus can create jobs across various skill levels, fostering community engagement while advancing regional energy independence [57].

In terms of overall energy costs, optimizing the hydrogen transport system through pipelines helps stabilize energy prices and increases market competition. Efficient pipeline systems ensure a steady flow of hydrogen, essential for market pricing dynamics in the energy market and fostering customer confidence in hydrogen as a sustainable alternative fuel [23]. This stable supply helps mitigate price volatility that can be associated with more fragmented delivery modes, bolstering the attractiveness of hydrogen over its competitors.

Continuing the examination of economic advantages, Capelle et al. indicate that economic modeling suggests hydrogen pipelines can achieve economies of scale as deployment increases, thus lowering costs [42], consequently, these hydrogen pipeline systems not only serve individual users but aggregate demand, ultimately making hydrogen a more viable choice for energy consumers.

1.8 Global Policy Landscape and Strategic Roadmaps

The global landscape for hydrogen policies is rapidly evolving, driven by the pressing need to transition to sustainable energy systems and mitigate climate change impacts. This section examines the strategic roadmaps various nations have developed to incorporate hydrogen into their energy matrices, showcasing the policies, frameworks, and incentives that facilitate this transition. It will highlight the approaches taken by G20 nations, specific case studies, and regulatory trends shaping the hydrogen economy.

1.8.1 The Emergence of Hydrogen Policies

The global shift towards hydrogen can be attributed to its potential as a clean energy carrier that significantly contributes to reducing carbon emissions across various sectors. National strategies increasingly identify hydrogen as a central element, aligned with international climate commitments such as the Paris Agreement. For instance, Yalamati et al. [25] argue that G20 nations are pivotal in advancing green hydrogen strategies to achieve net-zero emissions, underscoring the geopolitical importance of hydrogen technology in their energy policies. This transition encompasses not only environmental benefits but also economic and energy security considerations, as countries seek to enhance their energy autonomy while fostering low-carbon technologies [58].

1.8.2 Strategic Roadmaps in Key Regions

Countries have responded with tailored strategic roadmaps to unlock hydrogen's potential. For example, the European Union has laid out an ambitious Hydrogen Strategy aiming for a climate-neutral Europe by 2050, which includes plans for large-scale hydrogen production and infrastructure development [59]. The strategy emphasizes the importance of establishing hydrogen hubs and integrating hydrogen networks with the broader energy system to facilitate the transition from fossil fuels.

In Asia, Japan is leading with a hydrogen roadmap that focuses on utilizing hydrogen for both energy storage and as an international energy carrier [59]. The country has implemented policies incentivizing the import of liquefied hydrogen and developing domestic hydrogen generation capabilities, aimed at diversifying its energy supply while adhering to stringent greenhouse gas reduction targets [60]. Similarly, China's approach, as outlined by Gong et al. [61], emphasizes building regional hydrogen hubs and encouraging local experiments to create a robust hydrogen economy that can meet its vast energy demand efficiently.

1.8.3 Frameworks and Regulations

The regulatory frameworks being developed around hydrogen are crucial for fostering an environment conducive to innovation and investment. Countries are increasingly adopting policies that offer incentives for hydrogen production, including tax credits, renewable hydrogen subsidies, and grants for research and development projects aimed at reducing production costs [62, 63]. The establishment of emissions certification systems is also imperative for ensuring transparent accounting, as highlighted by White et al. These systems will facilitate international trade in hydrogen and promote environmental integrity in the supply chain [64].

Comparative analysis shows that while the EU favors a detailed regulatory framework with specific quotas for renewable hydrogen, the United States focuses on offering incentives without restricting hydrogen production methods, thereby encouraging a competitive market [61]. Such differences reflect varying national priorities, yet all underscore the significance of collaboration and policy coherence in creating an effective hydrogen economy.

1.8.4 International Cooperation and Global Markets

International cooperation is essential in facilitating the global hydrogen market. The interconnected nature of hydrogen production, transport, and consumption necessitates collaborative efforts among countries to overcome technological and infrastructural barriers. G20 nations, as evidenced by Yalamati et al. [25], are increasingly engaging in discussions on policies and frameworks to share best practices, harmonize standards, and invest in hydrogen technology together.

The development of a hydrogen market also requires considered approaches towards creating supply chains for the trade of hydrogen. This entails addressing logistical challenges related to hydrogen storage and transportation, including adopting innovative solutions such as liquid carriers for shipping hydrogen over long distances [65]. Policy initiatives must therefore encompass the entire value chain, from production to distribution to end-use applications, which is essential for fostering economic competitiveness while promoting sustainability.

1.8.5 Future Directions and Implementation Challenges

As nations pivot towards hydrogen as a cornerstone of their energy strategies, challenges remain. Assessing the actual environmental benefits of hydrogen against the backdrop of its multifaceted production methods is critical for policymakers [66]. Furthermore, leveraging various forms of hydrogen—green, blue, and grey—while managing the associated carbon footprints is vital for making informed policy decisions that effectively balance economic and environmental goals. Moreover, strategic roadmaps should encompass plans for research and development to encourage innovations in hydrogen technology. The predictive modeling conducted by Daniel et al. highlights the importance of analyzing future cost trajectories of green hydrogen production, signifying that effective forecasting and financial mechanisms are necessary for supporting investments in hydrogen infrastructure [67].

1.9 Environmental and Societal Implications of Hydrogen Networks

The expansion of hydrogen networks presents both significant environmental benefits and complex societal implications that shape perceptions and acceptance of hydrogen as a viable energy source. This section will examine the environmental impacts of hydrogen infrastructure, focusing on its role in reducing greenhouse gas emissions and advancing sustainability, while also addressing societal aspects, including public perception, job creation, and energy equity.

1.9.1 Environmental Benefits of Hydrogen Networks

Hydrogen is increasingly recognized as a pivotal element in achieving a sustainable energy future, particularly due to its potential to decarbonize hard-to-abate sectors such as transportation, industry, and heating. As highlighted by Zemīte et al. [68], blending hydrogen with natural gas has been identified as an effective strategy for reducing carbon emissions in existing gas networks, with the potential for blends of 5–20% hydrogen by volume. This integration of hydrogen helps minimize the carbon footprint associated with gas combustion, promoting a gradual transition towards a hydrogen-based economy while leveraging existing infrastructure.

The environmental advantages of hydrogen networks extend beyond direct emissions reductions. Hamed et al. [69] explore the thermodynamic implications of hydrogen networks, underscoring that well-designed hydrogen supply chains can lead to lower overall energy consumption and reduced pollutant emissions. Moreover, as pipelines and infrastructure are developed, the increasing reliance on hydrogen sourced from renewable resources—such as wind and solar—further mitigates environmental impacts, especially when compared to conventional fossil fuels [70].

In the context of a broader lifecycle assessment (LCA), the production and utilization of hydrogen yield varying environmental outcomes based on the production methods employed. Burns et al. [71] note that green hydrogen, derived from renewable energy sources, exhibits significantly lower environmental impacts compared to blue or grey hydrogen, which relies on fossil fuels. Transitioning towards hydrogen production methods that minimize carbon emissions is crucial in enhancing the overall sustainability of hydrogen networks, further supporting policies aimed at climate neutrality [69].

Beyond greenhouse gas reduction, the thoughtful integration of hydrogen into existing energy systems can lead to improved air quality and public health outcomes. Instances of lower emissions from industrial processes and reduced reliance on conventional fossil fuels can translate to fewer pollutants in the atmosphere and subsequently better respiratory health for communities, particularly in urban settings [72]. This public health perspective highlights the multifaceted benefits of hydrogen networks, resonating with public interests and concerns regarding energy consumption and environmental degradation.

1.9.2 Societal Implications of Hydrogen Adoption

The societal implications of hydrogen networks are equally important, as they encompass job creation, community engagement, and energy equity. The establishment of hydrogen infrastructure offers significant economic development opportunities, generating jobs in manufacturing, installation, and maintenance. According to Engelen et al. [73], the successful deployment of hydrogen fuel infrastructure can yield positive dividends concerning employment and local economic stimulation. With substantial investment in hydrogen-related projects, communities could witness revitalization, particularly in regions traditionally reliant on fossil fuels.

The potential for hydrogen technology to enhance energy security fuels public interest and support. Hydrogen networks can facilitate decentralized energy production, delivering energy to remote or underserved communities that may have limited access to conventional energy systems [69]. This reliance on indigenous renewable resources to produce hydrogen not only reduces dependence on imported fuels but also fosters local energy independence and resilience. However, public perception of hydrogen technology remains critical for achieving successful implementation. Misconceptions about hydrogen safety, environmental benefits, and its role in energy transition can all lead to resistance. To cultivate acceptance, effective communication around the safety measures and regulatory frameworks governing hydrogen networks is essential. Both Pellegrini et al. and Butturi et al. [70, 74] emphasize the necessity for transparency and community involvement in shaping energy policies around hydrogen, ensuring that stakeholders understand the benefits and challenges associated with hydrogen adoption. Energy equity must also be at the forefront of hydrogen initiatives to ensure that the transition does not aggravate existing social inequalities. Policymakers should actively engage diverse communities in decision-making and planning processes for hydrogen infrastructure development. This inclusive approach can help identify the unique energy needs of various populations while promoting equitable access to hydrogen's benefits.

The promotion of hydrogen as a clean energy carrier aligns with broader sustainable development goals, fostering socio-environmental synergies that can enhance both community well-being and environmental sustainability. The deployment of hydrogen technology is set against the backdrop of competitive energy markets, and establishing a robust hydrogen economy entails addressing the socio-economic hurdles inherent in large-scale transitions. Public support could be further mobilized through strategic investments from governments, focused education initiatives, and private sector partnerships that underscore the shared benefits of transitioning to hydrogen networks.

1.10 The Strategic Importance of Hydrogen Pipelines in the Energy System

Hydrogen is increasingly recognized as a pivotal element within the transition to sustainable energy systems. Pipelines designed for hydrogen transport are crucial for integrating this versatile energy carrier into established energy networks, facilitating its utilization across various sectors including transportation, heating, and industrial applications. This strategic importance lies not solely in hydrogen's capacity to substitute fossil fuels but also in its ability to serve as a key link between renewable energy generation and consumption, allowing for a more resilient, balanced, and low-carbon energy ecosystem [75, 76].

The pathway toward a hydrogen-managed energy future necessitates significant investments in hydrogen pipeline infrastructure, which can expedite the distribution of hydrogen derived from renewable sources and help in stabilizing energy systems during periods of variable supply from renewables such as wind and solar power [77]. Additionally, the integration of hydrogen pipelines can alleviate some of the logistical challenges currently faced in energy transportation, allowing for reduced carbon footprints and enhanced economic efficiency [77]. This reflects a broader understanding that hydrogen pipelines are not just conduits but integral components of a future-focused energy strategy that prioritizes sustainable practices.

The environmental benefits associated with hydrogen pipelines cannot be overlooked. Transporting gaseous hydrogen through pipelines is estimated to generate a smaller environmental impact compared to road transport or other methods of hydrogen delivery, significantly reducing the overall greenhouse gas footprint within hydrogen's value chain [77]. Notably, pipelines can deliver hydrogen safely over long distances, facilitating access to decarbonized energy in regions that may otherwise be dependent on fossil fuels [77]. These characteristics underscore hydrogen's unique potential as a cornerstone of a decarbonized energy grid, particularly in urban settings where air quality and reduced atmospheric pollutants are of increasing concern.

Recent studies emphasize that integrating hydrogen production and usage with existing energy infrastructure ensures that the transition to low-carbon technologies does not incur prohibitive economic costs. Instead, it aids in maintaining energy system reliability while promoting new economic opportunities in hydrogen production, storage, and distribution sectors [75, 76]. The advancing landscape suggests that breakthroughs in hydrogen technology could yield economically viable solutions that enhance socio-political acceptance, thereby supporting the wider adoption of hydrogen systems [78]. The evolution towards hydrogen pipelines thus signifies a comprehensive approach to addressing the dual pressures of climate change and energy security, particularly in the context of geopolitical uncertainties surrounding traditional fossil fuel supply routes.

References

1. Kourougianni F et al (2024) A comprehensive review of green hydrogen energy systems. Renew Energy 120911
2. Vahidinasab V, Mohammadi-Ivatloo B, Lim JS (eds) (2024) Green hydrogen in power systems. Springer Nature
3. Su Y et al (2022) Prediction of mixing uniformity of hydrogen injection in natural gas pipeline based on a deep learning model. Energies 15(22):8694
4. Agency IE (2025) Global hydrogen review 2025. International Energy Agency
5. Kumar S, Bera A (2025) Prospects and challenges of underground hydrogen storage. In: Subsurface hydrogen energy storage, pp 387–417
6. Li J, Xie B, Gong L (2024) Numerical research on leakage characteristics of pure hydrogen/hydrogen-blended natural gas in medium-and low-pressure buried pipelines. Energies 17(12):2951
7. Abbas AJ et al (2024) Transitioning to a hydrogen economy: exploring the viability of adapting natural gas pipelines for hydrogen transport through a case study on compression versus Looping. Gases 4(2):74–96
8. Zhang C et al (2023) Key technologies of pure hydrogen and hydrogen-mixed natural gas pipeline transportation. ACS Omega 8(22):19212–19222
9. Genovese M et al (2023) Power-to-hydrogen and hydrogen-to-X energy systems for the industry of the future in Europe. Int J Hydrog Energy 48(44):16545–16568
10. Vijayakumar V et al (2022) Creating a global hydrogen economy: review of international strategies, targets, and policies with a focus on Japan, South Korea, California and Germany. National Center for Sustainable Transportation
11. Reigstad GA et al (2022) Moving toward the low-carbon hydrogen economy: experiences and key learnings from national case studies. Adv Appl Energy 8:100108
12. Kovač A, Paranos M, Marciuš D (2021) Hydrogen in energy transition: a review. Int J Hydrog Energy 46(16):10016–10035
13. Lebrouhi B et al (2022) Global hydrogen development-a technological and geopolitical overview. Int J Hydrog Energy 47(11):7016–7048
14. Hassan Q et al (2024) Green hydrogen: a pathway to a sustainable energy future. Int J Hydrog Energy 50:310–333
15. Kethamukkala K, Liu Y (2023) Information fusion and data augmentation for risk-based maintenance optimization of hydrogen gas pipelines. In: 15th Annual conference of the prognostics and health management society, PHM 2023. Prognostics and Health Management Society

16. Abbas AJ et al (2021) An investigation into the volumetric flow rate requirement of hydrogen transportation in existing natural gas pipelines and its safety implications. Gases 1(4):156–179
17. Wang Y, Su C, Xie M (2024) Optimizing inspection plan for corroded pipeline with considering imperfect maintenance. Proc Inst Mech Eng Part O: J Risk Reliabil 238(2):417–428
18. Hussain M, Zhang T (2023) Potential of big data analytics for energy pipeline integrity management. Corros Manag (Jan/Feb Issue):31–33
19. Hussain M et al (2024) Energy pipeline degradation condition assessment using predictive analytics–challenges, issues, and future directions. J Pipeline Sci Eng 100178
20. Boretti A, Pollet BG (2024) Hydrogen economy: paving the path to a sustainable, low-carbon future. Int J Hydrog Energy 93:307–319
21. Mahajan D et al (2022) Hydrogen blending in gas pipeline networks—A review. Energies 15(10):3582
22. Cerniauskas S et al (2020) Options of natural gas pipeline reassignment for hydrogen: cost assessment for a Germany case study. Int J Hydrog Energy 45(21):12095–12107
23. André J et al (2014) Time development of new hydrogen transmission pipeline networks for France. Int J Hydrog Energy 39(20):10323–10337
24. Chen X et al (2024) Research on standards and standard system of hydrogen pipeline in China. In: E3S web of conferences 520:04016. EDP Sciences
25. Yalamati HPS, Vij RK, Srivastava R (2024) Green hydrogen revolution: mapping G20 nations' policies and geopolitical strategies in the net-zero emission era. Wiley Interdiscip Rev: Energy Environ 13(5):e538
26. Li Q et al (2024) Hydrogen impact: a review on diffusibility, embrittlement mechanisms, and characterization. Materials 17(4):965
27. Algayyim SJM et al (2024) Influence of natural gas and hydrogen properties on internal combustion engine performance, combustion, and emissions: a review. Fuel 362:130844
28. Meda US et al (2023) Challenges associated with hydrogen storage systems due to the hydrogen embrittlement of high strength steels. Int J Hydrog Energy 48(47):17894–17913
29. Sun B et al (2024) Current challenges in the utilization of hydrogen energy-a focused review on the issue of hydrogen-induced damage and embrittlement. Adv Appl Energy 100168
30. Rolo I, Costa VA, Brito FP (2023) Hydrogen-based energy systems: current technology development status, opportunities and challenges. Energies 17(1):180
31. Ahad MT et al (2023) An overview of challenges for the future of hydrogen. Materials 16(20):6680
32. Le TT et al (2024) Fueling the future: a comprehensive review of hydrogen energy systems and their challenges. Int J Hydrog Energy 54:791–816
33. Sofian M et al (2024) A review on hydrogen blending in gas network: insight into safety, corrosion, embrittlement, coatings and liners, and bibliometric analysis. Int J Hydrog Energy 60:867–889
34. Sadeq AM et al (2024) Hydrogen energy systems: technologies, trends, and future prospects. Sci Total Environ 173622
35. Hydrogen Council and McKinsey & Company (2024) Hydrogen Insights 2024
36. Andrews J, Shabani B (2014) The role of hydrogen in a global sustainable energy strategy. Wiley Interdiscip Rev: Energy Environ 3(5):474–489
37. Zhong L, Wu Y (2024) Probabilistic deployment pathways of scaling up distributed green hydrogen systems for urban residential communities in North America. Preprints
38. Bekele E et al (2024) Hydrogen valleys for local energy system decarbonization: an assessment of the environmental and economic aspects. J Phys: Conf Ser 2893:012085 (IOP Publishing)
39. Büsch L et al (2024) HyPLANT100: industrialization from assembly to the construction site for gigawatt electrolysis. Hydrogen 5(2):185–208
40. Ocko IB, Hamburg SP (2022) Climate consequences of hydrogen emissions. Atmos Chem Phys 22(14):9349–9368
41. Yang K et al (2024) Risk modelling of hydrogen-enriched natural gas on pipelines and gas-electric coupled systems. IET Energy Syst Integr 6(3):253–267

42. Capelle J et al (2008) Sensitivity of pipelines with steel API X52 to hydrogen embrittlement. Int J Hydrog Energy 33(24):7630–7641
43. Javaheri V (2023) Steel pipeline for the hydrogen storage and delivery: metallurgical viewpoint for Finnish ecosystem. Future Technol 2(1):58–61
44. Noussan M et al (2021) The role of green and blue hydrogen in the energy transition—A technological and geopolitical perspective. Sustainability 13(298):2021
45. Klopčič N et al (2022) Refurbishment of natural gas pipelines towards 100% hydrogen—A thermodynamic-based analysis. Energies 15(24):9370
46. Ott B et al (2023) Ensuring natural gas infrastructure is suitable for hydrogen service. Process Saf Prog 42(2):213–224
47. Stöhr T et al (2024) Hydrogen quality in used natural gas pipelines: An experimental investigation of contaminants according to ISO 14687: 2019 standard. Int J Hydrog Energy 67:1136–1147
48. Cavaliere P (2023) Safety issues and regulations. Water electrolysis for hydrogen production. Springer, pp 729–791
49. Šimunović J et al (2024) Environmental and social impact assessment (ESIA). 2024-2027 ZEAS consortium
50. Olsen K, Shulhan G, Di Zanno P (2022) Methodologies for Conversion of new natural gas pipelines to hydrogen service in North America. In: International pipeline conference. American Society of Mechanical Engineers
51. Alssalehin E, Holborn P, Pilidis P (2025) Assessment of hydrogen storage and pipelines for hydrogen farm. Energies 18(5):1167
52. Raj A et al (2024) Evaluating hydrogen gas transport in pipelines: current state of numerical and experimental methodologies. Int J Hydrog Energy 67:136–149
53. Wang C et al (2023) Minireview on the leakage ignition and flame propagation characteristics of hydrogen: advances and perspectives. Energy Fuels 37(8):5653–5666
54. Mohitpour M, Solanky H, Vinjamuri GK (2004) Materials selection and performance criteria for hydrogen pipeline transmission. In: ASME pressure vessels and piping conference
55. De Kleijne K et al (2024) Worldwide greenhouse gas emissions of green hydrogen production and transport. Nat Energy 9(9):1139–1152
56. Fekete JR, Sowards JW, Amaro RL (2015) Economic impact of applying high strength steels in hydrogen gas pipelines. Int J Hydrog Energy 40(33):10547–10558
57. Lee H, Lee S (2022) Economic analysis on hydrogen pipeline infrastructure establishment scenarios: case study of South Korea. Energies 15(18):6824
58. Lockard DW (2015) A framework for evaluating global policy on sustainability. J Glob Responsibil 6(2):215–228
59. Shiraishi K, Park WY, Kammen DM (2024) The role of hydrogen as long-duration energy storage and as an international energy carrier for electricity sector decarbonization. Environ Res Lett 19(8):084011
60. Doğrul M, Takayuki Y (2025) The political economy of Japan's net-zero vision in the context of energy security. Ege Acad Rev 25(1):241–254
61. Gong X, Quitzow R, Boute A (2024) Developing China's hydrogen economy: national regulation through local experimentation. Transnatl Environ Law 13(2):337–367
62. Danish MSS (2023) Exploring metal oxides for the hydrogen evolution reaction (HER) in the field of nanotechnology. RSC Sustain 1(9):2180–2196
63. Omotoye GB et al (2024) Navigating global energy markets: a review of economic and policy impacts. Int J Sci Res Arch 11(1):195–203
64. White LV et al (2021) Towards emissions certification systems for international trade in hydrogen: the policy challenge of defining boundaries for emissions accounting. Energy 215:119139
65. Dickson R et al (2022) Global transportation of green hydrogen via liquid carriers: economic and environmental sustainability analysis, policy implications, and future directions. Green Chem 24(21):8484–8493

66. Singh G, Slack N, Sharma S (2022) Politics–administration dichotomy: insight from a developing country. In: Farazmand A (eds) Global Encyclopedia of Public Administration, Public Policy, and Governance. Springer, Cham, pp 9850–9856
67. Daniel T et al (2024) Potential of progressive and disruptive innovation-driven cost reductions of green hydrogen production. Energy Fuels 38(11):10370–10380
68. Zemite L et al (2023) Blending hydrogen with natural gas/biomethane and transportation in existing gas networks. Latv J Phys Tech Sci 60(5):43–55
69. Hamed AM et al (2023) A review on blue and green hydrogen production process and their life cycle assessments. In: IOP conference series: earth and environmental science. IOP Publishing
70. Pellegrini M, Guzzini A, Saccani C (2020) A preliminary assessment of the potential of low percentage green hydrogen blending in the Italian natural gas network. Energies 13(21):5570
71. Roos G (2024) An overview of the arguments in literature, for and against the use of green hydrogen for the production of direct reduced iron. Preprints
72. Ghimire A et al (2015) A review on dark fermentative biohydrogen production from organic biomass: process parameters and use of by-products. Appl Energy 144:73–95
73. Engelen P-J, Kool C, Li Y (2016) A barrier options approach to modeling project failure: the case of hydrogen fuel infrastructure. Resour Energy Econ 43:33–56
74. Butturi MA, Gamberini R (2020) Urban–industrial symbiosis to support sustainable energy transition. Int J Energy Prod Manag 5(4):355–366
75. Kut P, Pietrucha-Urbanik K, Zeleňáková M (2024) Assessing the role of hydrogen in sustainable energy futures: a comprehensive bibliometric analysis of research and international collaborations in energy and environmental engineering. Energies 17(8):1862
76. Alves C et al (2024) Hydrogen technologies: recent advances, new perspectives, and applications. In: Abdallah Z, Aldoumani N (eds) Hydrogen technologies - advances, insights, and applications. IntechOpen
77. Revinova S et al (2024) Hydrogen in energy transition: the problem of economic efficiency, environmental safety, and technological readiness of transportation and storage. Resources 13(7):92
78. Fan Z (2024) The role of hydrogen in achieving sustainable energy systems: challenges and opportunities. Highlights Sci Eng Technol 116:237–240

Chapter 2
Overview of Hydrogen Pipeline Infrastructure

2.1 Current Status of Hydrogen Pipeline Networks

Natural gas pipelines have been in operation for decades and are designed to transport methane, a molecule significantly larger than hydrogen. This presents unique challenges when considering the retrofitting process, as hydrogen's physical and chemical properties require adaptations in pipeline materials and system design [1]. The existing natural gas network is extensive; for instance, approximately 5.4 million kilometers of pipelines serve major regions in the U.S. and Canada, carrying natural gas to millions of homes and businesses [2]. This established infrastructure can potentially serve as a backbone for hydrogen distribution, provided that modifications address both safety and material compatibility concerns. Hydrogen, recognized for its potential as a clean energy carrier, presents unique infrastructure requirements compared to conventional fossil fuels. Most existing natural gas pipelines are not fully compatible with hydrogen transport due to differences in chemical properties and material interactions. Hydrogen embrittlement, for instance, is a significant challenge since it can lead to premature failure of materials used in existing pipelines [3, 4]. Thus, while the current hydrogen pipeline infrastructure is still developing, utilizing existing natural gas networks may provide a viable transition pathway, although modifications will be necessary to accommodate hydrogen's properties [5, 6].

A consensus among researchers indicates that an incremental approach to utilizing existing natural gas pipelines for hydrogen transport is preferable. Zemīte et al. [7], Bdioui et al. [8] and Quintino et al. [9] suggest that blending hydrogen with natural gas can ease the transition to a hydrogen economy by reducing the immediate need for entirely new infrastructure investment. The capabilities of existing pipelines to manage hydrogen mixtures have been researched extensively, with findings indicating that many systems can handle blends of up to 20% hydrogen by volume without requiring significant upgrades [6]. Kigle et al. [10] suggest potential cost savings and reduced barriers to the widespread deployment of hydrogen in the natural gas grid.

M. Hussain et al., *Hydrogen Pipeline Integrity*, Green Energy and Technology,
https://doi.org/10.1007/978-981-95-5609-0_2

Despite these promising pathways, substantial infrastructural investments and regulatory frameworks must support the transition toward a hydrogen economy. For instance, building dedicated hydrogen pipelines may eventually become essential, particularly for high-purity hydrogen applications in various sectors, including industry and transportation [11, 12]. According to Agarwal et al. [13] and Hassan et al. [14], safety protocols must be robust, given the higher flammability and permeation characteristics of hydrogen compared to natural gas. The broader acceptance of hydrogen as an energy source also depends on public and stakeholder confidence in the safety of hydrogen infrastructure, which has been challenged by past accidents involving hydrogen station failures [15].

Research into pipeline material suitability for hydrogen transport emphasizes the need to select and retrofit existing infrastructure. Current investigations have focused on the performance of various materials under hydrogen exposure, with attention given to the phenomenon of hydrogen embrittlement, which can compromise traditional steel pipeline integrity [16]. Regular evaluation and monitoring of pipeline conditions will be vital as hydrogen networks expand, as the implications of material degradation directly affect safety and operational efficacy [17, 18].

The feasibility of hydrogen as a fuel source is closely tied to economic considerations. The costs associated with establishing hydrogen refueling stations and dedicated transport pipelines are high, often deterring rapid deployment [19, 20]. The competitiveness of hydrogen is influenced not only by production costs, which currently present a barrier but also by utility pricing strategies and market demand generated through governmental and environmental policies aimed at decarbonization [21–23]. The transition necessitates a well-planned investment strategy that addresses both the physical infrastructure, and the technological enhancements needed to optimize hydrogen production and distribution [24, 25].

Globally, countries are exploring innovative hydrogen applications, supported by various pilot projects focused on hydrogen mobility and infrastructure development [26, 27]. In regions like Europe, there is substantial political momentum for advancing hydrogen economy frameworks, resulting in strategies that integrate hydrogen into existing energy systems [28, 29]. Kountouris et al. [30] and Zemīte et al. [31] highlight the EU's intent to integrate hydrogen widely into energy markets, emphasizing the need for robust infrastructure and a clear, harmonized regulatory framework across member states.

In terms of logistics, the complexities of hydrogen supply chains amplify the challenge of creating a reliable delivery network. Alvarez Coomonte et al. [32] and Ichimura et al. [20] state that solutions involving multi-modal transportation methods including road, rail, and pipeline systems—must be considered, while also taking into account regional energy demands and infrastructural constraints that could hinder progress. Ultimately, addressing the challenges surrounding hydrogen pipeline networks requires a multidisciplinary approach involving chemistry, economics, policy making, and engineering. Stakeholder collaboration and comprehensive planning will be essential to overcoming resistance and uncertainty in the transition toward a hydrogen-based energy future [33]. The resulting hydrogen infrastructure will not only support market demand for clean energy solutions but will also help enhance energy security as jurisdictions seek to diversify energy sources and mitigate climate change impacts.

2.2 Existing Hydrogen Pipelines Versus Repurposed Natural Gas Pipelines

The transition toward a hydrogen economy is increasingly pertinent in the context of global energy demands and environmental concerns. The transportation of hydrogen, which can be achieved through specialized pipelines, poses significant challenges and opportunities, particularly when evaluating the feasibility of using existing natural gas pipeline infrastructure for hydrogen transport. This analysis explores the characteristics of both dedicated hydrogen pipelines and repurposed natural gas pipelines, referencing a spectrum of recent studies and developments in this domain.

Gu et al. [34] note that the construction of dedicated hydrogen pipelines remains costly, with estimates suggesting that the investment per unit length is approximately three times higher than that of natural gas pipelines. Abbas et al. [35] suggest that, given the high expense, optimizing existing infrastructure is often a more financially viable option for hydrogen transport. As highlighted by Hoffart, the desire to repurpose existing pipelines reflects the drive towards achieving a lower-cost solution in an era marked by rapid energy transition and decarbonization efforts [36]. Abbas et al. [6] assert that, according to various economic analyses, utilizing existing natural gas pipelines rather than developing new hydrogen-specific systems—could substantially reduce the overall costs associated with hydrogen transport infrastructure.

The repurposing of natural gas pipelines comes with its own technical challenges, primarily concerning the compatibility of hydrogen with the materials and design of existing pipelines [37]. Su et al. [38] point out that hydrogen's smaller molecular size compared to methane can lead to higher leakage rates, necessitating rigorous safety assessments and potential adaptations to address the increased risks associated with hydrogen transport. As depicted in Zhao and Cheng's research, the uniqueness of hydrogen demands specialized modeling approaches to ensure structural integrity during its movement through modified pipelines [37]. This is also corroborated by the findings of Ban et al. [39], who documented the inherent vulnerabilities in the welds of natural gas pipelines, which pose significant risks when hydrogen is introduced into the system.

The studies surrounding hydrogen blending indicate a general consensus on the feasibility of utilizing existing natural gas pipelines, coupled with an acknowledgment of the necessary advancements in pipeline integrity monitoring and rehabilitation [40]. Although safety must remain paramount, successful implementation could serve as a catalyst for broader adoption and infrastructural transformation. Tian et al. [41] demonstrate that, with modern analytical models ranging from computational fluid dynamics to advanced statistical method predictive maintenance can provide valuable insights into the operational integrity of repurposed pipelines.

From an engineering perspective, the compatibility of materials used in natural gas pipelines with hydrogen is a pivotal factor. Abubakar et al. [42] are conducting ongoing research involving computational thermodynamic analyses to evaluate the effects of temperature and pressure on pipeline materials, thereby enriching our understanding of material degradation and longevity factors critical to the reliability of hydrogen transportation systems. As these investigations progress, they will assure stakeholders that existing pipeline systems can evolve to accommodate a blended hydrogen economy.

2.3 Physical and Chemical Behavior of Hydrogen in Pipelines

The physical and chemical behavior of hydrogen in pipelines is a critical area of study, particularly given hydrogen's unique properties, which differ fundamentally from those of other gases like natural gas. Hydrogen, being the lightest and smallest molecule, exhibits rapid diffusion characteristics that influence its behavior in pipeline systems. Understanding these properties is vital for the safety, efficiency, and integrity of hydrogen transport infrastructure. As elucidated in various studies, hydrogen's interactions with pipeline materials, particularly through phenomena such as embrittlement, dictate the design and material selection for safe transportation systems.

One of the primary concerns when transporting hydrogen through pipelines is hydrogen embrittlement (HE). Hydrogen can diffuse into materials, particularly metals like steel, and lead to significant degradation of their mechanical properties. Studies indicate that microstructural changes induced by hydrogen exposure can result in a loss in ductility and toughness, thus increasing the susceptibility of pipeline materials to cracking and failure [43, 44]. For example, research on X80 pipeline steel has demonstrated that hydrogen not only penetrates but can also alter the microstructural integrity of the steel by promoting cracks and other forms of damage when exposed to high-pressure hydrogen environments [44, 45]. The mechanisms through which HE operates are complex and involve the interaction of hydrogen atoms with the material's lattice structure, causing changes in phase properties and stress distribution within the steel [46, 47].

The diffusion of hydrogen in pipeline materials is significantly influenced by several factors, including grain size, temperature, and the presence of defects or impurities [46, 47]. The behavior of hydrogen within steel can vary depending on the microstructural characteristics of the alloy, such as the presence of nanosized precipitates which act as trapping sites for hydrogen atoms [48]. In particular, fine-grained structures enhance diffusion due to increased pathways along grain boundaries, though they simultaneously introduce trapping sites that can hinder the flow of hydrogen and promote localized embrittlement [46, 49]. Current research suggests a two-fold effect of grain boundaries, in which diffusion is both enhanced and retarded, emphasizing the necessity for optimizing the microstructure of steel to mitigate hydrogen-related risks.

2.4 Key Differences Between Hydrogen and Natural Gas Pipelines

The transportation of hydrogen and natural gas through pipelines involves distinct considerations due to their differing physical and chemical properties. Notably, hydrogen has a lower energy density and a smaller molecular size compared to natural gas, leading to unique challenges for pipeline infrastructure originally designed for natural gas. This response highlights the key differences between hydrogen and natural gas pipelines, focusing on aspects such as material compatibility, pressure and leakage characteristics, blending practices, and economic implications.

2.4.1 Material Compatibility and Mechanical Properties

Hydrogen's effects on pipeline materials, particularly regarding hydrogen embrittlement, are significant when considering the infrastructure used for natural gas. Ban et al. [39] discuss the heightened risks of mechanical property deterioration in pipeline steel due to hydrogen exposure, which increases the risks of failure. Zhang et al. [3] also note that the integrity of existing pipeline materials can be compromised under high-pressure hydrogen conditions, emphasizing the need for comprehensive evaluations of material compatibility and safety standards.

2.4.2 Pressure Characteristics and Leakage

The pressure characteristics differ markedly between hydrogen-enriched natural gas and pure natural gas. The volumetric flow rate required for hydrogen transport is significantly higher, necessitating modifications or expansions of existing pipeline infrastructures. Studies indicate that to transport an equivalent energy amount, a three-fold increase in flow rate is needed for hydrogen compared to natural gas [35]. Su et al. [38] and Zhang et al. [3] point out that hydrogen's smaller molecular size results in increased leakage rates, necessitating the investigation of improved sealing materials and techniques within existing pipelines. The leakage behavior of hydrogen blends in pipelines has emerged as a critical concern, leading research to focus on enhancing the sealing and durability of pipeline systems based on comparative analyses to natural gas transport setups.

2.4.3 Blending Practices

Blending hydrogen with natural gas is considered an interim solution while dedicated hydrogen pipelines are developed. Abbas et al. [6] highlight that blending hydrogen into existing natural gas pipelines not only offers a potential pathway for hydrogen's integration but also helps to leverage the significant existing natural gas infrastructure. This approach, which could involve varying hydrogen proportions, might optimize both acute operational efficiency and compliance with safety regulations while transitioning to a hydrogen economy [1].

2.4.4 Economic Implications

The economic feasibility of transitioning natural gas pipelines for hydrogen transport involves assessing high initial costs associated with modifying existing infrastructure versus constructing new pure hydrogen pipelines. Research conducted by Lee and Lee [40] indicates that while modifying natural gas pipelines is cost-effective, long-term strategies would likely necessitate investment in dedicated hydrogen infrastructure, which may be disproportionately higher. The blended approach can thus serve as a transitional strategy, considering the high capital expenditures associated with new infrastructure [1].

2.5 Hydrogen Pipeline Materials and Types

The effective transportation of hydrogen is pivotal for harnessing its potential as a clean energy source. Hydrogen can be distributed via pipelines, which present a cost-effective solution for both short- and long-distance transport. However, integrating hydrogen into existing infrastructure poses several challenges, including the selection of appropriate materials and the need for modifications to current systems [3, 12]. The primary materials used for hydrogen pipelines include steel, polyethylene, and fiber-reinforced polymers, each possessing distinct properties that determine their suitability for hydrogen transport.

Steel is widely utilized due to its high strength and durability. However, it presents challenges such as susceptibility to hydrogen embrittlement, where hydrogen diffuses into the steel, leading to decreased ductility and increased brittleness [50]. Research has focused on assessing various steel grades and coatings to improve their resistance to hydrogen damage. For example, Cerniauskas et al. [51] have examined natural gas pipeline reassignment for hydrogen, highlighting the importance of utilizing specialized protective coatings to mitigate degradation risks.

Polyethylene, another critical material, offers advantages such as low hydrogen permeability, making it suitable for hydrogen distribution networks. Its flexibility and lightweight characteristics further contribute to its favorable properties for use in pipelines [52]. However, the long-term behavior of polyethylene in contact with hydrogen, as well as its performance under varying pressure and temperature conditions, requires continued investigation to ensure safety and reliability over service life [53].

Fiber-reinforced polymers have emerged as a promising alternative to traditional metal pipelines. They are noted for their cost-effectiveness, with estimates indicating a potential 20% reduction in costs compared to steel pipelines [50]. These materials are significant for providing lightweight solutions that can be easily integrated into existing networks without extensive modifications. Nevertheless, further research is required to optimize their mechanical properties and ensure they meet the long-term demands of hydrogen transport [3].

2.6 Design Differences of Hydrogen Pipelines Compared to Natural Gas Pipelines

When considering the design differences between hydrogen pipelines and natural gas pipelines, it is essential to recognize not only the inherent physical and chemical properties of hydrogen but also the implications for infrastructure adaptation, safety, and material performance. Hydrogen, possessing unique characteristics compared to natural gas (primarily methane), necessitates significant changes to pipeline design and operation to promote safe and efficient transportation. These differences span material selection, structural integrity, leakage characteristics, and operational requirements.

2.6.1 Material Differences and Mechanical Properties

One of the primary concerns with hydrogen pipelines is the susceptibility of pipeline materials to hydrogen embrittlement. Hydrogen embrittlement affects many materials used in pipeline construction, particularly steels and other metallurgical composites. Studies have indicated that while some materials, such as X65 and X80 steels, can withstand hydrogen concentrations up to 10–15% without significant integrity issues, higher concentrations can lead to a pronounced decrease in mechanical strength and an increase in crack propagation rates under stress [54]. Consequently, developing robust materials and coatings specifically designed for hydrogen transport becomes critical to mitigate these risks.

The mechanical challenges presented by hydrogen are compounded by pressure requirements, as hydrogen needs to be transported at higher pressures compared to natural gas to achieve similar energy densities [38]. This necessitates the use of thicker pipeline walls or advanced composite materials that can tolerate higher stress while preventing premature failure due to hydrogen-induced cracking [39]. Moreover, future applications may require entirely new standards and specifications for pipeline materials tailored for hydrogen service environments [55].

2.6.2 *Safety and Leakage Considerations*

Safety emerges as a paramount concern in hydrogen transportation, as research highlights that hydrogen's small molecular size results in a significantly higher escape velocity compared to methane. This property increases the risk of leaks, which could lead to flammable concentrations in confined spaces [56]. Additionally, leakage from hydrogen pipelines poses unique risks due to the potential for flame propagation and explosive mixtures with air. As such, the design must incorporate advanced leak detection systems and stringent safety monitoring protocols to detect even low concentrations of hydrogen promptly.

One notable aspect is the importance of maintaining pipeline integrity. Studies show that leakage from hydrogen-blended natural gas pipelines can lead to significant operational challenges due to varying density and flow characteristics of the mixture [35]. Research on leakage dynamics indicates that the behavior of the gas under varying pressure conditions requires updated computational fluid dynamics models to predict accurately how hydrogen will behave in existing natural gas infrastructure [38]. This modeling is critical in developing operational strategies for retrofitting existing natural gas pipelines for hydrogen transportation, which can mitigate risks associated with increased leakage.

2.6.3 *Operational and Design Optimization*

Optimizing the design and layout of hydrogen pipelines diverges significantly from existing natural gas infrastructure due to different thermal-hydraulic properties. The transportation of hydrogen-admixed natural gas, or hydrogen-enriched natural gas (HENG), affects the energy content and heating value, requiring adjustments in pressure drop calculations and flow rate management [57]. Operationally, integrating hydrogen requires enhanced compressor capacity and fluid dynamic assessments to ensure efficient mixing and flow across pipeline networks. Moreover, as hydrogen transport systems evolve, the need for cost-effective modifications to existing infrastructure without compromising safety and efficiency will drive innovation in pipeline design. In this regard, many studies advocate for leveraging machine learning approaches and advanced simulation techniques to enhance pipeline dispatching systems and detect any operational inefficiencies or safety risks in real-time [5, 35]. Research indicates that improved resistance to hydrogen embrittlement and leakage through the application of artificial intelligence could facilitate safer and more efficient hydrogen transport networks [58].

2.6.4 Regulatory Framework and Standardization

Establishing a regulatory framework specifically addressing hydrogen pipelines is essential. Current standards primarily governing natural gas pipelines may not suffice given the different properties and risks associated with hydrogen transport. Consequently, international standards and safety codes must be re-evaluated and updated to reflect the unique characteristics of hydrogen, its interaction with pipeline materials, and the associated operational challenges. Countries like China and others are actively working on developing and implementing these new standards [44, 55].

2.7 Infrastructure Integration and Expansion

The transition towards a hydrogen-based energy system is increasingly becoming a focal point in modern energy discourse, particularly as concerns about climate change and sustainability gain traction. A key component of this transition involves the integration of hydrogen into existing natural gas infrastructure, an approach that presents both opportunities and challenges. This synthesis will explore the blending of hydrogen with natural gas, the viability of dedicated hydrogen pipelines versus retrofitting existing pipelines, and the implications of each choice on energy systems.

Blending hydrogen with natural gas offers a pathway to decarbonize existing energy systems. Reports indicate that many countries are exploring the potential of incorporating hydrogen into their natural gas networks as a method to mitigate the infrastructural and financial barriers associated with building dedicated hydrogen pipelines [59, 60]. Economic models suggest that blending can facilitate a more gradual transition towards a hydrogen economy while ensuring continued use of existing infrastructure [59]. Studies indicate that this approach helps retain the benefits of existing natural gas systems and contributes to reducing the overall carbon footprint [60].

The debate over dedicated hydrogen pipelines versus retrofitting existing infrastructure reveals a divergence in strategic approaches. Dedicated hydrogen pipelines tend to offer optimal safety and efficiency, particularly for large-scale hydrogen distribution [61]. However, the implications of constructing new lines are often considerable in terms of cost and development time [62]. In contrast, retrofitting existing natural gas pipelines allows for immediate hydrogen integration into the energy mix, significantly lowering capital expenditures. This intermediate solution is particularly advantageous during the formative years of hydrogen market development [59].

The literature describes methods to assess the performance of both retrofitted and dedicated hydrogen networks, indicating that planning and operational models are essential for evaluating their feasibility and long-term sustainability [61].

The synergy of renewable energy sources and hydrogen production is another compelling reason to consider blending and retrofitting infrastructure. The integration of excess renewable energy for hydrogen production, particularly through Power-to-Gas (PtG) systems, presents pathways for storing excess energy and enhancing grid stability [63]. Moreover, models demonstrate that blending hydrogen can increase the overall energy delivery capacity of the existing gas networks, providing both technical and economic advantages in a multi-source energy scenario [61].

Notably, the regulatory environment presents unique challenges for both approaches to hydrogen infrastructure. Current regulations may not be adequately aligned with innovative hydrogen solutions, creating barriers to widespread implementation [64]. The need for harmonized codes and standards is emphasized across the literature, illustrating that effective governance will be crucial in facilitating the transition to a hydrogen economy [63]. This alignment will guide infrastructure development and ensure the safe integration of hydrogen into energy systems. As hydrogen technologies advance, the strategic planning of hydrogen infrastructure must incorporate considerations for scalability and adaptability to future energy demands [23]. Table 2.1 summarize the primary aspects of blending with natural gas, dedicated hydrogen pipelines, and retrofitted pipelines, including specific points on infrastructure costs, technical feasibility, safety, material compatibility, regulatory challenges, and potential impacts on carbon emissions.

2.8 Retrofitting and Comparisons with Natural Gas Infrastructure

The transition to a hydrogen economy necessitates the consideration of existing natural gas infrastructure, particularly the feasibility of retrofitting these systems to accommodate hydrogen transport. Retrofitting existing pipelines offers a cost-effective and time-efficient method to expand hydrogen delivery capabilities without the need for extensive new construction. Various studies suggest that the retrofitting of hydrogen-compatible components within existing infrastructure can facilitate this transition [65].

2.8.1 Hydrogen Embrittlement and Material Considerations

One of the key challenges in retrofitting natural gas pipelines for hydrogen transport is the phenomenon of hydrogen embrittlement (HE). Research indicates that the lower molecular weight of hydrogen compared to methane allows it to diffuse more readily

Table 2.1 Comparison of hydrogen integration approaches

Criteria	Blending hydrogen with natural gas	Dedicated hydrogen pipelines	Retrofitted existing pipelines
Infrastructure cost	Lower initial investment due to existing infrastructure; gradual integration	High capital investment required for new pipelines	Medium cost; involves retrofitting existing infrastructure
Technical feasibility	Technically feasible with existing systems; requires blending ratio management	Full system design required; specific materials need to be utilized	Need to assess existing pipeline conditions; may require significant upgrades
Safety concerns	Reduced safety risks in lower blending ratios; requires monitoring for hydrogen embrittlement	High confidence in safety if designed for hydrogen, but unknowns in legacy systems	Safety dependent on the integrity of existing infrastructure and material compatibility
Material compatibility	Potential issues with existing materials; ongoing research on embrittlement	Designed specifically for hydrogen; materials optimized for reduced risks	Compatibility checks needed, possible material changes required
Regulatory challenges	Lack of established blending regulations; evolving standards	Regulatory clarity needed for new infrastructure; may face delays	May leverage existing regulations but necessitates updates for hydrogen transport
Impact on carbon emissions	Helps reduce emissions gradually; transitional approach aligns with mixed energy systems	Potential for substantial emissions reductions with full hydrogen adoption	Emission impact varies based on pipeline conditions and hydrogen adoption levels

into materials, potentially compromising the structural integrity of the pipeline [66]. The impact of HE on commonly used pipeline steels, such as those conforming to API 52 specifications, requires careful evaluation to determine necessary upgrades or replacements for aging infrastructure [63]. Notably, studies have shown that while existing materials can handle low levels of hydrogen blending, significant concentrations may mandate a transition to more hydrogen-resistant alloys or materials that are less prone to HE effects [66].

2.8.2 *Economic Implications of Retrofitting*

From an economic perspective, the integration of hydrogen into existing natural gas systems is viewed as a viable strategy to reduce greenhouse gas emissions while leveraging pre-existing assets. The costs associated with constructing new hydrogen pipelines are substantial; thus, retrofitting existing infrastructure represents a lower-cost alternative that could minimize operational expenditures during the transition period [6, 59]. Economic modeling suggests that blending hydrogen within natural gas networks could significantly reduce capital investment while allowing for an incremental transition as hydrogen becomes more prevalent in the energy economy [8]. Furthermore, blending hydrogen at low concentrations introduces a transitional phase that may facilitate increased hydrogen production and advancement in related technologies.

2.8.3 Safety Considerations in Hydrogen Blending

Nevertheless, safety concerns are paramount when blending hydrogen with natural gas. Hydrogen presents a different combustion risk profile, being more flammable and having a higher flame velocity than natural gas. Therefore, the safety standards employed for natural gas systems may need revisiting to adapt to the different hazard profiles associated with hydrogen. Reports suggest that hydrogen concentrations above certain thresholds could lead to safety challenges, including increased risk of combustion incidents in appliances and modifications to burner designs [9, 67]. This necessitates public awareness initiatives and regulatory adjustments to ensure safe blending practices are established [68].

2.8.4 Ongoing Research and Development

Ongoing research is crucial to understand the interactions between hydrogen and existing pipeline materials comprehensively. Researchers have been investigating the impacts of various hydrogen blending rates on pipeline equipment, appliance performance, and safety at the consumer level [63, 69]. Case studies, such as the UK's HyDeploy project, aim to assess the implications of blending hydrogen at rates approaching 20% in domestic applications, which have thus far demonstrated minimal disruption to consumers [9]. Additionally, numerical models are being developed to better predict the behavior of hydrogen in both blended and pure states within existing pipeline infrastructures [65, 70].

2.9 Global Trends in Hydrogen Pipeline Deployment

The global hydrogen landscape has been rapidly evolving, driven by a confluence of technological advancements, policy support, and the urgent need to transition toward a low-carbon energy system. Hydrogen pipelines are central to this transition, providing the necessary infrastructure for transporting hydrogen from production sites to end users. The deployment of hydrogen pipelines reflects broader trends in energy systems that prioritize integration, efficiency, and sustainability.

Countries around the world are increasingly recognizing hydrogen as a key player in their energy strategies. A critical trend is the integration of hydrogen into existing natural gas networks, which allows for a phased transition to cleaner energy sources while utilizing existing infrastructure. Reports indicate that many nations are actively exploring hydrogen blending—introducing hydrogen into existing natural gas pipelines—as a way to decarbonize their energy systems [71, 72]. This blending strategy is particularly appealing because it leverages current investments in natural gas infrastructure and expedites the delivery of renewable hydrogen to consumers.

In Europe, comprehensive strategies to develop hydrogen infrastructure have been initiated, with significant investments earmarked for creating hydrogen hubs that connect production, storage, and transport. The European Hydrogen Strategy outlines ambitious targets for hydrogen deployment, aiming for a capacity of up to 10 million tons of renewable hydrogen production by 2030. This initiative includes developing hydrogen pipelines that connect with renewable energy sources, facilitating the transportation of hydrogen across borders [71, 73]. Such cross-border projects highlight the importance of regional cooperation in achieving hydrogen deployment goals and ensuring supply security.

Technological advancements are making the retrofitting of existing infrastructures for hydrogen transport more feasible. Research and development efforts have produced materials and technologies that can withstand hydrogen's unique properties, such as embrittlement, which are critical for maintaining the integrity and safety of hydrogen pipelines [71, 74]. Innovations in materials science are crucial as they provide effective solutions to mitigate the risks associated with hydrogen transport, thereby encouraging broader acceptance and investment in hydrogen infrastructure.

The global expansion of hydrogen pipelines is further supported by robust policy frameworks targeting sustainable energy transitions. In many countries, government policies are aligned to incentivize investments in hydrogen production technologies, as well as the infrastructure necessary for distribution. For instance, nations are increasingly focused on policies that promote renewable hydrogen production, thereby ensuring that hydrogen can be generated sustainably and economically while also enhancing energy security [74, 75]. These policies often include financial incentives such as subsidies, grants, and tax credits for hydrogen development projects, encouraging private investment in hydrogen infrastructure.

The integration of hydrogen into transportation networks is emerging as a critical focus area. Hydrogen is being viewed not just as an energy carrier but as a crucial component in the decarbonization of transport systems. Studies highlight that hydrogen-fueled vehicles (HFCVs) can provide significant carbon reductions compared to traditional fossil fuels, which promotes the adoption of hydrogen in the transport sector [75, 76]. As more hydrogen refueling stations are constructed, enabled by connecting pipelines, the infrastructure to support hydrogen-powered transport systems continues to grow.

In Asia, significant advancements in hydrogen pipeline deployment are occurring, particularly in countries like Japan and South Korea, where hydrogen is regarded as a central pillar of future energy strategies. Japan's commitment to becoming a "hydrogen society" exemplifies this trend, with the country actively investing in hydrogen infrastructure and technological development. Similarly, the South Korean government has set ambitious targets to create a nationwide hydrogen economy, which includes deploying extensive hydrogen pipeline networks [77, 78].

Recent assessments of hydrogen deployment trends point toward a shift in energy patterns, where hydrogen is increasingly integrated into the broader energy economy. This integration is facilitated by coupling electricity systems with hydrogen production, allowing for a more efficient use of renewable energy [79]. Hydrogen can absorb excess electricity generated from renewables during peak production times, mitigating the issue of curtailment commonly associated with solar and wind energy [80]. This element not only enhances grid stability but also creates an additional revenue stream for renewable energy producers.

References

1. Klopčič N et al (2022) Refurbishment of natural gas pipelines towards 100% hydrogen—A thermodynamic-based analysis. Energies 15(24):9370
2. Glanville P et al (2022) Impact of hydrogen/natural gas blends on partially premixed combustion equipment: NOx emission and operational performance. Energies 15(5):1706
3. Zhang C et al (2023) Key technologies of pure hydrogen and hydrogen-mixed natural gas pipeline transportation. ACS Omega 8(22):19212–19222
4. Ilyushechkin A et al (2023) Material challenges and hydrogen embrittlement assessment for hydrogen utilisation in industrial scale. Hydrogen 4(3):599–619
5. Kethamukkala K, Liu Y (2023) Information fusion and data augmentation for risk-based maintenance optimization of hydrogen gas pipelines. In: 15th Annual conference of the prognostics and health management society, PHM 2023. Prognostics and Health Management Society
6. Abbas AJ et al (2024) Transitioning to a hydrogen economy: exploring the viability of adapting natural gas pipelines for hydrogen transport through a case study on compression versus Looping. Gases 4(2):74–96
7. Zemite L et al (2023) Blending hydrogen with natural gas/biomethane and transportation in existing gas networks. Latv J Phys Tech Sci 60(5):43–55
8. Bdioui H et al (2023) Feasibility study on hydrogen blending into Tunisian natural gas distributing system. Preprint
9. Quintino FM, Nascimento N, Fernandes EC (2021) Aspects of hydrogen and biomethane introduction in natural gas infrastructure and equipment. Hydrogen 2(3):301–318
10. Kigle S et al (2025) TransHyDE-Sys: an integrated systemic approach for analyzing and supporting the transformation of energy systems and hydrogen infrastructure development. Energy Technol 13:2300828
11. Fetisov V, Davardoost H, Mogylevets V (2023) Technological aspects of methane–hydrogen mixture transportation through operating gas pipelines considering industrial and fire safety. Fire 6(10):409
12. Javaheri V (2023) Steel pipeline for the hydrogen storage and delivery: metallurgical viewpoint for Finnish ecosystem. Future Technol 2(1):58–61
13. Agarwal R (2022) Transition to a hydrogen-based economy: possibilities and challenges. Sustainability 14(23):15975
14. Hassan Q et al (2023) Hydrogen fuel cell vehicles: opportunities and challenges. Sustainability 15(15):11501

15. Lee J-S et al (2022) Review of hydrogen gas sensors for future hydrogen mobility infrastructure. Appl Sci Converg Technol 31(4):79–84
16. Sigen A, Li X (2024) Strategic analysis of past and modern hydrogen storage methods and prospects for its future. Innov Sci Technol 3(2):14–20
17. Zakgeym D et al (2023) Better through oxygen functionality? The benzophenone/dicyclohexylmethanol LOHC-system. Sustain Energy Fuels 7(5):1213–1222
18. Makaryan IA et al (2022) A comprehensive review on the prospects of using hydrogen–methane blends: challenges and opportunities. Energies 15(6):2265
19. De Wolf D, Smeers Y (2023) Comparison of battery electric vehicles and fuel cell vehicles. World Electr Veh J 14(9):262
20. Ichimura T, Kasai H, Oka K (2025) Dihydrolevoglucosenone (CyreneTM) as a bio-derived liquid organic hydrogen carrier. ChemPlusChem 90(4):e202400639
21. Fleiter T et al (2025) Hydrogen infrastructure in the future CO_2-neutral European energy system—How does the demand for hydrogen affect the need for infrastructure? Energy Technol 13(2):2300981
22. Cerniauskas S et al (2019) Future hydrogen markets for transportation and industry: the impact of CO_2 taxes. Energies 12:4707
23. Solomon MD et al (2024) Cost optimization of compressed hydrogen gas transport via trucks and pipelines. Energy Technol 12(1):2300785
24. Litvinenko VS et al (2020) Barriers to implementation of hydrogen initiatives in the context of global energy sustainable development. Записки Горного Института 244:428–438
25. Yusuf N, Al-Ansari T (2023) Current and future role of natural gas supply chains in the transition to a low-carbon hydrogen economy: a comprehensive review on integrated natural gas supply chain optimisation models. Energies 16(22):7672
26. Fladvad B (2023) Infrastructuring environmental (in) justice: green hydrogen, Indigenous sovereignty and the political geographies of energy technologies. Geographica Helvetica 78(4):493–505
27. Moon H et al (2022) Urban hydrogen production model using environmental infrastructures to achieve the net zero goal. Energies 15(24):9293
28. Ameli H et al (2024) A review of the role of hydrogen in the heat decarbonization of future energy systems: insights and perspectives. Energies 17(7):1688
29. Kılkış B, Kılkış Ş (2018) Hydrogen economy model for nearly net-zero cities with exergy rationale and energy-water nexus. Energies 11(5):1226
30. Kountouris I et al (2024) A unified European hydrogen infrastructure planning to support the rapid scale-up of hydrogen production. Nat Commun 15(1):5517
31. Zemite L et al (2023) A comprehensive overview of the Europen and Baltic landscape for hydrogen applications and innovations. Latv J Phys Tech Sci 60(3):33–53
32. Álvarez Coomonte A et al (2024) Review of the planning and distribution methodologies to locate hydrogen infrastructure in the territory. Energies 17(1):240
33. Hjort A et al (2023) Fuelling the future: assessing multifuel filling stations for hydrogen and other renewable fuels through life cycle analysis. Energy Sci Eng 11(9):3033–3041
34. Gu S et al (2025) Optimal design of hydrogen-blended natural gas pipeline network considering separation systems. AIChE J 71(2):e18648
35. Abbas AJ et al (2021) An investigation into the volumetric flow rate requirement of hydrogen transportation in existing natural gas pipelines and its safety implications. Gases 1(4):156–179
36. Hoffart FM (2022) Building new H_2 pipelines or repurposing natural gas pipelines for H_2 admix-ture?–An economic perspective on effective climate mitigation. Energy 2004:2965
37. Zhao J, Cheng F (2023) Finite element modeling of the hydrogen atom distribution on dented pipeline for hydrogen transport under cyclic loading. Int J Fract 246:181–201
38. Su Y et al (2022) Prediction of mixing uniformity of hydrogen injection in natural gas pipeline based on a deep learning model. Energies 15(22):8694
39. Ban J et al (2023) Research progress and prospects on hydrogen damage in welds of hydrogen-blended natural gas pipelines. Processes 11(11):3180

40. Lee H, Lee S (2022) Economic analysis on hydrogen pipeline infrastructure establishment scenarios: case study of South Korea. Energies 15(18):6824
41. Tian Y et al (2024) Non-destructive testing technology for corrosion wall thickness reduction defects in pipelines based on electromagnetic ultrasound. Front Earth Sci 12:1432043
42. Abubakar YK et al (2025) A two-parameter computational thermodynamic analysis of hydrogen-impurity mixtures in a repurposed pipeline. Adv Sci Technol 160:33–40
43. Briottet L, Moro I, Lemoine P (2012) Quantifying the hydrogen embrittlement of pipeline steels for safety considerations. Int J Hydrog Energy 37(22):17616–17623
44. Wang A et al (2025) Experimental study on hydrogen-induced crack propagation of X80 steel under alternating pressure fluctuations. Materials 18(5):947
45. Hutsaylyuk V et al (2019) Mechanical properties of gas main steels after long-term operation and peculiarities of their fracture surface morphology. Materials 12(3):491
46. Yazdipour N, Dunne D, Pereloma EV (2012) Effect of grain size on the hydrogen diffusion process in steel using cellular automaton approach. Mater Sci Forum (Trans Tech Publ) 706–769:1568–1573
47. Thomas A, Szpunar JA (2020) Visualisation of diffusion sites and measurement of hydrogen traps in hot-rolled pipes. Mater Sci Technol 36(17):1870–1882
48. Cui Q et al (2017) Effect of nanosized NbC precipitates on hydrogen diffusion in X80 pipeline steel. Materials 10(7):721
49. Cai L, Zhao LM (2018) Effect of hydrogen trapping and poisons on diffusion behavior of hydrogen in low carbon steel. Key Eng Mater 764:3–10
50. Panda PK, Sahoo B, Ramakrishna S (2023) Hydrogen production, purification, storage, transportation, and their applications: a review. Energy Technol 11(7):2201434
51. Cerniauskas S et al (2020) Options of natural gas pipeline reassignment for hydrogen: Cost assessment for a Germany case study. Int J Hydrog Energy 45(21):12095–12107
52. Klopffer M, Flaconneche B, Odru P (2007) Transport properties of gas mixtures through polyethylene. Plast Rubber Compos 36(5):184–189
53. Kane MC et al (2008) Permeability, solubility, and interaction of hydrogen in polymers-an assessment of materials for hydrogen transport. WSRC-STI-2008-00009, Rev. 0. Savannah River Site (SRS), Aiken, SC (United States)
54. Titov AI et al (2019) Hydrogen accumulation and distribution in pipeline steel in intensified corrosion conditions. Materials 12(9):1409
55. Xiaolu C et al (2024) Research on standards and standard system of hydrogen pipeline in China. In: E3S web of conferences 520:04016. EDP Sciences
56. Bu F et al (2024) Analysis of leakage and diffusion characteristics and hazard range determination of buried hydrogen-blended natural gas pipeline based on CFD. ACS Omega 9(37):39202–39218
57. Zhang H et al (2021) Effects of hydrogen blending on hydraulic and thermal characteristics of natural gas pipeline and pipe network. Oil Gas Sci Technol-Revue d'IFP Energies Nouvelles 76:70
58. Weber AC, Papageorgiou LG (2018) Design of hydrogen transmission pipeline networks with hydraulics. Chem Eng Res Des 131:266–278
59. Zacepins A et al (2024) Economic modelling of mixing hydrogen with natural gas. Processes 12(2):262
60. Tawfik Z, El-Sheltawy S, Abdelghany A (2024) Decarbonizing natural gas infrastructure: blending hydrogen for sustainable energy. In: The international conference on chemical and environmental engineering. Military Technical College
61. Qiu Y et al (2022) Multi-stage flexible planning of regional electricity-HCNG-integrated energy system considering gas pipeline retrofit and expansion. IET Renew Power Gener 16(15):3339–3367
62. Löhr L et al (2022) Nested decomposition approach for dispatch optimization of large-scale, integrated electricity, methane and hydrogen infrastructures. Energies 15(8):2716
63. Francesconi M et al (2024) Impact of hydrogen blending on a real-world gas distribution network with a non-uniform elevation profile. J Phys: Conf Ser 2893:012067 (IOP Publishing)

64. de Castro FA et al (2024) Green hydrogen: perspectives and challenges in using the natural gas network in Ceará/Brazil. J Geosci Environ Protect 12(3):70–94
65. Li J, Xie B, Gong L (2024) Numerical research on leakage characteristics of pure hydrogen/hydrogen-blended natural gas in medium-and low-pressure buried pipelines. Energies 17(12):2951
66. Capelle J et al (2008) Sensitivity of pipelines with steel API X52 to hydrogen embrittlement. Int J Hydrog Energy 33(24):7630–7641
67. Leicher J et al (2022) The impact of hydrogen admixture into natural gas on residential and commercial gas appliances. Energies 15(3):777
68. Martin P et al (2024) A review of challenges with using the natural gas system for hydrogen. Energy Sci Eng 12(10):3995–4009
69. Panu M et al (2021) Integration of excess renewable energy with natural gas infrastructure for the production of hydrogen and chemicals. Process Integr Opt Sustain 5:487–504
70. Ogbe E et al (2019) Integrated design and operation optimization of hydrogen commingled with natural gas in pipeline networks. Ind Eng Chem Res 59(4):1584–1595
71. Kut P, Pietrucha-Urbanik K, Zeleňáková M (2024) Assessing the role of hydrogen in sustainable energy futures: a comprehensive bibliometric analysis of research and international collaborations in energy and environmental engineering. Energies 17(8):1862
72. Ogarek P, Wojtoń M, Słyś D (2023) Hydrogen as a renewable energy carrier in a hybrid configuration of distributed energy systems: bibliometric mapping of current knowledge and strategies. Energies 16(14):5495
73. Wu T, Wang J (2022) Reliability evaluation for integrated electricity-gas systems considering hydrogen. IEEE Trans Sustain Energy 14(2):920–934
74. Wan J et al (2024) Research on scenario construction and economic analysis for electric-hydrogen coupling. J Phys: Conf Ser 2728:012075 (IOP Publishing)
75. Masan SE et al (2023) Impact of hydrogen coverage trend on methyl formate adsorption on MoS_2 surface: a first principles study. ACS Omega 8(7):6523–6529
76. Clegg S, Mancarella P (2015) Integrated modeling and assessment of the operational impact of power-to-gas (P2G) on electrical and gas transmission networks. IEEE Trans Sustain Energy 6(4):1234–1244
77. Zhou Y, Chen S, Chen J (2024) A comprehensive survey of low-carbon planning and operation of electricity, hydrogen fuel, and transportation networks. IET Energy Syst Integr 6(2):89–103
78. Fu P, Pudjianto D, Strbac G (2020) Integration of power-to-gas and low-carbon road transport in great Britain's future energy system. IET Renew Power Gener 14(17):3393–3400
79. Li Z et al (2020) Development of renewable energy multi-energy complementary hydrogen energy system (A Case Study in China): a review. Energy Explor Exploit 38(6):2099–2127
80. Sun Q et al (2022) Multi-stage co-planning model for power distribution system and hydrogen energy system under uncertainties. J Modern Power Syst Clean Energy 11(1):80–93

Chapter 3
Integrity Management Programs (IMP)

This chapter provides an in-depth exploration of Hydrogen Pipeline Integrity Management Programs (PIMP), emphasizing the strategic frameworks, regulatory landscapes, performance monitoring mechanisms, and stakeholder engagement processes essential for ensuring the safe and reliable operation of hydrogen pipeline infrastructure. As hydrogen emerges as a key component in the transition to cleaner energy systems, the integrity of its transportation networks is paramount. This chapter presents a structured and forward-looking approach to managing the unique challenges posed by hydrogen pipelines, such as hydrogen embrittlement, high diffusivity, and safety risks.

The chapter begins with an outline of the Framework and Key Components of PIMP, focusing on the implementation of Risk-Based Inspection (RBI) and management cycles. These methodologies prioritize inspection and maintenance activities based on likelihood and consequence of failure, enabling efficient resource allocation and proactive risk mitigation. This section also defines roles and responsibilities, clarifying the accountability of operators, engineers, safety personnel, and management teams within the PIMP framework to ensure consistent oversight and execution.

The next section addresses Regulatory Requirements and Compliance, providing a comprehensive overview of the key codes and standards governing hydrogen pipeline operations, including ASME, ISO, and national safety regulations. It discusses the importance of reporting and documentation, including the development of inspection records, maintenance logs, and incident reports, which serve both operational needs and compliance with regulatory mandates. The chapter emphasizes the need for organizations to stay current with evolving hydrogen-specific guidelines as global energy policies continue to shift.

Performance Indicators and Continuous Improvement are the focus of the third section, where the chapter introduces a set of relevant Key Performance Indicators (KPIs) for hydrogen pipeline integrity. These may include failure rates, inspection intervals, leak detection metrics, and repair times, all of which help quantify system performance. Furthermore, this section details how audits and feedback loops

M. Hussain et al., *Hydrogen Pipeline Integrity*, Green Energy and Technology,
https://doi.org/10.1007/978-981-95-5609-0_3

contribute to continuous improvement by identifying system inefficiencies, validating corrective actions, and ensuring lessons learned are incorporated into future planning cycles.

Finally, the chapter explores the critical role of Stakeholder Engagement and Communication in the long-term success of PIMPs. It outlines mechanisms for reporting to investors and regulators, ensuring transparency, risk disclosure, and alignment with public and environmental expectations. It also emphasizes transparency and trust building, particularly with communities located near pipeline infrastructure, by promoting open dialogue, public education, and ethical communication strategies.

3.1 Framework and Key Components of IMP

The construction and maintenance of a Hydrogen Pipeline Integrity Management Program (PIMP) necessitate a comprehensive understanding of various infrastructural, technological, and regulatory components. A well-structured PIMP integrates several key elements crucial for ensuring pipeline integrity, safety, and operational efficiency, as shown in Fig. 3.1.

This framework is vital for managing the complexities surrounding the transportation of hydrogen through pipelines, especially given its unique material properties and associated risks.

1. ***Regulatory Framework and Standards***

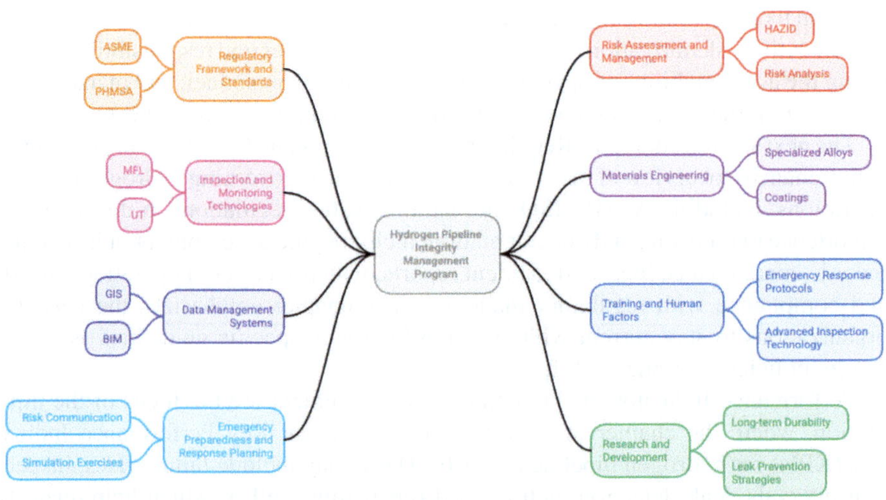

Fig. 3.1 Hydrogen pipeline integrity management

The foundation of any integrity management program is a robust regulatory framework. This framework provides guidelines that govern the design, construction, operation, and maintenance of hydrogen pipelines. Existing standards are often adapted to accommodate hydrogen's specific properties, including its potential for causing material embrittlement in steel and other alloys [1]. Organizations such as the American Society of Mechanical Engineers (ASME) and the Pipeline and Hazardous Materials Safety Administration (PHMSA) are instrumental in developing these regulations to mitigate risks associated with hydrogen transport [2]. As such, adherence to these guidelines ensures that hydrogen pipelines are designed and operated in compliance with safety and environmental standards, minimizing the risk of leaks, ruptures, and catastrophic failures [3].

2. ***Risk Assessment and Management***

An essential component of PIMP is comprehensive risk assessment strategies. This process involves identifying potential hazards associated with hydrogen transport, such as leaks due to material failures or external threats. Risk management techniques, including Hazard Identification (HAZID), Risk Analysis (RA), and Risk Control (RC), are implemented to address these concerns [4]. Modern methodologies often integrate artificial intelligence and machine learning algorithms to predict and mitigate risks more effectively by analyzing historical data and identifying patterns that could indicate impending failures [5]. The application of predictive maintenance—derived from these analyses—ensures proactive management of pipeline integrity, reducing downtime and maintenance costs.

3. ***Inspection and Monitoring Technologies***

Regular inspection and monitoring are fundamental to maintaining pipeline integrity. Non-destructive testing methods, such as Magnetic Flux Leakage (MFL) and Ultrasonic Testing (UT), play a critical role in identifying internal and external corrosion, cracks, and other anomalies in pipeline systems [6]. The integration of real-time monitoring systems, such as smart sensors and Internet of Things (IoT) technologies, allows for continuous assessment of pressure, flow rates, and potential leak detection. These advanced monitoring capabilities not only enhance safety but also improve operational efficiency by enabling timely intervention when anomalies are detected.

4. ***Materials Engineering***

The choice of materials used in constructing hydrogen pipelines is essential for preventing failures due to hydrogen-induced embrittlement (HIE) and stress corrosion cracking (SCC). Research emphasizes the utilization of specialized alloys and coatings that can withstand the unique challenges posed by hydrogen transport [7]. The use of advanced computational methods can assist engineers in selecting suitable materials and evaluating their long-term performance under various environmental conditions. Innovations in materials science, such as carbon fiber reinforced composites and nanostructured materials, are being explored to enhance the performance and reliability of pipeline systems.

5. ***Data Management Systems***

Effective data management is crucial for the operational success of PIMP. The integration of Geographic Information Systems (GIS) and Building Information Modeling (BIM) facilitates better visualization and management of pipeline networks [8]. The development of comprehensive data pipelines allows for the seamless incorporation of data from various sources, promoting informed decision-making. These sophisticated databases capture the essential elements of pipeline systems, including environmental data, historical performance indicators, and real-time monitoring results, leading to enhanced risk assessment and management capabilities [9].

6. ***Training and Human Factors***

Human factors significantly influence the effectiveness of a PIMP. Comprehensive training programs must be developed to ensure personnel are well-versed in the specific operational challenges posed by hydrogen pipelines. This encompasses understanding the physics of hydrogen behavior, emergency response protocols, and mastery of advanced inspection and monitoring technology. By fostering a culture of safety and continuous improvement, organizations can enhance team competence and preparedness, reducing the likelihood of human error that contributes to pipeline incidents [10].

7. ***Emergency Preparedness and Response Planning***

An integral part of PIMP is establishing emergency preparedness and response plans. These strategies dictate how organizations should respond to incidents involving pipeline failures, including leakages and accidents. Plans must include risk communication strategies to inform the public and first responders effectively about the potential hazards associated with hydrogen [11]. Additionally, incorporating simulation exercises and drills can enhance the preparedness of all stakeholders involved, allowing for a more efficient, coordinated response in the event of an emergency.

8. ***Research and Development***

Continuous research and development play an influential role in the evolution of PIMP. Embracing new technologies and methodologies ensures that the management program adapts to emerging risks and advances in engineering practices. Collaborations between industry, academia, and regulatory bodies facilitate knowledge sharing and innovation [12]. Focus areas for R&D include investigating the long-term durability of pipeline materials, improving hydrogen detection technologies, and optimizing leak prevention strategies [13, 14]. This ongoing evaluation allows systems to remain at the forefront of safety and efficiency in hydrogen pipeline operations.

3.1.1 Risk-Based Inspection (RBI) and Management Cycles

Risk-based inspection (RBI) methodologies have become a cornerstone of integrated pipeline integrity management, particularly in the context of hydrogen transport. The complexity of hydrogen pipelines necessitates a framework that allows for systematic risk identification, assessment, and inspection prioritization to ensure safe and reliable operation. The fundamental principle behind RBI is to correlate the probability of failure (PoF) and the consequences of such failures, thus guiding inspection strategies based on quantifiable risk factors.

Conceptual Framework of RBI: RBI involves a multi-faceted approach that includes qualitative and quantitative assessments of potential risks associated with pipeline operations. The RBI process typically begins with identifying potential failure modes, followed by an assessment of their likelihood and the subsequent evaluation of consequences [15]. This allows for the prioritization of inspection efforts, allocating resources where they can yield the greatest safety and reliability improvements, thereby optimizing maintenance and operational costs. The integration of historical data and operational parameters enhances the reliability of risk models and inspection schedules.

Quantitative Risk Assessment: Quantitative risk assessments form the backbone of RBI methodologies. They provide a mathematical basis for evaluating risks associated with pipeline failures and enable the establishment of metrics to guide inspection cycles. One remarkable case involves the quantitative assessment of gas riser pipelines in offshore facilities, where analysis of the probability and consequences of failures informed a more optimal inspection strategy [15]. By using quantitative methods, operators can develop strategies to mitigate risks effectively, making informed decisions about maintenance interventions.

Integration of Reliability Engineering: The integration of reliability engineering principles into RBI practices further enhances its effectiveness. Recognizing the reliability of inspection techniques is crucial for ensuring the accuracy and effectiveness of inspections. An effective RBI framework must encompass the reliability and performance of various inspection methods, accounting for uncertainties inherent in pipeline operations. By emphasizing reliability, organizations can prioritize inspection intervals based on the condition of specific assets rather than generic time-based cycles, thus improving operational efficiency and safety outcomes.

Machine Learning and Predictive Analytics: Recent advancements in machine learning (ML) and data analytics have significantly impacted RBI methodologies for pipeline integrity management. ML models can analyze vast datasets, identifying patterns and anomalies that may indicate potential risks or failures [16]. By applying predictive analytics, operators can move from reactive inspection protocols to more proactive management strategies, anticipating issues before they occur. Implementing such techniques alongside traditional RBI approaches can provide a more comprehensive understanding of the factors that influence pipeline integrity, aiding in better decision-making regarding maintenance schedules and inspection regimes.

Implementation of Management Cycles: The management cycles associated with RBI involve continuous evaluation and adaptation of inspection strategies based on evolving operational conditions and risk profiles. This cyclical process includes the phases of planning, execution, evaluation, and improvement [17]. During the planning phase, risk assessments inform the establishment of inspection intervals and strategies. Following inspections, the results are analyzed to evaluate the effectiveness of the strategies employed and to identify areas requiring further attention. Finally, the insights gained are used to refine and optimize future inspection plans, creating a feedback loop that enhances safety and operational performance.

Collaboration and Stakeholder Engagement: Effective implementation of RBI principles within pipeline integrity management is facilitated through collaboration among various stakeholders. Engaging with regulators, industry experts, and operational personnel fosters a culture of safety and promotes the sharing of best practices and lessons learned. This collaborative approach ensures that the RBI framework is continually updated to reflect the latest technological advancements and regulatory requirements, thereby maintaining its relevance and effectiveness in a rapidly evolving energy landscape [18].

3.2 Regulatory Requirements and Compliance

The regulatory landscape surrounding hydrogen pipeline transport is crucial for ensuring both safety and environmental protection. As the deployment of hydrogen infrastructure expands, particularly in the context of energy transition towards cleaner fuels, adherence to established regulations and compliance mechanisms becomes increasingly important. The development and implementation of a comprehensive regulatory framework that governs the entire lifecycle of hydrogen pipelines—from design and construction to operation and decommissioning, as shown in Fig. 3.2—are paramount for mitigating risks associated with hydrogen transport [19].

Fig. 3.2 Navigating the regulatory landscape of hydrogen pipelines

The development of specific hydrogen standards has been initiated, addressing the unique characteristics and risks associated with hydrogen transport, including its compatibility with various pipeline materials and potential embrittlement issues. Comprehensive regulations, such as the Technical Regulation on Onshore Oil and Gas Pipelines (RTDT) in Brazil, serve as useful benchmarks for ensuring safe operational practices across diverse geographical and operational contexts [20].

Operators are required to develop inspection protocols that not only comply with regulatory mandates but also integrate advanced technological applications, ensuring that inspections effectively identify potential failures before they occur. This proactive compliance strategy is essential in managing the integrity of hydrogen pipelines, particularly given the material challenges posed by hydrogen transport [21]. These international frameworks encourage countries to share best practices and collaborate on research initiatives aimed at improving safety and efficiency in hydrogen pipeline management. Furthermore, adherence to internationally recognized standards can facilitate cross-border hydrogen trade, aligning with broader economic and environmental goals across regions [19].

3.2.1 Key Codes and Standards

The key codes and standards relevant to hydrogen pipeline integrity management programs (PIMPs) is briefly discussed in Table 3.1.

These codes and standards, along with other relevant national and international guidelines, form the regulatory framework that governs the integrity management of hydrogen pipeline infrastructure.

3.3 Performance Indicators and Continuous Improvement

In the context of hydrogen pipeline integrity management, performance indicators are vital for assessing the efficiency of operations and the effectiveness of compliance with regulatory requirements. Continuous improvement involves adapting and enhancing processes based on performance assessments and feedback from various stakeholders. Following this framework, organizations involved in hydrogen pipeline transport can better ensure safety, minimize risks, and promote sustainable practices.

1. ***Defining Key Performance Indicators (KPIs)***

The identification and definition of key performance indicators (KPIs) are crucial for effectively monitoring the integrity of hydrogen pipelines [22]. KPIs should encompass various dimensions, including safety, reliability, environmental impact, and operational efficiency. For instance, metrics such as failure rates, incident reports, and corrective action response times are essential for evaluating safety protocols in pipeline operations. The implementation of real-time monitoring technologies can

Table 3.1 Key codes and standards

Code/standard	Scope/coverage	Key relevance to hydrogen pipelines
ASME B31.12—Hydrogen piping and pipelines	Design, materials, fabrication, assembly, testing, inspection, and operation of hydrogen piping and pipeline systems	Addresses hydrogen embrittlement, ensures safe hydrogen transport
PHMSA regulations (49 CFR Part 192 & 193)	U.S. regulations for hazardous materials and pipeline safety	Covers design, construction, operation, and maintenance to ensure public and environmental safety
ISO 19880-1—Gaseous hydrogen fueling stations	Guidelines for design, installation, and operation of hydrogen fueling stations & infrastructure	Focus on safety, material compatibility, and inspection in hydrogen supply chain
EN 17124—Hydrogen fuel: product specification & quality assurance	Quality standards and test methods for hydrogen fuel in transport applications	Ensures hydrogen purity and safety for fuel cells and hydrogen-powered equipment
RTDT—Technical regulation on onshore oil & gas pipelines (Brazil)	Brazilian regulation for design, construction, operation, and maintenance of onshore pipelines	Includes inspection, community engagement, and incident investigation for hydrogen pipelines
ASME boiler & pressure vessel code (BPVC), Sect. VIII, Div. 1	General requirements for design, fabrication, and inspection of pressure vessels	Relevant to components used in hydrogen pipeline systems

significantly improve the accuracy of KPIs by providing immediate data on pipeline conditions, leading to timely interventions.

2. ***Safety Performance Indicators***

Safety performance indicators are paramount in hydrogen pipeline management due to the potential hazards associated with hydrogen transport. Metrics such as the number of reportable incidents, leak detection response times, and emergency response effectiveness should be continuously monitored [23]. Compliance with safety performance metrics is associated with enhanced safety outcomes and reflects broader quality management within operations. Organizations must establish a baseline for these indicators, referencing historical data to track improvements over time and elucidate patterns that may necessitate enhanced safety measures.

3. ***Reliability and Operational Efficiency Metrics***

Reliability metrics can include the number of operational days without incidents or failures, while operational efficiency may be measured by throughput and the frequency of scheduled maintenance or inspections. Establishing benchmarks and trends in these metrics provides actionable insights into the operational health of pipeline systems.

4. ***Environmental Compliance Metrics***

In light of the growing emphasis on corporate social responsibility and environmental accountability, environmental compliance metrics are gaining importance. These metrics could include emissions leakage rates, adherence to environmental regulations, and the effectiveness of strategies to mitigate environmental impacts [24]. Regular reporting on these aspects enables organizations to demonstrate their commitment to sustainability, which has becomc increasingly relevant to stakeholders and regulators alike.

5. ***Incorporating Continuous Improvement Cycles***

Adopting a continuous improvement cycle involves systematically applying performance indicators and feedback to enhance operational practices. The Plan-Do-Check-Act (PDCA), see Fig. 3.3, cycle is a widely recognized framework that facilitates this process. Organizations can initiate planning efforts based on analyzed performance indicators, execute changes in operations, verify the effectiveness of those changes through post-implementation reviews, and refine processes accordingly. This iterative approach ensures dynamic adaptation to operational challenges, regulatory shifts, and changes in stakeholder expectations.

6. ***Stakeholder Engagement and Communication***

Engaging stakeholders in the development and monitoring of performance indicators is crucial for fostering a culture of accountability and transparency. By actively seeking input from employees, regulators, and the communities impacted by hydrogen pipeline operations, organizations can identify gaps in performance and areas for improvement. Effective communication of performance metrics and progress towards goals reinforces trust and enables collective learning, promoting best practices across the industry.

7. ***Leveraging Technology for Performance Monitoring***

The integration of advanced technologies, such as Internet of Things (IoT) sensors and big data analytics, can significantly enhance performance monitoring capabilities. Such technologies facilitate real-time data collection, allowing for predictive maintenance and proactive decision-making [25]. By analyzing data trends on pipeline performance and integrity, organizations can quickly identify anomalies and address potential issues before they escalate, ultimately leading to improved safety and reduced operational disruptions.

8. ***Training and Development for Compliance***

Investment in workforce training is essential for ensuring compliance with established performance indicators and operational procedures. Regular training programs focusing on regulatory requirements, operational best practices, and safety protocols are vital for enhancing employee competency [26]. Ensuring that personnel are equipped with the necessary skills to navigate compliance challenges reduces the likelihood of failures and fosters a culture of safety within the organization.

9. ***Benchmarking and Industry Comparisons***

Fig. 3.3 Continuous improvement cycle

Benchmarking against industry standards and competitors can provide valuable insights into an organization's performance relative to peers. Understanding competitive positioning helps identify opportunities for improvement and establishes realistic targets for performance indicators. Regularly engaging with industry associations or partnerships can enhance knowledge sharing and promote the adoption of best practices.

3.3.1 KPIs for Pipeline Integrity

Key Performance Indicators (KPIs) play a crucial role in managing and maintaining the integrity of hydrogen pipelines refer (see Table 3.2). These indicators facilitate a comprehensive evaluation of the operations, safety, and environmental sustainability of pipeline systems.

1. ***Safety Performance Indicators***

Safety is paramount in hydrogen pipeline operations, given the potential hazards associated with hydrogen transport. Key safety performance indicators include:

- **Incident Rate**: Measures the number of incidents per operational hour or mile of pipeline. This KPI helps in assessing the overall safety record of operations and pinpointing areas in need of improvement.

Table 3.2 Key performance indicators (KPIs) for hydrogen pipeline integrity

KPI	Description	Measurement method	Target/ benchmark	Frequency of monitoring
Leak detection rate	Number of leaks detected per length of pipeline	Leak detection sensors, inspections	Zero leaks or minimal leak rate	Continuous/ Monthly
Corrosion rate	Rate of pipeline wall thickness reduction	Ultrasonic testing, corrosion probes	Below threshold set by standards	Quarterly/ Semi-annual
Pipeline pressure stability	Maintaining pipeline pressure within safe limits	Pressure sensors	±5% of operating pressure	Continuous
Integrity test completion	Percentage of scheduled integrity tests completed	Inspection records	100% completion	Annually
Incident response time	Time taken to respond to detected anomalies	Incident logs	Under defined response time (e.g., 1 h)	Per incident
Hydrogen embrittlement rate	Occurrence of embrittlement-related defects	Material testing, inspections	Zero or minimal occurrences	Annual/after major events
Pipeline repair frequency	Number of repairs required per pipeline length	Maintenance records	Decreasing trend preferred	Monthly/ Quarterly
Safety compliance rate	Compliance with safety and regulatory standards	Audit reports	100% compliance	Annual/after audits
Operational downtime	Time pipeline is non-operational due to integrity issues	Operations logs	Minimized downtime	Monthly
Customer complaints related to pipeline integrity	Number of complaints indicating pipeline issues	Customer service logs	Zero or minimal complaints	Monthly

- **Response Time to Incidents**: Tracks the average time taken to respond to safety incidents, including leak detection and emergency repairs. Quick response times are critical for minimizing damage.
- **Leak Detection Rate**: Represents the percentage of leaks detected versus those that occur. Effective leak detection systems are vital for maintaining safety and minimizing environmental impact.

These safety indicators provide essential insights into the effectiveness of safety practices and highlight areas requiring attention or improvement.

2. ***Reliability Metrics***

Reliability metrics focus on the functionality of the pipeline and its ability to carry out its intended operations without failure. Key reliability KPIs include:

- **Mean Time Between Failures (MTBF)**: This metric calculates the average time between failures for the pipeline system. A higher MTBF indicates greater reliability and efficiency in operations.
- **Number of Unscheduled Downtimes**: Tracks how often unplanned outages occur due to equipment failures or infrastructure issues. Reducing unscheduled downtime is critical for maintaining the integrity of hydrogen transport.
- **Inspection Effectiveness**: Measures the percentage of inspections that lead to proactive identification of potential issues. This indicator is pivotal for assessing the efficacy of maintenance strategies.

Tracking these reliability indicators helps organizations understand the operational health of their hydrogen pipeline systems and fosters continual enhancement of reliability practices.

3. ***Environmental Compliance Indicators***

With increasing focus on sustainability and reducing environmental impact, environmental compliance indicators have become crucial for hydrogen pipeline management. These KPIs include:

- **Emissions Monitoring**: Measures the volume of greenhouse gases and other pollutants emitted from pipeline operations. This indicator is essential for assessing compliance with environmental regulations and improving sustainability practices.
- **Impact Assessment of Spills and Leaks**: Evaluates the extent of environmental damage caused by pipeline leaks or incidents. This metric is important for determining response effectiveness and improving practices to prevent future incidents.
- **Waste Management Efficiency**: Assesses how effectively materials and by-products are managed throughout the hydrogen supply chain. This overall efficiency reflects an organization's commitment to sustainable practices.

By focusing on environmental compliance metrics, organizations can enhance their sustainability efforts and mitigate the ecological risks associated with hydrogen transport.

4. ***Operational Efficiency Metrics***

Operational efficiency metrics assess how effectively resources are utilized within pipeline operations. Key KPIs for measuring operational efficiency include:

- **Pipeline Utilization Rate**: This metric calculates the percentage of the pipeline's capacity utilized. Higher utilization rates suggest efficient operations and greater profitability.
- **Maintenance Costs per Mile of Pipeline**: Evaluates the average expenditure on maintenance activities for each mile of pipeline. Lower costs can indicate improved operational efficiency and effective resource management.
- **Average Repair Time**: Measures the time taken to address and resolve pipeline issues. Quick repair times are crucial for maintaining operational continuity.

These operational efficiency indicators enable organizations to streamline operations effectively and improve cost-efficiency within their pipeline management systems.

5. ***Stakeholder Satisfaction Metrics***

While often overlooked, stakeholder satisfaction is an essential aspect of pipeline integrity management. KPIs related to stakeholder satisfaction include:

- **Community Engagement Frequency**: Monitors how often organizations engage with local communities to address concerns and convey operational changes. Regular engagement fosters trust and transparency.
- **Public Feedback Ratings**: Captures community attitudes towards pipeline operations through surveys or feedback mechanisms. Positive ratings reflect effective communication and responsibility in handling community relations.

Engaging stakeholders and understanding their perceptions can significantly enhance an organization's reputation and lead to more productive operations.

6. ***Continuous Improvement through KPIs***

The role of KPIs extends beyond mere measurement; they serve as a foundation for continuous improvement initiatives. Implementing a feedback loop involving the PDCA (Plan-Do-Check-Act) cycle enables organizations to analyze KPIs and develop strategies for enhancement. For example:

- **Analysis of Incident Data**: Regular review of safety performance indicators alongside historical incident data can identify trends and lead to interventions that enhance safety protocols.
- **Operational Audit and Benchmarking**: Comparing performance metrics against industry standards can highlight gaps in efficiency and provide a path for operational enhancements.

Through diligent monitoring of these KPIs and a commitment to continuous improvement, organizations can enhance the integrity of hydrogen pipelines and promote sustainable practices.

3.3.2 Audits and Feedback Loops

In the management of hydrogen pipeline integrity, audits and feedback loops play integral roles in ensuring ongoing compliance with safety standards and the continual improvement of operational practices. Effective auditing processes help organizations assess their pipeline integrity management systems, identify areas for improvement, and drive quality enhancements. Concurrently, feedback loops serve to reinforce learning and adapt practices based on audit findings, promoting a culture of continuous improvement.

1. ***The Auditing Process***

The auditing process typically involves systematic evaluations of pipeline operations to determine adherence to established standards and best practices. In the context of hydrogen pipeline integrity, audits can be categorized into two main types: internal and external audits. Internal audits are conducted by the organization's personnel to assess compliance with internal policies and procedures, while external audits are performed by third-party entities to ensure compliance with regulatory standards and provide an impartial evaluation [27].

2. ***Implementing Feedback Loops***

Feedback loops are critical for creating a responsive and adaptive pipeline management system, as depict in Fig. 3.4. They involve the continuous process of collecting, analyzing, and acting upon both audit findings and operational data. The functionality of a feedback loop in pipeline integrity management can be illustrated as follows:

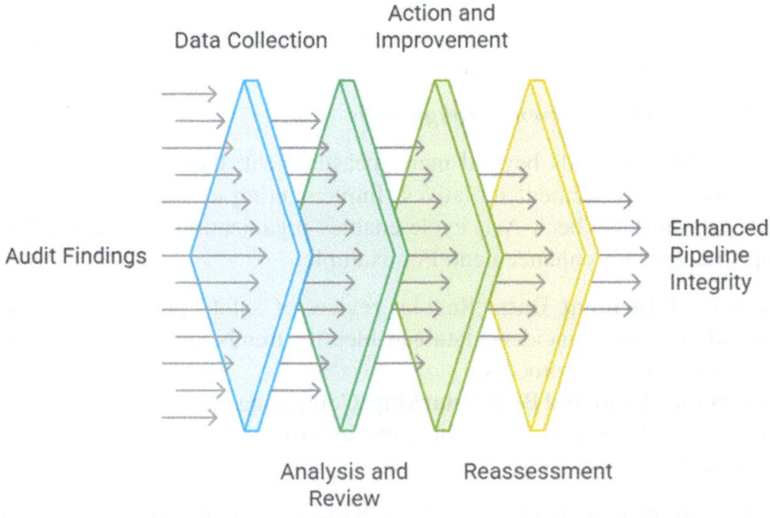

Fig. 3.4 Continuous improvement in pipeline integrity

- **Data Collection**: Gathering data from audits, incident reports, inspections, and operational metrics is the first step in the feedback process. For example, metrics related to leak detection effectiveness and response times can help pinpoint areas requiring immediate attention [28].
- **Analysis and Review**: The collected data should be analyzed to identify trends, inconsistencies, and potential risks. This analysis allows organizations to understand the effectiveness of their current practices, leading to informed decision-making. For instance, identifying a recurring failure in leak response protocols through data analysis can facilitate targeted training and re-evaluation of procedures.
- **Action and Improvement**: Based on the analysis, organizations must implement corrective actions to address any deficiencies identified during audits or through operational metrics. For example, if an audit reveals inadequate leak detection capacity, investments in better sensor technologies or enhanced training for personnel may be warranted [29].
- **Reassessment**: After corrective measures have been implemented, reassessment through subsequent audits and data evaluations is crucial to determine whether improvements have taken effect. This cycle of continuous improvement is vital for maintaining the integrity of hydrogen pipeline systems [29].

3. ***Creating a Culture of Continuous Improvement***

To foster a culture of continuous improvement, organizations must embrace audit findings and the feedback loop as part of their operational ethos. This cultural shift can be facilitated through several strategies:

- **Training and Development**: Empowering staff through training programs that emphasize the importance of audits and the value of feedback can foster greater engagement and accountability. Providing education on compliance standards, safety protocols, and best practices is crucial for building a competent workforce [30].
- **Open Communication Channels**: Encouraging open communication regarding audit results and operational feedback promotes transparency. It enables team members to share insights, improvements, and challenges, which can collectively enhance pipeline integrity management strategies.
- **Performance Accountability**: Establishing accountability measures for staff regarding adherence to safety protocols and operational standards ensures that all employees understand their roles in upholding pipeline integrity. Recognizing and rewarding teams for successful audit outcomes can motivate continued compliance and improvement [31].
- ***The Role of Technology in Auditing and Feedback***

The integration of technology has revolutionized the auditing and feedback processes within pipeline management. Utilizing automated systems for data collection and analysis enhances the accuracy and efficiency of audits. Several technological advancements contribute to this evolution:

- **Data Analytics**: Leveraging big data analytics enables organizations to monitor pipeline operations in real time, providing immediate feedback on conditions and performance [32]. By implementing data-driven insights, organizations can identify trends and design predictive maintenance strategies to mitigate risks.
- **Auditing Software**: The use of specialized auditing and compliance management software streamlines processes by automating data collection, reporting, and follow-up actions. This software can facilitate easier access to historical audit data, making it simpler to track continuous improvement over time [33].
- **Remote Auditing Technologies**: With increased reliance on remote monitoring systems, auditors can assess pipeline integrity without needing to be physically present on-site. This capability not only enhances efficiency but also reduces costs associated with traditional auditing methods [33].

3.4 Stakeholder Engagement and Communication

Stakeholder engagement is a fundamental component in the management of hydrogen pipeline integrity, particularly in fostering transparent communication, enhancing public trust, and facilitating collaboration among various parties involved in hydrogen transportation. The successful implementation of stakeholder engagement strategies has significant implications for the operational efficiency and regulatory compliance of hydrogen pipeline systems.

1. ***Understanding Stakeholder Roles***

Identifying and understanding the roles of various stakeholders is crucial for effective engagement. Stakeholders in hydrogen pipeline projects typically include government authorities, regulatory bodies, community representatives, environmental groups, industry players, and the general public. As noted by Yusif and Hafeez-Baig [34], determining the best approach to stakeholder engagement enables organizations to better understand stakeholder needs and expectations, which is critical for fostering cooperative relationships and aligning interests.

2. ***Types of Communication Channels***

Effective communication channels are essential for engaging stakeholders throughout the lifecycle of hydrogen pipeline projects. The choice of communication methods can affect the level of engagement and the clarity of the information shared. Various channels to communicate with stakeholders may include:

- **Public Meetings and Workshops**: Hosting community meetings allows stakeholders to voice concerns and ask questions directly related to hydrogen pipeline operations. This face-to-face interaction fosters trust and enhances collaboration.
- **Online Platforms**: Websites, social media, and email newsletters can serve as effective tools for disseminating information about project developments, safety protocols, and community impacts, enabling stakeholders to stay informed and engaged [35].

- **Surveys and Feedback Mechanisms**: Regularly soliciting feedback from stakeholders provides organizations with insights into public perceptions and concerns related to hydrogen projects. This approach helps to address potential issues proactively and adapt to stakeholder preferences [36].
- ***Best Practices for Effective Stakeholder Engagement***

Establishing best engagement practices can enhance the depth and quality of stakeholder interactions. These practices include:

- **Dynamic Interaction**: As emphasized by Gould [37], fostering dynamic interaction among stakeholders facilitates knowledge sharing and collaboration, which are essential for developing innovative solutions to challenges associated with hydrogen transport.
- **Transparency**: Maintaining open lines of communication and providing stakeholders with clear information about decisions, risks, and project impacts can enhance trust and credibility. Organizations should ensure that updates regarding operational changes and safety measures are communicated clearly to all stakeholders.
- **Capacity Building**: Engaging stakeholders in capacity-building initiatives can empower them with knowledge and skills relevant to hydrogen pipeline management. This approach can create a more informed stakeholder base capable of contributing constructively to discussions and decisions.
- ***Measuring Stakeholder Engagement Outcomes***

To gauge the effectiveness of stakeholder engagement efforts, organizations should establish metrics that reflect stakeholder satisfaction and the degree of involvement. Potential metrics may include:

- **Engagement Participation Rates**: Tracking the number of stakeholders participating in meetings, surveys, and other engagement activities is an indicator of interest and involvement in hydrogen projects.
- **Feedback Quality**: Assessing the quality of feedback received from stakeholders, including suggestions for improvements or concerns raised, can inform areas for enhancement in communication practices [35].
- **Trust Levels**: Measuring shifts in public trust toward hydrogen pipeline operations can indicate the success of engagement efforts and guide future strategies [38].
- ***The Role of Stakeholder Engagement in Crisis Management***

Effective stakeholder engagement is particularly critical in crisis situations, such as incidents involving leaks or safety concerns. Well-established engagement practices can facilitate swift and effective communication with stakeholders during emergencies, enabling rapid dissemination of information and mitigation of public concerns. For example, clear and timely communication can help prevent misinformation and foster public confidence in the organization's ability to manage crises effectively [39].

3.4.1 Reporting to Investors and Regulators

Effective stakeholder engagement is crucial for reporting to investors and regulators in the context of hydrogen pipeline integrity management. Organizations must establish transparent and comprehensive communication channels to ensure that all relevant stakeholders are informed about the operational performance, safety measures, and compliance status of hydrogen pipeline systems.

Reporting to Investors Investors are key stakeholders who require detailed information about the financial and operational aspects of hydrogen pipeline projects. Reporting to investors should include the following elements:

1. **Financial Performance**: Detailed financial statements, including capital expenditures, operational costs, and revenue projections, to demonstrate the viability and profitability of the hydrogen pipeline infrastructure.
2. **Operational Efficiency**: Metrics related to pipeline utilization, throughput, and maintenance costs to showcase the operational efficiency and reliability of the hydrogen transport system.
3. **Risk Management**: Comprehensive risk assessment and mitigation strategies to assure investors about the organization's ability to manage potential hazards and ensure the safety of hydrogen pipelines [40].
4. **Sustainability and Environmental Impact**: Information on the organization's efforts to minimize the environmental impact of hydrogen transport, including emissions monitoring, waste management, and compliance with relevant regulations [37].
5. **Stakeholder Engagement**: Details on the organization's stakeholder engagement initiatives, such as community outreach, public feedback mechanisms, and collaboration with industry partners, to demonstrate a commitment to transparency and accountability.

Reporting to Regulators Regulatory bodies play a crucial role in ensuring the safety and compliance of hydrogen pipeline operations. Reporting to regulators should encompass the following:

1. **Regulatory Compliance**: Detailed documentation of the organization's adherence to applicable codes, standards, and regulations governing the design, construction, operation, and maintenance of hydrogen pipelines.
2. **Safety Performance**: Comprehensive reporting on safety metrics, including incident rates, emergency response times, and leak detection effectiveness, to demonstrate the organization's commitment to safety [41].
3. **Inspection and Maintenance**: Detailed records of pipeline inspections, maintenance activities, and corrective actions taken to address any identified issues, in line with regulatory requirements.
4. **Incident Reporting and Investigation**: Thorough reporting on any pipeline incidents, including root cause analyses and corrective measures implemented to prevent future occurrences, as mandated by regulatory bodies [42].

5. **Stakeholder Engagement and Communication**: Information on the organization's stakeholder engagement strategies, particularly with local communities and regulatory agencies, to ensure transparent and collaborative relationships.

By adopting a comprehensive and transparent approach to reporting, organizations can effectively communicate their commitment to safety, operational excellence, and environmental responsibility to both investors and regulators. This, in turn, can enhance trust, facilitate regulatory compliance, and support the long-term viability of hydrogen pipeline infrastructure.

3.4.2 Transparency and Trust Building

Effective stakeholder engagement relies on establishing transparency and building trust between organizations and their stakeholders, see Fig. 3.5. Transparency enables open communication and accountability, while trust fosters collaborative relationships and enhances the credibility of the organization's actions.

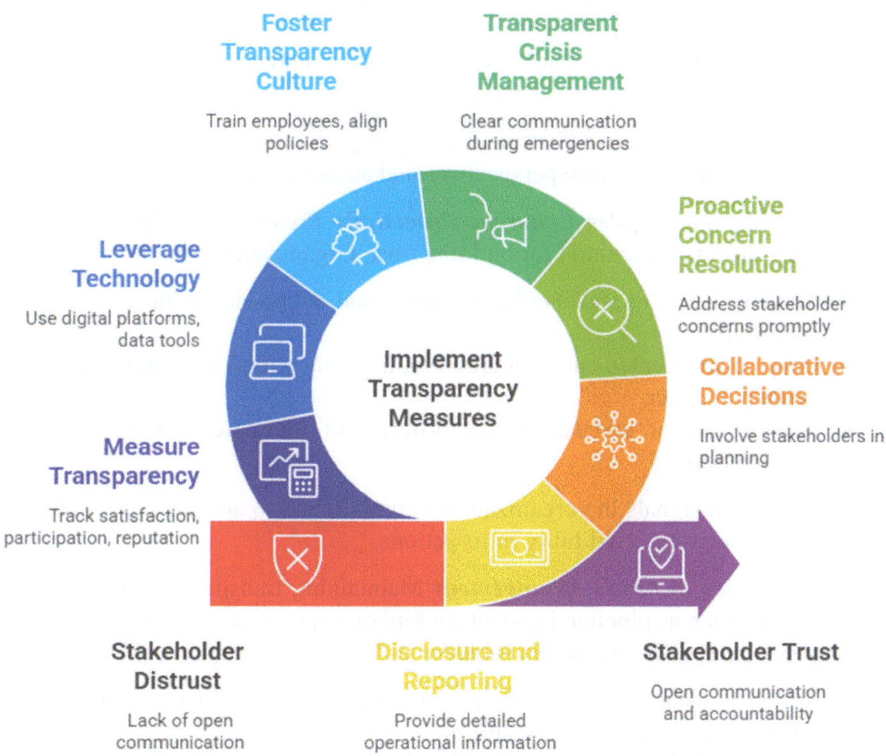

Fig. 3.5 Building transparency and trust

1. ***Transparency through Disclosure and Reporting*** Transparency is a fundamental principle that underpins effective stakeholder engagement. Organizations can demonstrate transparency through comprehensive disclosure and reporting practices. This includes:

   - Providing detailed information about pipeline operations, safety protocols, and environmental impact assessments [43].
   - Regularly publishing performance metrics, incident reports, and corrective actions taken to address stakeholder concerns.
   - Engaging stakeholders in the development of reporting frameworks to ensure their needs and expectations are reflected [44].

Transparent reporting enhances accountability and builds trust by demonstrating the organization's commitment to open communication.

2. ***Collaborative Decision-Making Processes*** Transparency in decision-making processes is crucial for building trust with stakeholders. Organizations should:

   - Involve stakeholders in the planning, design, and implementation of hydrogen pipeline projects.
   - Clearly communicate the rationale behind decisions and how stakeholder input has been incorporated.
   - Establish feedback mechanisms that allow stakeholders to voice their concerns and influence future decisions [45].

By fostering collaborative decision-making, organizations can demonstrate their willingness to consider diverse perspectives and address stakeholder interests.

3. ***Addressing Stakeholder Concerns Proactively*** Proactively addressing stakeholder concerns is essential for building trust. Organizations should:

   - Actively listen to stakeholder feedback and acknowledge their issues and perspectives.
   - Develop and implement strategies to mitigate identified risks and concerns in a timely manner.
   - Provide regular updates on the progress of mitigation efforts and their effectiveness.

This approach signals the organization's commitment to addressing stakeholder needs and enhances the credibility of its actions.

4. ***Transparency in Crisis Management*** Maintaining transparency during crisis situations, such as pipeline incidents or emergencies, is crucial for building and preserving trust. Organizations should:

   - Establish clear communication protocols to provide timely and accurate information to stakeholders [46].
   - Engage stakeholders in the development of emergency response plans and ensure their concerns are addressed.

- Conduct thorough investigations into incidents and share the findings and corrective actions with stakeholders [47].

Transparent crisis management demonstrates accountability and commitment to the safety and well-being of the affected communities.

5. ***Fostering a Culture of Transparency and Trust*** Embedding a culture of transparency and trust-building within the organization is essential for sustaining effective stakeholder engagement. This can be achieved through:

- Providing training and resources to employees on the importance of transparency and stakeholder engagement.
- Aligning organizational policies, procedures, and incentives to reinforce the value of transparency and trust.
- Regularly reviewing and updating engagement strategies based on stakeholder feedback and evolving expectations.

By cultivating a transparent and trustworthy organizational culture, the hydrogen pipeline operator can enhance its credibility and foster long-term, collaborative relationships with stakeholders [48].

6. ***Leveraging Technology for Transparency*** Emerging technologies can enhance transparency and facilitate trust-building in stakeholder engagement. Organizations can leverage:

- Digital platforms and social media to facilitate real-time information sharing and interactive communication.
- Data visualization tools to present complex information clearly and accessibly.
- Blockchain-based systems to ensure the integrity and traceability of data and decision-making processes [49].

The strategic application of technology can strengthen transparency, improve stakeholder understanding, and demonstrate the organization's commitment to open and accountable practices.

7. ***Measuring Transparency and Trust*** Establishing metrics to assess the effectiveness of transparency and trust-building efforts is crucial for continuous improvement. Potential indicators may include:

- Stakeholder satisfaction surveys and feedback.
- Participation rates in engagement activities and decision-making processes.
- Perceived credibility and reputation of the organization among stakeholders.

By regularly monitoring and evaluating these metrics, organizations can identify areas for enhancement and adapt their strategies accordingly.

References

1. Ban J et al (2023) Research progress and prospects on hydrogen damage in welds of hydrogen-blended natural gas pipelines. Processes 11(11):3180
2. Ott B et al (2023) Ensuring natural gas infrastructure is suitable for hydrogen service. Process Saf Prog 42(2):213–224
3. Fan Y, Feng X-X (2023) Research on integrity management of long distance pipeline. In: E3S web of conferences. EDP Sciences
4. Tan J et al (2025) Data analysis and modeling of gas pipeline intelligent management system based on machine learning algorithm. J Comput Methods Sci Eng 14727978251324145
5. Ogbe E et al (2019) Integrated design and operation optimization of hydrogen commingled with natural gas in pipeline networks. Ind Eng Chem Res 59(4):1584–1595
6. Khwaja SA, Paul S (2022) Inspection of coated hydrogen transportation pipelines. Appl Sci 12(19):9503
7. Ahad MT et al (2023) An overview of challenges for the future of hydrogen. Materials 16(20):6680
8. Huang Y et al (2023) A research on data integration and application technology of urban comprehensive pipe gallery based on three-dimensional geographic information system platform. IET Smart Cities 5(2):111–122
9. Feng Z et al (2025) Intelligent measurement switch full performance testing pipeline operation and maintenance based on digital twin technology. In: International conference on computer graphics, artificial intelligence, and data processing (ICCAID 2024). SPIE
10. Khanal A et al (2024) Review of hydrogen-related accidents: root causes, mitigation strategies, and recommendations for secure utilization. In: IOP conference series: earth and environmental science. IOP Publishing
11. Russo P, De Marco A, Parisi F (2020) Assessment of the damage from hydrogen pipeline explosions on people and buildings. Energies 13(19):5051
12. Hussain M et al (2024) Application of artificial intelligence in the oil and gas industry. Engineering applications of artificial intelligence. Springer, pp 341–373
13. Kuczyński S et al (2019) Thermodynamic and technical issues of hydrogen and methane-hydrogen mixtures pipeline transmission. Energies 12(3):569
14. Mahajan D et al (2022) Hydrogen blending in gas pipeline networks—A review. Energies 15(10):3582
15. Asfar MIY et al (2021) Quantitative risk-based inspection on gas riser pipelines at offshore facilities. Teknomekanik 4(2):78–84
16. Amadhe F, Anjorin R, Uwoghiren F (2021) Advancements in machine learning for pipeline integrity management: a comprehensive review of predictive and optimization techniques. Cogn J Multidiscip Stud 4(11)
17. Rahman OHOS, Pratama FW, Siradj ES (2022) Risk indentification on superheater pipeline boiler of 600 MW power plants using a risk based inspection (RBI) method. Jurnal Pendidikan Teknologi Kejuruan 5(4):111–114
18. Sun Y, Cheng F (2024) Dissociative adsorption of hydrogen molecules at Al_2O_3 inclusions in steels and its implications for gaseous hydrogen embrittlement of pipelines. Corros Mater Degrad 5(2):200–223
19. Chen X et al (2024) Research on standards and standard system of hydrogen pipeline in China. In: E3S web of conferences. EDP Sciences
20. Silva BF, Filho PPDM (2025) Analysis of a third-party action incident in a gas pipeline: a case study of the Cuiabá Lateral Pipeline in Brazil. Process Safety Progr 44(1):114–121
21. Giannini L et al (2023) Materials for hydrogen storage and transport: implications for risk-based inspection. Key Eng Mater 959:221–230
22. Nicotra G et al (2024) Process safety & asset integrity key performance indicators (PS&AI KPIs): an operative model for strengthening the asset safety barriers. In: SPE international conference and exhibition on health, safety, environment, and sustainability. SPE

23. Johnson OB et al (2024) Developing real-time monitoring models to enhance operational support and improve incident response times. Int J Eng Res Dev 20(11):1296–1304
24. Arvanitopoulos T, Garsous G, Agnolucci P (2021) Carbon leakage and agriculture: a literature review on emissions mitigation policies. OECD food, agriculture and fisheries papers, No. 169, OECD Publishing, Paris
25. Hussain M, Zhang T, Seema M (2023) Adoption of big data analytics for energy pipeline condition assessment-a systematic review. Int J Press Vessels Pip 206:105061
26. Olonilua O, Aliu JO (2025) Assessing workforce training strategies in critical infrastructure: insights and recommendations. Institute for Homeland Security, Sam Houston State University
27. Hurst JR et al (2020) National clinical audit for hospitalised exacerbations of COPD. ERJ Open Res 6(3):00208
28. Zahid MJ et al (2023) Assessing adherence to Royal College of Surgeons guidelines: a closed-loop audit of operation notes in a tertiary healthcare unit. Cureus 15(9):e45743
29. Lampa S et al (2019) SciPipe: a workflow library for agile development of complex and dynamic bioinformatics pipelines. GigaScience 8(5):giz044
30. Frendy, Takeda F (2023) Employing string similarity metrics of partners to estimate audit team continuity: determinant and its effects on audit outcomes and pricing. J Account Lit 45(2):314–339
31. Shin IH, Lee MG, Park W (2013) Implementation of the continuous auditing system in the ERP-based environment. Manag Audit J 28(7):592–627
32. Ingen-Housz-Oro S et al (2013) Dermatosurgery: total quality management in a dermatology department. Dermatology 225(3):204–209
33. Lins S et al (2015) What is really going on at your cloud service provider? Creating trustworthy certifications by continuous auditing. In: 2015 48th Hawaii international conference on system sciences. IEEE
34. Yusif S, Hafeez-Baig A (2024) Impact of stakeholder engagement strategies on managerial cognitive decision-making: the context of CSP and CSR. Soc Responsib J 20(6):1101–1121
35. Pizzi S et al (2021) Social media as stakeholder engagement tool: CSR communication failure in the oil and gas sector. Corp Soc Responsib Environ Manag 28(2):849–859
36. Kaur A, Lodhia S (2018) Stakeholder engagement in sustainability accounting and reporting: a study of australian local councils. Account Audit Account J 31(1):338–368
37. Wayne Gould R (2012) Open innovation and stakeholder engagement. J Technol Manag Innov 7(3):1–11
38. Dyczkowska J, Dyczkowski T (2020) Building stakeholder relations through ongoing engagement and constructive dialogue: lessons from large biopharmaceutical companies. Eur Res Stud J XXIII(2):733–746
39. Walling AM et al (2024) Implementing patient-centered outcomes research Institute stakeholder engagement principles in models of palliative care delivery and advance care planning research. Med Care 62(10):693–700
40. Omoya OA, Papadopoulou KA, Lou E (2019) Reliability engineering application to pipeline design. Int J Quality Reliabil Manag 36(9):1644–1662
41. Day S et al (2018) Stakeholder engagement to inform HIV clinical trials: a systematic review of the evidence. J Int AIDS Soc 21:e25174
42. Mårtensson T, Ståhl D, Bosch J (2019) Test activities in the continuous integration and delivery pipeline. J Softw: Evolut Process 31(4):e2153
43. Dasinapa MB (2024) The integration of sustainability and ESG accounting into corporate reporting practices. Adv Appl Account Res 2(1):13–25
44. Adigwe CS et al (2024) Leading in a time of crisis: the coronavirus effect on leadership in America. Asian J Econ Bus Account 24(4):1–20
45. Habibipour A (2024) Responsible living labs: what can go wrong? J Inf Commun Ethics Soc 22(2):205–218
46. Martínez J et al (2022) Operationalizing stakeholder engagement through the stakeholder-centric engagement charter (SCEC). J Gen Intern Med 37(Suppl 1):105–108

47. Hyndman N, McConville D (2018) Making charity effectiveness transparent: building a stakeholder-focussed framework of reporting. Financ Account Manag 34(2):133–147
48. Concannon TW et al (2014) A systematic review of stakeholder engagement in comparative effectiveness and patient-centered outcomes research. J Gen Int Med 29(12):1692–1701
49. Perko T, Martell M, Turcanu C (2020) Transparency and stakeholder engagement in nuclear or radiological emergency management. Radioprotect Paris 55:S243–S248

Chapter 4
Materials for Hydrogen Pipeline Applications

4.1 Introduction

The role of materials in hydrogen pipeline applications is critical and multi-faceted, primarily due to the unique characteristics of hydrogen as an energy carrier. Hydrogen's small molecular size allows it to permeate through materials more easily than other gases, which can lead to significant issues such as hydrogen embrittlement and material degradation [1]. The lightweight and reactive nature of hydrogen necessitates the use of specialized materials that can withstand not only the mechanical stresses of pipeline operation but also the corrosive and embrittling effects of hydrogen itself. Consequently, understanding the interactions between hydrogen and pipeline materials is essential for ensuring the long-term integrity and reliability of hydrogen transport systems [2].

Research has highlighted the significant impact of hydrogen embrittlement, a process whereby hydrogen atoms diffuse into the metal lattice of pipeline materials, causing a reduction in ductility and strength. This vulnerability is particularly pronounced in high-strength steels commonly used in pipeline constructions [1]. For instance, the study by Hejazi et al. [3] shows that exposure to hydrogen can enhance the susceptibility to brittle fracture at lower stress levels compared to when the same materials are tested in environments without hydrogen. Therefore, the development of materials that either resist hydrogen absorption or mitigate its damaging effects is a primary focus in the design of hydrogen pipelines [3]. Additionally, factors such as the microstructure of the materials and the conditions under which they are used including temperature, pressure, and the presence of impurities—play pivotal roles in determining their vulnerability to hydrogen embrittlement [2]. For example, the influence of microstructural constituents on hydrogen embrittlement resistance has been explored by various researchers, indicating that the arrangement and type of phases within a material can alter the way hydrogen interacts with it [2]. The research

M. Hussain et al., *Hydrogen Pipeline Integrity*, Green Energy and Technology,
https://doi.org/10.1007/978-981-95-5609-0_4

by Cai et al. [4] demonstrates that mechanical properties such as ductility and toughness are gradually compromised in hydrogen environments due to the complex interplay of these factors. Thus, a comprehensive understanding of material properties, coupled with tailored designs emphasizing resistance to hydrogen, is crucial for the development of safe and efficient hydrogen pipelines [5].

In addressing hydrogen embrittlement, studies have investigated various methodologies to enhance material resilience, such as through chemical additives and coatings designed to limit hydrogen ingress [6]. These protective strategies are essential not only in preventing direct hydrogen-induced damage but also in prolonging the lifespan of pipeline materials under operational stresses. For instance, some protective coatings have demonstrated significant effectiveness in reducing permeation rates of hydrogen, leading to improved overall performance of the pipeline materials [7]. Furthermore, the consideration of operational conditions—such as acidity, impurities, and environmental stresses—can influence material choices and maintenance strategies for pipelines [8].

4.2 Hydrogen-Induced Damage Mechanisms

Hydrogen-induced damage mechanisms in pipelines, primarily constituted of steel, pose significant challenges as natural gas pipelines transition to accommodate hydrogen transport. Numerous studies have documented the various forms of damage that can arise from hydrogen exposure, including hydrogen embrittlement, stress corrosion cracking, and loss of mechanical integrity, quantified through a multitude of interrelated factors.

Hydrogen embrittlement (HE) significantly compromises the mechanical properties of pipeline materials, particularly under high-pressure conditions, such as in hydrogen-blended natural gas pipelines. Experimental data suggests that the susceptibility of steel to HE is influenced by several factors, including mechanical loading conditions, environmental exposure, and material characteristics, which dynamically interact to affect pipeline integrity [9, 10]. The multi-faceted nature of hydrogen embrittlement necessitates a systematic elucidation of the underlying mechanisms, specifically concerning weld performance, which is vulnerable due to the concentrated stress in these areas [11]. The interplay of hydrogen with other atmospheric constituents, such as carbon dioxide, exacerbates mechanical property degradation in such welds involved in hydrogen transportation [11].

The permeation behavior of hydrogen through pipeline steels is another critical factor influencing degradation mechanisms. Studies have highlighted that internal pipeline surfaces typically suffer from hydrogen-induced cracking due to the ingress of hydrogen atoms, which can create voids and micro-cracks, leading to failure under load [12]. This permeation process is further complicated by external conditions such as soil moisture and chemistry, which can catalyze additional corrosion processes, leading to external stress corrosion cracking [13]. Cerniauskas et al. [14] indicated that these synergistic interactions often culminate in the generation of catastrophic through-wall.

Long-term operational experience has revealed that pipelines exposed to gaseous hydrogen for extended periods undergo notable degradation, manifested as a reduction in toughness and an increase in brittleness [15]. Increased fatigue crack growth rates have also been documented under varying hydrogen concentrations, indicating that daily operational fluctuations, such as pressure cycling and temperature changes, significantly impact structural integrity [16]. It has been observed that cyclic loading experienced during daily operations compounds the effects of hydrogen embrittlement, heightening the risk of failure [16]. The brittle fracture behavior of pipeline steel is closely associated with the absorption of hydrogen, underscoring the need for improved monitoring and risk modeling approaches to assess and mitigate these risks effectively [17].

The modeling of hydrogen distribution in pipeline systems has also gained considerable attention. Issues related to the buoyancy effect of hydrogen—where hydrogen accumulates at higher elevations within pipes due to its lower density compared to natural gas—may lead to inconsistent fuel mixtures, further complicating the operational reliability of hydrogen transport pipelines [18]. Numerical analyses have suggested that reducing the risk of hydrogen accumulation and optimizing pipeline design can enhance safety measures [13]. Furthermore, studies have demonstrated that the microstructural constituents of steel play a pivotal role in determining how susceptible these materials are to hydrogen embrittlement, hence leading to differentiated performance across various steel grades utilized in pipeline construction [19].

Operational strategies, such as the adoption of high-strength steels and appropriate polymer coatings, have been suggested to mitigate hydrogen-induced degradation. It has been posited that machine learning approaches could optimize assessments of materials' susceptibility to hydrogen embrittlement, given the critical role of steel microstructure in this degradation phenomenon [9]. Moreover, concerns have been raised about existing risk-based inspection standards being inadequate for evaluating hydrogen susceptibility, emphasizing the necessity for comprehensive guidelines that accommodate the realities of hydrogen environments [20].

4.3 Mechanisms of Hydrogen Embrittlement and Crack Propagation

Hydrogen embrittlement (HE) is a significant concern in materials used for hydrogen pipeline applications, and understanding the mechanisms that underpin this phenomenon is critical for developing materials able to resist the deleterious effects of hydrogen exposure. HE results in a reduction of ductility and toughness, leading to premature failure in high-strength materials, particularly under mechanical stress. Numerous theoretical models have been proposed to elucidate the mechanisms of

HE, highlighting various pathways through which hydrogen interacts with metallic materials to induce embrittlement.

4.3.1 Theoretical Models of Hydrogen Embrittlement

Several models have been proposed to explain hydrogen embrittlement phenomena, with the most notable being the hydrogen-enhanced decohesion (HEDE) model and the hydrogen-enhanced local plasticity (HELP) model [21]. The HEDE model posits that hydrogen reduces the cohesive strength of the metal matrix at grain boundaries, promoting intergranular cracking as hydrogen is concentrated along these weak interfaces. This pathway suggests that, upon hydrogen absorption, the hydrogen atoms cluster at grain boundaries and facilitate crack propagation by weakening atomic bonds, making it easier for cracks to initiate and grow.

On the other hand, the HELP model focuses on the interaction between hydrogen and dislocations, proposing that hydrogen enhances dislocation mobility, which can lead to localized deformation and cracking under load [22]. The HELP mechanism implies that hydrogen can alter the plastic deformation behavior of metals, especially in conjunction with applied stress, facilitating the formation of micro voids and subsequent crack propagation. This interaction often results in a ductile-to-brittle transition as the presence of hydrogen compromises the material's ability to deform plastically.

The hydrogen-enhanced strain-induced vacancy (HESIV) mechanism suggests that hydrogen can induce the formation of vacancy clusters that interact with dislocations, ultimately contributing to crack propagation and growth. These hydrogen-induced vacancies are believed to facilitate the development of microstructural defects, leading to an accelerated rate of failure under tensile or cyclic loading conditions.

4.3.2 Crack Initiation and Growth

Crack initiation in materials subjected to hydrogen exposure is heavily influenced by mechanical stress and microstructural features. Studies have shown that regions of high stress, such as notches or inclusions, are particularly prone to the accumulation of hydrogen, leading to localized crack formation. For example, 316L stainless steel specimens displayed substantial crack growth that aligned with the accumulation of hydrogen at the stress concentrators, suggesting that hydrogen contributes to premature failure through localized degradation [23]. Similarly, Qu et al. [24] highlighted that cracks in X80 steel propagating in the heat-affected zone exhibited intergranular characteristics facilitated by hydrogen, indicating that the geometry of the microstructure influences hydrogen-assisted crack growth.

The process of crack propagation is further exacerbated under cyclic loading conditions, which can facilitate the dynamic accumulation of hydrogen at crack tips and promote accelerated crack growth rates. Studies propose that under cyclic loads, hydrogen diffusion rates increase significantly, leading to steeper crack propagation trajectories as dislocations interact with hydrogen atoms. This phenomenon is critical for pipeline applications, where materials are frequently subjected to fluctuating loads due to operational pressures.

4.3.3 Interaction of Microstructures with Hydrogen

The microstructural characteristics of materials play a crucial role in their response to hydrogen exposure. For instance, the presence of certain alloying elements can enhance resistance to hydrogen-induced degradation. Research indicates that steels with refined microstructures or specific alloy compositions demonstrate improved hydrogen tolerance [25]. Conversely, higher strength materials often exhibit pronounced sensitivity to HE due to increased dislocation density, which can trap hydrogen atoms and promote embrittlement.

The formation of voids or cracks as a precursor to failure is a well-documented phenomenon in high-strength materials exposed to hydrogen. The voids initiate in highly stressed regions where hydrogen accumulates, and as loading continues, these voids can coalesce, leading to catastrophic failure. Advanced techniques such as electron backscatter diffraction and in-situ monitoring have enhanced our understanding of these processes by allowing real-time observation of hydrogen-induced changes in microstructure [26].

4.3.4 Experimental Observations and Mechanistic Insights

Empirical studies have corroborated the theoretical frameworks of hydrogen-assisted cracking, providing insights into the conditions under which HE occurs. Under experimental conditions involving hydrogen charging, materials exhibit clear signs of embrittlement, including reduced fracture toughness and increased vulnerability to crack initiation. The concentration of hydrogen induced through surface treatments such as cathodic protection exacerbates the embrittlement process by increasing the local hydrogen concentration in stressed regions.

Advanced methodologies combining finite element simulations with experimental data facilitate the exploration of hydrogen diffusion dynamics and crack propagation mechanisms. The integration of such methodologies reveals the critical parameters influencing the hydrogen embrittlement process, providing a robust framework for predicting material performance under operational conditions [27].

4.4 Evaluating Material Performance

The transition towards a hydrogen economy necessitates the development and assessment of hydrogen transportation systems, particularly pipelines. This includes the evaluation of material performance under the unique challenges presented by hydrogen and hydrogen blends. Hydrogen presents distinct properties that can influence pipeline integrity, most notably through mechanisms such as hydrogen embrittlement (HE), leakage, and the adaptability of existing infrastructure.

When assessing hydrogen pipelines, material performance can be significantly impacted by the characteristics of hydrogen. Hydrogen's small molecular size can lead to higher diffusion rates compared to natural gas, presenting concerns about leakage and embrittlement of pipeline materials. Numerous studies highlight that materials used in pipeline construction must be resistant to HE to prevent catastrophic failures during usage under high-pressure conditions. For instance, Paterlini et al. [28] discuss how T95 low-alloy steel exhibited a toughness reduction due to hydrogen exposure. Similarly, Ghadiani et al. [16] emphasize the critical importance of understanding the fatigue characteristics of pipeline steels in a hydrogen environment to ensure structural integrity.

The compatibility of different steel grades with hydrogen is paramount, particularly when considering retrofitting existing natural gas infrastructure. Existing materials like API 5L X42 and X52 have been recommended due to their proven performance in both natural gas and hydrogen environments, as outlined by Cai et al. [4]. The standards governing these materials must consider prolonged exposure to hydrogen, as studies indicate that impurity gases within natural gas blends can exacerbate HE issues [29].

Research has indicated that replacing natural gas pipelines with hydrogen-specific materials may yield long-term benefits despite initial economic hurdles. For example, the investment required for specific hydrogen pipelines is significantly higher, but the potential for lower operational costs makes it an attractive option in the long run [30]. Zhang et al. elaborate on how the costs per unit length for pure hydrogen pipelines can be approximately three times higher than those for traditional natural gas pipelines, necessitating a careful examination of cost–benefit scenarios over the lifespan of the materials used [31].

The application of advanced hybrid sensing systems to detect leaks emphasizes the importance of incorporating technology that can adapt to the unique attributes of hydrogen. Wang et al. propose a novel leakage sensing framework that enhances the overall safety of hydrogen transportation systems [32]. Enhanced inspection and monitoring techniques are crucial for maintaining the integrity of pipeline systems, and ongoing research in these areas could lead to significantly improved safety outcomes.

It is essential to recognize that the operational environments of hydrogen pipelines are subject to significant fluctuations in pressure, which enhances the risk of material fatigue. Wang et al. further elaborate on how alternating pressure fluctuations can influence crack propagation patterns in pipeline steels [33]. This dynamic demands materials capable of withstanding both the mechanical stresses associated with cyclic loading and the aggressive chemical environment posed by hydrogen.

The intricacies of material degradation under hydrogen-enhanced conditions are accentuated by differing strain rates and loading conditions. Research indicates a need for further investigations into the effects of slow strain rates on hydrogen migration behaviors within pipeline steels to better understand the link between strain conditions and HE [34]. Understanding these interactions aids in the development of new materials designed to mitigate hydrogen's adverse effects. Moreover, assessing the performance of existing pipeline materials under hydrogen-enriched conditions could lead to profound implications for the retrofitting of current natural gas pipelines. Studies exploring different methods of adapting these structures reveal that spending on innovative technologies for inspection and maintenance is critical for ensuring the long-term viability of the hydrogen transport infrastructure [35].

Ultimately, the successful transportation of hydrogen through pipelines pivots on a holistic approach that integrates advanced material technologies with rigorous safety and efficiency standards. The importance of conducting comprehensive risk assessments, as emphasized by Li et al. [36], cannot be overstated. Such evaluations are essential for identifying the vulnerabilities of pipeline materials and implementing measures to enhance their performance.

4.5 Material Selection Framework

The selection of materials for hydrogen pipelines is a crucial factor in the development of safe and efficient hydrogen infrastructure as shown in Fig. 4.1.

Hydrogen possesses unique properties that challenge conventional materials due to phenomena such as hydrogen embrittlement, diffusion, and solubility, which significantly impact material performance under high-pressure conditions. Various studies have evaluated the compatibility of different materials with hydrogen and provided a framework for understanding the implications of these interactions.

A primary concern in selecting materials for hydrogen pipelines is material compatibility, defined as a material's ability to withstand hydrogen ingress without exhibiting mechanical degradation such as embrittlement. Research has indicated that certain metals, particularly martensitic stainless steels, exhibit varying degrees of hydrogen solubility and diffusivity, supporting their potential use in high-pressure environments. For instance, Fayek et al. [37] demonstrated that the diffusivity of hydrogen in martensitic stainless steel is relatively low, which suggests good hydrogen compatibility, especially in materials that also maintain high strength. Kimura et al. [38] also emphasized the necessity of establishing standardized testing methods to assess material hydrogen compatibility, particularly for high-pressure applications, thereby underscoring the need for comprehensive material selection strategies.

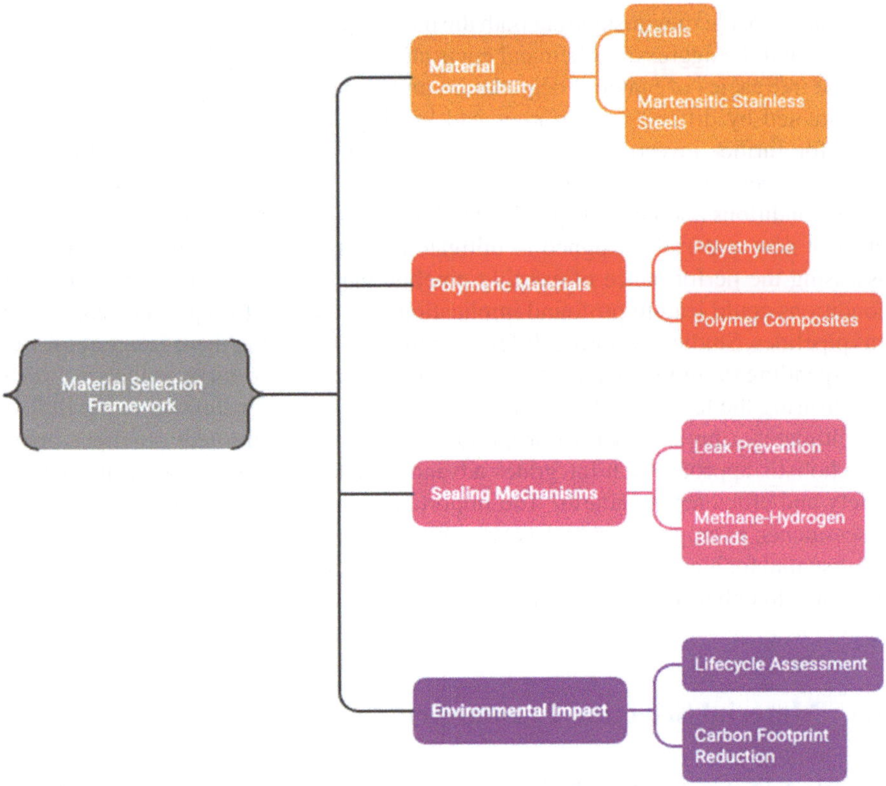

Fig. 4.1 Material selection framework for hydrogen pipelines

In addition to metals, polymeric materials are gaining attention for hydrogen pipelines, especially in sealing applications. Research by Balasooriya et al. [39] indicates that while polymeric materials may be susceptible to degradation in gaseous hydrogen environments, they show promise for use in high-pressure hydrogen applications when properly formulated and optimized. Polymers such as polyethylene are generally compatible with hydrogen gas and perform effectively in hydrogen environments. Specific polymer composites have demonstrated enhanced performance characteristics in high-pressure settings, thereby warranting further investigation into their applications within pipeline systems [40].

Compatibility assessments are reinforced by studies detailing the tribological behavior of materials in hydrogen environments. The work of Theiler and Gradt [41] examined several polymer materials to understand their mechanical performance and stability under hydrogen exposure, highlighting the need to evaluate friction and wear under realistic conditions. Investigations extend to commonly used polymer components in hydrogen infrastructure, affirming that their mechanical properties and resistance to hydrogen-induced degradation must be thoroughly assessed to ensure pipeline durability and reliability [42].

Sealing mechanisms present additional challenges in hydrogen transport. The necessity for effective sealing materials that can prevent hydrogen leaks is highlighted in studies conducted by San Marchi and Somerday [43] which address the associated risks with hydrogen pipelines. Leak prevention is critical due to hydrogen's flammable nature; therefore, the compatibility of sealing materials with both hydrogen and methane-hydrogen blends is essential for ensuring safety and operational integrity [44]. Developing proactive strategies for assessing and optimizing sealing solutions is crucial, particularly as the energy sector transitions to hydrogen as a primary energy carrier. Moreover, ongoing research is exploring innovative materials that enhance the performance of hydrogen pipeline infrastructures. The review by Alvine et al. [45] discusses the evolving landscape of materials science, including the increased applications of new composite materials that exhibit strong mechanical properties along with excellent hydrogen compatibility. The study of zenith steels concerning their fatigue resistance under hydrogen exposure also underscores efforts to improve material performance [46]. Thus, employing advanced material science principles is vital for developing more reliable and efficient hydrogen transport solutions.

Another critical area of focus in material selection for hydrogen pipelines involves the environmental impact and lifecycle assessment of materials used in hydrogen production, storage, and transportation. The comprehensive analysis by Osman et al. [47] sheds light on the lifecycle impacts of various hydrogen production pathways and their implications for material selection, emphasizing that sustainability considerations will increasingly drive future material choices. Transitioning to environmentally sustainable materials not only helps comply with rigorous regulations but also aligns with broader goals of reducing the carbon footprint associated with hydrogen infrastructure.

Additionally, as stated by San Marchi et al. [48], ongoing advancements in research and technology provide a strong scientific foundation for enhancing hydrogen technology codes and standards. Establishing rigorous testing and qualification processes is crucial for building confidence in material performance, especially as regulatory scrutiny evolves alongside technological advancements. Implementing systematic assessment approaches for materials under conditions reflective of actual operational environments is key to guiding material selection for hydrogen pipelines.

4.6 Selection of Steels, Alloys, and Composite Materials

The selection of appropriate steels, alloys, and composite materials is crucial for the design and utilization of pipelines intended for hydrogen transport. This requirement stems from the unique challenges posed by hydrogen, particularly its propensity to induce hydrogen embrittlement (HE), which compromises structural integrity and mechanical performance. In selecting materials for hydrogen pipelines, it is essential to consider several factors including mechanical properties, microstructural characteristics, and resistance to environmental degradation.

4.6.1 Microstructural Considerations

Microstructural characteristics significantly influence the hydrogen susceptibility of various steels. For example, research indicates that advanced high-strength steels (AHSS) such as dual-phase (DP) and transformation-induced plasticity (TRIP) steels exhibit distinct responses to hydrogen due to their unique microstructures [49]. The transformation of retained austenite into martensite during deformation increases susceptibility to HE, particularly under slow strain rate conditions. Specifically, TRIP steels have demonstrated significant susceptibility to HE, making their microstructural composition a vital factor in material selection [50]. High-Mn austenitic steels, such as TWIP steels, are another focus due to their exceptional mechanical properties.

4.6.2 Mechanical Properties and Strength

Strength is generally associated with increased susceptibility to hydrogen embrittlement. Higher strength materials such as 18Cr10Mn–0.4N exhibit greater ductility loss when subjected to hydrogen exposure. This correlation between high strength and increased HE susceptibility is crucial when selecting materials for hydrogen applications, particularly as the mechanical demands increase with pipeline class and usage parameters [51]. Therefore, understanding the balance between strength and ductility is vital; materials must be chosen not only for their load-bearing capabilities but also for their resilience against hydrogen-induced degradation.

For example, high-strength steels with hardness values beyond 390 HV are identified as particularly sensitive to hydrogen embrittlement [52]. Consequently, while high-strength steel is desirable for its mechanical performance, it necessitates thorough evaluations of potential HE risks. A balance must be achieved to ensure that pipeline materials maintain adequate toughness and ductility without sacrificing the strength necessary to support high operational pressures.

4.6.3 Alloys and Composite Materials

To mitigate the effects of hydrogen, innovations in alloy design are increasingly implemented. The inclusion of elements such as chromium has been shown to influence hydrogen resistance positively. For instance, adding chromium to ultra-high-strength steels results in enhanced resistance to delayed fracture under hydrogen exposure [53]. Similarly, advanced alloying techniques and the use of modern composite materials incorporate engineered properties to minimize hydrogen ingress and improve overall durability against embrittlement. Moreover, recent investigations into the properties of low alloy steels like API 5L grades have indicated that variations in elemental composition can significantly alter the hydrogen-induced cracking behavior. For instance, the incorporation of specific alloying elements can improve both strength and resistance to hydrogen attack, allowing for tailored solutions based on operational environments.

Composite materials are also emerging as promising candidates for improving hydrogen resistance in pipeline applications. Their hybrid structures can be designed to resist not only mechanical but also chemical degradation, thereby enhancing overall performance and safety in harsh environments.

4.6.4 Performance Under Stress and Corrosion

In addition to mechanical and microstructural properties, the performance of steel and alloy materials must also be evaluated concerning corrosion and stress conditions. Environments containing hydrogen sulfide (H_2S) can exacerbate hydrogen embrittlement; understanding the interplay between stress corrosion cracking and hydrogen embrittlement is essential in material selection [54]. Specifically, studies on steels exposed to H_2S reveal that even minimal hydrogen concentration can lead to significant damage, highlighting the need for rigorous testing under various environmental scenarios.

The design and application of protective coatings is a strategy currently under investigation to improve corrosion resistance and mitigate hydrogen diffusion in pipeline steels. These coatings offer a barrier against hydrogen permeation, thus preserving the mechanical properties and extending the life of the pipeline [55]. However, it is important to ensure that these coatings do not significantly impede structural integrity or lead to unexpected failure mechanisms.

4.7 Strategies to Mitigate Material Degradation

Mitigating material degradation, especially in the context of advanced applications such as fuel cells, batteries, and other energy-harvesting systems, has become a focal point of research and development across multiple fields. This is critically important as materials are often subjected to harsh operational conditions that could lead to performance losses and eventual failures. A comprehensive approach brings together various strategies, including the development of new materials, structural modifications, use of protective coatings, and the integration of encapsulation methods. Each of these strategies addresses specific degradation mechanisms and facilitates an extension of the material lifecycle.

One of the prominent strategies includes the implementation of protective coatings, which can effectively shield materials from corrosive environments and mechanical wear. For instance, Wierzbicki et al. [56] discuss the potential of radical scavenging strategies to mitigate oxidative degradation in anion-exchange membrane fuel cells. This encapsulation is critical for enhancing the durability of thin films, which often suffer from oxidative degradation when exposed to moisture or pollutants.

Radical scavenging is another significant strategy for mitigating material degradation, particularly in proton-exchange membrane (PEM) fuel cells. Wierzbicki et al. [56] highlighted the potential of radical scavenging strategies in anion-exchange membrane fuel cells, which are often plagued by oxidative degradation due to radical formation. By neutralizing these radicals before they can react with the membrane materials, the overall lifespan of the fuel cells can be significantly enhanced.

The innovation in material synthesis also routes toward enhancing stability. Tsipoaka et al. [57] emphasized the design of degradation-mitigating composite membranes that provide superior power densities while maintaining structural integrity under dry conditions, a common operational challenge for fuel cells. These enhancements can be attributed to not only improvements in material chemistry but also advances in fabrication processes such as layer-by-layer assembly that promote better structural organization.

Integrating smart operational strategies also presents a viable pathway to mitigate degradation. Controlled environments that adapt to dynamic operational requirements prevent scenarios that tend to accelerate degradation [58]. For instance, distributing power in a nonlinear manner can help suppress current peaks that lead to localized overheating—an occurrence known to compound material fatigue and degradation rates.

Furthermore, researchers have identified the value of machine learning and artificial intelligence in predicting material performance degradation patterns and optimizing operational parameters to prolong lifespan [59]. Algorithms can analyze operational data to identify critical stress conditions that lead to rapid degradation, allowing for timely interventions before significant damage occurs.

The choice of raw materials should also reflect degradation mitigation objectives. The implementation of alternative materials, as discussed by Zhang et al. [60], offers better durability and contributes to reducing the environmental impact of energy systems through sustainable design approaches. This aligns with the broader objectives of reducing the carbon footprint associated with conventional materials used in energy applications.

Advanced materials design, such as the development of degradation-resistant polymers or composite coatings enriched with radical scavengers, shows promise in further improving performance integrity. Research indicates that engineered polymer layers exhibiting different functional characteristics can greatly enhance corrosion resistance while maintaining desirable electrical conductivity—an essential requirement for many electrochemical applications [61].

4.8 Emerging Materials and Innovations

The advent of hydrogen as a pivotal component in the global transition to sustainable energy is driving significant advancements in the materials and technologies related to hydrogen pipelines. The development of new materials, as well as innovations in transportation techniques, is critical for ensuring the efficient and safe transport of hydrogen, which has distinct challenges due to its low density and high flammability. This section synthesizes current research findings on emerging materials for hydrogen pipelines, focusing on their efficacy and the innovations that pave the way for a robust hydrogen transport infrastructure.

The use of metal–organic frameworks (MOFs) and covalent organic frameworks (COFs) has become increasingly prominent in the field of hydrogen storage and transport. These advanced materials are characterized by their high porosity and selective gas adsorption capabilities. For instance, Carrera et al. [62] research has shown that MOFs can significantly enhance hydrogen storage capacities, which is essential for pipeline applications that require high energy density and safe handling. Recent advancements in the design of MOFs have led to exceptionally high isosteric heats of adsorption, allowing for efficient hydrogen storage at ambient conditions [63]. Such innovative materials are not just an enhancement but a necessity, as they directly address the challenges of conventional storage methods.

In addition to storage, the integrity and reliability of pipelines transporting hydrogen are critical concerns, especially regarding material interactions with hydrogen. The recent findings on hydrogen embrittlement highlight the importance of selecting materials that can withstand the unique corrosive properties of hydrogen [64]. Studies have examined how hydrogen affects various pipeline steels, emphasizing that specific alloys need to be developed to mitigate the detrimental effects associated with hydrogen transport [65]. As hydrogen pipelines are increasingly repurposed from natural gas systems, understanding the mechanical properties of existing materials becomes essential to ensure safety and longevity.

Hydrogen's role as an energy carrier also necessitates the development of innovative pipeline technologies. The integration of smart pipeline management systems utilizing artificial intelligence (AI) can optimize the logistics of hydrogen transport, providing real-time data on system performance and safety [66]. Such technologies improve operational efficiency while minimizing the risk of leaks and failures. Innovations in pipeline materials that can self-heal or provide real-time pressure monitoring can further enhance the safety and reliability of hydrogen transport systems [67]. These advancements are crucial as hydrogen infrastructure expands globally, needing systems that are resilient to failures.

As research continues into novel composites for pipeline applications, biocomposite materials are emerging as a sustainable alternative to traditional fiberglass and steel pipes. These materials can offer lightweight advantages while being more resistant to environmental degradation, which is crucial given the potential for hydrogen leakage and its environmental impacts [68]. The incorporation of renewable resources in the manufacturing of biocomposites significantly reduces the carbon footprint, aligning with the broader goals of decarbonization and the establishment of a circular economy in hydrogen transport technologies [69].

Innovations in hydrogen pipeline technologies also align with sustainability efforts, reinforcing the dual goal of efficiency and eco-friendliness. Enhanced methods for hydrogen production from renewable sources, such as solar or wind energy, are being coupled with advancements in pipeline systems to create a more integrated hydrogen economy [70]. The strategic development of hydrogen infrastructure is underpinned by the need to build out capabilities that can efficiently deliver hydrogen to end-users, from industrial applications to residential energy systems. This multifaceted approach not only supports energy transitions but also fosters economic growth within the emerging hydrogen sector.

The increasing deployment of hydrogen fuel cell technology across various sectors underscores the urgency of developing efficient pipeline systems. The transportation and storage of hydrogen must keep pace with the rapid growth of demand for hydrogen fueling stations and associated infrastructure [71]. Political and economic incentives are playing a significant role in this transition, driving investment in technologies that minimize operational risks while maximizing efficiency [72]. Policies that advocate for research into advanced materials and innovative hydrogen transport technologies are essential for realizing a sustainable hydrogen economy.

Finally, multidimensional studies assessing the lifecycle impacts of hydrogen pipeline materials must be integrated into the decision-making processes surrounding infrastructure development and technology deployment. Comprehensive assessments can ensure that the chosen materials not only meet performance criteria but also adhere to environmental sustainability guidelines [73]. By coupling environmental assessments with advancements in pipeline materials, stakeholders can better align hydrogen transport innovations with overarching climate goals.

4.9 Innovations in Material Engineering for Sustainability and Performance

The integration of innovative materials in the engineering sector, especially for pipelines intended to transport hydrogen, is pivotal for achieving sustainability and enhancing overall performance. The advancements in material science focus on developing solutions that are resilient and efficient in transporting hydrogen while being environmentally sound. Innovations include the utilization of composite materials, bioinspired engineering, and recycling methodologies that define the future of sustainable construction materials.

4.9.1 Composite Materials and Their Sustainability Potential

The adoption of composite materials is becoming increasingly prevalent in engineering applications aimed at improving both performance and sustainability. For instance, fibers derived from natural sources, like hemp, are being explored for their potential as sustainable reinforcements in composite structures [74]. These materials provide excellent mechanical properties while minimizing the carbon footprint associated with conventional synthetic fibers. Their biodegradable nature promotes resource conservation and aligns with the growing demand for eco-friendly alternatives in engineering practices.

Further innovations in composite technology involve the bio fabrication of materials using fungi. Recent studies highlight how mycelium can be cultivated on low-value organic substrates, transforming them into resilient materials for insulation, packaging, and construction [31]. This bio-based approach significantly reduces reliance on petroleum-derived polymers, addressing sustainability challenges while providing a novel avenue for material production that leverages natural processes for environmental benefits.

4.9.2 The Role of Recycling in Material Engineering

Recycling is a critical strategy for achieving sustainability in material engineering, particularly in the context of hydrogen pipeline applications. The use of recycled materials, such as reclaimed asphalt pavement (RAP) in road construction, illustrates how civil engineering can reduce environmental impact while maintaining performance standards [75]. By incorporating recycled materials into new construction, not only is the demand for virgin resources diminished, but the energy consumption associated with material processing is also significantly lowered.

Further exploration into the recycling of construction waste is vital for minimizing landfill usage and reducing the overall ecological footprint of the construction industry. For example, the integration of waste-based geopolymers in asphalt pavements is gaining traction as a sustainable alternative that enhances performance and durability while addressing waste management challenges [76]. This innovation reflects a broader transition towards a circular economy in engineering, where materials are reused and recycled, ensuring that their lifecycle is extended and resource waste is minimized.

4.9.3 Advanced Engineering Solutions for Infrastructure Resilience

Engineering innovations increasingly emphasize the need for materials that exhibit not only performance and durability but also self-healing capabilities. Epoxy-based vitrimers are one such innovation that emphasizes sustainability by allowing for the recycling and restoration of material properties under stress [77]. These materials can adapt to their environment by changing their viscosity, which allows for self-healing after being damaged. Implementing such smart materials in hydrogen pipelines could significantly enhance their longevity and safety, reducing the need for frequent repairs and resource expenditures associated with conventional materials.

The development of multifunctional materials that serve a primary structural purpose while providing additional benefits such as antimicrobial properties or thermal insulation is gaining increased attention [78]. These features contribute to a building's overall sustainability by reducing energy consumption and maintaining indoor environmental quality. By integrating these technologies into the design process, engineers can develop solutions that address multiple objectives simultaneously—enhancing the structural, environmental, and economic performance of pipelines.

4.9.4 Sustainable Practices and Values in Engineering

A concerted effort to redefine the priorities in material selection is essential. As engineering practices shift towards sustainability, value engineering emerges as an important planning tool that incorporates environmental considerations into project assessments [79]. This approach fosters innovations that align with local and international sustainability standards. By embedding sustainable practices into the decision-making process, engineers have the opportunity to enhance project value while minimizing negative environmental impacts.

Integrating sustainability themes in the education of engineering students is critical to ensuring that future generations are equipped with the knowledge and tools needed to develop sustainable materials and practices [80, 81]. By fostering a culture of sustainability in engineering curricula, future engineers will be more adept at making environmentally conscious decisions in their designs and material selections, reinforcing the idea that engineering can and should align with broader ecological goals.

References

1. Cabrini M et al (2019) Hydrogen embrittlement evaluation of micro alloyed steels by means of J-Integral curve. Materials 12(11):1843
2. Kim S-G, Kim J-Y, Hwang B (2023) Effect of tempering temperature on hydrogen embrittlement of SCM440 tempered martensitic steel. Materials 16(16):5709
3. Hejazi D et al (2016) Effect of gaseous hydrogen charging on the tensile properties of standard and medium Mn X70 pipeline steels. Mater Sci Technol 32(7):675–683
4. Cai L et al (2022) Experimental investigation on the hydrogen embrittlement characteristics and mechanism of natural gas-hydrogen transportation pipeline steels. Mater Res Express 9(4):046512
5. Huang L, Zhang L (2024) Effect of hydrogen on high cycle fatigue properties of L360 pipeline steel notched specimens. Materials 17(22):5612
6. Li S et al (2025) Fracture failure analysis of safety valve spring in nuclear power plant. J Phys: Conf Ser (IOP Publishing)
7. Juliawati A, Razak NAA (2013) Hydrogen embrittlement susceptibility of pipeline steel. Appl Mech Mater 315:820–824
8. Xu Q, Zhang J (2017) Novel methods for prevention of hydrogen embrittlement in iron. Sci Rep 7(1):16927
9. Subedi A et al (2023) Evaluation of the factors determining hydrogen embrittlement in pipeline steels: an artificial intelligence approach. In: Proceedings of the 33rd European safety and reliability conference
10. Bu F et al (2024) Analysis of leakage and diffusion characteristics and hazard range determination of buried hydrogen-blended natural gas pipeline based on CFD. ACS Omega 9(37):39202–39218
11. Ban J et al (2023) Research progress and prospects on hydrogen damage in welds of hydrogen-blended natural gas pipelines. Processes 11(11):3180
12. Dey S et al (2021) Study of electrochemical behavior, hydrogen permeation and diffusion in pipeline steel. Mater Sci Forum (Trans Tech Publ) 1019:145–156
13. Li J, Xie B, Gong L (2024) Numerical research on leakage characteristics of pure hydrogen/hydrogen-blended natural gas in medium-and low-pressure buried pipelines. Energies 17(12):2951
14. Cerniauskas S et al (2019) Future hydrogen markets for transportation and industry: the impact of CO_2 taxes. Energies 12(24):4707
15. Summers E et al (2024) Offshore wind-to-hydrogen: the impact of intermittency on hydrogen production and transport. In: International conference on offshore mechanics and arctic engineering. American Society of Mechanical Engineers
16. Ghadiani H et al (2024) Assessing hydrogen embrittlement in pipeline steels for natural gas-hydrogen blends: implications for existing infrastructure. Solids 5(3):375–393
17. Koren E et al (2024) Investigating electrochemical charging conditions equivalent to hydrogen gas exposure of X65 pipeline steel. Mater Corros 75(3):315–321
18. Xu W et al (2024) Simulation study on hydrogen concentration distribution in hydrogen blended natural gas transportation pipeline. Plos One 19(12):e0314453
19. Shin S-H et al (2024) EffEct of Microstructural constituEnts on HydrogEn EMbrittlEMEnt rEsistancE of aPi X60, X70, and X80 PiPElinE stEEls. Arch Metall Mater 39–43
20. Giannini L et al (2023) Materials for hydrogen storage and transport: implications for risk-based inspection. Key Eng Mater 959:221–230
21. Wasim M, Djukic MB, Ngo TD (2021) Influence of hydrogen-enhanced plasticity and decohesion mechanisms of hydrogen embrittlement on the fracture resistance of steel. Eng Fail Anal 123:105312
22. Song J, Curtin W (2014) Mechanisms of hydrogen-enhanced localized plasticity: an atomistic study using α-Fe as a model system. Acta Mater 68:61–69
23. Roberts E (2021) High resolution characterisation of H on stress corrosion cracking in nuclear materials [PhD Thesis]. University of Oxford

24. Qu J et al (2019) Hydrogen-assisted crack growth in the heat-affected zone of X80 steels during in situ hydrogen charging. Materials 12(16):2575
25. Zhang D et al (2019) Effect of microstructure refinement on hydrogen-induced damage behavior of low alloy high strength steel for flexible riser. Mater Sci Eng A 765:138278
26. Soundararajan CK (2023) Hydrogen-induced degradation behavior of nickel alloy 625, studied using multiscale in-situ experiments. Mater Sci Eng A 865:144635
27. Djukic MB et al (2016) Hydrogen embrittlement of industrial components: prediction, prevention, and models. Corrosion 72(7):943–961
28. Paterlini L et al (2025) Hydrogen embrittlement of a T95 low-alloy steel charged by electrochemical method. Materials 18(5):1047
29. Zhou C, Zhou H, Zhang L (2024) The impact of impurity gases on the hydrogen embrittlement behavior of pipeline steel in high-pressure H2 environments. Materials 17(9):2157
30. Gu S et al (2025) Optimal design of hydrogen-blended natural gas pipeline network considering separation systems. AIChE J 71(2):e18648
31. Zhang C et al (2023) Key technologies of pure hydrogen and hydrogen-mixed natural gas pipeline transportation. ACS Omega 8(22):19212–19222
32. Wang Y et al (2024) A novel leakage sensing system of hydrogen transportation pipeline based on hybrid UWFBG array. In: Proceedings of advanced sensor systems and applications XIV. SPIE 13243
33. Wang A et al (2025) Experimental study on hydrogen-induced crack propagation of X80 steel under alternating pressure fluctuations. Materials 18(5):947
34. Peng Z et al (2023) Effect of slow strain rates on the hydrogen migration and different crack propagation modes in pipeline steel. Steel Res Int 94(8):2300070
35. Kethamukkala K, Liu Y (2023) Information fusion and data augmentation for risk-based maintenance optimization of hydrogen gas pipelines. In: 15th Annual conference of the prognostics and health management society, PHM 2023. Prognostics and Health Management Society
36. Li J, Song F, Zhang X (2024) A review on hazards and risks to pipeline operation under transporting hydrogen energy and hydrogen-mixed natural gas. Sci Technol Energy Trans 79:9
37. Fayek P et al (2021) Investigation of the pressure dependent hydrogen solubility in a martensitic stainless steel using a thermal agile tubular autoclave and thermal desorption spectroscopy. Metals 11(2):231
38. Kimura M et al (2021) Test method to establish hydrogen compatibility of materials in high pressure hydrogen gas environments for fuel cell vehicles. ISIJ Int 61(4):1333–1336
39. Balasooriya W et al (2022) A review on applicability, limitations, and improvements of polymeric materials in high-pressure hydrogen gas atmospheres. Polym Rev 62(1):175–209
40. Morsbach S et al (2022) Hydrogen compatibility of polymers for fuel cell vehicles. Energ Technol 10(9):2200018
41. Theiler G, Gradt T (2023) Comparison of the sliding behavior of several polymers in gaseous and liquid hydrogen. Tribol Online 18(5):217–231
42. Duranty ER et al (2018) In situ high pressure hydrogen tribological testing of common polymer materials used in the hydrogen delivery infrastructure. J Vis Exp: JoVE 133:56884
43. San Marchi CW, Somerday BP (2012) Technical reference for hydrogen compatibility of materials. Sandia National Laboratories (SNL), Albuquerque, NM, and Livermore, CA
44. Makaryan IA et al (2022) A comprehensive review on the prospects of using hydrogen–methane blends: challenges and opportunities. Energies 15(6):2265
45. Alvine KJ et al (2010) High-pressure hydrogen materials compatibility of piezoelectric films. Appl Phys Lett 97(22)
46. Ogawa Y, Iwata K (2023) Fatigue crack propagation in pearlitic steel under pressurized gaseous hydrogen: influences of microstructure size and strength level. ISIJ Int 63(7):1251–1262
47. Osman AI et al (2024) Life cycle assessment of hydrogen production, storage, and utilization toward sustainability. Wiley Interdiscip Rev: Energy Environ 13(3):e526
48. San Marchi C et al (2017) Overview of the DOE hydrogen safety, codes and standards program, part 3: advances in research and development to enhance the scientific basis for hydrogen regulations, codes and standards. Int J Hydrog Energy 42(11):7263–7274

49. Liu L, He B, Huang M (2018) The role of transformation-induced plasticity in the development of advanced high strength steels. Adv Eng Mater 20(6):1701083
50. Alza VA, Chavez VP (2022) TRIP steels: factors influencing their formation, mechanical properties and microstructure—A review. J Mech Civil Eng 19:37–60
51. Sakib AN et al (2025) Comprehensive safety assessment of hydrogen: from production to application in energy systems. Int J Energy Res 2025(1):8857513
52. Krella A (2025) Hydrogen-induced degradation of metallic materials—A short review. Materials 18(3):597
53. Venezuela J et al (2016) A review of hydrogen embrittlement of martensitic advanced high-strength steels. Corros Rev 34(3):153–186
54. Vakili M, Koutník P, Kohout J (2024) Addressing hydrogen sulfide corrosion in oil and gas industries: a sustainable perspective. Sustainability 16(4):1661
55. Al Madan A, Hussein A, Akhtar SS (2025) A review on internal corrosion of pipelines in the oil and gas industry due to hydrogen sulfide and the role of coatings as a solution. Corros Rev 43(2):189–208
56. Wierzbicki S et al (2023) Operando EPR study of radical formation in anion-exchange membrane fuel cells. ACS Catal 13(4):2744–2750
57. Tsipoaka M, Aziz MA, Shanmugam S (2021) Degradation-mitigating composite membrane that exceeds a 1 W cm^{-2} power density of a polymer electrolyte membrane fuel cell operating under dry conditions. ACS Sustain Chem Eng 9(7):2693–2704
58. Chu S et al (2024) Integrating graceful degradation and recovery through requirement-driven adaptation. In: Proceedings of the 19th international symposium on software engineering for adaptive and self-managing systems
59. Fu P, Pudjianto D, Strbac G (2020) Integration of power-to-gas and low-carbon road transport in great Britain's future energy system. IET Renew Power Gener 14(17):3393–3400
60. Zemite L et al (2023) Blending hydrogen with natural gas/biomethane and transportation in existing gas networks. Latv J Phys Tech Sci 60(5):43–55
61. Ates M (2016) A review on conducting polymer coatings for corrosion protection. J Adhes Sci Technol 30(14):1510–1536
62. Carrera M et al (2025) Rational design of 7-Azaindole-based robust microporous hydrogen-bonded organic framework for gas sorption. Angew Chem Int Ed 64(1):e202412981
63. Ramirez-Vidal P et al (2022) Modeling high-pressure hydrogen uptake by nanoporous metal–organic frameworks: implications for hydrogen storage and delivery. ACS Appl Nano Mater 5(1):759–773
64. Allendorf MD et al (2022) Challenges to developing materials for the transport and storage of hydrogen. Nat Chem 14(11):1214–1223
65. Bae D-S et al (2022) Effect of electrochemical hydrogen charging time on hydrogen embrittlement of the hot-rolled and accelerated cooling treated API X70 steel. Metals Mater Int 1–9
66. Zhang T, Bai H, Sun S (2022) Intelligent natural gas and hydrogen pipeline dispatching using the coupled thermodynamics-informed neural network and compressor Boolean neural network. Processes 10(2):428
67. Alves C et al (2024) Hydrogen technologies: recent advances, new perspectives, and applications. In: Abdallah Z, Aldoumani N (eds) Hydrogen technologies - advances, insights, and applications. IntechOpen
68. Habbar G et al (2023) Failure analysis of biocomposite sandwich pipe under internal pressure–Application for high pressure gas transportation pipelines MEDGAZ. Int J Press Vessels Pip 202:104891
69. Shardeo V, Sarkar BD (2024) Adoption of hydrogen-fueled freight transportation: a strategy toward sustainability. Bus Strateg Environ 33(2):223–240
70. Mokrzycki E, Gawlik L (2024) The development of a green hydrogen economy. Energies 17(13):3165
71. Vadivel N, Murthy AP (2024) Recent developments in membrane-free hybrid water electrolysis for low-cost hydrogen production along with value-added products. Small 20(52):2407845

72. Marouani I et al (2023) Integration of renewable-energy-based green hydrogen into the energy future. Processes 11(9):2685
73. Pereira J et al (2024) Hydrogen production, transporting and storage processes—A brief review. Clean Technol 6(3):1260–1313
74. Akter M, Uddin MH, Tania IS (2022) Biocomposites based on natural fibers and polymers: a review on properties and potential applications. J Reinf Plast Compos 41(17–18):705–742
75. Jiang Q, Liu W, Wu S (2024) Technological advances and challenges of reclaimed asphalt pavement (RAP) application in road engineering—A bibliometric analysis from 2000 to 2022. Environ Sci Pollut Res 31(24):35519–35552
76. Milad A et al (2021) Utilisation of waste-based geopolymer in asphalt pavement modification and construction—A review. Sustainability 13(6):3330
77. Lee MK et al (2025) Epoxy-based vitrimers for sustainable infrastructure: emphasizing recycling and self-healing properties. Polymers 17(3):373
78. Wu Y-C et al (2024) Lignin-based functional hydrogels: an eco-friendly bulk material. ACS Sustain Chem Eng 12(50):17952–17976
79. Khan AM, Alaloul WS, Musarat MA (2024) A critical review of digital value engineering in building design towards automated construction. Environ Dev Sustain 1–46
80. Quelhas OLG et al (2019) Engineering education and the development of competencies for sustainability. Int J Sustain High Educ 20(4):614–629
81. Davidson CI et al (2010) Preparing future engineers for challenges of the 21st century: sustainable engineering. J Clean Prod 18(7):698–701

Chapter 5
Pipeline Design Considerations for Hydrogen

5.1 Introduction

Engineering and design principles serve as the cornerstone for the conception, development, and operation of infrastructure systems, particularly within the energy sector. These principles underpin the creation of systems that are not only functional and efficient but also safe, reliable, and resilient throughout their operational lifespans. In an era characterized by rapid technological advancement, increasing environmental awareness, and progressively stringent regulatory frameworks, it is imperative that engineering practices evolve to address these multifaceted challenges. This chapter provides an in-depth examination of the fundamental considerations and design principles that govern the development of hydrogen pipeline systems, emphasizing their role in ensuring the integrity, efficiency, and sustainability of hydrogen transport infrastructure within the broader context of the global energy transition.

Central to this discourse is the imperative to uphold the highest standards of safety and reliability. Engineering codes and standards provide a framework within which designs are validated to withstand operational stresses, environmental conditions, and unforeseen contingencies [1]. These codes are not static; rather, they continuously evolve in response to new scientific insights, technological advancements, and lessons learned from past incidents. The application of appropriate safety margins and compliance with these standards is essential to mitigate risks, prevent catastrophic failures, and protect both human life and the environment.

The integration of alternative fuels, particularly hydrogen, into existing natural gas infrastructure epitomizes the contemporary challenges faced by engineers and designers. Hydrogen's distinct physical and chemical properties—such as its lower energy density, diffusivity, and propensity for embrittlement of metallic components—necessitate a comprehensive re-evaluation of conventional design methodologies. The blending of hydrogen with natural gas offers potential pathways to decarbonize existing energy systems; however, it simultaneously presents technical

M. Hussain et al., *Hydrogen Pipeline Integrity*, Green Energy and Technology,
https://doi.org/10.1007/978-981-95-5609-0_5

challenges related to material compatibility, system integrity, combustion characteristics, and leakage detection [2, 3]. Addressing these challenges demands a rigorous application of engineering principles, supported by advanced modeling, experimental validation, and adherence to evolving regulatory landscapes.

The contemporary energy landscape is undergoing a profound transformation driven by the urgent need to decarbonize energy systems and mitigate climate change. Hydrogen has emerged as a key enabler of this transition due to its potential to serve as a clean, versatile, and storable energy carrier. However, the widespread deployment of hydrogen infrastructure—particularly pipeline networks—presents unique engineering and design challenges. Unlike conventional natural gas systems, hydrogen pipelines must contend with hydrogen's distinct physical and chemical properties, including its low molecular weight, high diffusivity, wide flammability range, and tendency to cause embrittlement in certain metallic materials. These characteristics necessitate a re-evaluation of traditional design methodologies, material selection criteria, and operational strategies to ensure that safety and performance standards are not compromised.

Addressing these complexities requires a multidisciplinary approach that integrates knowledge from mechanical, chemical, and materials engineering, as well as fluid dynamics, thermodynamics, and corrosion science. Design engineers must balance innovation with the need to comply with established codes, standards, and best practices that govern pipeline safety and reliability. Organizations such as ASME, ISO, and EN are actively developing and refining hydrogen-specific standards to account for emerging knowledge on material compatibility, pressure containment, and risk management. The iterative nature of these standards—continuously updated in response to new research findings, field data, and incident analyses—underscores the dynamic relationship between engineering science and practical implementation.

Safety and reliability remain the guiding tenets of hydrogen pipeline design. The application of appropriate safety margins, redundant monitoring systems, and advanced integrity management frameworks is crucial for preventing failures and minimizing the potential consequences of leaks or ruptures. Furthermore, the design process must anticipate operational stresses, environmental factors, and potential degradation mechanisms that may arise over decades of service. The ability to predict, detect, and mitigate these risks is vital not only for protecting human life and property but also for maintaining public confidence in hydrogen as a safe and viable energy carrier.

Another critical dimension shaping modern pipeline design is the integration of digital technologies. The adoption of advanced sensors, data analytics, and automated control systems enables real-time monitoring of pressure, flow, and material condition, significantly enhancing system performance and predictive maintenance capabilities. However, this digital transformation introduces new vulnerabilities related to cybersecurity and system resilience. The protection of digital control and communication systems from malicious attacks or operational failures must therefore be embedded into the design philosophy from the outset.

5.2 Pipeline Design Parameters: Pressure, Temperature, Flow Dynamics

In the design and operation of pipelines, several essential parameters play a critical role in ensuring both safety and efficiency. These parameters include pressure dynamics, temperature control, and flow characteristics. Understanding the interplay between these factors is vital for optimizing pipeline performance, safeguarding infrastructure, and complying with regulatory standards.

5.2.1 Pressure Dynamics

Pressure is one of the most crucial parameters in pipeline design, as it directly affects the integrity and performance of the system. The pressure within pipelines must be maintained within specified limits to avoid the risks of leaks or ruptures. Optimal pressure design involves determining the Maximum Allowable Operating Pressure (MAOP) which considers factors such as material strength, external conditions, and fluid characteristics [4]. For instance, the design of high-pressure pipelines, particularly in hydropower stations, requires careful optimization of hydraulic parameters to ensure stability and minimize risks associated with transient pressure fluctuations during operation [5].

In addition to static pressure considerations, transient pressure responses must also be analyzed, especially during events such as valve closures or pump shutdowns, which can lead to pressure surges or "water hammer" effects. These phenomena necessitate the incorporation of surge control mechanisms and the careful design of pipeline bends and fittings to mitigate risks associated with pressure transients [6]. Computational fluid dynamics (CFD) plays a critical role here, allowing engineers to model pressure behavior accurately under various operational scenarios, thereby enhancing overall system reliability [6, 7].

5.2.2 Temperature Control

Temperature is another crucial factor influencing pipeline operations. Variations in temperature can affect the viscosity and density of the transported fluid, as well as the thermal expansion of the pipeline materials. In the context of CO_2 transport pipelines, for instance, temperature fluctuations can lead to variable flow resistance and influence the performance of pumps and compressors [8]. Therefore, understanding the thermal profiles along the pipeline is essential for designing systems capable of accommodating such variations while maintaining operational efficiency.

The impact of temperature on pipeline materials cannot be overstated; for example, certain alloys may exhibit reduced strength at elevated temperatures, increasing the risk of deformation or failure [9]. Thus, materials must be selected not only for their strength and durability but also for their ability to handle the temperature ranges expected during operation. Advanced modeling techniques can be utilized to predict the thermal behavior of pipeline systems, assisting in the selection of appropriate materials and insulation strategies [10].

5.2.3 Flow Dynamics

Flow characteristics are equally important in pipeline design. The flow behavior of the transported fluids dictates design considerations, including pipe diameter, roughness, and gradient. Hydraulic modeling is essential for optimizing these parameters to ensure efficient flow while minimizing pressure losses due to friction [11]. The Darcy-Weisbach equation is commonly employed to estimate pressure losses in fluid flow systems, enabling engineers to design for optimal flow conditions and ensure the system operates efficiently under varying conditions. Furthermore, accurate flow measurement is critical in maintaining pipeline operations. Flow meters and sensors must be integrated into pipeline systems to monitor flow rates and detect any irregularities that could indicate leaks or blockages. In addition to ensuring operational efficiency, robust flow monitoring systems enhance safety by providing early warnings of potential failures, allowing for immediate corrective action [12].

5.3 Structural Codes, Safety Margins, and Compliance Standards

The structural integrity of pipeline systems is paramount for ensuring safe operations in various industries, particularly in the oil and gas sector, where the failure of pipelines can result in catastrophic environmental and economic consequences. Following rigorous structural codes, applying appropriate safety margins, and adhering to compliance standards are essential components of pipeline design and management. Several standards and practices are in place globally to govern engineering principles related to pipeline integrity, safety, and efficiency, particularly under various operational conditions.

One of the foremost aspects of pipeline design is the incorporation of structural codes that provide guidelines for material selection, design specifications, and safety assessments. Standards such as the American Petroleum Institute (API) and the American Society of Mechanical Engineers (ASME) provide comprehensive protocols to define maximum allowable stress, required yield strength, and material fatigue limits. These codes are designed to mitigate risks associated with pressure surges, environmental impacts, and material degradation due to corrosion or other operational stresses [13]. Specifically, codes like API 5L and ASME B31.8 specify engineering practices that ensure the safe transportation of fluids while accommodating particular challenges encountered in the field [14].

Safety margins are determined based on the principles outlined in these structural codes, encompassing a range of factors, including mechanical properties of materials, operational conditions, and environmental influences. Engineering practices adopt a probabilistic approach to safety margins, allowing engineers to consider variability and uncertainty in operational parameters. This aspect is particularly critical in aging pipeline infrastructures, where corrosion and external stressors may lead to unexpected failures [15]. For instance, pipelines must endure pressures beyond normal operational parameters to provide an adequate buffer against sudden changes that could lead to rupture. The application of finite element analysis and probabilistic models has become fundamental in assessing the reliability of pipeline systems [16].

Regulatory compliance is a vital consideration that dictates the structuring of safety protocols and integrity monitoring mechanisms. Organizations are required to comply with local and international regulations that govern pipeline operations, including environmental protection laws and public safety mandates. Ensuring compliance often involves integrating continuous monitoring technologies capable of real-time assessments of pipeline conditions. The use of advanced methodologies for integrity management such as using in-line inspection data combined with software simulations facilitates adherence to these guidelines by providing actionable insights into the structural health of pipelines. Furthermore, continuous advancements in technology necessitate ongoing revisions of compliance standards, which must adapt to new findings in material science and engineering practices [17].

Structural integrity is critically evaluated through assessments of potential defects that could compromise pipeline safety, such as corrosion, dents, and weld failures. Employing external corrosion defect assessments (ECDA) and utilizing data analytics for predictive modeling are essential steps in this preventative strategy. Structural assessments also need to consider external factors such as natural disasters and landslide occurrences, which could apply additional loads on pipeline structures. Special designs and protective measures, such as adequate wall thickness and appropriate coating systems, are devised based on standards such as DNV-OS-F101, which emphasizes the importance of safety across all phases from design to decommissioning [18].

There exists a critical relationship between maintenance and compliance standards. Regular inspections and preventive maintenance are mandated by regulatory bodies to ensure pipelines remain within acceptable safety limits. Periodic testing, including burst pressure tests and leak detection methods, are pivotal in validating the pipeline's operational integrity. Proactive maintenance strategies, supported by comprehensive data collected through modern diagnostic tools, can significantly reduce the risk of pipeline failures caused by corrosion or undetected anomalies [19].

5.4 Mechanical Design Challenges

One of the foremost challenges is the material compatibility of existing pipeline infrastructure. Hydrogen embrittlement (HE) is a significant concern for the integrity and mechanical properties of pipeline steels. Research indicates that HE can lead to premature failures in steel pipes due to hydrogen atoms diffusing into the steel matrix, affecting ductility and toughness, particularly in high-pressure environments [20, 21]. Pipeline materials originally designed for natural gas exhibit vulnerabilities when exposed to hydrogen, necessitating thorough evaluations and potential material upgrades to withstand the unique stresses imposed by hydrogen transport [22]. This consideration extends to the need for robust design codes that account for the hydrogen impact on mechanical properties.

The economics of hydrogen pipelines are influenced by high initial investment costs necessary for constructing new hydrogen-specific pipelines. The installation cost for a dedicated hydrogen pipeline can be substantially higher—by approximately three times—compared to that of natural gas pipelines [23, 24]. Consequently, leveraging existing natural gas pipelines by blending hydrogen with natural gas has emerged as a feasible option to reduce costs while transitioning to a hydrogen economy [24, 25]. However, blending introduces its own set of challenges, as the different physical properties of hydrogen and natural gas can alter flow dynamics, potentially resulting in safety issues such as increased leakage rates [26].

Another significant challenge is maintaining operational pressures. Hydrogen requires compression to high pressures for effective transport, which incurs substantial energy costs and necessitates advanced compressor technologies [27]. Continuous pressurization is essential to keep the gas flow consistent and within safe operational ranges, which translates into increased complexity in pipeline management [28]. Fluctuating pressure due to variable hydrogen production exacerbates this issue, highlighting the need for effective pressure regulation systems to maintain pipeline integrity [29].

Leakage control and monitoring remain critical aspects of hydrogen pipeline design and operation. The lighter molecular structure of hydrogen compared to natural gas results in higher escape rates when leaks occur, presenting new challenges for gas distribution networks [26, 30]. Increased scrutiny is required for safety protocols in monitoring hydrogen leaks due to the flammability and potential explosive nature of hydrogen when mixed with air [31, 32]. Innovations in detection technologies such as hybrid fiber optic sensors and advanced computational fluid dynamics modeling are being explored to enhance monitoring capabilities in hydrogen transport systems [33].

The development of an integrated techno-economic framework that accommodates various hydrogen production pathways is vital for the successful transition to a hydrogen economy. The viability of hydrogen pipelines hinges not just on their mechanical integrity, but also on their ability to efficiently connect hydrogen production sites to demand centers while maintaining economic feasibility [34]. Life cycle assessments that consider both environmental impacts and economic costs are essential for guiding infrastructure investment decisions and shaping future hydrogen transport projects [35, 36].

5.5 Welding, Joining, and Fabrication

The welding, joining, and fabrication processes of pipelines intended for hydrogen transportation present significant technical challenges, primarily due to the unique mechanical issues posed by hydrogen. As the energy landscape shifts towards a hydrogen economy, the methodologies used for fabricating hydrogen-specific pipeline systems must be thoroughly assessed to ensure safety, performance, and reliability. This section discusses the techniques utilized in welding and joining pipeline components, with a focus on the challenges related to hydrogen's effects on welded joints.

In welded pipeline constructions, girth welds are critical weak points and account for a significant portion of failures in pipeline systems, particularly when transporting hydrogen. Studies show that hydrogen embrittlement is a major concern, wherein hydrogen atoms diffuse into the steel, significantly affecting welds due to their microstructure and the heat-affected zones (HAZ) created during welding [37]. The susceptibility of pipelines to hydrogen embrittlement necessitates the use of advanced welding techniques to minimize hydrogen introduction into the weld zone during the process. Various welding techniques, such as gas metal arc welding (GMAW) and friction stir welding (FSW), have been researched extensively for their effectiveness in mitigating these issues [38].

High-energy laser welding has emerged as a promising technique for pipeline fabrication, offering advantages such as reduced heat-affected zones, enhanced microstructural control, and improved mechanical properties in the welded joint. Research on laser-welded joints of X100 pipeline steel has demonstrated a significant gradient in microstructures that can improve joint properties while reducing the risk of hydrogen-induced failures [39]. Simulations and experimental analyses indicate that optimizing welding parameters can produce joints with lower susceptibility to hydrogen embrittlement [40].

An essential aspect of welding in hydrogen pipelines is the selection of appropriate filler materials. The microstructure and mechanical properties of the joint are heavily influenced by the type of filler used and the welding parameters applied. Different electrodes can lead to varying hydrogen concentrations in the weld pool, thereby affecting weld quality and integrity [41]. The use of flux-cored arc welding has gained popularity as it provides high deposition rates vital for pipeline construction while also managing hydrogen levels effectively [42].

The implementation of automated and semi-automated welding processes significantly enhances productivity and quality assurance in pipeline joining. Automated welding mitigates human error and can adaptively control parameters such as travel speed, arc stability, and heat input, which are crucial for minimizing residual stresses and preventing defects like lack of fusion [43]. For example, the advancement of welding robots designed specifically for underwater applications shows promise for constructing subsea pipelines, where traditional techniques are complex [44].

Post-welding treatment also plays a crucial role in restoring the mechanical properties of welded joints. Processes like post-weld heat treatment (PWHT) can relieve residual stresses induced during welding and enhance the toughness of the heat-affected zone. The use of PWHT has been shown to significantly improve the corrosion resistance and mechanical properties of welded components, making them more suitable for hydrogen transport [45]. These treatments must be tailored to the specific materials and operational conditions of the pipeline.

There is growing attention towards non-destructive testing (NDT) methods for assessing weld quality, which has become increasingly important with the evolution of welding technologies. Techniques such as X-ray diffraction, ultrasonic testing, and magnetic flux leakage are being developed to improve monitoring of weld integrity, allowing for real-time assessments during and after construction [46, 47]. These methods ensure that potential defects such as cracks or porosity are detected promptly, thus preventing catastrophic failures in operational pipelines.

5.6 Coatings, Linings, and Corrosion Protection

The selection and application of protective coatings, linings, and corrosion protection systems for hydrogen pipelines are critical to ensuring long-term integrity and performance. The specific challenges posed by hydrogen's physical and chemical properties necessitate the development of tailored strategies that promote compatibility with hydrogen environments, mitigate corrosion, and enhance the lifespan of the pipeline infrastructure.

One of the primary concerns in hydrogen environments relates to the corrosion mechanisms that affect pipeline materials. Recent studies indicate that hydrogen can exacerbate certain types of corrosion, particularly under high-temperature and pressure conditions common in hydrogen transport systems [24]. The presence of hydrogen can increase the corrosion rates of pipeline materials due to phenomena such as hydrogen-induced cracking and stress corrosion cracking. Consequently, the design of protective coatings must account for the vulnerabilities introduced by hydrogen, making traditional coatings insufficient without additional considerations [48].

Material selection plays a crucial role in the effective corrosion protection of pipelines. Advanced materials such as epoxy, polyurethane, and specialty polymer coatings have been investigated for their ability to provide barrier protection against corrosive environments while maintaining compatibility with hydrogen. For instance, polymer-based coatings exhibit excellent adhesion properties and flexibility, which are essential for accommodating the physical expansion and contraction of the pipeline materials subjected to dynamic operating conditions [48]. Additionally, hybrid coatings combining organic and inorganic elements can significantly enhance the corrosion resistance of metals in hydrogen-rich environments by leveraging the beneficial properties of both materials [49].

Innovative nanotechnology applications are emerging as promising solutions for enhancing corrosion-resistant properties. Nanostructured coatings, which incorporate materials like graphene or carbon nanotubes, demonstrate remarkable protective qualities by significantly increasing the barrier properties and mechanical strength of the coatings [50]. These novel coatings also reduce the risk of permeation by hydrogen, which can otherwise lead to premature degradation of the material beneath the coating layer. Therefore, the advancement of nanotechnology in protective coatings not only provides enhanced performance but also opens pathways to explore novel materials compatible with hydrogen environments [51].

The compatibility of coatings and linings with hydrogen environments is also pivotal for maintaining safety standards. Research indicates that certain polymeric materials exhibit susceptibility to embrittlement upon exposure to hydrogen, which can lead to reduced performance of protective coatings. For example, the study by Morsbach et al. [48] highlighted how prolonged exposure to pressurized hydrogen can lead to microstructural modifications in elastomers, compromising their sealing functions and overall integrity. Therefore, materials must not only resist corrosion but also remain unaltered and durable amidst hydrogen exposure.

Reliable methods for evaluating the performance of protective coatings in hydrogen environments are essential. Corrosion testing, adhesion testing, and stress testing are crucial for assessing the efficacy of coatings before their application on pipeline systems. For instance, accelerated aging tests that replicate the conditions of constant hydrogen exposure can provide insights into the long-term viability of the coatings under actual service conditions [52]. In designing testing standards, it is vital to establish methodologies that incorporate the unique challenges posed by hydrogen to develop protective solutions that meet the rigorous demands of pipeline operations.

5.7 Design for Inspection and Maintenance

The design for inspection and maintenance of hydrogen pipelines is critical in ensuring their integrity, reliability, and safety. Given the unique challenges associated with hydrogen as a transportable gas, comprehensive strategies must be developed that facilitate effective access to inspection points and integrate advanced monitoring technologies.

Accessibility and inspection points are fundamental to effective maintenance strategies in pipeline operations. Pipelines designed with accessible inspection points reduce the time and cost associated with routine maintenance and emergency repairs. Research indicates that adopting risk-based inspection (RBI) strategies can enhance maintenance operations by allowing focus on high-risk areas, thus making it imperative to integrate adequate inspection points at critical sections of the pipeline [53]. Moreover, the design should accommodate advanced non-destructive testing (NDT) methods capable of evaluating the structural integrity of materials without interrupting service [54]. This necessitates a thorough understanding of potential locations for corrosion and mechanical failures, particularly in hydrogen pipelines where such failures can be catastrophic.

In-line inspection tools, such as pipeline inspection gauges (PIGs), can be equipped with dedicated sensors to facilitate continuous monitoring and maintenance. Recent advancements in smart PIG technology have demonstrated improved capabilities for detecting internal anomalies through machine learning algorithms and automated analysis methods [55]. Furthermore, integrating robotic solutions that can traverse the inner walls of pipelines enhances inspection capabilities, improving access to hard-to-reach areas and ensuring comprehensive evaluations of pipeline integrity [56]. Such technological innovations not only improve rapid assessments but also provide valuable data for real-time performance monitoring, which is crucial in hydrogen environments known for unique corrosion mechanisms.

Integrating smart monitoring devices into the inspection regime fosters a proactive approach to pipeline maintenance. Recent developments in wireless sensor networks and IoT technologies have transformed pipeline monitoring by enabling continuous data collection and analysis [57]. These systems facilitate the implementation of predictive maintenance strategies, utilizing data analytics to predict when maintenance should occur before critical failures happen, thus minimizing downtime and associated costs [58]. Additionally, incorporating machine learning techniques allows for better interpretation of large datasets from routine inspections, providing insights into the long-term performance trends of pipeline systems during hydrogen transport [59].

Advancements in drone technologies for aerial inspections have emerged as a promising solution for monitoring accessible sections of hydrogen pipelines [58]. Drones equipped with specialized cameras and sensors can cover extensive areas quickly, capturing high-resolution images and real-time data to inform maintenance strategies. This remote assessment capability complements on-ground inspection efforts, optimizing labor resources and improving overall safety. The compatibility of smart monitoring systems with existing pipeline infrastructure is vital for effective implementation. As many hydrogen pipelines serve dual purposes, the integration of new technologies must align with traditional maintenance practices. Studies have shown that adopting a unified framework for pipeline asset management can significantly enhance operational efficiency, integrating traditional monitoring methodologies with innovative smart solutions [60].

Lastly, worker training and engagement are essential components of the successful deployment of inspection and maintenance technologies. Ensuring that personnel are adequately trained in using sophisticated monitoring tools and data analysis enhances the overall effectiveness of maintenance strategies. It is crucial to foster an organizational culture focused on maintenance excellence, equipping staff with the necessary skills to respond effectively to the challenges posed by hydrogen pipelines [61].

References

1. Yazdi M (2024) Reliability-centered design and system resilience. Advances in computational mathematics for industrial system reliability and maintainability. Springer, pp 79–103
2. Sofian M et al (2024) A review on hydrogen blending in gas network: insight into safety, corrosion, embrittlement, coatings and liners, and bibliometric analysis. Int J Hydrog Energy 60:867–889
3. Abdin Z (2024) Bridging the energy future: the role and potential of hydrogen co-firing with natural gas. J Clean Prod 436:140724
4. Kalil I et al (2025) Dynamic pressure management for well integrity in subsea wells: defining safe operating limits through the annulus operating envelope. In: SPE/IADC drilling conference and exhibition. SPE
5. Sotoodeh K (2023) The design of pressure safety and relief valves for overpressure protection: essential considerations. Trans Indian Natl Acad Eng 8(2):273–287
6. Guo Q et al (2024) Dynamic responses in a pipe surrounded by compacted soil suffering from water hammer with fluid–structure–soil interactions. Water 16(18):2668
7. Wang FZ et al (2024) Recent advancements in fluid dynamics: drag reduction, lift generation, computational fluid dynamics, turbulence modelling, and multiphase flow. Arab J Sci Eng 49(8):10237–10249
8. Wu F et al (2024) Influence of natural gas composition and operating conditions on the steady-state performance of dry gas seals for pipeline compressors. Lubricants 12(6):217
9. Middleton C, Timmins R, Townsend R (1996) The integrity of materials in high temperature components; performance and life assessment. Int J Press Vessels Pip 66(1–3):33–57
10. Reda A, Shahin MA, Montague P (2025) Review of material selection for corrosion-resistant alloy pipelines. Eng Sci 33:1373
11. Karadirek IE et al (2012) Implementation of hydraulic modelling for water-loss reduction through pressure management. Water Resour Manag 26(9):2555–2568
12. Adepoju AH et al (2022) Advancing monitoring and alert systems: a proactive approach to improving reliability in complex data ecosystems. IRE J 5(11):281–282
13. Sotoodeh K (2024) The prevention of piping mechanical failures by stress analysis: a review of codes and standards. JMST Adv 6(1):23–35
14. Rosenfeld MJ (2012) Transportation pipelines, including ASME B31.4, B31.8, B31.8S, B31G, and B31Q codes. In: Rao KR (eds) Companion guide to the ASME boiler and pressure vessel and piping codes, vol 2, 4th edition
15. Amaya-Gómez R et al (2023) Corrosion and reliability assessment of inspected pipelines. Springer
16. Shahzamanian M et al (2021) Systematic literature review of the application of extended finite element method in failure prediction of pipelines. J Pipeline Sci Eng 1(2):241–251
17. Lu Y, Morris KC, Frechette S (2016) Current standards landscape for smart manufacturing systems. Natl Inst Stand Technol, NISTIR 8107(3):1–39
18. D'Angelo L et al (2016) Safety level on different offshore pipeline design criteria: a comparison between DNV-OS-F101 and API RP-1111 codes. In: International pipeline conference. American Society of Mechanical Engineers
19. Hussain M et al (2024) Review of prediction of stress corrosion cracking in gas pipelines using machine learning. Machines 12(1):42
20. Amaro RL et al (2018) Development of a model for hydrogen-assisted fatigue crack growth of pipeline steel. J Pressure Vessel Technol 140(2):021403
21. Cai L et al (2022) Experimental investigation on the hydrogen embrittlement characteristics and mechanism of natural gas-hydrogen transportation pipeline steels. Mater Res Express 9(4):046512
22. Oesterlin H, Fischer C, Michler T (2025) Evaluation of lifetime predictions for future hydrogen pipelines by different fracture mechanics-based design codes. Energ Technol 13(2):2301012

23. An YW et al (2023) Performance analysis of multiple structural parameters of injectors for hydrogen-mixed natural gas using orthogonal experimental methods. Phys Fluids 35(11):117119
24. Abbas AJ et al (2024) Transitioning to a hydrogen economy: exploring the viability of adapting natural gas pipelines for hydrogen transport through a case study on compression vs. looping. Gases 4(2):74–96
25. Gu S et al (2025) Optimal design of hydrogen-blended natural gas pipeline network considering separation systems. AIChE J 71(2):e18648
26. Arunagiri K, Turssline JM, Arges CG (2024) Purifying hydrogen from dilute hydrogen-natural gas mixtures using HT-PEM electrochemical hydrogen pumps. ACS Energy Lett 9(6):2912–2919
27. Bu F et al (2024) Analysis of leakage and diffusion characteristics and hazard range determination of buried hydrogen-blended natural gas pipeline based on CFD. ACS Omega 9(37):39202–39218
28. Lee H, Lee S (2022) Economic analysis on hydrogen pipeline infrastructure establishment scenarios: case study of South Korea. Energies 15(18):6824
29. Wang A et al (2025) Experimental study on hydrogen-induced crack propagation of X80 steel under alternating pressure fluctuations. Materials 18(5):947
30. Summers E et al (2024) Offshore wind-to-hydrogen: the impact of intermittency on hydrogen production and transport. In: International conference on offshore mechanics and arctic engineering. American Society of Mechanical Engineers
31. Zhou C, Zhou H, Zhang L (2024) The impact of impurity gases on the hydrogen embrittlement behavior of pipeline steel in high-pressure H_2 environments. Materials 17(9):2157
32. Kethamukkala K, Liu Y (2023) Information fusion and data augmentation for risk-based maintenance optimization of hydrogen gas pipelines. In: 15th annual conference of the prognostics and health management society, PHM 2023. Prognostics and Health Management Society
33. Li F et al (2024) Towards a future hydrogen supply chain: a review of technologies and challenges. Sustainability 16(5):1890
34. Xie Z et al (2024) A review of hydrogen storage and transportation: progresses and challenges. Energies 17(16):4070
35. Solomon MD et al (2024) Cost optimization of compressed hydrogen gas transport via trucks and pipelines. Energ Technol 12(1):2300785
36. Qiu Y et al (2022) Multi-stage flexible planning of regional electricity-HCNG-integrated energy system considering gas pipeline retrofit and expansion. IET Renew Power Gener 16(15):3339–3367
37. Lee J et al (2019) Hydrogen-induced cracking of laser beam and gas metal arc welds on API X65 steel. Korean J Metals Mater 57(8):491–498
38. Ban J et al (2023) Research progress and prospects on hydrogen damage in welds of hydrogen-blended natural gas pipelines. Processes 11(11):3180
39. Wang G et al (2019) The evolution and distribution of microstructures in high-energy laser-welded X100 pipeline steel. Materials 12(11):1762
40. Chen K et al (2022) Study on corrosion resistance and hydrogen permeation behavior in inter-critically reheated coarse-grained heat-affected zone of X80 pipeline steel. Metals 12(7):1203
41. Wang C et al (2024) Research on automatic welding process of mid-diameter pipeline construction. J Phys: Conf Ser 2951:012001
42. Odhiambo V et al (2025) A review on advances on flux cored arc welding of pipes and petrochemical pipelines: Ein Überblick über die Fortschritte beim Fülldrahtschweißen von Rohren und petrochemischen Rohrleitungen. Materialwiss Werkstofftech 56(4):549–564
43. Ngo GV (2020) Automated orbital welding of carbon and low-alloy steels pipelines with small diameter. Mater Sci Forum 989:766–771
44. Yingchao F et al (2022) Stress analysis of the effect of additional load on the butt weld of suspended pipeline with variable wall thickness. Front Energy Res 9:792508
45. Ren T, Zhang JM, Niu XW (2024) Research on welding process and performance of prefabricated girth welded joints for double-connected pipes of X80M pipeline. Mater Sci Forum 1136:109–118

46. Feng Q et al (2016) Literature review: theory and application of in-line inspection technologies for oil and gas pipeline girth weld defection. Sensors 17(1):50
47. Geng L et al (2022) Image classification method based on improved deep convolutional neural networks for the magnetic flux leakage (MFL) signal of girth welds in long-distance pipelines. Sustainability 14(19):12102
48. Morsbach S et al (2022) Hydrogen compatibility of polymers for fuel cell vehicles. Energ Technol 10(9):2200018
49. Huang L, Zhang L (2024) Effect of hydrogen on high cycle fatigue properties of L360 pipeline steel notched specimens. Materials 17(22):5612
50. Avdeev YG et al (2024) Complex protection of some steels in sulfuric acid solutions by 1,2,4-triazole derivatives. Materials 17(19):4728
51. Rehman A et al (2024) Work-function-dependent reduction of transition metal nitrides in hydrogen environments. J Phys Chem Lett 15(46):11462–11467
52. Kimura M et al (2021) Test method to establish hydrogen compatibility of materials in high pressure hydrogen gas environments for fuel cell vehicles. ISIJ Int 61(4):1333–1336
53. Soedarsono JW et al (2023) Development of risk based inspection of 28-years-old subsea sales gas pipelines to support the energy demand. East-Eur J Enterp Technol 122(3)
54. Ma Q et al (2021) Pipeline in-line inspection method, instrumentation and data management. Sensors 21(11):3862
55. Freitas VCGD et al (2022) Velocity prediction of a pipeline inspection gauge (PIG) with machine learning. Sensors 22(23):9162
56. Daniyan I et al (2022) Development of an inline inspection robot for the detection of pipeline defects. J Facil Manag 20(2):193–217
57. Wang Z et al (2019) Compressed sensing method for health monitoring of pipelines based on guided wave inspection. IEEE Trans Instrum Meas 69(7):4722–4731
58. Ravishankar P et al (2022) Darts—drone and artificial intelligence reconsolidated technological solution for increasing the oil and gas pipeline resilience. Int J Disaster Risk Sci 13(5):810–821
59. Mgbemena CE, Onuoha DO, Godwin HC (2023) Development of a novel virtual reality-enabled remote monitoring device for maintenance of cathodic protection systems on oil and gas pipelines. Sci Rep 13(1):15874
60. Jiang T et al (2017) Application of FBG based sensor in pipeline safety monitoring. Appl Sci 7(6):540
61. Liu S et al (2018) A novel algorithm for pipeline displacement and bending strain of in-line inspection based on inertia measurement technology. Adv Mech Eng 10(12):1687814018816755

Chapter 6
Corrosion and Degradation Mechanisms

6.1 Overview of Corrosion in Hydrogen Pipelines

Corrosion in hydrogen pipelines presents a significant challenge for the development of hydrogen infrastructure, especially given the increasing reliance on hydrogen as a clean energy source. Understanding the complexities and potential degradation mechanisms is crucial for minimizing risks associated with hydrogen transport. This overview discusses key aspects of corrosion in hydrogen pipelines, emphasizing hydrogen embrittlement, material compatibility, leakage issues, and adaptations necessary for existing pipeline infrastructure.

One of the primary concerns regarding hydrogen transport through pipelines is hydrogen embrittlement (HE), a phenomenon where hydrogen atoms infiltrate the metal lattice of pipeline materials, leading to a reduction in mechanical properties. This degradation is particularly pronounced in steels used for natural gas pipelines, such as API X60, X70, and X80, which can suffer significant losses in tensile strength and ductility when exposed to hydrogen environments [1, 2]. Studies show that even relatively low concentrations of hydrogen can initiate embrittlement, which becomes more severe as hydrogen concentration increases. For instance, research indicates that the fatigue life of pipeline steels can dramatically decrease from thousands of cycles in nitrogen environments to mere hundreds when hydrogen is present [2].

The microstructural characteristics of pipeline materials significantly impact their susceptibility to hydrogen embrittlement. For instance, finer grain structures tend to exhibit a higher sensitivity to hydrogen ingress compared to coarser ones, as the grain boundaries provide pathways for hydrogen diffusion [3]. Moreover, variations in welding techniques and the resultant microstructural properties can further influence the degree of embrittlement, leading to failures if not appropriately managed [1]. Thus, extensive research focusing on the interplay between microstructure and HE is critical for developing heat treatments or coatings that can enhance hydrogen resistance [4].

M. Hussain et al., *Hydrogen Pipeline Integrity*, Green Energy and Technology,
https://doi.org/10.1007/978-981-95-5609-0_6

Another significant aspect of corrosion in pipelines designed or retrofitted for hydrogen usage is the leakage characteristics owing to the unique properties of hydrogen. Hydrogen has a much smaller molecular size and lower density compared to natural gas, which increases its tendency to diffuse through pipeline materials and leads to potential leakage issues [5]. Studies conducted using computational fluid dynamics have shown that the blending of hydrogen with natural gas can substantially alter leakage rates, raising economic and safety concerns [5]. Furthermore, the permeation of hydrogen through pipeline materials can lead to localized pressure build-ups, increasing the risk of cracking or failure [6]. Recent modeling has indicated that existing pipeline materials may require re-evaluation to ensure they can safely handle hydrogen without compromising structural integrity [7].

As hydrogen blending becomes more common in natural gas pipelines, it necessitates the examination of the compatibility of current materials with hydrogen-rich environments. The transition involves addressing various challenges related to mechanical integrity, corrosion resistance, and the overall performance of the pipelines [8]. Retrofitting existing natural gas pipelines may involve applying protective coatings or selective repairs to mitigate the risks associated with hydrogen exposure [1, 9]. Moreover, considerations must be given to the chemical reactions that can occur, such as sulfide stress cracking in the presence of hydrogen sulfide, which can complicate the integrity of pipeline systems and necessitate rigorous inspection regimes [2].

Operational adjustments, including modifications to transportation processes and pressure management systems, will also be vital in adapting pipelines for hydrogen transport. The differences in energy density and viscosity between hydrogen and natural gas influence the operational efficiency and safety of transport systems [10, 11]. For example, as hydrogen is injected into existing natural gas networks, adjustments in pressure and flow rates must be carefully managed to maintain system integrity and prevent failures caused by sudden changes in operational conditions [12]. The potential for chemical reactions within steel under high-pressure hydrogen conditions further complicates these challenges and requires ongoing research into the long-term durability of these materials [13]. Through these discussions, it becomes evident that developing effective strategies to prevent corrosion and manage the risks associated with hydrogen pipelines is imperative. The complexity and costs associated with building entirely new hydrogen pipelines drive the industry towards retrofitting existing natural gas infrastructure [13]. This transition must be supported by comprehensive studies that investigate material properties, environmental conditions, and their interactions under hydrogen exposure to ensure safe and effective hydrogen transport.

As the world gravitates towards a hydrogen economy, it is essential to prioritize research and development efforts focused on understanding corrosion mechanisms within hydrogen pipelines. These efforts will not only improve the resilience of our energy infrastructures but also facilitate the wider adoption of hydrogen as a clean and sustainable energy source, aligning with global decarbonization goals [14].

6.1.1 Types of Corrosion: Internal and External

Corrosion in hydrogen pipelines can be broadly categorized into internal and external corrosion. Internal corrosion arises from the exposure of the pipeline materials to the hydrogen gas, which can interact with any residual contaminants like water or corrosive species contained in the gas. Conversely, external corrosion occurs due to environmental factors affecting the outer surfaces of the pipelines, including moisture, soil conditions, and microbial activity. The distinction between internal and external corrosion is critical, as each type necessitates different strategies for monitoring, assessment, and mitigation.

The internal environment of hydrogen pipelines is unique compared to natural gas pipelines. For instance, the presence of moisture and impurities in hydrogen can accelerate corrosion rates. When water is present inside the pipeline, it can facilitate reactions between hydrogen and impurities leading to the formation of corrosive species that attack metal surfaces. Additionally, if hydrogen is mixed with other gases containing sulfur or chlorine, the potential for localized corrosion increases due to the formation of corrosive compounds that can attack the pipeline materials more aggressively. Studies indicate that under certain conditions, hydrogen can induce localized corrosion even in relatively benign environments, emphasizing the need for careful monitoring of internal conditions through the use of corrosion inhibitors or appropriate gas drying methods.

On the other hand, external corrosion is influenced by environmental conditions such as soil composition and moisture content. Pipelines buried in soils are at considerable risk from external corrosion due to electrochemical processes that can occur in the presence of moisture, leading to pitting and eventual failure of the pipeline material. The corrosivity of soil can vary significantly based on its electrolyte content, moisture levels, and temperature, making it critical to assess soil characteristics in locations where pipelines are installed. Cathodic protection is often employed as a mitigation measure against external corrosion, utilizing electrical systems to inhibit the electrochemical processes that lead to degradation. Selection of appropriate coatings and insulations is also vital, as these materials can act as barriers to moisture and corrosive agents from penetrating the pipeline surface.

The interactions between internal and external corrosion processes can be complex. For example, a pipeline's susceptibility to external corrosion can be exacerbated by internal corrosion, particularly if water or contaminants accumulate at points vulnerable to external electrolyte intrusion. Regular integrity assessments, including cathodic protection monitoring, and corrosion detection systems, are necessary to keep both internal and external corrosion in check. Such evaluations can guide maintenance planning and prioritize remediation efforts to ensure the continued safe operation of hydrogen pipelines.

Ultimately, understanding the mechanisms underpinning internal and external corrosion will enable pipeline operators to develop more effective corrosion management strategies. Continuous research and development in corrosion monitoring technologies and advanced materials science will be instrumental in enhancing the resilience of hydrogen pipeline infrastructure.

6.1.2 Role of Environment and Operating Conditions

The environment and operating conditions play a significant role in the corrosion mechanisms affecting hydrogen pipelines. Environmental factors include temperature, humidity, soil chemistry, and atmospheric conditions, all of which can significantly influence corrosion rates. For example, elevated temperatures can accelerate corrosion processes, as they often increase reaction rates and the electrochemical activity on pipeline surfaces. It is well documented that increased temperature can significantly decrease passive film formation rates on metallic surfaces, making them more susceptible to corrosion.

Hydrogen's interaction with other materials can also be contingent upon the environment, particularly in the presence of moisture or CO_2, which can promote the formation of hydrogen carbonate or other corrosive compounds, exacerbating the degradation mechanisms [15]. Externally, the presence of chlorides in the environment, often found in coastal areas or de-icing salts in colder climates, poses a risk for localized corrosion where cracks or defects may exist, providing pathways for corrosive agents to penetrate and initiate corrosion.

Operating conditions, including pressure and flow rates, have profound implications for corrosion behavior in hydrogen pipelines. High operating pressures facilitate greater diffusion of hydrogen into the pipeline material, intensifying the risk of hydrogen embrittlement and localized corrosion. Influence of flow rates is multifaceted; variations can lead to turbulence within the pipeline, increasing erosion rates and potentially contributing to mechanical degradation combined with electrochemical actions. Generally, operation at higher flow velocities can lead to the erosion of protective oxide layers that may otherwise inhibit corrosion.

The contributions of cathodic protection systems and the presence of corrosion inhibitors need to be evaluated within the context of the operating environment. Cathodic protection, while effective at reducing external corrosion rates, must be optimized to avoid over-protection, which can lead to the risk of hydrogen embrittlement in certain pipeline materials. Likewise, the selection of appropriate corrosion inhibitors is often contingent on operating conditions. These inhibitors need to be examined under the specific pressures, temperatures, and chemical environments present within hydrogen pipelines to evaluate their efficacy accurately.

Given these variables, it becomes clear that understanding the interplay between environmental factors and operating conditions is critical in developing comprehensive maintenance and risk management strategies for hydrogen pipelines. This will require a combination of theoretical modeling and empirical data collection, enabling the development of predictive maintenance schedules tailored to specific pipeline conditions. Furthermore, advancing sensor technologies and automated data collection approaches can help track real-time conditions, allowing for the timely intervention and adjustment of operational parameters to mitigate corrosion risks effectively.

6.2 Hydrogen-Specific Corrosion Mechanisms

Hydrogen-specific corrosion mechanisms are critical in evaluating the integrity and durability of pipelines that transport hydrogen or hydrogen-blended gas mixtures. These mechanisms vary significantly from traditional corrosion processes seen in pipelines carrying other gases, primarily due to hydrogen's unique physicochemical properties and its behavior under different environmental conditions. This section will delve into the specific corrosion phenomena associated with hydrogen, covering hydrogen embrittlement, stress corrosion cracking, the role of diffusion, and the interaction of hydrogen with pipeline materials.

One of the most prominent hydrogen-specific corrosion mechanisms is hydrogen embrittlement (HE). This phenomenon arises when hydrogen atoms penetrate the metallic lattice of materials, particularly high-strength steels typically used in pipelines. The infiltration of hydrogen into the metal can lead to significant reductions in ductility and tensile strength, thereby increasing the risk of catastrophic failure in pipelines [16, 17]. HE is exacerbated under conditions of high-pressure hydrogen, where the likelihood of hydrogen ingress via adsorptive mechanisms is enhanced. Giarola et al. [16] demonstrated in their investigations that a concentration of hydrogen can induce severe micro-cracking and deterioration of the mechanical properties of the pipeline material.

Another critical aspect of hydrogen-related corrosion is stress corrosion cracking (SCC). This form of corrosion occurs when tensile stress and a corrosive environment are present, facilitating crack propagation. Metal alloys exposed to hydrogen-rich environments are particularly susceptible to SCC, as hydrogen can weaken metallic bonds at the crack tips [18]. Experimental studies confirm that the presence of hydrogen accelerates the crack growth rates in steel pipelines, and these effects are often synergistic with other stressors like mechanical loading or environmental factors [18]. The challenge of SCC in hydrogen pipelines necessitates rigorous monitoring and control strategies, particularly at joints and welds where stress concentrations are more likely to occur.

The diffusion of hydrogen in metals, particularly steel, adds complexity to understanding hydrogen corrosion mechanisms. Hydrogen atoms, being the smallest and lightest atoms, can diffuse through most metals relatively easily, and their mobility is influenced by several factors such as temperature, pressure, and the material microstructure [19]. For example, Ghadiani et al. [2] highlight that the diffusion rates of hydrogen can be substantially different in various steels and can lead to localized degradation or the development of hydrogen blisters when concentrations exceed the material's threshold tolerance. The unique setup of pipelines implies that the pressure and temperature during operation significantly affect the degree of diffusivity and, as such, must be taken into account when assessing pipeline integrity [20].

The role of environmental conditions cannot be overstated when discussing hydrogen-specific corrosion mechanisms. Factors such as pH, temperature, and the presence of contaminants like chlorides can significantly influence not just corrosion rates but the type of corrosion experienced [20, 21]. For instance, in acidic soils, the availability of hydrogen ions can intensify the migration of hydrogen into pipeline materials, leading to accelerated embrittlement [15]. Detailed studies have shown that maintaining a neutral pH in environments surrounding pipelines can help mitigate some of the risks associated with hydrogen corrosion [21], although challenges remain in achieving optimal conditions across extensive pipeline networks. Moreover, when hydrogen is blended with natural gas, additional mechanisms may emerge due to the interactions between different gas species. Studies reveal that the introduction of hydrogen into natural gas pipelines modifies the electrochemical environment, potentially leading to enhanced corrosion due to shifts in local pH and the formation of new corrosive byproducts [22]. Thus, the risk assessment of currently operational pipelines must include analyses of blended gas effects, particularly in older infrastructure that was not designed for hydrogen transport [22].

Notably, recent advancements have focused on barrier technologies aimed at preventing hydrogen ingress into pipeline materials. Coatings and surface treatments that significantly reduce hydrogen permeability have been developed as a means to enhance the resilience of pipeline materials against hydrogen-induced failures. For example, for welding operations, the application of coatings has shown promise in providing a protective barrier that mitigates hydrogen diffusion into the base material, thereby reducing the incidence of HE [23]. The successful implementation of such protective measures requires a comprehensive understanding of the operational dynamics of pipelines, including factors such as flow rates and operational pressures, to adequately tailor the protective strategies.

The monitoring of hydrogen corrosion mechanisms necessitates advanced technologies for assessing the integrity and serviceability of pipelines. Non-destructive testing techniques, such as magnetic anisotropy methods for detecting hydrogenated regions within materials, are being explored as part of a broader strategy to enhance pipeline safety [24]. Continued innovation in detection and monitoring technologies is crucial for the ongoing safe operation of pipelines in environments where hydrogen is present, particularly as the push for reduced greenhouse gas emissions drives the increased utilization of hydrogen energy systems.

6.2.1 Hydrogen Embrittlement Corrosion

Hydrogen embrittlement corrosion represents a particularly insidious failure mechanism affecting pipeline steels exposed to hydrogen environments. As hydrogen diffuses into the metal's microstructure, it leads to a gradual reduction in mechanical properties, culminating in the risk of sudden and catastrophic failure. The fundamental mechanisms of HE can be categorized into two primary theories: hydrogen-enhanced decohesion (HEDE) and hydrogen-enhanced localized plasticity (HELP) [2, 21]. HEDE posits that hydrogen weakens the atomic bonds at grain boundaries, promoting crack nucleation, while HELP suggests that hydrogen facilitates plastic deformation, which ultimately leads to fracture under stress.

The susceptibility of pipelines to hydrogen embrittlement is influenced by a variety of factors, including material composition, microstructural characteristics, and environmental conditions. Research has shown that the inclusion of certain alloying elements (e.g., nickel, manganese) can mitigate HE, while higher strength steels often display increased susceptibility [16]. Advanced microstructural examinations through electron backscatter diffraction (EBSD) and transmission electron microscopy (TEM) have revealed critical insights into how microstructural features, such as grain size and shape, influence hydrogen diffusion pathways and trapping mechanisms [24].

The degree of hydrogen embrittlement can exhibit a marked dependency on the operational parameters of the pipeline. Higher pressures and temperatures typically facilitate increased hydrogen permeation and induce significant alterations in failure modes. For instance, studies conducted under varying pressure conditions demonstrate that the fracture, when subjected to higher hydrogen pressures, transitions from ductile features to brittle characteristics marked by intergranular and transgranular cracking [2]. The intricate relationship between operational conditions and material responses underscores the necessity for robust testing protocols aimed at predicting the failure thresholds of pipeline materials under specific hydrogen exposure scenarios.

Buried pipelines in particular face unique challenges concerning HE due to the compounded effects of environmental aging and stress concentrations introduced during operation. Electrode potentials can shift significantly in soil environments, exacerbating HE phenomena in underground installations where moisture levels fluctuate and cathodic protection strategies may fluctuate or become compromised [22]. Ongoing monitoring techniques need to be employed to address these challenges, ensuring long-term integrity in buried hydrogen pipelines.

6.2.2 Sulfide Stress Cracking and Other Forms

Sulfide stress cracking (SSC) is another critical aspect of hydrogen-specific corrosion mechanisms that affect pipelines, particularly those exposed to sour environments containing hydrogen sulfide (H_2S). The presence of H_2S is notorious for exacerbating SCC and contributes to the complexity of corrosion management in hydrogen pipelines. SSC arises when hydrogen is present alongside tensile stress and a sour environment, typically leading to the occurrence of brittle fracture at significantly lower stress levels than would occur in non-sour conditions.

The interaction between hydrogen and the sulfide ions can fundamentally alter the electrochemical environment and may precipitate crack growth processes. Studies indicate that the absorption of hydrogen within steel in the presence of H_2S can significantly reduce the stress threshold required for crack propagation, highlighting the need to consider both hydrogen embrittlement and sulfide interactions in the evaluation of pipeline integrity. This necessitates tailored approaches to material selection and maintenance practices for pipelines operating in environments where H_2S is encountered.

In addition to SSC and HE, pipelines may also experience other forms of degradation stemming from hydrogen exposure. For example, hydrogen blistering is a unique phenomenon where localized pockets of hydrogen accumulate, leading to pressure-induced blisters beneath the surface of the material. This can occur especially in regions where there are preexisting defects or microstructural weaknesses [16]. Strategies to combat these forms of corrosion include regular monitoring and tailored pipeline design approaches that always account for the presence of hydrogen and the synergistic effects of contaminants such as H_2S.

It's essential to consider that other operational factors can combine with hydrogen to create complex corrosion scenarios. For instance, the introduction of other corrosive contaminants can further exacerbate corrosion mechanisms present in hydrogen environments. With the increasing use of hydrogen as a fuel source, comprehensive strategies encompassing preventive, predictive, and mitigative measures will be critical to ensure long-term pipeline integrity and safety.

6.3 Detection and Monitoring of Corrosion

Corrosion in various industrial applications, especially in hydrogen pipelines, poses significant risks necessitating effective detection and monitoring methodologies. Various technologies and techniques have been developed to assess corrosion, tailor applications for diverse materials, and optimize maintenance strategies. This section will explore contemporary methods of detecting and monitoring corrosion, including traditional physical evaluation techniques, advanced non-destructive testing (NDT) methods, and sensor technology.

6.3.1 Visual, NDT, and Sensor-Based Techniques

Traditional methods for corrosion detection typically include visual inspections, physical testing, and chemical analyses, which enable engineers to evaluate the condition of materials visually or through laboratory analyses [25]. A proposed process for corrosion detection is shown in Fig. 6.1. Visual inspections are often the first step in assessing corrosion; however, they may not be sufficient alone for comprehensive evaluations, especially for materials where corrosion is not easily visible.

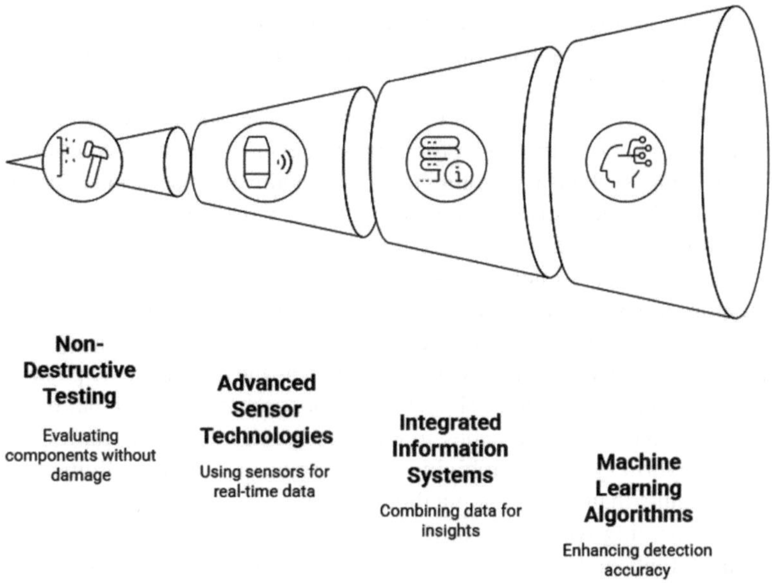

Fig. 6.1 Corrosion detection process

For instance, corrosion may be situated beneath coatings or within concrete structures, emphasizing the importance of combining visual assessments with advanced methodologies to ascertain the extent of degradation [26].

Non-destructive testing (NDT) techniques have gained increasing popularity in the realm of corrosion monitoring due to their reliability and the ability to evaluate components without causing damage. Techniques such as ultrasonic testing, eddy current testing, and acoustic emission testing are widely employed for real-time monitoring of corrosion [27]. For instance, acoustic emission (AE) monitoring utilizes the detection of elastic waves generated by the rapid release of energy, allowing for identification of corrosion fatigue and crack growth in pipeline materials [27]. Similarly, ultrasonic testing entails the propagation of sound waves through materials to detect internal flaws or gauge thickness, which is critical for evaluating the condition of steel pipelines [28, 35, 36].

Among advanced NDT methods, fiber Bragg grating (FBG) sensors have found applications in monitoring corrosion in reinforced concrete and steel structures. These sensors use optical fibers to measure changes in strain and temperature, providing real-time data on the potential for corrosion within the monitored structures [29]. This approach enables the early detection of corrosion while ensuring minimal disruption to the structures in which the sensors are installed.

Recent developments in corrosion monitoring also include novel technologies such as infrared thermography and pulsed eddy current (PEC) methods. Infrared thermography allows for the visualization of heat patterns on the surface of materials, thereby identifying areas of corrosion without direct contact [30]. Meanwhile, pulsed eddy current technologies have demonstrated efficacy in detecting corrosion under insulation in pipelines, which is critical given the challenges associated with visually monitoring insulated pipes [31].

Integrated information systems leveraging various sensor technologies have been employed to provide real-time data for corrosion evaluation and prediction metrics [32]. For example, systems that combine electrochemical sensors and data analytics can provide in-situ monitoring of corrosion rates in structures exposed to aggressive environments, automatically processing data to generate actionable insights for maintenance and repair strategies [33, 37].

Developing reliable and efficient methods for non-destructive evaluation (NDE) that emphasize long-term monitoring capabilities is essential in reducing economic losses associated with corrosion. Techniques such as the galvanostatic pulse method and linear polarization resistance (LPR) tactics are commonly used, but researchers continually explore new approaches to enhance sensitivity and accuracy [25, 34]. For instance, hybrid systems combining the strengths of various NDE methods may yield better results than individual methods alone.

Another promising avenue for corrosion detection centers upon the use of machine learning algorithms and advancements in digital image analysis. Combining traditional non-destructive techniques with modern machine learning approaches can significantly enhance the accuracy of corrosion assessments by automating detection and classifying corrosion types based on processed data from visual inspections [26]. Technologies such as YOLOv5 have emerged for the enhancement of corrosion detection capabilities on coated metal surfaces, revealing the intersection between materials science and machine learning [26].

Ultimately, as awareness of the implications of corrosion intensifies in industries using hydrogen transport systems, refining existing methodologies and adopting innovative approaches will be vital. This pursuit aims to improve detection accuracy and establish protocols that can effectively forecast corrosion challenges before they lead to catastrophic failures.

6.3.2 Corrosion Rate Measurement and Modeling

Understanding and accurately measuring the rate of corrosion is critical for implementing effective maintenance strategies and ensuring the structural integrity of pipelines, especially in environments where hydrogen is present. The corrosion rate can be quantified through various methods, including weight loss measurements, electrochemical techniques, and analytical modeling approaches. Each technique presents distinct advantages and limitations, necessitating a comprehensive analysis of the conditions and materials involved to select the most suitable corrosion rate measurement method.

One of the most straightforward approaches to corrosion rate measurement involves the weight loss method, where test specimens are exposed to corrosive environments for defined periods. The weight change is then measured, allowing for the calculation of corrosion rates in terms of mass loss per surface area over time. However, this method is often limited to laboratory settings since it requires specimen removal and may not account for localized corrosion that can occur in pipeline systems.

Electrochemical techniques have emerged as powerful tools for real-time measurement of corrosion rates, providing insights into corrosion processes as they occur in situ. Methods such as linear polarization resistance (LPR) and electrochemical impedance spectroscopy (EIS) allow for the analysis of corrosion behavior under various operational conditions. LPR relies on the application of a small perturbation voltage to measure the resultant current, generating data that can be correlated to the corrosion rate. EIS, on the other hand, involves the application of a sinusoidal voltage to the corrosion system, capturing the response to assess electrochemical properties. These techniques not only provide instantaneous corrosion rates but also yield information about the electrochemical conditions influencing corrosion behavior.

6.4 Corrosion Mitigation Strategies

Corrosion remains a critical challenge in the maintenance and operation of pipelines, particularly those transporting hydrogen or blended gases. Mitigating corrosion is essential for enhancing the longevity and reliability of these infrastructures. This section discusses various strategies for corrosion mitigation, encompassing coatings, cathodic protection, corrosion inhibitors, and environmentally-friendly approaches.

6.4.1 Coatings for Corrosion Protection

Protective coatings represent one of the most effective strategies for preventing corrosion in metal components. These coatings act as barriers between the metal surface and the corrosive environment, greatly reducing the rate of corrosion. For example, the application of epoxy coatings has become widespread due to their excellent adhesive properties and resistance to moisture and chemical attack [38]. Such coatings can effectively seal metal surfaces, preventing corrosive agents from contacting the substrate.

Recent advancements in nanotechnology have led to the development of nanocoatings that provide enhanced protection against corrosion. These coatings, utilizing materials such as aluminum oxide or titanium dioxide, not only resist corrosion but also improve the mechanical properties of the coated material [39]. Research indicates that these coatings can be engineered to exhibit self-healing properties, thereby restoring their integrity upon damage [39]. Moreover, hybrid sol–gel coatings have emerged as a promising solution, combining the benefits of both inorganic and organic materials to deliver effective corrosion resistance [37]. Studies have shown that sustainable coatings derived from natural substances, such as chitosan, can provide environmentally friendly alternatives while being effective corrosion inhibitors [40].

6.4.2 Cathodic Protection

Cathodic protection (CP) is a well-established electrochemical technique utilized to control corrosion on metallic surfaces. This method involves making the protected metal the cathode of an electrochemical cell, effectively preventing oxidation reactions that result in corrosion. Two primary forms of CP are sacrificial anode systems and impressed current systems.

Sacrificial anode systems use more anodic metals, such as zinc or magnesium, which corrode preferentially, thereby protecting the steel infrastructure [41]. These systems are particularly useful in practical applications like pipelines buried in soil or submerged in water.

Impressed current cathodic protection (ICCP) systems involve applying an external electric current to the metal surface, enhancing its cathodic characteristics. Research has shown that ICCP is particularly effective in environments where high chloride concentrations are present, such as coastal or de-icing applications [42]. For instance, the use of ICCP in chloride-contaminated concrete has demonstrated significant effectiveness in mitigating corrosion rates of embedded steel reinforcement [43].

6.4.3 Corrosion Inhibitors

Corrosion inhibitors are chemical substances that, when added in small concentrations to corrosive media, can significantly decrease or prevent metallic corrosion. Various studies have highlighted the use of organic inhibitors, biomaterials, and green inhibitors derived from plant extracts as viable corrosion mitigation options [44]. Their mechanisms often involve adsorption onto the metal surface, which can modulate the electrochemical reactions that lead to corrosion.

For example, vegetable extracts, including tannins and other polyphenols, have demonstrated effective corrosion protection properties due to their ability to form protective films on metal surfaces [45]. Additionally, studies have shown that some polysaccharides derived from plants can offer effective passive protection against corrosion in various environments [46]. Furthermore, electrochemical corrosion inhibitors have gained popularity for their effectiveness in acidic environments, often encountered in industrial settings. Compounds like thiazole and other heterocyclic compounds have shown promising results in reducing corrosion rates of various steels in aggressive acidic media [47].

6.4.4 Environmentally Friendly Approaches

With a growing emphasis on sustainability, environmentally friendly corrosion mitigation strategies are gaining traction. Notably, using biomass-derived coatings and corrosion inhibitors exemplifies a significant shift toward greener practices in corrosion management [44]. These natural materials exhibit a lower environmental impact compared to traditional synthetic chemicals while demonstrating remarkable effectiveness as corrosion protectants in various scenarios.

Recent advancements in conducting polymers and bio-based coatings, such as chitosan and lignin, provide an effective means to enhance corrosion resistance while minimizing ecological impact [40]. These materials show promise in various applications due to their biodegradability and ability to provide enhanced protective qualities against corrosive agents.

6.4.5 Advanced Surface Modification Techniques

Advanced surface modification techniques have also shown great potential in mitigating corrosion. Methods such as plasma electrolytic oxidation (PEO), which create a highly porous ceramic-like film on the metallic surface, improve wear and corrosion resistance [48]. Similarly, the application of micro-nano structures to create superhydrophobic surfaces has been shown to enhance corrosion resistance by reducing water adhesion and the likelihood of moisture accumulation on the metal surface [49].

Notably, electrochemical methods to form protective oxide layers, such as anodizing in the case of aluminum alloys, have proven effective in preventing corrosion in aggressive environments [50]. Research into hybrid coatings that integrate both organic and inorganic materials further enhances the protective capabilities of these surfaces, potentially leading to long-lasting corrosion resistance under various operational conditions [51].

6.5 Operational Practices to Minimize Corrosion

Operational practices play a crucial role in minimizing corrosion and enhancing the lifespan of infrastructure, particularly in environments where pipelines transport hydrogen or other corrosive materials. A comprehensive strategy encompassing design considerations, material selection, regular monitoring, environmental controls, and maintenance practices is essential for mitigating corrosion risks effectively. This section discusses several operational practices that can be implemented to minimize corrosion in pipeline systems as shown in Fig. 6.2.

Fig. 6.2 Cycle of operational practices for corrosion minimization

6.5.1 Design Considerations and Material Selection

Choosing the appropriate materials and designing pipelines to withstand corrosive environments is a fundamental aspect of corrosion management. Material selection should prioritize corrosion-resistant alloys, coatings, and composites that can endure specific environmental conditions. For instance, using high-strength stainless steels or nickel-based alloys in environments with high hydrogen sulfide (H_2S) concentrations can mitigate corrosion risks significantly [52]. Additionally, adopting design principles that allow for adequate drainage, minimize stagnant water, and enhance accessibility for maintenance can further reduce corrosion risks.

Incorporating protective features into design phases, such as sacrificial anodes, cathodic protection systems, and moisture barriers, adds an extra layer of security against corrosion [53]. Incorporating advanced techniques like finite element analysis (FEA) can help predict where stress concentrations may occur, leading to localized corrosion, thus enabling engineers to modify designs accordingly [54]. Additionally, ensuring that joints and welds are well-engineered can minimize corrosion-prone areas, addressing one of the major risk factors in pipeline integrity.

6.5.2 Corrosion Monitoring and Assessment

Regularly assessing the condition of pipelines through monitoring is key to identifying corrosion issues early. Implementing corrosion monitoring programs can provide valuable data on the operational conditions affecting corrosion rates, facilitating proactive management. Monitoring techniques, such as electrochemical potential surveys and corrosion rate measurements, can be employed to evaluate the effectiveness of protective measures [55].

Recent advancements in machine learning and artificial intelligence provide promising avenues for enhancing corrosion monitoring. Predictive models can analyze data from various sources, such as historical performance, environmental conditions, and material properties, to identify high-risk pipelines and prioritize inspections and maintenance activities effectively [56]. For instance, the ability to use remote sensing and GIS data in conjunction with monitoring technologies can yield deeper insights into corrosion susceptibility within specific environmental contexts [57].

6.5.3 Environmental Control Measures

Controlling the environmental factors that contribute to corrosion is essential for minimizing risks, particularly in pipelines subject to aggressive conditions. For example, maintaining appropriate temperature and humidity levels can dramatically reduce the potential for corrosion. In operational contexts such as oil refineries or chemical plants, optimizing fluid compositions to minimize corrosive contaminants like chlorides or acids is vital [58].

Deploying dehumidification systems or effective drainage constructs in buried pipeline installations can significantly limit moisture accumulation, reducing the likelihood of corrosion occurring due to moisture persistence [59]. Applying water-repellent coatings or hydrophobic treatments to surfaces exposed to moisture and corrosive agents may further improve resistance to corrosion [60]. These environmental controls can minimize corrosion initiation and propagation within infrastructures, ensuring prolonged operational lifespans.

6.5.4 Regular Maintenance and Repair Practices

Establishing a routine maintenance schedule that includes regular inspections, assessments, and timely repairs is critical for managing corrosion effectively. Operators should routinely inspect for signs of corrosion or damage, including visual inspections and utilizing advanced non-destructive testing (NDT) techniques to detect early corrosion stages [55]. Establishing a robust maintenance plan helps identify and rectify issues before they escalate into costly failures or require extensive repair work.

Implementing a failure management system allows operators to learn from past issues by maintaining detailed records and analyses of any corrosion failures encountered [61]. By analyzing the causes and patterns of past corrosion incidents, operators can adapt their maintenance strategies and design considerations to minimize future risks effectively. Additionally, utilizing advanced technologies such as corrosion inhibitors during maintenance can bolster protection levels while addressing environmental concerns related to chemical usage [62].

6.5.5 Education and Training

Promoting education and training within operational teams regarding corrosion awareness and control measures is an integral component of effective corrosion management. Ensuring that personnel are familiar with the best practices for corrosion prevention, the significance of compliance with safety protocols, and the proper use of preventative materials can significantly contribute to the reduction of corrosion risks [63]. Regular training sessions and workshops can help keep teams abreast of the latest advancements in corrosion management technologies and methodologies [64].

Additionally, fostering a culture of proactive maintenance within organizations, whereby all personnel acknowledge their roles in combating corrosion, can enhance the overall effectiveness of corrosion management systems. The incorporation of feedback loops and communication can further nurture this culture, where individuals are empowered to report concerns and improvements regarding equipment conditions [63].

6.5.6 Control of Moisture and Contaminants

Effective control of moisture and contaminant exposure is crucial in reducing corrosion rates in hydrogen pipelines. Moisture acts as a medium for electrochemical reactions that can facilitate corrosion processes. Implementing measures to minimize moisture within storage and transport systems is paramount; this may include the installation of drain systems and insulating materials to keep pipelines dry. Furthermore, the use of corrosion-resistant linings in storage tanks and piping systems can contribute to moisture control, thereby reducing corrosion susceptibility.

The presence of contaminants such as salts, acids, or biological agents can significantly accelerate corrosion. Regular monitoring of the chemical composition of the environments in which pipelines operate is essential, as changes may necessitate adjustments to corrosion control strategies. Moreover, filtrating and treating operating fluids to remove harmful contaminants before they enter pipelines can have significant effects on corrosive attack rates.

In areas prone to environmental conditions presenting high moisture or contaminants, implementing regular cleaning and drying protocols may prove beneficial. Using desiccants or dehumidifiers in enclosed environments, such as pump stations, also represents a valuable approach for maintaining low humidity levels. By ensuring that moisture and contaminants are controlled, pipeline operators can significantly project the longevity and stability of their systems.

6.5.7 Pressure and Flow Management

Effective pressure and flow management within pipelines is essential for minimizing corrosion-related risks. High-pressure conditions can exacerbate corrosion processes, primarily through mechanical impacts on pipe walls and increased diffusion rates of corrosive agents into materials. Maintaining optimal pressure limits according to material specifications is critical. Operational practices should include regular monitoring of pressure levels throughout the system and adjustments to maintain a consistent and safe operating environment.

Flow conditions also greatly influence corrosion rates. Stagnation or dead zones, where fluid movement is limited, can create pockets of corrosive environments that facilitate localized corrosion. Implementing strategies to ensure uniform flow rates and minimize turbulence will help mitigate these risks. Methods such as regular inspection of flow patterns and the use of flow-control devices can contribute to improved fluid dynamics within the pipeline.

Transient conditions, such as rapid pressurization or depressurization, can also significantly influence the integrity of pipelines and contribute to enhanced corrosion rates. Therefore, maintaining steady state operating conditions and carefully managing startup and shutdown procedures will help mitigate the risks associated with transient flow conditions. Furthermore, innovative solutions like data analytics can optimize flow management by incorporating real-time monitoring systems to detect anomalies in pressure or flow rates quickly. By ensuring proper control of pressure and flow, operators are better positioned to reduce corrosion risk and enhance the operational safety of pipeline systems.

References

1. Shin S-H et al (2024) Effect of microstructural constituents on hydrogen embrittlement resistance of API X60, X70, and X80 pipeline steels. Arch Metall Mater 39–43
2. Ghadiani H et al (2024) Assessing hydrogen embrittlement in pipeline steels for natural gas-hydrogen blends: implications for existing infrastructure. Solids 5(3):375–393
3. Yazdipour N, Dunne D, Pereloma EV (2012) Effect of grain size on the hydrogen diffusion process in steel using cellular automaton approach. Mater Sci Forum 706–709:1568–1573
4. Wang C et al (2025) Research on automatic welding process of mid-diameter pipeline construction. J Phys: Conf Ser 2951:012001
5. Bu F et al (2024) Analysis of leakage and diffusion characteristics and hazard range determination of buried hydrogen-blended natural gas pipeline based on CFD. ACS Omega 9(37):39202–39218
6. Dey S et al (2021) Study of electrochemical behavior, hydrogen permeation and diffusion in pipeline steel. Mater Sci Forum 1019:145–156
7. Abbas AJ et al (2024) Transitioning to a hydrogen economy: exploring the viability of adapting natural gas pipelines for hydrogen transport through a case study on compression vs looping. Gases 4(2):74–96
8. Qiu Y et al (2022) Multi-stage flexible planning of regional electricity-HCNG-integrated energy system considering gas pipeline retrofit and expansion. IET Renew Power Gener 16(15):3339–3367
9. Koren E et al (2024) Investigating electrochemical charging conditions equivalent to hydrogen gas exposure of X65 pipeline steel. Mater Corros 75(3):315–321
10. Mahajan D et al (2022) Hydrogen blending in gas pipeline networks—a review. Energies 15(10):3582
11. Kuczyński S et al (2019) Thermodynamic and technical issues of hydrogen and methane-hydrogen mixtures pipeline transmission. Energies 12(3):569
12. Abubakar YK et al (2025) A two-parameter computational thermodynamic analysis of hydrogen-impurity mixtures in a repurposed pipeline. Adv Sci Technol 160:33–40
13. Rasty J, Parker O, Mills M (2022) Forensic engineering investigation of factors contributing to the explosion of an international natural gas pipeline. J Natl Acad Forensic Eng 39(2):82–89
14. Tawfik Z, El-Sheltawy S, Abdelghany A (2024) Decarbonizing natural gas infrastructure: blending hydrogen for sustainable energy. In: The international conference on chemical and environmental engineering. Military Technical College
15. Titov AI et al (2019) Hydrogen accumulation and distribution in pipeline steel in intensified corrosion conditions. Materials 12(9):1409

16. Giarola JM et al (2022) The effect of hydrogen on the fracture toughness of friction-stir welded API 5L X70 pipeline steels. Fatigue Fract Eng Mater Struct 45(10):3009–3024
17. Alric L, Pluvinage G, Capelle J (2024) Influence of hydrogen embrittlement on the Wierbiecki-Xu failure strain criterion-application to a local strain-based design. Preprints
18. Volgina NI, Shulgin AV, Khlamkova SS (2021) Confirmation of hydrogen embrittlement mechanism for stress corrosion cracking of gas main lines. Defect Diffus Forum 410:572–577
19. Ban J et al (2023) Research progress and prospects on hydrogen damage in welds of hydrogen-blended natural gas pipelines. Processes 11(11):3180
20. Mijim JKA, Pluvinage G (2021) Maximum allowable service pressure for steel pipes used for transport of hydrogen pure or blended with natural gas. Eng Sci Technol 61–82
21. Janulionis R et al (2015) Degradation mechanisms and evaluation of failure of gas pipelines. Mechanics 21(5):352–360
22. Guy P, Laszlo T, Julien C (2021) Effects of hydrogen addition on design, maintenance and surveillance of gas networks. Processes 9(7):1219
23. Shi K et al (2021) MXene coatings: novel hydrogen permeation barriers for pipe steels. Nanomaterials 11(10):2737
24. Fekete JR, Sowards JW, Amaro RL (2015) Economic impact of applying high strength steels in hydrogen gas pipelines. Int J Hydrog Energy 40(33):10547–10558
25. Vasagar V et al (2024) Non-destructive techniques for corrosion detection: a review. Corros Eng, Sci Technol 59(1):56–85
26. Yu Q et al (2024) Detection and analysis of corrosion on coated metal surfaces using enhanced YOLO v5 algorithm for anti-corrosion performance evaluation. J Mar Sci Eng 12(7):1090
27. Hanafi Z et al (2012) Acoustic emission study of corrosion fatigue and fatigue for API 5L X70 gas pipeline steel. Appl Mech Mater 138:635–639
28. Zhang H et al (2021) Effects of hydrogen blending on hydraulic and thermal characteristics of natural gas pipeline and pipe network. Oil Gas Sci Technol-Revue d'IFP Energies Nouvelles 76:70
29. Deng F, Huang Y, Azarmi F (2019) Corrosion behavior evaluation of coated steel using fiber Bragg grating sensors. Coatings 9(1):55
30. Mulaveesala R, Dua G, Arora C (2019) Applications of infrared thermography for non-destructive characterization of concrete structures. In: Hassan MHM (eds) Advances in structural health monitoring. IntechOpen
31. Mohamed MH et al (2022) Tunnel-magnetoresistive-based pulsed eddy current probe for inspection of corrosion under insulation. In: IOP conference series: materials science and engineering. IOP Publishing
32. Dong GH et al (2013) Implementation of corrosion intelligent monitoring and durability early warning expert system for the large marine environmental engineering concrete structures. Adv Mater Res 610:1155–1161
33. Matthiesen H, Wonsyld K (2010) In situ measurement of oxygen consumption to estimate corrosion rates. Corros Eng, Sci Technol 45(5):350–356
34. ur Rahman MS, Hassan OS, Abou-Khousa MA (2022) Crack detection and corrosion mapping using loaded-aperture microwave probe. IEEE Open J Instrum Meas 1:1–11
35. Zhang H et al (2016) The non-destructive test of steel corrosion in reinforced concrete bridges using a micro-magnetic sensor. Sensors 16(9):1439
36. Tian Y et al (2024) Non-destructive testing technology for corrosion wall thickness reduction defects in pipelines based on electromagnetic ultrasound. Front Earth Sci 12:1432043
37. Figueira RB (2017) Electrochemical sensors for monitoring the corrosion conditions of reinforced concrete structures: a review. Appl Sci 7(11):1157
38. Fayyaz O et al (2021) Enhancement of mechanical and corrosion resistance properties of electrodeposited Ni–P–TiC composite coatings. Sci Rep 11(1):5327

39. Lee J et al (2017) Oil-impregnated nanoporous oxide layer for corrosion protection with self-healing. Adv Func Mater 27(15):1606040
40. Aguilar-Ruiz AA et al (2023) Chitosan-based sustainable coatings for corrosion inhibition of aluminum in seawater. Coatings 13(9):1615
41. Byrne A, Holmes N, Norton B (2016) State-of-the-art review of cathodic protection for reinforced concrete structures. Mag Concr Res 68(13):664–677
42. Zhang EQ et al (2018) Effect of the paste–anode interface under impressed current cathodic protection in concrete structures. Mater Corros 69(8):1104–1116
43. Zhu J-H et al (2016) Mechanical and electrochemical performance of carbon fiber reinforced polymer in oxygen evolution environment. Polymers 8(11):393
44. Wang Q et al (2023) Application of biomass corrosion inhibitors in metal corrosion control: a review. Molecules 28(6):2832
45. Benea L, Dănăilă E, Dumitraşcu VM (2016) Vegetable extracts as inhibitors of carbon steel corrosion in acidic environment. Adv Mater Res 1139:46–51
46. Subedi A et al (2023) Evaluation of the factors determining hydrogen embrittlement in pipeline steels: an artificial intelligence approach. In: Proceedings of the 33rd European safety and reliability conference
47. Assad H et al (2024) Assessment of the inhibitory efficacy of a thiazole derivative as an efficient corrosion inhibitor for augmenting the resistance of MS in acidic environments. Langmuir 40(31):16367–16383
48. Donatus U, Thompson G, Zhou X (2016) Effect of prior sputter deposition of pure aluminium on the corrosion behaviour of anodized friction stir weld of dissimilar aluminium alloys. Scripta Mater 123:126–129
49. Chen L et al (2018) Superhydrophobic micro-nano structures on silicone rubber by nanosecond laser processing. J Phys D Appl Phys 51(44):445301
50. Zuchry M et al (2023) Effect of anodizing on aluminum alloy 2024 with boric sulfate acid in medium 3.5% NaCl. East-Eur J Enterp Technol 4(6(124)):41–50
51. Kumar VR, Muthupandi V, Sivaprasad K (2019) Effect of type and concentration of aqueous solutions on corrosion behaviour of plasma electrolytic oxide films on ZM21 Mg alloy. Mater Sci Forum 969:309–314
52. Vakili M, Koutnik P, Kohout J (2024) Addressing hydrogen sulfide corrosion in oil and gas industries: a sustainable perspective. Sustainability 16(4):1661
53. Jungjohann KL et al (2016) Steel corrosion mechanisms during pipeline operation: in situ characterization. Microsc Microanal 22(S3):1564–1565
54. Cobanoglu MM, Kermanshachi S, Damnjanovic I (2016) Statistical modeling of corrosion failures in natural gas transmission pipelines. Pipelines 2016:195–204
55. Bęben D, Steliga T (2023) Monitoring and preventing failures of transmission pipelines at oil and natural gas plants. Energies 16(18):6640
56. Rayhana R et al (2024) Towards next-generation NDE: predictive analysis of pipeline integrity using machine learning. In: NDE 4.0, predictive maintenance, communication, and energy systems: the digital transformation of NDE II. SPIE 12952
57. Ali MA (2024) Entrepreneurial mindset: fostering innovation in business management. Adv J Econ Financ 1(3):1–9
58. Subramanian C (2021) Corrosion prevention of crude and vacuum distillation column overheads in a petroleum refinery: a field monitoring study. Process Saf Prog 40(2):e12213
59. Matilla AL et al (2024) Analysis of the effectiveness of the application of corrosion inhibitors to steel re-bars embedded in concrete. Appl Sci 14(8):3364
60. Zhao J, Cheng YF (2023) Finite element modeling of the hydrogen atom distribution on dented pipeline for hydrogen transport under cyclic loading. Int J Fract 246:181–201
61. Silva A et al (2024) Towards resilient pipeline infrastructure: lessons learned from failure analysis. Discover Appl Sci 6(11):585

62. Sesia R et al (2023) Natural polyphenols and the corrosion protection of steel: Recent advances and future perspectives for green and promising strategies. Metals 13(6):1070
63. Groysman A (2024) Corrosion risk for process safety in the chemical industry. Afinidad 81(601):10–24
64. Odunlami O et al (2025) A review of corrosion threat in marine industry. Key Eng Mater 1012:67–78

Chapter 7
Inspection Methods for Hydrogen Pipelines

7.1 Introduction

The continuous advancements in inspection technologies are critical for ensuring the integrity and safety of hydrogen pipelines. Hydrogen, being a highly flammable gas with unique material properties, presents distinct challenges that necessitate robust inspection protocols. Emerging approaches leverage non-destructive testing (NDT), robotics, and novel sensor technologies to assess the condition of hydrogen pipelines effectively while minimizing risks associated with human inspections in hazardous environments.

Historically, the inspection of pipelines primarily relied on traditional methods, often involving physical inspections by trained personnel. While effective to some extent, these manual approaches are not only labor-intensive but also inherently limited in terms of detection sensitivity and operational efficiency. Recent studies demonstrate a paradigm shift towards advanced inspection methodologies, emphasizing automation through technologies such as unmanned aerial vehicles (UAVs), machine learning algorithms, and real-time data analytics, which enhance the ability to predict and prevent infrastructure failures [1].

As further evidence of the evolving landscape of inspection technologies, the review by Prisutova et al. highlights the increasing utilization of fiber-optic sensors for monitoring pipeline conditions [2]. These sensors are capable of providing real-time data on various environmental factors such as pressure, temperature, and strain, which are critical for ensuring the operational safety of hydrogen pipelines. The ability to continuously monitor these parameters significantly enhances the management of infrastructure integrity, enabling timely interventions that mitigate risk and prevent catastrophic failures.

The cost implications of hydrogen pipeline inspections continue to play a crucial role in shaping the methodologies employed. Recent economic analyses have indicated that the integration of automated technologies within the inspection process

M. Hussain et al., *Hydrogen Pipeline Integrity*, Green Energy and Technology,
https://doi.org/10.1007/978-981-95-5609-0_7

could yield substantial cost savings, particularly when balancing the initial technological investments against the long-term savings from reduced maintenance needs and improved operational efficiencies [3]. Enabling real-time monitoring capabilities is anticipated to greatly enhance the predictivity of pipeline failures, thereby optimizing maintenance strategies and extending the lifespan of critical hydrogen infrastructure.

The diversity of inspection technologies is reflected in the literature, which outlines various applications of unmanned systems for pipeline surveillance. These technologies encompass UAVs equipped with advanced imaging systems that offer high-resolution visual inspections, potentially reducing human effort in hazardous environments whilst ensuring thorough assessments of pipeline conditions. Through developments in these systems, the barriers traditionally posed by inaccessible areas and challenging environmental conditions could be surmounted, thereby advancing the operational capabilities of hydrogen pipeline inspections.

Utilizing UAVs for pipeline monitoring fundamentally transforms the inspection landscape by incorporating automation and data analytics, ultimately allowing for a more data-driven approach. The literature emphasizes the significance of machine learning capabilities embedded within UAVs to enhance defect detection and assess pipeline conditions effectively [4]. These advancements not only foster a more proactive maintenance culture but also align with broader sustainability objectives by minimizing the ecological footprint associated with infrastructure inspections.

7.2 Principles of Pipeline Inspection

First and foremost, a critical starting point in the inspection process is the implementation of rigorous standards that specify testing protocols for hydrogen pipelines. The standards governing hydrogen transport have undergone significant development, particularly in regions such as China where early applications have revealed substantial insights into effective inspection practices [5]. Escalating attention towards hydrogen's material interactions prompts the establishment of norms that not only address conventional integrity assessments but also adapt to hydrogen-specific concerns like embrittlement in materials such as steel [5].

A comprehensive knowledge of defect types commonly encountered in hydrogen pipelines is essential. The prevalent issues include corrosion, mechanical defects, and welding failures, each requiring distinct detection approaches [6]. Understanding local environmental factors and pipeline operating conditions also plays a crucial role in determining the appropriate assessment techniques. The impact of external stresses and environmental conditions on pipeline integrity further emphasizes the significance of context in inspection.

Inspection techniques can be classified broadly into direct (NDT) and indirect methods. Non-destructive testing methods, such as magnetic flux leakage (MFL), ultrasonic testing (UT), and radiographic testing (RT), have proven effective in identifying internal and superficial defects without compromising the structural integrity of the pipeline [7]. It is essential that these traditional methods are complemented by advances in technology, particularly in light of the increased safety demands associated with hydrogen transport.

The application of pipe inspection gauges (PIGs) is one of the most effective strategies for continuous monitoring of pipeline conditions. PIGs currently incorporate various sensors that facilitate the measurement of geometric and material integrity, allowing for the identification of corrosion, dents, and leaks [8]. Maintaining an up-to-date inventory of PIG technology enables pipeline operators to optimize maintenance schedules based on acquired inspection data, ensuring a proactive approach to infrastructure management [7].

The risk-based inspection (RBI) approach offers a systematic methodology to prioritize inspection efforts according to the potential risk associated with different pipeline segments [9]. This approach focuses resources on areas deemed to present the highest hazard potential based on operational history and probabilistic assessments. The incorporation of statistical methods and predictive data analytics into RBI strategies has allowed for enhanced decision-making frameworks that can guide future investments in inspection technologies [8]. Furthermore, given the stringent requirements associated with hydrogen transport, the development of hybrid inspection techniques that combine multiple NDT methods is increasingly prioritized to achieve comprehensive assessments of pipeline integrity [10]. Such approaches not only capitalize on the respective advantages of each technique but also mitigate the weaknesses inherent in using a singular method [11]. For instance, combining MFL with ultrasonic sensing may provide a more thorough understanding of pipeline conditions and defects present at various depths and orientations.

The successful implementation of effective inspection methodologies relies inherently on harmonizing expertise among various disciplines, including materials science, engineering, and data analytics. Collaborative efforts across these fields can pave the way for developing customized solutions that cater specifically to the needs of hydrogen pipeline systems, as highlighted by studies emphasizing the importance of interdisciplinary cooperation in shaping industry practices [12].

7.2.1 Inspection Objectives and Frequency

The inspection of hydrogen pipelines is driven by various objectives critical to maintaining safety, operational efficiency, and regulatory compliance. The primary goal is to ensure that the pipelines remain within defined safety thresholds while minimizing the risk of leaks, ruptures, or environmental contamination. Regular inspections are fundamental to achieving these objectives, as they help identify material degradation, mechanical defects, and corrosion, particularly under the unique stressors associated with hydrogen transport.

One significant objective of inspections is the detection of leaks, which can pose substantial safety hazards due to hydrogen's flammability and its ability to diffuse rapidly in the atmosphere. Effective leak detection requires the implementation of sophisticated sensor technology capable of providing real-time monitoring and alerts should hydrogen concentrations exceed thresholds deemed acceptable. The prior establishment of these thresholds is often informed by quantitative risk assessments that take into consideration both the operational history and environmental conditions impacting the pipeline's integrity.

The frequency of inspections varies based on several factors, including the age and material of the pipelines, operating conditions, and historical performance data. Regulatory bodies often stipulate minimum inspection intervals, which can range from annual to multi-year assessments depending on the assessed risk levels associated with specific pipeline segments. In the case of critical pipelines, more frequent inspections may be mandated. For instance, the introduction of real-time monitoring systems can complement scheduled inspections, enabling a shift toward more dynamic and responsive inspection regimes that operate based on operational data trends rather than fixed intervals.

Integrating a risk-based approach to the inspection frequency can yield substantial benefits. By applying data analytics to identify trends and predict potential failure points, operators can implement a more tailored inspection schedule that accounts for evolving conditions rather than relying solely on a one-size-fits-all model. This adaptability becomes particularly critical in high-stakes environments where the implications of failure can be dire, emphasizing the need for a continuously evaluated inspection framework that evolves alongside the pipeline's operational context.

7.2.2 Challenges Specific to Hydrogen Pipelines

One of the most pertinent challenges arises from hydrogen's unique material properties, notably its small molecular size and high diffusivity. These properties enhance the risk of permeation and embrittlement, particularly in traditional pipeline materials like steel. As a result, specialized inspection techniques and continuous monitoring systems must be employed to mitigate the associated risks and detect potential failures in real-time.

Another challenge follows from hydrogen's highly reactive nature, which suggests that even small leaks can have dangerous consequences. Hydrogen can facilitate combustion under relatively low ignition energy, increasing the complexity of inspection methodologies and necessitating strict adherence to safety protocols during inspections. Inspectors may require specialized training to understand the risks associated with hydrogen pipelines fully, as traditional inspection practices may not always account for the volatility inherent to hydrogen.

The prevailing operating conditions within hydrogen pipelines can be challenging. High pressures and varying temperatures encountered during hydrogen transport can result in a multitude of defects that differ from those typically observed in pipelines for other utility gases. These environmental variables necessitate sophisticated and often bespoke inspection technologies capable of withstanding harsh conditions while maintaining accuracy in defect detection. The lack of comprehensive data on hydrogen pipeline performance under sustained operational loads remains a significant barrier. This information gap complicates risk assessments and hinders the development of universally applicable inspection standards. Inspection methodologies must therefore evolve continually based on expanded empirical evidence collected from operational pipelines and field data.

The integration of advanced decision-making algorithms into inspection frameworks poses another logistical challenge. While machine learning and artificial intelligence applications offer promising enhancements to sensors and automated inspection systems, the accuracy of predictive models relies heavily on the volume and quality of input data. Thus, advanced data analytics tools must be aligned with reliable sensor systems to yield actionable insights, necessitating investment in both hardware and software evolution.

The inherent complexities discussed necessitate comprehensive collaborations across multiple disciplines, including material science, engineering, and environmental health. Concerted efforts to address these unique challenges will foster the development of innovative solutions and operational protocols that prioritize safety while optimizing maintenance and inspection efficiencies. The multi-faceted nature of the hydrogen sector mandates a cohesive and integrated approach; wherein technological advancements must be aligned with evolving safety standards and regulatory frameworks.

Lastly, public perception and acceptance of hydrogen as an energy carrier can create socio-political challenges, particularly regarding its safety. Engaging stakeholders and the public to foster understanding and awareness of hydrogen pipelines and their inspection protocols is crucial in establishing a consensus on their role in the future energy landscape. This aspect is vital not only for regulatory compliance but also for securing investments into the hydrogen sector, ultimately shaping the evolution of inspection practices that center around safety, reliability, and transparency.

7.3 Pipeline Inspection Methods

In the realm of inspecting hydrogen pipelines, various methods have been developed to address the unique challenges posed by hydrogen transportation. One of the primary concerns in these pipelines is the formation of defects, particularly in coated infrastructures. Khwaja et al. [13] provide a comprehensive evaluation of inspection methods tailored for detecting such defects, detailing the prevalent types seen in coated hydrogen pipelines and discussing blended hydrogen-natural gas pipelines. This foundational work underscores the importance of adopting effective inspection practices tailored to the distinct characteristics of hydrogen transportation systems.

In-line inspection (ILI) techniques are especially prominent in the context of pipeline integrity management. These methods rely on the deployment of Pipeline Inspection Gauges (PIGs), which facilitate inspections such as detecting corrosion and structural deformations. According to Liu et al. [14], PIGs utilize several integrated sensor technologies to perform non-destructive evaluations of the pipeline's structural integrity. This integration of technologies enhances the inspection's reliability and accuracy.

The magnetic anisotropy method discussed by Bolobov et al. [15] presents an innovative approach to identifying hydrogenated sections of steel pipelines. This method exploits the relationship between hydrogen concentration in the metal and the stresses experienced during hydrogenation, highlighting ongoing advancements in pipeline inspection methodologies focused specifically on hydrogen-related concerns.

Supplementary to these advanced sensing techniques, ultrasonic testing (UT) and electromagnetic methods have also gained traction. Yang et al. [16] note that utilizing sensor arrays can significantly enhance the efficiency and resolution of various inspection modalities, such as pulsed eddy current inspection tailored for thermally insulated pipelines. Likewise, studies indicate that combining different non-destructive testing methods, including magnetic flux leakage (MFL) and ultrasonic testing, can provide comprehensive solutions for pipeline inspections [17].

7.3.1 In-line Inspection Technologies

In-line inspection (ILI) technologies play a critical role in ensuring the integrity and safety of pipelines, especially regarding the unique challenges associated with hydrogen transportation. Techniques such as Magnctic Flux Lcakagc (MFL) and Ultrasonic Testing (UT) are utilized; their key strengths and limitations are summarized in Table 7.1. ILI technologies are essential for identifying and characterizing defects that could lead to significant operational risks.

7.3.1.1 Magnetic Flux Leakage (MFL) Tools

MFL inspection tools are well-regarded for their efficiency in detecting corrosion and other forms of metal loss in pipelines. The MFL technique operates by magnetizing the pipeline wall and detecting magnetic fields that escape from regions where defects are present [18]. This method has been successfully adapted for various types of pipelines, including those carrying oil and gas. Research indicates that MFL tools demonstrate high reliability in assessing the corrosion integrity of pipelines, providing essential information regarding maintenance needs [19]. The reliability of MFL in pipeline inspections has been further enhanced by advancements such as three-dimensional defect modeling, which improves the capability to reconstruct defect profiles accurately [5].

Recent simulations have shown that three-axis MFL tools can enhance detection capabilities, making them particularly valuable in complex hydrogen environments [20]. The precision of MFL inspection has also been shown to improve with the integration of techniques such as machine learning, which can analyze MFL data

Table 7.1 In-line inspection technologies

Technology	Principle	Applications	Strengths	Limitations	Adaptations for hydrogen environments
Magnetic flux leakage (MFL)	Magnetizes pipe wall; detects magnetic field leakage caused by metal loss	• Corrosion detection • Metal loss sizing	• Fast inspection speed • Effective for ferrous materials	• Not suitable for crack detection • Limited to ferrous pipes	• Use of hydrogen-compatible magnets and sensor shielding
Ultrasonic testing (UT)	Uses ultrasonic waves to detect wall thickness and defects	• Corrosion and crack detection • Wall thickness measurement	• High-resolution data • Accurate sizing of defects	• Needs liquid couplant • Slower than MFL	• Sensor materials adapted for hydrogen exposure • Adjusted calibration for hydrogen-affected materials
Adapted inspection tools	Includes advanced UT and EMAT for hydrogen environments	• Integrity management in hydrogen pipelines	• Enhanced detection of hydrogen damage • Compatibility with hydrogen gas	• Emerging field with ongoing development	• Use of hydrogen tolerant sensors • Improved electronics sealing • Non-contact EMAT options

more effectively [21]. Such advancements underscore the importance of MFL as a crucial tool in pipeline integrity management and its adaptability to hydrogen transport conditions.

7.3.1.2 Ultrasonic Testing (UT) Tools

Conversely, Ultrasonic Testing (UT) tools utilize high-frequency sound waves to detect internal flaws and measure wall thickness, making them particularly effective for identifying cracks and corrosion. UT is recognized for its ability to provide precise location and size measurements of defects, which is critical for assessing structural integrity [22]. Notably, UT techniques, including guided wave ultrasonic testing, are essential for pipelines and are recognized in various applications, including those involving hydrogen, where detecting micro-defects is paramount [23].

The integration of intelligent pigs equipped with UT sensors has further increased the efficacy of inspections by facilitating the rapid and accurate assessment of long stretches of pipelines [24]. In the context of hydrogen pipelines, modifications in ultrasonic testing methods, such as adapting equipment for detecting changes in sound velocity due to hydrogen embrittlement, reflect ongoing innovation in inspection practices.

7.3.1.3 Adaptations for Hydrogen Environments

The application of MFL and UT technologies specifically to hydrogen environments necessitates careful consideration due to the unique physical and chemical properties of hydrogen. Research indicates that the design of inspection tools must account for the potential impact of hydrogen on material integrity, requiring adaptations in traditional inspection methods to ensure accuracy and reliability [22]. The development of standards governing hydrogen pipeline operations is essential for effectively implementing these ILI technologies in such environments [5].

Advancements in computational modeling and machine learning could significantly enhance the operational safety and efficiency of pipeline inspections, particularly in the increasingly relevant field of hydrogen transport [18]. As the hydrogen economy continues to expand, ongoing refinement of these technologies remains crucial in mitigating potential risks associated with hydrogen pipelines.

7.3.2 Non-destructive Testing (NDT) Techniques

Non-Destructive Testing (NDT) techniques are essential for assessing the integrity and reliability of structures without causing damage, particularly in contexts such as hydrogen transportation pipelines. Among the widely used NDT techniques are radiography, eddy current testing, and acoustic emission monitoring. New methodologies specific to hydrogen environments are emerging to deal with the unique challenges posed by hydrogen's properties.

Radiography involves the use of X-rays or gamma rays to produce images of a pipeline's internal structure. This technique is particularly effective for detecting internal defects such as cracks or voids in materials. Dwivedi et al. [25] indicates that radiographic NDT techniques can provide high resolutions of internal structures, which is crucial for materials used in hydrogen pipelines. Utilizing radiography can enable proactive measures for maintenance and ensure the safe operation of infrastructure, particularly given hydrogen's propensity for creating embrittlement and stress corrosion cracking in certain materials.

Eddy Current Testing (ECT) utilizes electromagnetic induction to detect surface and subsurface defects in conductive materials. This method is particularly effective for assessing conductive pipelines made of steel, a common material in hydrogen transportation. Studies indicate that the implementation of advanced eddy current techniques enhances the detection of small cracks and fatigue failures that may not be visible through visual inspections [26]. Given hydrogen's adverse effects on metal fatigue, such adaptations are particularly critical for maintaining pipeline integrity.

Acoustic Emission (AE) is another vital NDT method that involves monitoring stress waves produced during the deformation of materials. AE can be beneficial in detecting active corrosion processes or crack growth in pipelines. This method can offer real-time monitoring capabilities, which allows for the early detection of defects as they develop [27]. The adoption of AE in pipeline inspections is increasingly popular, particularly with advancements in digital signal processing and data analytics, which enhance defect identification accuracy.

Emerging NDT Methods for Hydrogen Environments

Given the specific threats presented by hydrogen, such as hydrogen-induced cracking (HIC) and stress corrosion cracking (SCC), traditional NDT methods are being supplemented or modified to address these risks effectively. For instance, the application of advanced ultrasonic phased array techniques has been highlighted as an innovative approach for inspecting welds and detecting internal flaws in hydrogen pipelines [28]. These methods leverage sophisticated algorithms and imaging techniques to improve defect characterization and sizing.

Developing sensors capable of real-time data acquisition specifically tailored for hydrogen environments is critical. This includes approaches such as impedance-based NDT methods that can detect potential debonding in composite structures used in hydrogen storage or transportation [29]. These innovative strategies often combine several NDT techniques to maximize results, allowing for comprehensive assessments of pipeline integrity.

The deployment of emerging technologies such as machine learning and artificial intelligence further enhances NDT methods. The data collected from various NDT techniques can be analyzed and interpreted using these advanced algorithms to predict potential failures before they occur, providing a proactive maintenance framework that is particularly necessary in the context of hydrogen infrastructure [26].

7.3.3 Robotics and Drone-Based Inspections

Robotics and drone-based inspections are emerging as transformative technologies in the field of pipeline monitoring, particularly regarding the inspection of hydrogen pipelines. The advancement of these technologies enhances the efficiency, safety, and accuracy of inspection processes while minimizing human exposure to hazardous environments.

Robotics for Pipeline Inspection

Robotic systems designed for in-pipe inspection have gained traction due to their capacity to operate in environments that are often inaccessible or unsafe for human inspectors. Adegboye et al. highlight that these systems utilize sensors and intelligent computational algorithms to effectively monitor the internal condition of pipelines, further supporting the use of these technologies in remote monitoring endeavours [30]. Robotic inspection devices can capture data on surface corrosion, material degradation, and other structural anomalies, significantly enhancing routine maintenance protocols [31].

In terms of design, robots utilized for pipeline inspections face several challenges, particularly when navigating through complex piping systems. Elankavi et al. present a wheeled-type inspection robot that can maneuverer through curved pipes and has been adapted to meet the dynamic requirements of pipeline inspections, such as measuring bends and maintaining stability [32]. Furthermore, adaptations for enhanced autonomy and communication capabilities in robots ensure that inspections can be conducted efficiently under various conditions, including live gas flow scenarios [33].

Drone-Based Inspections

On the other hand, drone technology complements robotic systems, especially when inspecting above-ground pipeline segments. Drones can be equipped with high-resolution cameras and sensors to visually assess large lengths of pipeline infrastructure from the air. This capability allows for rapid assessments of pipeline conditions and can significantly reduce inspection times compared to conventional methods [34].

The integration of drone technology with robotic systems has also been explored. For example, combining drones with autonomous in-pipe robots can facilitate comprehensive inspections, covering both external and internal pipeline conditions in a single operational cycle [35]. This multi-faceted approach not only enhances inspection coverage but also amplifies data collection processes, enabling better predictive maintenance.

Innovations and Environmental Considerations

Innovative methodologies, such as tele-robotics and advanced motion planning systems, have been developed to assist in identifying pipeline defects more efficiently [36]. Tele-robotic systems enable human–robot interactions that allow for semi-autonomous operations, crucial in environments where real-time decision-making is necessary. Furthermore, advancements in artificial intelligence enable robots to learn from inspection data, thereby improving their operational effectiveness over time [21].

Given the unique challenges associated with hydrogen transportation, ensuring that robotic and drone inspection systems are explicitly tailored for the specific conditions posed by hydrogen is paramount. These systems must not only be robust enough to withstand operation conditions but also integrate specialized sensors capable of detecting potential leakages and identifying material vulnerabilities due to hydrogen embrittlement [17].

7.3.4 Fiber-Optic Sensing and Real-Time Monitoring

The use of fiber-optic sensing technology for real-time monitoring of pipelines has emerged as a powerful solution for ensuring the integrity and safety of pipeline systems, including those dedicated to hydrogen transportation. Fiber-optic sensors offer unmatched sensitivity and the capability to perform continuous, real-time monitoring over extensive distances. Here, we synthesize current advancements in fiber-optic sensing technologies, focusing on their applications in pipeline monitoring.

Distributed Optical Fiber Sensing (DOFS)

Distributed optical fibre sensing (DOFS) employs the principles of Rayleigh, Brillouin, and Raman scattering to monitor changes along an entire length of optical fibre, thereby providing spatially resolved data Lu et al. [37]. This technology allows for real-time detection of structural anomalies such as strain, temperature variations, and acoustic vibrations, making it highly suited for pipeline environments.

The deployment of DOFS in pipeline monitoring systems has significantly enhanced sensitivity, allowing for early detection of issues such as leaks, third-party intrusions, and corrosion. For instance, studies highlight the ability of phase-sensitive optical time domain reflectometry (Φ-OTDR) to conduct real-time acoustic vibration measurements with high precision, effectively detecting sounds associated with potential pipeline breaches. This advancement contributes not only to continuous monitoring but also to improved safety measures in pipeline operations [17].

Applications in Pipeline Monitoring

In pipeline safety, distributed acoustic sensing (DAS) systems, a type of DOFS, are being utilized to monitor leakage and structural integrity with heightened efficiency. For example, integrating acoustic sensors within pipelines, either externally or internally, enables the rapid detection of acoustic events, thereby ensuring timely responses to potential issues. While deployment challenges associated with internal installations have been recognized, the benefits of heightened monitoring sensitivity often justify these efforts.

Lalam et al. [38] discuss the implementation of phase-OTDR technology in field tests for monitoring natural gas pipelines, demonstrating that fibre-optic systems are economically viable and field-ready for real-world applications. The ability to provide continuous data streams ensures that operators can maintain awareness of the pipeline's condition and rapidly respond to any detected anomalies.

Innovations and Future Directions

The evolution of fiber-optic sensing technologies has not only focused on the physical sensing capabilities but also on sophisticated data analytics methods. Machine learning algorithms, discussed by Yang et al. have been employed to process data from distributed optical fiber sensors, allowing for real-time identification of damage events under various operational conditions [39]. This integration of advanced analytics maximizes the utility of the sensing data, enabling operators to predict failures rather than only react to incidents.

As research continues in this field, the potential of fiber-optic sensing technologies for comprehensive monitoring of pipelines, particularly those designed for hydrogen transportation, appears promising. These technologies align well with increasing safety regulations and the demand for sustainable energy solutions, making them invaluable contributors to the monitoring of future pipeline infrastructure.

7.4 Sensor Technologies and Real-Time Monitoring

The integration of advanced sensor technologies into pipeline monitoring systems has become increasingly critical in ensuring the safety, reliability, and efficiency of pipeline infrastructure, particularly in the context of oil, gas, and hydrogen transport, a brief details and benefits are shown in Table 7.2.

7.4.1 Leak Detection Systems

Leak detection presents one of the most significant challenges in pipeline management. Various sensor technologies have emerged to address this issue, primarily encompassing gas concentration detection and pressure/flow analysis methods. Hou et al. discussed two main approaches for real-time leakage monitoring: directly

Table 7.2 Sensor technologies and real-time monitoring for hydrogen pipeline safety and performance

Technology	Brief Description	Benefits
Leak detection systems	Use advanced sensors (e.g., fiber-optic, acoustic, or laser-based) to detect minute hydrogen leaks	• Detects even small leaks due to hydrogen's high diffusivity • Prevents safety hazards and explosions • Minimizes hydrogen loss and environmental risk
Pressure and flow monitoring	Employs high-sensitivity sensors to monitor variations in pressure and flow specific to hydrogen	• Identifies pressure drops and flow irregularities caused by leaks or blockages • Prevents hydrogen embrittlement risks through controlled pressure • Supports early fault detection
Smart pipeline systems and IoT integration	Integrates hydrogen-specific sensors with IoT platforms for remote, real-time monitoring and analytics	• Enhances predictive maintenance using real-time data • Enables rapid response to abnormal events • Facilitates compliance with hydrogen safety standards • Supports automated shutdown and control systems

detecting gas concentration along pipelines using diverse sensors, including catalytic bead sensors and infrared point sensors, and monitoring pressure changes within the pipeline [40]. Among these technologies, the use of distributed optical fiber sensing (DOFS) for leak detection has gained traction, delivering high sensitivity and spatial resolution, as shown in studies by Zuo et al. [41], which detail the applicability of optical fiber acoustic sensing systems in real-time environments.

Lalam et al. [38] emphasized the importance of hybrid sensing methodologies in improving leak detection accuracy. Their work explored the deployment of distributed optical fiber sensors to monitor the integrity of gas pipelines, illustrating successful pilot-scale implementations. The efficacy of combining multiple sensor types—such as acoustic sensors and DOFS—has been demonstrated to enhance leak detection capabilities, providing comprehensive insights necessary for prompt remediation actions [41].

7.4.2 Pressure and Flow Monitoring

Another critical aspect of pipeline monitoring involves pressure and flow measurement, essential for maintaining operational integrity and safety. Continuous monitoring of pressure fluctuations can be achieved through smart sensors that provide real-time data, enabling operators to detect anomalous variations indicative of potential leaks or blockages. Liu et al. [42] highlighted methodologies integrating pressure sensors with predictive modeling based on flow data analysis, facilitating better maintenance strategies.

The implementation of smart control methodologies, such as predictive modeling, augments real-time pressure and flow monitoring systems. Technologies leveraging the Internet of Things (IoT) can connect pressure and flow sensors to centralized data hubs, enabling trend analysis and machine learning for anomaly detection. As operational demands increase, integrating advanced analytics into monitoring systems has become a standard practice across various industries [43].

7.4.3 Smart Pipeline Systems and IoT Integration

The advent of IoT technologies has revolutionized pipeline monitoring by enabling seamless data exchange and remote access to essential operational metrics. Smart pipeline systems utilize arrays of interconnected sensors that provide comprehensive data on various parameters, facilitating real-time monitoring and analysis. The integration of IoT enhances operational visibility and establishes a framework for automated alerts to detect potential issues.

Singh et al. [44] highlighted the use of IoT in oil pipeline monitoring systems, where a combination of Zigbee and long-range architectures facilitates reliable data communication across extensive networks. Their findings suggest that this connectivity significantly enhances the ability to monitor numerous pipeline sections in real time, offering greater oversight in identifying leaks or pressure anomalies promptly.

Further advancements in wireless sensor networks (WSN) have also been introduced to improve the reliability of leak detection methods. Amran et al. [45] discussed utilizing ground-penetrating radar in conjunction with WSNs to identify leaks efficiently, indicating the potential for adapting similar approaches in gas and oil pipelines, which highlights how different technologies can converge to enhance overall monitoring capabilities.

7.5 Data Analytics and Digital Twins for Integrity Management

In managing the integrity of pipelines, particularly in the context of the hydrogen economy, leveraging data analytics and digital twin technologies has proven essential. These methodologies enable real-time monitoring, predictive analytics, and simulation, allowing for proactive and efficient pipeline management. As the global energy sector transitions toward low-carbon alternatives, hydrogen has emerged as a critical component of future energy systems. Its potential to decarbonize hard-to-abate sectors, such as heavy industry and transportation, has driven significant investments in hydrogen production, storage, and distribution infrastructure. Among the various transportation methods, pipelines offer an efficient and scalable solution for moving hydrogen across regions. However, the unique physical and chemical properties of hydrogen introduce distinct challenges for pipeline integrity, including hydrogen embrittlement, leak detection difficulties, and accelerated material degradation. Table 7.3 shows brief details about digital twins.

To address these challenges, the integration of advanced data analytics and digital twin technologies is gaining momentum in the energy industry. Data analytics enables real-time monitoring, anomaly detection, and predictive maintenance through the intelligent analysis of sensor and operational data. Meanwhile, digital twins—virtual replicas of physical pipeline systems—allow operators to simulate and assess pipeline behavior under various conditions, facilitating proactive decision-making and risk mitigation. Together, these technologies offer a powerful framework for enhancing the safety, reliability, and efficiency of hydrogen pipeline networks, supporting the broader transition to a hydrogen-based energy economy.

7.5.1 Data Collection and Processing

Effective integrity management heavily relies on comprehensive data collection and processing systems that can assimilate data from various sources, including in-line

Table 7.3 Data analytics and digital twin technologies for hydrogen pipeline integrity management

Technology	Brief description	Benefits
Data collection and processing	Gathers real-time data from sensors (e.g., pressure, temperature, leak detection) and processes it for insights	• Enables comprehensive monitoring • Supports accurate decision-making • Enhances data traceability and compliance
Predictive analytics for pipeline health	Uses AI/ML algorithms to analyze historical and real-time data to predict potential failures or degradation	• Identifies corrosion, hydrogen embrittlement, and fatigue early • Reduces unplanned downtime • Extends asset life
Digital twin models and simulation	Creates a virtual replica of the hydrogen pipeline system to simulate operations, stress, and failure scenarios	• Supports proactive maintenance planning • Validates operational strategies • Enhances safety and reliability via scenario testing

inspection (ILI) data, sensor information, and environmental conditions. Dakhel et al. [46] highlight that utilizing experimental data from fatigue and burst tests can significantly inform integrity assessments and facilitate the development of robust integrity management frameworks tailored for pipelines. The integration of these datasets allows operators to establish guidelines for maintenance, conduct integrity assessments, and calculate the residual life of pipeline sections, ensuring continuous operation with minimized risk.

The incorporation of advanced database management systems enhances the capability to manage extensive datasets, facilitating rapid access and analysis. Pipeline integrity management systems benefit from structured databases that can effectively analyze historical incidents, corrosion trends, and operational metrics, thereby supporting a data-driven approach to decision-making. This comprehensive data processing setup is vital for maintaining efficiencies in transportation and environmental protection.

7.5.2 Predictive Analytics for Hydrogen Pipeline Health

Predictive analytics plays a pivotal role in assessing the health of hydrogen pipelines by analyzing data trends to foresee potential failures before they occur. By employing machine learning algorithms and statistical models, operators can identify patterns indicative of deterioration, thereby facilitating early interventions. Fan and Feng [47] emphasize that such predictive methodologies not only augment the current integrity management protocols but also enhance the overall safety and efficiency of pipeline operation.

Machine learning models can process input data from pressure sensors, flow meters, and environmental monitoring tools to generate reliable predictions about pipeline performance and potential issues. Integrating these predictive models with real-time data allows for dynamic risk assessments and can guide preventive maintenance strategies aimed at minimizing downtime. For instance, the application of predictive analytics in monitoring corrosion rates or assessing the structural integrity of weld seams in pipelines can significantly reduce the risk of catastrophic failures.

7.5.3 Digital Twin Models and Simulation

Digital twin technology involves creating a virtual representation of physical pipeline systems, which can be used for real-time monitoring, simulation, and predictive maintenance. Digital twins allow for an unparalleled understanding of the pipeline's operational characteristics, as they integrate real-time data feeds with advanced computational models. Feng et al. describe how digital twins can enhance operation and maintenance by creating a comprehensive virtual model that reflects the pipeline's performance under various operational scenarios [48].

Simulation through digital twins can also support decision-making regarding integrity management, as these models can visualize stress and deformation patterns under different environmental conditions. Shardeo and Sarkar [49] investigated reliability analysis methods using digital twins, which provide crucial insights into the behaviour of corroded pipelines under various stressors. Similarly, digital twins can incorporate environmental data, operational parameters, and inspection results, allowing for holistic network analysis and optimizing safety strategies.

The potential of digital twins in predictive maintenance is profound, as real-time monitoring and simulation capabilities enable operators to implement condition-based maintenance strategies. By continuously updating the digital twin with live data, operators can make informed decisions based on the current state of the pipeline, reducing unexpected failures and improving operational efficiency [50].

7.6 Leak Detection Systems

Leak detection systems are essential for maintaining the safety, reliability, and environmental compliance of pipeline infrastructure. In hydrogen pipeline networks, the role of these systems becomes even more critical due to the unique physical characteristics of hydrogen, which increase the likelihood and potential impact of leaks. An effective leak detection system must not only detect a leak quickly but also accurately determine its location and magnitude to enable timely intervention.

Various technologies are employed in leak detection systems, each based on different detection principles such as mass balance, pressure monitoring, acoustic emissions, optical sensing, or direct gas detection. These systems can be deployed internally (within the pipeline) or externally (around the pipeline) and may operate continuously or on a scheduled basis. The selection of a suitable leak detection method depends on several factors, including pipeline design, pressure and flow conditions, location (e.g., buried or above ground), accessibility, and regulatory requirements.

Advanced leak detection systems increasingly incorporate automation, remote monitoring, and data analytics to enhance detection accuracy and response speed. Integration with Supervisory Control and Data Acquisition (SCADA) systems and Geographic Information Systems (GIS) further enables operators to visualize and manage potential leak scenarios in real-time.

7.6.1 Traditional Versus Advanced Leak Detection Methods

Traditional leak detection methods rely primarily on pressure drop analysis and visual inspections, which can be effective but often fail to provide timely and accurate leak localization, especially in extensive pipeline networks. Techniques such as flow monitoring and threshold pressure monitoring are common but may not adequately address smaller, undetected leaks or the complexities of hydrogen properties [51].

Conversely, advanced leak detection technologies leverage modern sensor technologies and data analytics to improve leak detection capabilities. Techniques such as acoustic emission monitoring and distributed acoustic sensing (DAS) can detect sound waves generated by leaks, offering higher sensitivity and real-time data. These sophisticated methods allow for the localization of leaks with greater precision compared to conventional approaches. For example, Nguyen et al. [52] presented a least squares deconvolution technique for leak localization, significantly enhancing the signal-to-noise ratio for detecting minor leaks.

7.6.2 Sensor Types: Electrochemical, Optical, Acoustic

Various sensor types play crucial roles in leak detection systems. Electrochemical sensors are effective for detecting hydrogen concentrations and can provide real-time monitoring of local environments within pipeline networks. These sensors leverage chemical reactions to accurately identify leaks.

Optical sensors, such as those utilizing fibre optic technology, can detect variations in light transmission caused by leaks and have emerged as effective solutions for long-distance monitoring. These sensors can be integrated into pipelines to continuously assess conditions, thus enhancing safety.

Acoustic sensors represent another vital technology, particularly in conjunction with DAS. Acoustic emission techniques measure the sound waves produced by leaks, allowing for the identification and location of leaks based on the frequency and characteristics of these emitted sounds. Research illustrates that using hydrophones or accelerometers, these systems can detect both fluid-borne and structure-borne waves generated by leaks, providing valuable insights into the nature of potential failures [53].

7.6.3 Gas Sensors and Distributed Acoustic Sensing (DAS)

DAS systems are among the most promising technologies for leak detection in hydrogen pipelines. They work by deploying optical fiber cables along the infrastructure, which monitor continuous acoustic signals and temperature variations. This technology provides spatially distributed measurements, significantly improving the ability to detect, pinpoint, and analyze leaks across long pipeline stretches.

The combination of gas sensors and DAS can be particularly effective; while gas sensors detect the presence of hydrogen at specific points, DAS provides a broader view of the entire pipeline system's health. This integration allows for more comprehensive monitoring strategies, combining localized detection with continuous analysis and feedback loops that enhance real-time response capabilities [51].

7.6.4 Integration of Leak Detection in Hydrogen Pipeline Networks

Integrating leak detection systems into existing hydrogen pipeline networks is essential for enhancing operational safety and efficiency. This integration often requires the deployment of hybrid systems that incorporate multiple detection methods, allowing for improved coverage and reliability. Advanced modeling techniques can optimize the installation strategies of sensors to ensure that high-risk sections of pipelines are sufficiently monitored.

Additionally, leveraging IoT technologies in conjunction with leak detection systems enables seamless data sharing and real-time response strategies. By using wireless communication and cloud platforms, operators can access real-time data from remote locations, allowing for immediate decisions in the event of a detection alarm [53].

7.6.5 AI and Machine Learning for Predictive Leak Detection

The integration of artificial intelligence (AI) and machine learning into leak detection systems represents a transformative shift toward more proactive management of pipeline integrity. By analyzing historical and real-time data, AI algorithms can identify patterns indicative of leaks, enabling predictive maintenance strategies that mitigate risks before they escalate into failures.

Research has demonstrated that machine learning models can enhance the accuracy of leak detection by processing vast datasets from various sensor types, allowing for improved anomaly detection. For instance, advanced machine learning approaches using neural networks have been shown to effectively predict leak occurrences based on acoustic signals and pressure variations, thereby allowing for quicker and more informed responses to potential threats [54].

References

1. Bruggemann TS, Ford JJ (2013) Automated aerial inspection guidance with improved turn planning. In: 2013 Australian control conference. IEEE
2. Prisutova J et al (2022) Use of fibre-optic sensors for pipe condition and hydraulics measurements: a review. Civ Eng 3(1):85–113
3. Odili PO et al (2024) Integrating advanced technologies in corrosion and inspection management for oil and gas operations. Eng Sci Technol J 5(2):597–611
4. Gibb S et al (2018) Nondestructive evaluation sensor fusion with autonomous robotic system for civil infrastructure inspection. J Field Robot 35(6):988–1004
5. Chen X et al (2024) Research on standards and standard system of hydrogen pipeline in China. In: E3S web of conferences 520:04016. EDP Sciences
6. Elankavi RS et al (2022) Design and motion planning of a wheeled type pipeline inspection robot. J Robot Control (JRC) 3(4):415–430
7. Chen J, Huang S, Zhao W (2015) Equivalent MFL model of pipelines for 3-D defect reconstruction using simulated annealing inversion procedure. Int J Appl Electromagnet Mech 47(2):551–561
8. Giannini L et al (2023) Materials for hydrogen storage and transport: implications for risk-based inspection. Key Eng Mater 959:221–230
9. Soedarsono JW et al (2023) Development of risk based inspection of 28-years-old subsea sales gas pipelines to support the energy demand. East-Eur J Enterp Technol 2(3(122)):17–27
10. Elmasry M, Zayed T, Hawari A (2019) Multi-objective optimization model for inspection scheduling of sewer pipelines. J Constr Eng Manag 145(2):04018129
11. Wang Z et al (2019) Compressed sensing method for health monitoring of pipelines based on guided wave inspection. IEEE Trans Instrum Meas 69(7):4722–4731
12. Huang L, Zhang L (2024) Effect of hydrogen on high cycle fatigue properties of L360 pipeline steel notched specimens. Materials 17(22):5612
13. Khwaja SA, Paul S (2022) Inspection of coated hydrogen transportation pipelines. Appl Sci 12(19):9503
14. Liu S et al (2018) A novel algorithm for pipeline displacement and bending strain of in-line inspection based on inertia measurement technology. Adv Mech Eng 10(12):1687814018816755
15. Bolobov VI et al (2023) Using the magnetic anisotropy method to determine hydrogenated sections of a steel pipeline. Energies 16(15):5585
16. Yang L et al (2023) Circular-arc array for the pulsed eddy current inspection of thermally insulated pipelines. Meas Sci Technol 34(12):125114
17. Ma Q et al (2021) Pipeline in-line inspection method, instrumentation and data management. Sensors 21(11):3862
18. Feng Q et al (2016) Literature review: theory and application of in-line inspection technologies for oil and gas pipeline girth weld defection. Sensors 17(1):50

19. San Marchi C et al (2017) Overview of the DOE hydrogen safety, codes and standards program, part 3: advances in research and development to enhance the scientific basis for hydrogen regulations, codes and standards. Int J Hydrog Energy 42(11):7263–7274
20. Durai M et al (2022) Analysis of leakage in a sustainable water pipeline based on a magnetic flux leakage technique. Sustainability 14(19):11853
21. Liu S, Wang H, Li R (2022) Attention module magnetic flux leakage linked deep residual network for pipeline in-line inspection. Sensors 22(6):2230
22. Salama MM et al (2013) Characterization of the uncertainties in the inspection results of ultrasonic intelligent pigs. In: International conference on offshore mechanics and arctic engineering. American Society of Mechanical Engineers
23. Shah J, El-Hawwat S, Wang H (2023) Guided wave ultrasonic testing for crack detection in polyethylene pipes: laboratory experiments and numerical modeling. Sensors 23(11):5131
24. Ramirez-Vidal P et al (2022) Modeling high-pressure hydrogen uptake by nanoporous metal–organic frameworks: implications for hydrogen storage and delivery. ACS Appl Nano Mater 5(1):759–773
25. Dwivedi SK, Vishwakarma M, Soni A (2018) Advances and researches on non destructive testing: a review. Mater Today: Proc 5(2):3690–3698
26. Noori Hoshyar A et al (2019) Algorithm development for the non-destructive testing of structural damage. Appl Sci 9(14):2810
27. Zhang J et al (2021) Non-destructive evaluation of coating thickness using water immersion ultrasonic testing. Coatings 11(11):1421
28. Raman RS et al (2024) Analysing indirect methods for comparatively determining the compressive strength of materials with various properties. In: E3S web of conferences 507:01018. EDP Sciences
29. Seo D-W et al (2021) Development of a new temporary attachment technique for detecting debonding of a composite structure using impedance based non-destructive testing method. Appl Sci 11(22):10763
30. Adegboye MA, Fung W-K, Karnik A (2019) Recent advances in pipeline monitoring and oil leakage detection technologies: principles and approaches. Sensors 19(11):2548
31. Jeon K-W et al (2024) Development of an in-pipe inspection robot for large-diameter water pipes. Sensors 24(11):3470
32. SuginàElankavi R et al (2024) Design of a wheeled-type in-pipe inspection robot to overcome motion singularity in curved pipes. J Ambient Intell Smart Environ 16(1):43–55
33. Jang H et al (2022) Development of modularized in-pipe inspection robotic system: MRINSPECT VII+. Robotica 40(5):1361–1384
34. Ibarguren A et al (2013) Thermal tracking in mobile robots for leak inspection activities. Sensors 13(10):13560–13574
35. Mirats Tur JM, Garthwaite W (2010) Robotic devices for water main in-pipe inspection: a survey. J Field Robot 27(4):491–508
36. Martínez-García EA, Martínez-Villafañe A, Mohan RE (2012) Tele-robotics for motion planning assistance to search pipeline defects. In: 2012 7th IEEE conference on industrial electronics and applications (ICIEA). IEEE
37. Lu P et al (2019) Distributed optical fiber sensing: review and perspective. Appl Phys Rev 6(4):041302
38. Lalam N et al (2024) Distributed optical fiber sensor systems: application to natural gas pipeline monitoring. In: Optical waveguide and laser sensors III. SPIE 13044
39. Yang K et al (2024) Risk modelling of hydrogen-enriched natural gas on pipelines and gas-electric coupled systems. IET Energy Syst Integr 6(3):253–267
40. Hou L et al (2017) Gas concentration detection via multi-channeled air sampling method. Sens Rev 37(2):187–195
41. Zuo J et al (2020) Pipeline leak detection technology based on distributed optical fiber acoustic sensing system. IEEE Access 8:30789–30796
42. Liu H et al (2024) Research on PID control method for predictive modeling of oil pipeline infrastructure under industrial internet of things driving. In: International conference on algorithms, high performance computing, and artificial intelligence (AHPCAI 2024). SPIE

43. Zhu J-H et al (2016) Mechanical and electrochemical performance of carbon fiber reinforced polymer in oxygen evolution environment. Polymers 8(11):393
44. Singh G, Slack NJ, Sharma S (2021) Politics-administration dichotomy: insight from a developing country. In: Farazmand A (eds) Global encyclopedia of public administration, public policy, and governance. Springer Nature, pp 9850–9856
45. Amran TT et al (2018) Monitoring underground water leakage pattern by ground penetrating radar (GPR) using 800 MHz antenna frequency. In: IOP conference series: materials science and engineering. IOP Publishing
46. Dakhel A et al (2023) Fatigue and burst tests of full-scale girth welded pipeline sections for safe operations. Weld World 67(5):1193–1208
47. Fan Y, Feng X-X (2023) Research on integrity management of long distance pipeline. In: E3S web of conferences 385:03011. EDP Sciences
48. Feng Z et al (2025) Intelligent measurement switch full performance testing pipeline operation and maintenance based on digital twin technology. In: International conference on computer graphics, artificial intelligence, and data processing (ICCAID 2024). SPIE
49. Shardeo V, Sarkar BD (2024) Adoption of hydrogen-fueled freight transportation: a strategy toward sustainability. Bus Strateg Environ 33(2):223–240
50. Li J et al (2022) Leakage simulation and acoustic characteristics based on acoustic logging by ultrasonic detection. Adv Geo-Energy Res 6(3):181–191
51. Wang W et al (2021) Experimental study on water pipeline leak using In-Pipe acoustic signal analysis and artificial neural network prediction. Measurement 186:110094
52. Nguyen STN et al (2018) Least squares deconvolution for leak detection with a pseudo random binary sequence excitation. Mech Syst Signal Process 99:846–858
53. Zhang K et al (2023) Experimental investigation on near-field acoustic propagation characteristics of leakage detection in submarine pipelines. J Mar Sci Eng 11(10):2012
54. Radzman MIR et al (2022) Pipe leakage detection system with artificial neural network. IAES Int J Artif Intell 11(3):977

Chapter 8
Sensor Technologies and Real-Time Monitoring

This chapter explores the critical role of sensor technologies and real-time monitoring in ensuring the integrity and safety of industrial systems, particularly in hydrogen infrastructure. It begins by highlighting the importance of real-time monitoring for risk reduction, early warning of potential failures, and compliance with evolving regulatory requirements. The chapter delves into hydrogen leak detection technologies, comparing fixed and portable sensors and emphasizing the advantages of networked sensor arrays and wireless systems for comprehensive coverage. It further discusses structural health monitoring (SHM) tools, including strain gauges, fiber optic sensors, ultrasonic arrays, and advanced inspection methods such as smart pigs and permanent monitoring systems. The chapter also addresses the integration of data analytics and predictive maintenance strategies, detailing how condition-based monitoring frameworks and sensor data can be leveraged to optimize maintenance planning and enhance system reliability. Through this comprehensive overview, the chapter underscores the transformative impact of sensor technologies on asset integrity management.

8.1 Importance of Real-Time Monitoring for Integrity

Real-time monitoring, enabled by advanced sensor technologies, plays a central role in ensuring the structural soundness, leak-tightness, and safe operation of hydrogen pipeline networks. The deployment of advanced sensor technologies facilitates the early detection of leaks, structural weaknesses, and other risk factors associated with pipeline operations, significantly enhancing safety protocols. Early warning systems that utilize sophisticated monitoring technologies can provide immediate alerts in the event of structural discrepancies or leakages, thus minimizing potential hazards associated with hydrogen transportation [1]. The significance of these systems is accentuated by hydrogen's high diffusivity and its propensity for forming

M. Hussain et al., *Hydrogen Pipeline Integrity*, Green Energy and Technology,
https://doi.org/10.1007/978-981-95-5609-0_8

combustible mixtures with air, which underscores the necessity for prompt detection and intervention [2].

Implementing robust monitoring solutions directly correlates to risk reduction in pipeline systems. In recent studies, the application of low-resolution satellite imagery and fiber optic sensors has shown promise in identifying abnormalities in pipeline operations. These technologies can monitor the geographical and environmental conditions surrounding pipelines, aiding operators in pre-emptively addressing hazardous situations [3]. For instance, the use of Distributed Optical Fiber Sensors (DOFS) can effectively detect vibrations that indicate a potential leak, allowing for immediate responses that could prevent catastrophic incidents [4]. Such technological advancements in monitoring systems are essential for dealing with the unique challenges posed by hydrogen pipelines, particularly given their susceptibility to material degradation and embrittlement [5].

Traditional pipeline integrity assessment methods, which rely on periodic inspections, are increasingly being supplanted by continuous monitoring systems that provide immediate data on operating conditions. Real-time monitoring enables the detection of micro-leaks, stress-induced damage, corrosion, and mechanical deformation before they evolve into major failures. In hydrogen pipelines, where small defects can propagate rapidly due to hydrogen embrittlement and the gas's permeation potential, the ability to detect anomalies in situ and in real time significantly enhances risk mitigation and operational reliability.

8.1.1 Risk Reduction and Early Warning

The complexities associated with hydrogen transport necessitate stringent risk reduction measures, making real-time monitoring a cornerstone of operational safety [6]. Hydrogen's unique physical properties, such as its high escape velocity and low molecular weight, amplify leakage risks compared to traditional hydrocarbons [2]. Studies indicate that the integration of modern leak detection systems can substantially enhance the safety margins by enabling swift responses to identified risks, thereby preventing large-scale incidents [5]. Regulatory bodies increasingly advocate for the adoption of such technologies, as they are pivotal in meeting both operational safety standards and environmental regulations aimed at minimizing greenhouse gas emissions [7].

Effective real-time monitoring also dovetails with compliance initiatives mandated by regulatory frameworks. In various jurisdictions, regulations are evolving to accommodate the integration of hydrogen into existing pipelines, establishing stringent requirements for monitoring systems capable of detecting leaks and failures quickly [6]. For instance, the Canadian Framework on Hydrogen Infrastructure emphasizes the importance of lifecycle management and consistent monitoring to uphold safety in transportation systems as hydrogen energy narratives gain traction.

Enhanced monitoring capabilities not only facilitate compliance with these regulatory drivers but also foster public trust in the safety of hydrogen transportation networks [8].

8.1.2 Regulatory Drivers

As the push for cleaner energy intensifies, regulatory drivers play a significant role in shaping monitoring practices across hydrogen pipeline infrastructures. Government regulations are increasingly focused on ensuring safety and environmental protection, necessitating rigorous monitoring systems for hydrogen leaks and structural integrity assessments [6]. The establishment of regulations governing hydrogen transport seeks to address the inherent risks involved in handling this volatile energy source, particularly in traditional natural gas infrastructure being adapted for hydrogen use [2]. The review of regulatory frameworks surrounding hydrogen blending in natural gas pipelines reveals a concerted effort to standardize monitoring practices that can effectively manage and mitigate risk, ensuring operational integrity and environmental safety [9].

Responsible hydrogen management aligns with regulatory aims to achieve carbon neutrality by establishing predefined safety protocols and operational standards for hydrogen infrastructures. Regulations are being formulated to obligate pipeline operators to implement advanced monitoring technologies that can meet the emerging safety challenges that hydrogen transportation represents [7]. This evolution in regulatory expectations not only drives the technological adoption necessary for safe operations but also reinforces the critical importance of real-time monitoring as an industry standard moving forward.

8.2 Hydrogen Leak Detection Technologies

The detection of hydrogen leaks in pipeline systems is essential to ensure safety and maintain the integrity of hydrogen transportation infrastructures. Due to hydrogen's physical properties, including its low molecular weight and high diffusivity, it poses unique challenges for leak detection, necessitating the integration of advanced monitoring technologies. As hydrogen is increasingly utilized as a clean energy source, effective leak detection becomes crucial to mitigate risks associated with pipeline operations [10].

Recent advancements in detection methodologies have prompted a reevaluation of existing technologies tailored for hydrogen service. Traditional leak detection systems typically used in hydrocarbon pipelines often fall short when applied to hydrogen due to its differing behavior. Therefore, a growing body of research is focused on developing specialized technologies that address the unique characteristics of hydrogen, including its propensity for embrittlement and the potential for combustion if not managed correctly [2].

Key aspects of hydrogen leak detection revolve around precise measurements of parameters such as pressure, flow rate, and acoustic vibrations, which indicate the presence of leaks. Innovative approaches, such as dynamic Bayesian networks, exhibit promising results in combining multiple sensor outputs to enhance leak localization accuracy [4]. Furthermore, the application of distributed acoustic sensing (DAS) technologies has shown substantial improvements in detecting leak-induced vibrations, allowing for real-time monitoring of pipeline conditions [11].

The urgency of developing and deploying effective leak detection systems is influenced by the regulatory environment surrounding hydrogen transportation. Regulatory bodies emphasize the need for safety and compliance in hydrogen infrastructures, making the integration of modern leak detection technologies not just a technical necessity but a legal obligation [1]. As pipelines are retrofitted for hydrogen service, understanding the differences in leak dynamics between hydrogen and traditional natural gas pipelines becomes crucial in developing comprehensive monitoring solutions. This emphasizes a proactive approach in engineering pipeline systems to anticipate leakage and enhance overall system reliability.

Given the challenges concerning pipeline integrity in hydrogen transport, continued investment in research and the adoption of advanced monitoring technologies will strengthen the safety frameworks that govern hydrogen pipeline operations. As the industry evolves, leveraging insights from interdisciplinary research across materials science, fluid dynamics, and sensor technologies will be essential for crafting robust leak detection systems tailored for the dynamic nature of hydrogen transport [12].

8.2.1 Fixed Versus Portable Sensors

In the realm of hydrogen leak detection technologies, the choice between fixed and portable sensors presents critical implications for pipeline safety and operational efficiency. Refer to Table 8.1 for more details. Fixed sensors are typically installed in strategic locations throughout a pipeline system. They provide continuous monitoring of hydrogen concentrations and alert operators to potential leaks, functioning effectively within specified environments and delivering real-time data on gas levels to control systems [13]. These sensors are essential in locations where the risk of leakage is significant, and regulatory standards necessitate constant oversight. Fixed sensors often feature robust designs that can withstand harsh conditions while sustaining long-term operation, making them invaluable for industrial settings [13].

On the other hand, portable sensors offer different advantages and applications. These compact, mobile devices enable technicians to conduct spot-checks and localized measurements of hydrogen concentrations, providing flexibility in monitoring areas of a pipeline system that might not be continuously surveyed [14]. Portable

Table 8.1 Fixed and portable sensors: differences, benefits, and limitations

Aspect	Fixed sensors	Portable sensors
Definition	Permanently installed at specific locations on equipment	Handheld or mobile devices used for periodic measurements
Installation	Requires upfront installation and setup	No permanent installation required
Data collection frequency	Continuous or high-frequency real-time data	Periodic/manual collection
Monitoring scope	Monitors specific, predefined points continuously	Can be used flexibly across multiple assets
Data accuracy	High and consistent due to fixed placement	Variable; may depend on operator skill or positioning
Cost	Higher upfront cost; scalable in large systems	Lower initial cost; may incur higher labor over time
Labor requirement	Low once installed; automated	High; requires skilled personnel for regular use
Use cases	Critical or high-value assets needing constant monitoring	Non-critical assets, troubleshooting, or route-based monitoring
Benefits	• Real-time alerts • Trend analysis • Remote access	• Flexibility • Cost-effective for small-scale use • Useful for diagnostics
Limitations	• High initial investment • Less flexible	• Labor intensive • Inconsistent data • Not suitable for 24/7 monitoring

sensors are particularly useful in scenarios where infrastructure is not conducive to fixed installations or where quick assessments are required in response to detected irregularities. The mobility of these devices facilitates rapid identification of leaks and assessment of conditions within confined and hazardous spaces. Furthermore, advancements in sensor technology have enabled the development of highly sensitive portable devices that provide accurate measurements on-site without necessitating extensive downtime for installation [15].

Both fixed and portable sensor technologies carry specific limitations and challenges. Fixed sensors may require considerable resources for maintenance and recalibration to ensure accuracy over time, especially in varying environmental conditions [16]. Their installation can also be costly, particularly if retrofitting existing infrastructures. In contrast, portable sensors may lead to inconsistencies in data collection, as they rely on manual operation and may suffer from operator error or variability based on environmental changes [17]. While they provide immediate feedback, their reliance on user interaction can impact data collection's frequency and reliability, necessitating careful training for personnel [18].

Balancing the benefits of fixed and portable sensors is crucial for developing a comprehensive hydrogen leak detection strategy. The ideal solution often involves integrating both types of sensors within a single monitoring framework to ensure continuous surveillance complemented by the flexibility of portable technologies for spot-check applications. This hybrid approach allows for continuous reassurance provided by fixed sensors while enabling rapid, localized assessments with portable options, facilitating a more robust defense against potential hydrogen leak hazards [19]. In an era where hydrogen energy systems are expanding and evolving, ensuring that the chosen sensors adequately respond to the needs of each specific application and operational context is paramount for enhancing safety and operational efficiency [20].

As the push for adopting hydrogen as a clean energy carrier continues, considerations surrounding sensor technology will undoubtedly enhance the efficacy of safety management systems and operational standards. Deploying a combination of fixed and portable sensors tailored to specific monitoring environments can establish a formidable line of defense against the dangers posed by hydrogen leaks, thus advancing the potential of hydrogen infrastructure while ensuring safety through robust, responsive technology [15].

8.2.2 Networked Sensor Arrays and Wireless Systems

In the context of modern pipeline monitoring, networked sensor arrays and wireless systems represent a transformative shift toward enhanced leak detection capabilities, as shown in Fig. 8.1. The proliferation of wireless sensor networks (WSNs) tailored for pipeline leak detection allows for real-time monitoring and assessment of critical infrastructure across extensive geographic areas. These networks consist of multiple sensor nodes that communicate wirelessly, facilitating the collection of data regarding environmental conditions and pipeline integrity, thereby elevating the operational efficiency of leak detection systems [21].

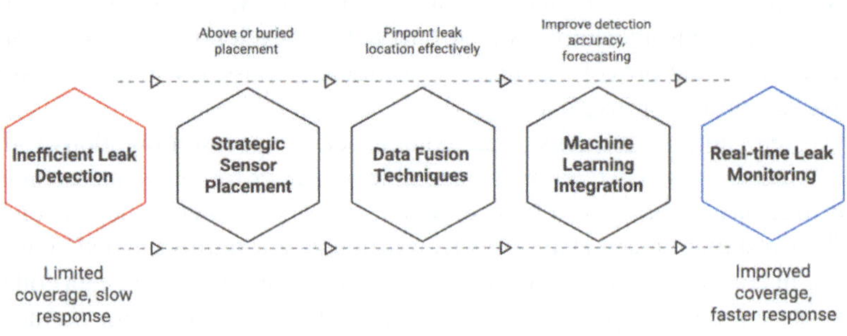

Fig. 8.1 Enhanced leak detection with WSNs

One of the primary benefits of deploying networked sensor arrays is their capacity to cover large geographical areas that traditional monitoring might struggle to address adequately. By using an array of interlinked sensor nodes, operators can monitor various parameters, such as pressure fluctuations, fluid flow rates, and acoustic signals indicative of leaks. For example, a study demonstrated that the use of a WSN to monitor pipelines enabled the detection of leaks in real-time and improved operator responses to potential hazards [22]. Furthermore, the sensor nodes can be strategically placed either above ground or buried within the pipeline environment, expanding the potential range of applications, particularly in remote or vulnerable locations where human access is limited.

Wireless systems also enhance the robustness and scalability of leak detection operations. They can be deployed quickly without the need for extensive wiring or infrastructural modifications, making them an attractive option for utilities and industries looking to retrofit existing pipeline networks. Coupled with advancements in battery technology and low-power electronics, modern sensors can operate over extended periods, minimizing maintenance requirements while still delivering reliable monitoring capabilities [23]. For example, utilizing low-power vibration sensors within a WSN framework has emerged as a preferred method as it allows for continuous monitoring with minimal energy consumption, which is critical given the often-expansive nature of pipeline networks [24].

The integration of wireless systems into networked sensor arrays presents significant opportunities for enhancing leak localization precision. Utilizing advanced data fusion techniques, information from multiple sensors can be analyzed to pinpoint the exact location of a leak much more effectively than isolated measurements [25]. Machine learning algorithms and data-driven models refine this process further, providing predictive capabilities that can assess historical data patterns to improve detection accuracy and forecasting of potential failures within the pipeline infrastructure [26]. For instance, by analyzing the acoustic emissions and pressure variations detected by multiple sensors, models can distinguish between normal operational noise and potential leak indicators [27].

Despite their numerous advantages, challenges such as signal interference, environmental factors, and the necessity for robust security protocols also accompany the adoption of networked sensor arrays and wireless systems [28]. Ensuring the integrity and reliability of communications within WSNs is fundamental to maintaining safety, as potential vulnerabilities could expose these systems to cyber threats or physical tampering. Therefore, continuous research is needed to further refine both the technologies used in these systems and the best practices for their deployment and maintenance [27].

8.3 Structural Health Monitoring (SHM)

Structural Health Monitoring (SHM) is an essential practice that involves the continuous assessment and evaluation of a structure's integrity, using advanced sensing technologies and analytical methodologies to detect damage and ensure safety [29]. The primary goal of SHM is to provide a systematic approach for the timely identification of changes in the mechanical and physical properties of structures, thereby facilitating maintenance decisions that extend their service life and enhance overall safety. The relevance of SHM grows as infrastructure ages, and both societal reliance upon complex structures and the demand for sustainable practices increase [30].

In essence, SHM integrates various sensing technologies—ranging from traditional sensors like accelerometers and strain gauges to more sophisticated methods such as Fiber Bragg Grating (FBG) sensors and piezoelectric transducers—to monitor structural responses under operational conditions [31]. By collecting data on parameters such as strain, displacement, and vibration, SHM systems provide insights not only into the existing state of a structure but also predict future performance and potential failure [32]. This predictive capability is paramount in critical infrastructure sectors like civil engineering, aerospace, and energy, where failures can lead to catastrophic consequences both financially and in terms of human safety [33].

The implementation of SHM systems is driven by technological advancements that allow for real-time data acquisition and processing, which have been made possible through wireless sensor networks (WSNs) and IoT-enabled devices [34]. These systems are designed to minimize human intervention, increase efficiency, and reduce the costs associated with manual inspections, which are often intrusive and time-consuming [29]. As a result, a more dynamic approach to infrastructure management emerges, where data is continuously gathered and analyzed to inform maintenance decisions proactively, rather than reactively addressing issues after they arise [35].

The journey towards effective SHM is laden with challenges that include data management, sensor reliability, and the interpretation of complex datasets gathered from diverse monitoring methods [36]. As various sensors produce large volumes of data, the integration of machine learning and artificial intelligence techniques into SHM frameworks has begun to gain traction, allowing for improved data processing, anomaly detection, and predictive analytics [37]. These methodologies enable the automatic identification of potential structural issues, resulting in earlier interventions that can prolong the lifespan of critical infrastructure [37].

SHM is not solely a retrospective task focused on damage detection; it also emphasizes its preventive aspect by facilitating condition-based maintenance. Such maintenance strategies prioritize interventions based on the actual condition of a structure rather than relying on fixed schedules, ensuring resources are allocated effectively [38]. By employing remote sensing techniques alongside traditional methods, the operational footprint of maintenance activities is reduced, enhancing the sustainability of infrastructure management practices [39].

The application of SHM also extends to unique structural forms and environments, including bridges, high-rise buildings, wind turbines, and even aerospace structures, each requiring tailored approaches to address specific challenges related to their materials, loading conditions, and operational environments [33]. For instance, wind turbine foundations have been shown to benefit significantly from SHM systems to manage the dynamic loads experienced over their operational lifespan, thereby optimizing energy production and maintaining structural integrity [30].

8.3.1 Strain Gauges, Fiber Optic Sensors, and Ultrasonic Arrays

Structural Health Monitoring (SHM) is a critical approach for assessing and ensuring the integrity of engineered structures over their lifespan. Among the various technologies employed in SHM, strain gauges, fiber optic sensors, and ultrasonic arrays stand out for their unique capabilities to measure and analyze physical changes within structures subjected to various stresses and environmental influences [40].

Strain Gauges are widely recognized for their effectiveness in detecting strain, crucial for understanding load distribution and potential failure points in structures. These devices operate on the principle of electrical resistance change, where the resistance of a conductive element varies in response to stretching or compressing forces applied to it. Advanced strain gauges have been developed using materials like graphene and carbon nanotubes, which enhance sensitivity and flexibility, enabling more accurate and reliable monitoring in diverse conditions [41]. The integration of strain gauges into a SHM framework has been reported to improve the ability to detect dynamic load changes and predict structural performance under various loading scenarios, including flexural and compressive loads in reinforced concrete beams and metal structures [42]. Additionally, wireless systems are transforming the deployment of strain gauges, allowing real-time data transmission that facilitates immediate analysis and decision-making [41].

Fiber Optic Sensors (FOS) represent another innovative technology within the SHM landscape, offering numerous advantages over traditional electronic sensors. FOS, specifically Fiber Bragg Grating (FBG) sensors, possess excellent sensitivity, are immune to electromagnetic interference, and can be embedded within composite materials without compromising structural integrity [31]. By measuring strain, temperature, and structural displacement along the fiber, FBG sensors enable comprehensive, distributed monitoring over long distances and across various structural elements, which is particularly beneficial for large infrastructure projects such as bridges and dams [43]. Their capacity for multiplexing—simultaneously measuring multiple locations using a single fiber—allows for cost-effective and efficient structural monitoring, surpassing the capabilities of point sensors [8]. Recent advancements in optical fiber technologies have led to the development of highly sensitive strain measurement systems, essential for identifying localized damage and assessing long-term structural performance [44].

Ultrasonic Arrays are integral to SHM methodologies, particularly for detecting internal flaws and assessing material properties through non-destructive testing (NDT). This technique uses high-frequency sound waves to identify anomalies within a structure. When ultrasonic waves propagate through a material, they reflect from discontinuities such as cracks, voids, and material boundaries. The integrity of these reflections provides valuable insights into structural health, enabling detailed mapping of defects and stresses not easily captured through other sensing modalities [45]. Unlike strain gauges and fiber optic sensors, ultrasonic arrays provide a comprehensive view of a structure's condition at multiple intervals and depths, making them particularly suitable for structural inspections prior to major construction or after significant loading events [46]. This capability, when complemented with advanced signal processing techniques, allows for effective monitoring of structural dynamics, contributing to improved safety management strategies.

8.3.2 Smart Pig Technologies and Permanent Monitoring

Smart pigs, also known as in-line inspection (ILI) tools, are autonomous or semi-autonomous devices that traverse the interior of pipelines to assess structural integrity. They provide high-resolution, wall-by-wall inspection data and remain indispensable for baseline assessment, regulatory compliance, and periodic condition evaluation.

Smart pigs such as magnetic flux leakage (MFL), ultrasonic testing (UT), electromagnetic acoustic transducer (EMAT), and geometry tools are used to detect metal loss, cracks, and mechanical deformation. UT and EMAT systems are particularly important for hydrogen service due to their ability to identify and size hydrogen-assisted and fatigue-related cracking. These inspections establish a baseline condition and support defect characterization, fitness-for-service evaluations, and regulatory compliance. Permanent monitoring systems complement ILI by providing real-time or near-real-time condition awareness. Technologies such as distributed fiber optic sensing, acoustic emission monitoring, corrosion and hydrogen permeation sensors, and high-frequency pressure and flow measurements enable early detection of leaks, crack activity, abnormal strain, and operational anomalies. Continuous data streams improve sensitivity to rapidly evolving damage mechanisms that may not be captured by periodic inspections alone. When integrated, smart pig data (i.e., ILI data) and permanent monitoring data provide essential information for establishing a closed-loop integrity management framework. ILI results guide sensor placement and the setting of alarm thresholds, while monitoring data track defect evolution and inform risk-based inspection intervals. For hydrogen pipelines, this combined strategy enhances safety, reduces uncertainty in defect growth prediction, and supports reliable long-term operation under demanding service conditions.

8.4 Data Analytics and Predictive Maintenance

The integration of data analytics into predictive maintenance represents a significant evolution in the management of industrial processes and infrastructure operations. Through the adoption of advanced analytics and machine learning techniques, organizations can transition from traditional time-based maintenance strategies to more refined, condition-based approaches that significantly reduce costs and enhance operational efficiency [47]. Predictive maintenance (PdM) relies on real-time data collection and analytics to forecast equipment failures before they occur, enabling proactive maintenance actions that mitigate downtime and extend asset life [48].

At the core of predictive maintenance is the ability to leverage big data analytics, which encompasses the collection, processing, and analysis of vast amounts of operational data. Effective predictive maintenance strategies utilize data gathered from various sources, including IoT devices, historical maintenance logs, and performance metrics, to identify trends and anomalies that signal potential issues. This data-driven decision-making process is essential in making informed maintenance and operational choices that can prevent unexpected equipment failures.

The frameworks that support predictive maintenance often include sophisticated algorithms capable of processing heterogeneous data inputs to generate actionable insights. For instance, machine learning approaches can analyze trends in operational data to predict the remaining useful life (RUL) of equipment, addressing both mechanical and electrical systems across various sectors, including manufacturing and energy [49]. By employing technologies such as artificial intelligence (AI) and deep learning, organizations enhance their prediction capabilities, allowing them to customize maintenance schedules based on actual equipment conditions rather than predetermined time intervals [50].

Deploying these advanced analytics systems is not without challenges. The integration of predictive maintenance requires a robust data infrastructure capable of supporting the high volumes of data generated from monitoring systems. Many organizations encounter hurdles related to data quality, interoperability, and the necessary skill sets for interpreting complex analytical outputs effectively. Additionally, cybersecurity concerns surrounding data protection and system integrity must be addressed to ensure the reliability of predictive maintenance solutions [51].

8.4.1 Condition-Based Monitoring Frameworks

Condition-based monitoring (CBM) frameworks are integral to modern maintenance strategies, particularly in industries where equipment reliability is crucial, see Fig. 8.2 and its cycle is shown in Fig. 8.3. These frameworks leverage real-time data from various sensors to monitor the health and performance of machinery, enabling organizations to implement maintenance activities based on the actual condition of assets rather than relying solely on predetermined schedules.

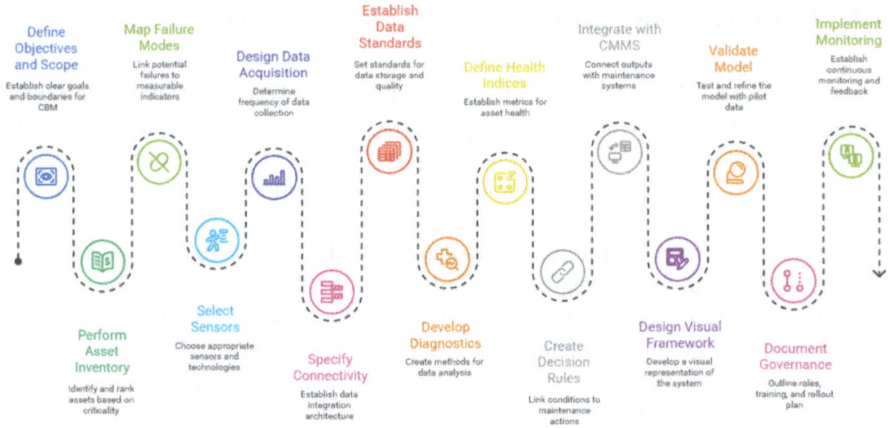

Fig. 8.2 Condition-based monitoring framework implementation

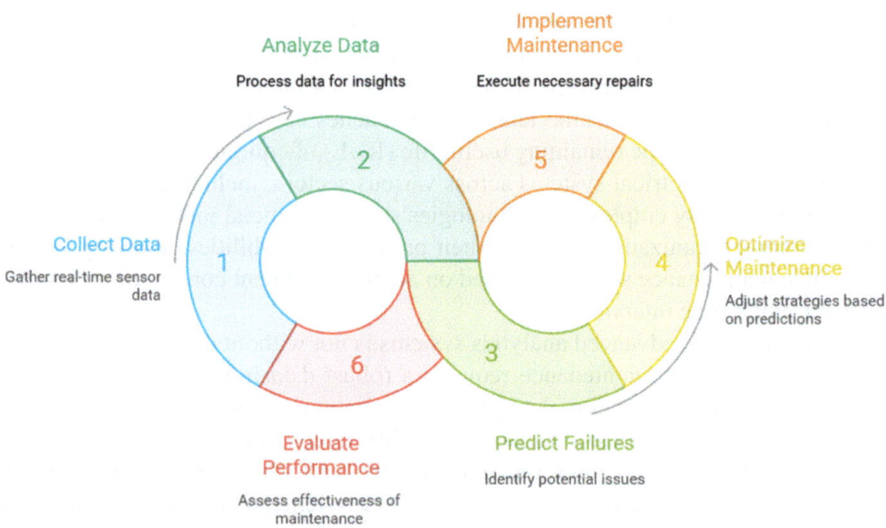

Fig. 8.3 Condition-based monitoring cycle

Such an approach enhances operational efficiency and reduces costs associated with unnecessary maintenance and unplanned downtimes [52]. At the heart of a condition-based monitoring framework lies the need for integrating data from diverse sources to facilitate a comprehensive understanding of equipment status. The integration of condition monitoring with process sensors presents a robust model for advancing operations and maintenance planning [52]. This framework employs techniques such as Multilevel Flow Modeling (MFM), which allows for causal reasoning about equipment states based on sensor readings. This capability is essential for predicting failures and optimizing operational workflows, ensuring that necessary repairs or adjustments can be made proactively [52].

In recent years, the demand for intelligent monitoring solutions has driven the development of data-driven methodologies that utilize advanced analytics, including machine learning algorithms, to continually assess the condition of equipment. For example, smart monitoring systems have been developed that employ novelty detection methods to analyze data collected from electromechanical systems across their operational lifespan. These data-driven approaches are pivotal for diagnosing potential vulnerabilities in machinery before they lead to costly failures.

CBM frameworks benefit significantly from advancements in artificial intelligence and incremental learning methodologies. As these systems learn from historical operational data, they become increasingly adept at identifying emerging faults and adapting maintenance strategies accordingly. The incorporation of real-time analysis capabilities, where sensor data is continuously evaluated against known fault patterns and operational parameters, enhances the ability to prevent failures [53].

Condition-based monitoring frameworks also address the uncertainties associated with prognosis and maintenance scheduling. With the increasing number of sensors being deployed, these systems support a transition from traditional corrective maintenance strategies to more predictive approaches that respond to real-time data. Such frameworks provide integrated solutions that facilitate timely interventions, thereby prolonging the lifespan of critical assets in environments that demand high reliability [54].

The framework can also encompass various methodologies tailored to specific industry needs, such as vibration-based monitoring in mechanical systems or corrosion detection in structural applications. For instance, a recent study developed a framework utilizing vibration signals from wind turbine gearboxes to assess their operational state, illustrating the versatility of condition monitoring systems across sectors [55].

As industries continue to adopt Industry 4.0 principles, the integration of Internet of Things (IoT) technologies into condition-based monitoring frameworks is becoming increasingly prevalent. By linking sensors to cloud platforms, organizations gain access to vast amounts of data that facilitate granular monitoring and analysis of system health in real-time. This interconnected approach enables multi-layered visibility into asset performance, further enhancing predictive capabilities and guiding directed maintenance efforts based on accurate assessments of equipment conditions [53].

8.4.2 Integrating Sensor Data with Maintenance Planning

The integration of sensor data into maintenance planning frameworks represents a significant advancement in predictive maintenance, ensuring that organizations can maintain operational efficiency and minimize downtime. The advent of the Internet of Things (IoT) has facilitated the widespread deployment of sensors across various industries, allowing for near real-time data collection and analysis that directly informs maintenance strategies [56]. This integration not only enhances decision-making processes regarding when and how maintenance should occur but also optimizes resource allocation and reduces overall maintenance costs.

The core principle of integrating sensor data with maintenance planning lies in the continuous collection and evaluation of operational data. By utilizing condition-based monitoring frameworks, organizations can assess the health of their assets in real-time. For instance, sensors that monitor vibration, temperature, and pressure can provide critical insights into the condition of machinery, enabling predictive maintenance teams to determine when a component might fail based on its operational state [57]. This data-centric approach allows maintenance strategies to shift from fixed schedules to more dynamic, condition-based methods, preventing costly downtime while enhancing operational reliability [58].

An exemplary case study of this integration can be observed in smart factories, where predictive maintenance driven by intelligent sensors serves as a cornerstone for operational excellence. These sensors collect vast amounts of data from equipment, and advanced analytics algorithms analyze patterns to forecast potential failures, informing maintenance personnel of necessary actions before an issue escalates [59]. Such readiness helps preserve machinery and extend asset life while ensuring maintenance is conducted efficiently, aligning operational needs with strategic goals.

The deployment of machine learning algorithms complements sensor data integration by enhancing predictive analytics capabilities. For example, data from various sensors can be analyzed using machine learning methods to identify anomalies or emerging trends that might indicate impending failures. This predictive capability allows maintenance teams to prioritize tasks based on real-time insights, improving operational efficiency and reducing the likelihood of unexpected breakdowns [60].

In conjunction with IoT technologies, cloud computing has further facilitated the integration of sensor data and maintenance planning. By utilizing cloud-based platforms, organizations can aggregate sensor data from disparate locations, providing a central repository for analysis and reporting [61]. This enables stakeholders to monitor equipment conditions, generate maintenance schedules, and swiftly adjust resource allocations in response to changing operational demands. The ability to visualize data collected from various sensors also empowers maintenance planners and technicians to make informed decisions based on comprehensive insights into equipment health and performance [62].

The ongoing development of smart technologies in maintenance contexts is evident in applications such as smart grids and automated facilities management. In these settings, integrating sensor networks plays a critical role in monitoring the health and performance of both mechanical systems and electrical assets, with predictive analytics feeding directly into maintenance planning frameworks [63]. Incorporating continuous feedback from smart sensors facilitates a proactive maintenance approach, mitigating risks inherent in traditional reactive methods [64].

The successful integration of sensor data into maintenance planning comes with challenges. Concerns regarding data quality, sensor calibration, and device interoperability must be effectively managed to ensure the reliability of gathered and analyzed information [65]. Establishing protocols for sensor maintenance and developing frameworks that can dynamically adapt to sensor outputs are essential for ensuring maintenance strategies remain effective and responsive.

References

1. Bu F et al (2024) Analysis of leakage and diffusion characteristics and hazard range determination of buried hydrogen-blended natural gas pipeline based on CFD. ACS Omega 9(37):39202–39218
2. Zhang C et al (2023) Key technologies of pure hydrogen and hydrogen-mixed natural gas pipeline transportation. ACS Omega 8(22):19212–19222
3. Lalam N et al (2024) Distributed optical fiber sensor systems: application to natural gas pipeline monitoring. In: Optical Waveguide and Laser Sensors III. SPIE
4. Wang Q et al (2024) Outline design of an atmospheric corrosion data monitoring system. In: E3S Web of Conferences 478:01028. EDP Sciences
5. Yang L et al (2023) Circular-arc array for the pulsed eddy current inspection of thermally insulated pipelines. Meas Sci Technol 34(12):125114
6. de Castro FA et al (2024) Green hydrogen: perspectives and challenges in using the natural gas network in Ceará/Brazil. J Geosci Environ Prot 12(3):70–94
7. Karplus VJ et al (2025) Risks in the design of regional hydrogen hub systems: a review and commentary. Risk Anal 45(3):581–599
8. Zhang K et al (2023) Experimental investigation on near-field acoustic propagation characteristics of leakage detection in submarine pipelines. J Mar Sci Eng 11(10):2012
9. Erdener BC et al (2023) A review of technical and regulatory limits for hydrogen blending in natural gas pipelines. Int J Hydrog Energy 48(14):5595–5617
10. Su Y et al (2022) Prediction of mixing uniformity of hydrogen injection in natural gas pipeline based on a deep learning model. Energies 15(22):8694
11. Zhu J et al (2023) Leakage and diffusion behavior of a buried pipeline of hydrogen-blended natural gas. Int J Hydrog Energy 48(30):11592–11610
12. Ghomashchi R (2023) Green energy revolution and substitution of hydrocarbons with hydrogen: distribution network infrastructure materials. Energies 16(24):8020
13. Lee H, Lee S (2022) Economic analysis on hydrogen pipeline infrastructure establishment scenarios: case study of South Korea. Energies 15(18):6824
14. Jamil S et al (2021) Cr_2O_3–TiO_2-modified filter paper-based portable nanosensors for optical and colorimetric detection of hydrogen peroxide. ACS Omega 6(36):23368–23377
15. Li S et al (2025) Fracture failure analysis of safety valve spring in nuclear power plant. J Phys: Conf Ser 2954:012101
16. Oh D-W, Kang K, Lee J-H (2023) Minimum detection concentration of hydrogen in air depending on substrate type and design of the 3ω sensor. Sensors 23(21):9009
17. Yun J et al (2024) Artificial intelligence assisted smart self-powered cable monitoring system driven by time-varying electric field using triboelectricity based cable deforming detection. Adv Energy Mater 14(27):2400156
18. Patel H, Pettitt M, Wilson JR (2012) Factors of collaborative working: a framework for a collaboration model. Appl Ergon 43(1):1–26
19. Yan K et al (2018) Fabrication of multiwall carbon nanotube sheet based hydrogen sensor on a stacking multi-layer structure. Nanotechnology 29(37):375503
20. Ahad MT et al (2023) An overview of challenges for the future of hydrogen. Materials 16(20):6680
21. Duru C, Ani C (2017) A statistical analysis on the leak detection performance of underground and overground pipelines with wireless sensor networks through the maximum likelihood ratio test. Sādhanā 42(11):1889–1899

22. Islam MT, Aslan S (2021) Leak detection and location pinpointing in water pipeline systems using a wireless sensor network. In: 2021 IEEE international symposium on circuits and systems (ISCAS). IEEE
23. Quiñones-Grueiro M et al (2018) An unsupervised approach to leak detection and location in water distribution networks. Int J Appl Math Comput Sci 28(2):283–295
24. Martini A, Troncossi M, Rivola A (2016) Leak detection in water-filled small-diameter polyethylene pipes by means of acoustic emission measurements. Appl Sci 7(1):2
25. El-Zahab S et al (2016) Collective thinking approach for improving leak detection systems. Smart Water 2(1):3
26. Kusriyanto M, Yulianto A, Kurniawan S (2018) Early detection of LPG gas leakage based wireless sensor networking. In: MATEC Web of Conferences 154, 01045 (2018). EDP Sciences
27. Mysorewala M (2019) Time and energy savings in leak detection in WSN-based water pipelines: a novel parametric optimization-based approach. Water Resour Manag 33(6):2057–2071
28. Utama INSA, Hadi S, Hariyadi IP (2022) Plume detection system based internet of things. Int J Eng Comput Sci Appl (IJECSA) 1(1):19–26
29. Sun M, Staszewski W, Swamy R (2010) Smart sensing technologies for structural health monitoring of civil engineering structures. Adv Civ Eng 2010(1):724962
30. Currie M et al (2013) Structural health monitoring for wind turbine foundations. Proc Inst Civ Eng-Energy 166(4):162–169
31. Karatas C et al (2020) Fibre Bragg grating sensor applications for structural health monitoring. Aircr Eng Aerosp Technol 92(3):355–367
32. Tarhini H et al (2018) Optimization of piezoelectric wafer placement for structural health-monitoring applications. J Intell Mater Syst Struct 29(19):3758–3773
33. Mghazli MO et al (2024) Experimental machine learning approach for building structural health monitoring application. J Phys: Conf Ser 2647:182031
34. Geara C et al (2019) Bayesian updating for uncertain condition state using permanent monitoring and sequential inspections. In: MATEC web of conferences 261:02005
35. Xu Q, Yuan S, Ren Y (2021) Gaussian mixture model based damage evaluation for aircraft structures. Mater Res Proc 18:154–160
36. Yi T-H et al (2015) Distributed sensor networks for health monitoring of civil infrastructures. Hindawi Publishing Corporation, p 271912
37. Bao Y, Li H (2021) Machine learning paradigm for structural health monitoring. Struct Health Monit 20(4):1353–1372
38. Bagnoli F, Livi R (2018) Michael faraday: a virtuous life dedi-cated to science. Substantia 2(1):121–134
39. Mutlib NK et al (2016) Ultrasonic health monitoring in structural engineering: buildings and bridges. Struct Control Health Monit 23(3):409–422
40. Basaran M, Turkmen HS, Yildiz M (2024) Sensor-enhanced thick laminated composite beams: manufacturing, testing, and numerical analysis. Sensors 24(16):5366
41. Anas M et al (2018) Structural health monitoring of GFRP laminates using graphene-based smart strain gauges. J Braz Soc Mech Sci Eng 40(8):397
42. Jayawickrema M et al (2023) Strain patterns of short span reinforced concrete beams under flexural loading: a comparison between distributed sensing and concrete damaged plasticity modelling. J Intell Mater Syst Struct 34(10):1123–1135
43. Li S, Wu Z, Zhou L (2010) Health monitoring of flexural steel structures based on distributed fibre optic sensors. Struct Infrastruct Eng 6(3):303–315
44. Hu X, Wang B, Ji H (2013) A wireless sensor network-based structural health monitoring system for highway bridges. Comput-Aided Civ Infrastruct Eng 28(3):193–209
45. Zhao J, Cheng F (2023) Finite element modeling of the hydrogen atom distribution on dented pipeline for hydrogen transport under cyclic loading. Int J Fract 246:181–201
46. Wang X, Chakraborty J, Niederleithinger E (2021) Noise reduction for improvement of ultrasonic monitoring using coda wave interferometry on a real bridge. J Nondestr Eval 40(1):14
47. Sang GM, Xu L, de Vrieze, P (2021) A predictive maintenance model for flexible manufacturing in the context of industry 4.0. Front Big Data 4:663466

48. Kaur S et al (2025) Emerging trends in industry 4.0 and predictive maintenance. Abhigyan 43(1):54–67
49. Alves F et al (2020) Deployment of a smart and predictive maintenance system in an industrial case study. In: 2020 IEEE 29th international symposium on industrial electronics (ISIE). IEEE
50. Korompili G, Mußbach G, Riziotis C (2024) Structural health monitoring of solid rocket motors: from destructive testing to perspectives of photonic-based sensing. Instruments 8(1):16
51. Razali MN et al (2020) Big data analytics for predictive maintenance in maintenance management. Prop Manag 38(4):513–529
52. Wu J, Zhang X (2024) Integrating condition-based monitoring with process sensors information for operation and maintenance in a functional modeling framework. Proc Inst Mech Eng, Part O: J Risk Reliab 238(3):502–522
53. Saucedo-Dorantes JJ et al (2020) Industrial data-driven monitoring based on incremental learning applied to the detection of novel faults. IEEE Trans Industr Inf 16(9):5985–5995
54. Wu X (2023) Research on Apple Inc. market winning case study. Adv Econ, Manag Polit Sci 24:130–136
55. Mauricio A, Qi J, Gryllias K (2019) Vibration-based condition monitoring of wind turbine gearboxes based on cyclostationary analysis. J Eng Gas Turbines Power 141(3):031026
56. Pech M, Vrchota J, Bednář J (2021) Predictive maintenance and intelligent sensors in smart factory. Sensors 21(4):1470
57. Abdallah M et al (2023) Anomaly detection and inter-sensor transfer learning on smart manufacturing datasets. Sensors 23(1):486
58. von Enzberg S et al (2020) Implementation and transfer of predictive analytics for smart maintenance: a case study. Front Comput Sci 2:578469
59. Dogea R, Yan XT, Millar R (2023) Implementation of an edge-fog-cloud computing IoT architecture in aircraft components. MRS Commun 13(3):416–424
60. Bing G, Karim AM, Karim AM (2024) Study on society awareness and smart city and facilities management: integrated approach. Int J Acad Res Bus Soc Sci 14(1):265–478
61. Sadiki S et al (2019) Running smart monitoring maintenance application using Cooja simulator. Int J Eng Res Afr 42:149–159
62. Rice J et al (2011) Enabling framework for structural health monitoring using smart sensors. Struct Control Health Monit 18(5):574–587
63. Pala S et al (2014) Smart sensors for condition based maintenance: a test case in the manufacturing industry. In: PHM Society European Conference, 2(1)
64. Shamsuddoha M et al (2021) Smart monitoring of a full-scale composite hydrofoil manufactured using automated fibre placement under high cycle fatigue. Smart Mater Struct 31(1):015025
65. Sim S-H, Lee J-J (2021) Special issue on "smart city and smart infrastructure." Sensors 21(21):7064

Chapter 9
Data Analytics and Digital Twins

This chapter explores the transformative role of data analytics and digital twins in enhancing the integrity management of hydrogen pipelines. It begins by examining the increasing influence of Big Data and the Internet of Things (IoT) in enabling data-driven decision-making for pipeline operations. The chapter highlights the operational and financial benefits these technologies offer to operators and investors, including improved efficiency, safety, and asset longevity.

The discussion progresses to the concept of digital twins—virtual replicas of physical pipeline systems—and details their key components and data requirements. It outlines how operational, inspection, and environmental data are integrated to create dynamic models that reflect real-time conditions. The chapter further delves into the use of machine learning for predictive modeling, enabling early detection of anomalies and accurate failure probability estimations.

Visualization tools such as dashboards and alert systems are presented as critical elements in supporting timely, informed decision-making. The integration of these tools with broader asset management platforms is also addressed, demonstrating how digital twins can be leveraged to optimize pipeline performance, reduce risk, and support long-term sustainability in hydrogen infrastructure.

9.1 Overview of Data-Driven Pipeline Integrity Management

One of the prominent areas where digital twins have gained traction is within healthcare systems. Researchers have noted that digital twins can significantly enhance patient care through real-time data integration and predictive analytics capabilities [1]. By employing machine learning algorithms alongside patient-specific data, healthcare providers can utilize digital twin technology to forecast potential health risks and devise proactive interventions.

M. Hussain et al., *Hydrogen Pipeline Integrity*, Green Energy and Technology,
https://doi.org/10.1007/978-981-95-5609-0_9

Reports indicate that this technology contributes to process optimization by enabling manufacturers to simulate and analyze operational scenarios, ultimately leading to heightened efficiency and reduced downtime [2]. For instance, digital twins facilitate predictive maintenance strategies by continuously monitoring equipment conditions through sensor data, thereby forecasting failures before they occur [3] and establishing maintenance schedules that maximize operational efficacy. Consequently, the fusion of digital twin technology with advanced analytics tools not only optimizes manufacturing processes but also enhances supply chain operations by creating digital replicas of logistical systems.

Digital twins can also play a critical role in the automation and optimization of complex systems within industries such as logistics, agriculture, and construction [4]. In agriculture, for example, digital twins can be employed to monitor crop conditions and optimize resource usage, thus enhancing yield and sustainability. Similarly, in construction, digital twins enable project managers to create simulations of building processes, identifying potential issues before they arise and ensuring timely project completion.

The integration of digital twins within industrial applications illustrates a broader trend toward the digitalization of various sectors. Companies are increasingly leveraging this technology to create a more adaptive and predictive organizational structure, leading to significant advancements in operational efficiency, quality control, and system reliability across various fields. It is widely acknowledged that as industries evolve, the adoption of digital twins will continue to play a crucial role in reshaping operational landscapes, enhancing competitive advantages, and fostering a culture of innovation and adaptability.

9.1.1 Role of Big Data and IoT

The integration of Big Data and the Internet of Things (IoT) has generated significant advancements across various domains, linking data collection and processing with operational efficiencies and enhanced decision-making capabilities, some of them are shown in Table 9.1. The synergy of these two technologies facilitates the collection of vast amounts of real-time data, which can be harnessed for predictive analytics, operational monitoring, and resource management across disciplines such as healthcare, smart cities, agriculture, and manufacturing.

The integration of IoT and Big Data is not without its challenges, particularly regarding data security, privacy, and interoperability among disparate systems, some of the challenges and proposed solutions are shown in Table 9.2.

Table 9.1 Role of big data and IoT

Aspect	Description
Integration of big data and IoT	Combines large-scale data collection with advanced processing to improve decision-making, operational efficiency, and real-time monitoring
Data generation	IoT devices (sensors, actuators, smart systems) continuously collect vast amounts of structured, semi-structured, and unstructured data
Analytical frameworks	Big Data platforms leverage AI and machine learning to process, analyze, and extract insights for predictive analytics and strategic decision-making
Applications	Healthcare (patient monitoring), Smart Cities (traffic and energy management), Agriculture (precision farming), Manufacturing (predictive maintenance, quality control)
Industrial impact	IIoT enables predictive maintenance, reduced downtime, cost efficiency, and improved product quality in manufacturing
Challenges	Data security, privacy, scalability, and interoperability across diverse systems remain critical obstacles
Solutions	Adoption of federated learning, cryptographic methods, and advanced data management strategies to safeguard and optimize data usage

Table 9.2 Challenges and solutions in big data–IoT integration

Challenges	Proposed solutions
Data security	Use of encryption, blockchain, and advanced intrusion detection systems
Privacy concerns	Federated learning and privacy-preserving data-sharing techniques
Interoperability issues	Development of standardized protocols and cross-platform integration frameworks
High data volume and velocity	Scalable cloud computing, edge computing, and distributed storage systems
Complex data structures	AI/ML-based algorithms for efficient data cleaning, classification, and analysis

9.1.2 Benefits for Operators and Investors

One significant advantage for operators is the facilitation of data-driven decision-making processes. With IoT devices continuously generating vast data streams, companies can analyze this information for more informed strategic choices, enabling timely interventions [5]. For instance, in manufacturing environments, real-time monitoring supported by IoT can optimize production schedules, reduce waste, and enhance quality control. This ability to optimize operations leads to improved resource allocation, directly contributing to cost savings and maximizing return on investment (ROI) for both operators and stakeholders [6].

Predictive analytics stemming from Big Data allows operators to foresee trends and identify emerging opportunities in their markets. By leveraging machine learning algorithms alongside historical and real-time data, organizations can derive actionable insights that help shape their business strategies. For example, companies in agriculture can use IoT sensors to track soil conditions and crop health, allowing farmers to implement precision farming techniques that improve yield and reduce input costs effectively [7]. This capacity for predictive analysis not only drives efficiency but also ensures better risk management, fostering investor confidence [8].

The financial implications of employing IoT and Big Data extend beyond immediate cost savings to encompass broader market influences, such as sustainability initiatives. As companies adopt eco-friendly practices driven by data insights, they can bolster their reputation and appeal to socially-conscious investors. Sustainable business practices through data reduction and efficiency foster loyalty among environmentally-aware consumers. Consequently, this creates an additional marketing advantage, positioning organizations favorably in competitive markets.

In operational environments like healthcare, the adoption of IoT and data analytics can streamline patient management processes, leading to reduced operational costs and improved healthcare delivery [9, 10]. By optimizing workflows and utilizing predictive analytics for patient care, healthcare providers can enhance their service quality while also reducing unnecessary expenditures. This not only leads to better outcomes for patients but also attracts investors looking for innovative solutions to prevalent healthcare challenges.

9.2 Building Digital Twins for Hydrogen Pipelines

The development of digital twins for hydrogen pipelines is expected to significantly enhance the hydrogen production and distribution sectors. These virtual replicas of physical assets allow for improved monitoring, predictive analytics, and operational optimization, which are critical as global demand for hydrogen increases. Hydrogen pipelines, vital for transporting hydrogen from production sites to consumption areas, require robust infrastructure management to ensure safety, efficiency, and cost-effectiveness.

Central to digital twin technology is the ability to integrate real-time data from various sources, including sensors and IoT devices, to reflect the physical state and performance of hydrogen pipelines. By continuously updating the digital model with data from the physical pipeline, operators can utilize real-time analytics to identify anomalies and inefficiencies that may signal problems such as leaks or pressure drops. This proactive monitoring enhances operational reliability and minimizes downtime, ultimately maximizing throughput and revenue.

The high-pressure nature of hydrogen transport makes it essential to manage risks effectively due to the flammability of hydrogen [11]. A digital twin can serve as a crucial tool for risk management, using predictive analytics to evaluate potential failure modes and their effects on pipeline integrity. This capability allows operators to implement preventive measures before critical failures, ensuring compliance with safety regulations and reducing the risk of accidents that could jeopardize operational continuity and public safety.

As the hydrogen economy expands, rapid scaling of production and distribution capabilities is essential. The digital twin model facilitates fast testing and iteration of pipeline designs and operations without the expense of physical prototyping or retrofitting existing infrastructure. Virtual simulations enable organizations to make informed decisions regarding upgrades or expansions while assessing the economic and technical implications of these changes.

The economic benefits of adopting digital twin technology extend beyond operational efficiencies. Integrating digital twins can lead to significant cost savings by preventing leaks and other disruptions. Additionally, by minimizing maintenance costs and ensuring efficient operations, companies can achieve a quicker return on investment, making the case for digital twins increasingly attractive to investors focusing on the growing hydrogen market.

9.2.1 Concept and Components

The concept of digital twins for hydrogen pipelines involves creating real-time virtual replicas of these essential infrastructures, facilitating extensive monitoring, analysis, and optimization of their operations. This technology allows for a holistic understanding of the pipelines, significantly improving the management of hydrogen transport—a crucial element in the energy transition landscape. By integrating various components such as IoT sensors, advanced analytics frameworks, and simulation models, digital twins serve as powerful tools in achieving operational efficiency, enhancing safety, and supporting sustainable energy strategies.

1. **Core Concept of Digital Twins**

At its essence, a digital twin is a digital replica of a physical entity. This includes the behavior and characteristics of hydrogen pipelines, represented using dynamic models that continually update based on real-time data [12]. The digital twin platform connects the digital and physical realms by ensuring that the virtual model accurately reflects the current status of the physical pipeline. This involves various data inputs, such as flow rates, pressure, temperature, and potential leak detection metrics, created through sensors strategically placed throughout the infrastructure. The digital twin's design incorporates elements of simulation, allowing operators to conduct various analyses and predictions related to the operation and maintenance of hydrogen pipelines [13].

2. **Components of Digital Twins for Hydrogen Pipelines**

The digital twin framework for hydrogen pipelines is composed of several essential components, each playing a critical role in the functionality and efficiency of the digital twin system. These components are shown in Fig. 9.1.

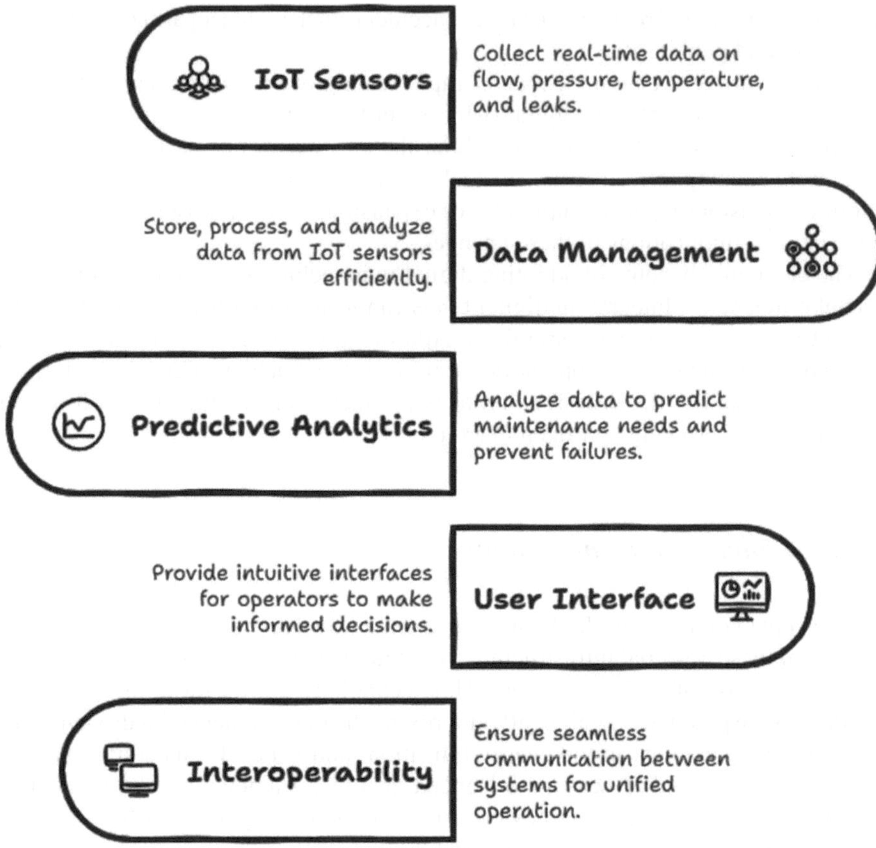

Fig. 9.1 Digital twin components

3. **Benefits of Digital Twins in Hydrogen Pipeline Management**

The use of digital twins in hydrogen pipelines is accompanied by numerous advantages that enhance both operational performance and investment value, as shown in Fig. 9.2. As stakeholders navigate the complexities of hydrogen infrastructures, digital twins offer a vital tool in ensuring safety, reliability, and efficiency [14].

9.2.2 Data Inputs: Operational, Inspection, and Environmental

The creation of digital twins for hydrogen pipelines hinges upon the integration of various types of data inputs, which are crucial for accurately reflecting the operational state of the physical infrastructure. These data inputs can be categorized into three

Fig. 9.2 Benefits of digital twins in hydrogen pipeline management

main groups: operational data, inspection data, and environmental data. Each of these data types plays a vital role in ensuring that the digital twin can effectively simulate pipeline behaviors, facilitate predictive analytics, and optimize overall operational performance.

1. ***Operational Data***

Operational data encompasses the real-time metrics obtained from the functioning of the hydrogen pipeline. This data is predominantly sourced from IoT sensors embedded throughout the infrastructure, which continually monitor the pipeline's performance. Key operational parameters may include:

- **Flow Rate**: Sensory monitoring of the hydrogen flow rate is essential for understanding the pipeline's throughput and ensuring that it operates within designated parameters. Real-time flow data aids in identifying unusual patterns that may signal operational disruptions or inefficiencies.
- **Pressure Levels**: Accurate pressure monitoring is critical, as hydrogen pipelines often operate at high pressures. Real-time data on pressure levels enables operators to ensure that the system functions safely and efficiently. Extreme deviations from normal pressure ranges can indicate potential leaks or equipment failures.
- **Temperature**: Temperature measurements are integral to monitoring the state of the hydrogen being transported. Changes in temperature can affect both the efficiency of the pipeline operation and the integrity of the materials used in construction.
- **Valve Status**: The operation of valves along the pipeline influences the flow of hydrogen. Data regarding valve positions (open or closed) and their operational status provide insight into the distribution dynamics of hydrogen within the network.

Operational data provides the real-time feedback needed to update the digital twin continuously. Such responsiveness allows operators to manage and control pipeline systems dynamically, enhancing reliability and efficiency.

2. ***Inspection Data***

Inspection data comprises results from various assessments conducted on the hydrogen pipeline, aimed at ensuring its integrity and safety. Regular inspections are necessary to monitor the physical state of the pipelines and to detect potential issues early. Key components of inspection data include:

- **Maintenance Records**: Historical data on maintenance activities is vital for understanding the lifecycle of pipeline components. These records provide insights into past repairs, replacements, and general upkeep operations, ultimately informing predictive maintenance strategies.
- **Leak Testing Results**: Standard leak detection methods, such as ultrasonic testing or pressure testing, yield data on the integrity of the pipeline. Results from these tests help identify areas that may be susceptible to failure, refining the digital twin's predictive capabilities.
- **Corrosion Assessments**: Inspection data on pipeline corrosion is critical, as hydrogen can lead to embrittlement and degradation of materials over time. Corrosion monitoring sensors provide data that influence the maintenance schedule and inform operators about pipeline health.
- **Visual Inspections and Non-Destructive Testing (NDT)**: Regular visual inspections, enhanced by NDT methods such as magnetic particle testing or radiography, contribute valuable data on the pipe surface, welds, and joints, ensuring that potential failure points are identified and addressed promptly.

This inspection data not only serves as a historical reference but also feeds into the operational analysis, allowing the digital twin to forecast when maintenance actions are needed based on the current condition of the pipeline.

3. ***Environmental Data***

Environmental data involves the various external factors influencing the performance and safety of hydrogen pipelines. This data helps contextualize the operational and inspection metrics while enabling comprehensive analysis regarding how environmental conditions may affect the infrastructure. Key environmental data components include:

- **Temperature and Humidity**: Fluctuations in ambient temperature and humidity levels can impact gas density and the performance of pipeline materials. Monitoring these variables allows operators to evaluate the potential influence on pipeline function.
- **Soil Conditions**: For underground pipelines, real-time data regarding soil characteristics can impact corrosion rates and overall structural integrity. Data on soil pH, moisture content, and composition informs decisions regarding protective measures and maintenance schedules.

- **Seismic Activity**: In areas prone to seismic events, monitoring data on ground motion and vibrations is essential. This information allows operators to assess potential impacts on pipeline integrity during and after seismic activities, enhancing safety measures.
- **Weather Conditions**: Real-time weather station data can affect operational decisions, as severe weather situations (e.g., storms or heavy snow) may necessitate temporary shutdowns or increased monitoring of pipeline conditions.

Integrating environmental data into the digital twin framework allows for improved simulations and assessments, enabling a more nuanced understanding of the operational context of the hydrogen pipeline. As a result, it becomes possible to anticipate the need for maintenance or operational adjustments based on external factors that might otherwise go unnoticed.

9.3 Predictive Models and Risk Forecasting

Predictive models and risk forecasting for hydrogen pipelines are central to ensuring safe and efficient operation of hydrogen transportation systems. As interest in hydrogen as a clean energy source grows, it is essential to employ sophisticated methodologies to assess risks associated with its transport. Predictive models facilitate the identification of potential hazards, enabling stakeholders to implement strategies that mitigate risks and enhance the overall safety of pipeline operations.

9.3.1 Predictive Models and Their Role

Predictive models utilize historical and real-time data alongside machine learning and statistical techniques to forecast various outcomes related to pipeline operations. These models analyze factors such as material properties, environmental conditions, flow rates, and historical incidents to predict potential risks related to hydrogen transportation. For example, the relative risk scoring (RRS) technique has been employed to formulate a risk profile based on critical factors such as corrosion, leakage, and atmospheric conditions, significantly improving risk assessment capabilities [15].

The application of predictive modeling allows operators to conduct quantitative risk analyses, estimating the likelihood of pipeline failures and their potential consequences [16]. By simulating various scenarios, the model can forecast potential hazards and inform strategies to mitigate or prevent them. Additionally, machine learning algorithms enhance the accuracy of these models, as they can identify patterns and correlations that might not be evident through traditional analytical methods.

9.3.2 *Risk Forecasting Techniques*

Risk forecasting is an essential component of predictive modeling, providing a systematic approach for quantifying and evaluating risks associated with hydrogen pipelines. Various techniques are used to model risk, as shown in Fig. 9.3.

Unlike retrospective risk assessment, which focuses on historical data and failure analysis, risk forecasting aims to predict the likelihood and potential consequences of future events based on statistical, physical, and probabilistic models. This predictive capability enables operators to optimize maintenance schedules, enhance safety performance, and guide infrastructure investments.

9.3.2.1 Quantitative Risk Assessment (QRA)

Quantitative Risk Assessment (QRA) is the foundation of hydrogen pipeline risk forecasting. It integrates failure probability, exposure frequency, and consequence severity into a unified risk metric. The general formulation is:

$$R = P_f \times C$$

where:

- R = Risk (expected loss or consequence per unit time or distance)
- P_f = Probability of failure (per km-year or per component-year)
- C = Consequence of failure (fatalities, environmental damage, or economic loss).

For hydrogen pipelines, P_f is determined using **statistical reliability models** (e.g., Weibull or exponential distributions) that account for embrittlement rates, pressure cycles, corrosion growth, and material fatigue.

The consequence term often relies on computational fluid dynamics (CFD) modeling to simulate hydrogen release, dispersion, ignition, and overpressure effects.

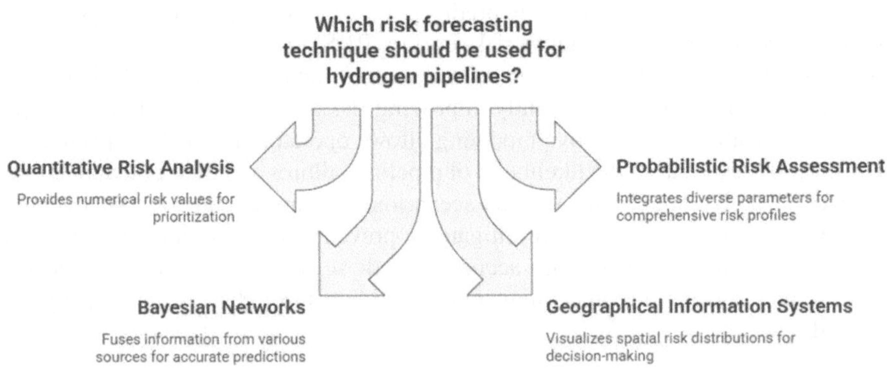

Fig. 9.3 Risk forecasting techniques

9.3.2.2 Probabilistic and Bayesian Modeling

Hydrogen pipeline risk forecasting benefits from probabilistic approaches, particularly Bayesian inference, which can incorporate both historical data and expert judgment to continuously update risk profiles as new information becomes available.

A Bayesian Network (BN) model represents the probabilistic relationships between failure causes (nodes) such as:

- Material degradation
- Pressure surge
- Weld defect occurrence
- Cathodic protection failure
- Environmental stressors (e.g., temperature cycles).

The Bayesian updating equation is:

$$P(H|E) = \frac{P(E|H) \cdot P(H)}{P(E)}$$

where $P(H \mid E)$ is the updated (posterior) probability of failure given new evidence E, such as detected microleaks or real-time strain data.

By integrating data from sensors, inspection reports, and operational records, Bayesian models enable real-time dynamic risk forecasting, adapting predictions as conditions evolve.

9.3.2.3 Reliability-Centered and Time-To-Failure Forecasting

Reliability-centered models focus on failure probability as a function of time, crucial for hydrogen pipelines where embrittlement and fatigue evolve gradually. The Weibull distribution is commonly used:

$$P_f(t) = 1 - e^{-(t/\eta)^\beta}$$

where:

- η = Characteristic life parameter
- β = Shape parameter ($\beta > 1$ indicates wear-out failure; $\beta < 1$ indicates early-life failures).

Parameters are estimated through field inspection data, hydrostatic test intervals, or accelerated aging tests in hydrogen environments. Using these models, maintenance schedules and inspection frequencies can be risk-optimized to prevent catastrophic failure while minimizing operational downtime.

9.3.2.4 Computational Fluid Dynamics (CFD) and Consequence Simulation

CFD-based models are essential for forecasting the spatial and temporal impact of hydrogen release scenarios. Because hydrogen disperses and ignites differently than methane, CFD simulations model:

- **Jet dispersion behavior** under various leak sizes and orientations
- **Buoyancy-driven flow** in open and confined spaces
- **Deflagration and detonation** potential depending on air-hydrogen mixture ratios
- **Thermal radiation contours** and pressure wave propagation.

These models use software such as ANSYS Fluent, OpenFOAM, or FLACS-Hydrogen to estimate overpressure zones, thermal dose, and fatality probability. Results are incorporated into risk contour maps, identifying high-risk regions along the pipeline corridor and guiding emergency response planning.

9.3.2.5 Machine Learning and Data-Driven Forecasting

With the proliferation of Internet of Things (IoT) sensors and smart pipeline technologies, data-driven risk forecasting is gaining prominence. Machine learning (ML) algorithms can process large volumes of real-time operational data—pressure fluctuations, acoustic emissions, vibration signals, and hydrogen concentration trends—to detect anomalies and predict failures.

Common ML techniques include:

- **Artificial Neural Networks (ANNs):** Predict nonlinear relationships between stress, temperature, and leak likelihood.
- **Random Forests:** Classify pipeline sections by risk level using multiple input features (material, age, coating condition).
- **Support Vector Machines (SVM):** Identify boundary conditions leading to hydrogen embrittlement onset.
- **Recurrent Neural Networks (RNN):** Model time-series degradation processes for long-term forecasting.

Integration of ML with **digital twins**—virtual replicas of pipeline systems—enables predictive maintenance through continuous simulation and data assimilation.

9.3.2.6 Multi-Criteria Decision Analysis (MCDA)

In strategic pipeline risk management, decisions often involve conflicting objectives: cost minimization, safety maximization, and environmental protection. **MCDA** frameworks provide a structured method to balance these objectives by assigning weights to key criteria such as:

- Probability of failure
- Societal impact
- Proximity to populated areas
- Cost of mitigation measures.

Techniques such as Analytic Hierarchy Process (AHP) or Technique for Order of Preference by Similarity to Ideal Solution (TOPSIS) are frequently employed to prioritize risk control investments and evaluate alternative pipeline routes or material upgrades.

9.3.2.7 Integrated Forecasting and Risk Visualization

Modern hydrogen pipeline operators increasingly employ integrated risk forecasting platforms, combining QRA, probabilistic modeling, CFD results, and ML analytics into a unified decision-support system. Geographic Information Systems (GIS) are used to visualize risk levels spatially, while temporal models project how risk evolves under different operating scenarios—such as hydrogen blending ratios, pressure variations, or climate conditions.

These integrated models enable proactive risk management, allowing early intervention before system integrity is compromised. Forecasted risk outputs are typically represented as:

- **Risk matrices** (likelihood vs. consequence)
- **Pipeline risk indices** (e.g., R-index per kilometer)
- **Dynamic dashboards** showing real-time probability maps.

3 **Key Data Inputs for Predictive Models**

To develop effective predictive models and risk assessments for hydrogen pipelines, several key inputs must be integrated:

a. **Operational Data**

Operational data consists of vital real-time metrics collected from sensors and monitoring devices along the pipeline. Important parameters include:

- **Flow Measurements**: Understanding flow rates and patterns aids in identifying potential operational inefficiencies that may lead to failures.
- **Pressure Levels**: Continuous monitoring of pressure helps detect sudden drops or spikes that might indicate leaks or blockages.
- **Temperature Readings**: Evaluating temperature changes is crucial as they can affect the physical properties of the hydrogen being transported, impacting safety and efficiency.

b **Inspection Data**

Inspection data encompasses the results of regular evaluations of the pipeline integrity. This data includes:

- **Maintenance Histories**: Records of past maintenance work guide predictive analytics in estimating future maintenance needs and potential points of failure.
- **Corrosion Assessments**: Data on corrosion-related wear helps operators understand material degradation rates, a significant risk factor in hydrogen environment exposure.

c **Environmental Data**

Environmental factors can considerably influence pipeline operation and safety. Relevant data includes:

- **Soil Characteristics**: Soil pH, moisture content, and composition affect corrosion rates and the long-term integrity of buried pipelines.
- **Weather Conditions**: Knowledge of prevailing weather patterns assists in planning operational adjustments during adverse conditions.

9.4 Machine Learning Approaches

Machine learning encompasses various algorithms that can learn from and make predictions based on data. In the context of hydrogen pipelines, these algorithms analyze historical performance data, operational metrics, and inspection results to identify patterns that correlate with pipeline failures and potential safety hazards. This predictive capability is essential for modern risk management practices, enabling proactive measures to be implemented before issues arise. Types of Machine Learning Approaches for hydrogen pipeline are shown in Fig. 9.4.

Characteristic	Supervised Learning	Unsupervised Learning	Reinforcement Learning
Data Labeling	Labeled datasets	Unlabeled datasets	Interactions with environment
Outcome Knowledge	Known outcomes	Unknown outcomes	Optimizes control policies
Application	Risk forecasting	Anomaly detection	Optimizing operations
Example Algorithm	Decision trees	K-means clustering	Control policies

Fig. 9.4 Machine learning approaches for hydrogen pipelines

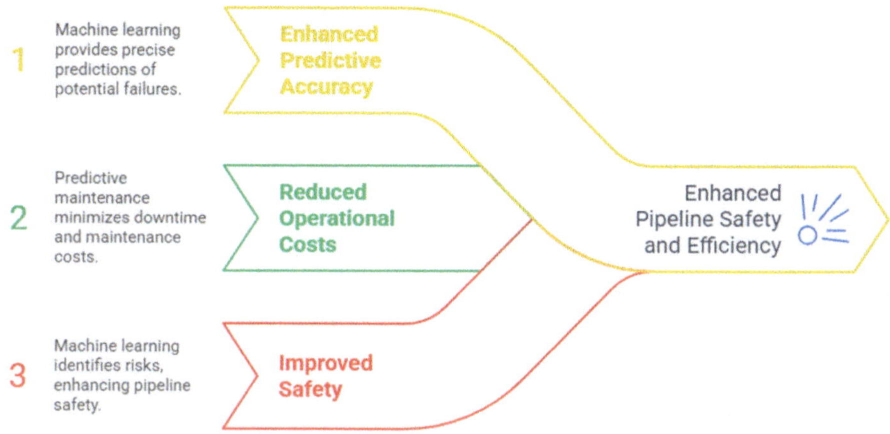

Fig. 9.5 Machine learning in hydrogen pipelines

Integration with Predictive Models

Machine learning algorithms integrate seamlessly with existing predictive models by enhancing data analysis capabilities. The fusion of predictive models with machine learning allows for:

- **Predictive Maintenance**: Algorithms analyze sensor data to forecast when components are likely to fail, allowing for timely maintenance actions that prevent unplanned downtime and costly failures.
- **Risk Modeling**: ML enhances the accuracy of risk assessments by incorporating multifactorial datasets, resulting in more robust predictions regarding pipeline integrity and associated hazards.
- **Environmental Adaptation**: Incorporating environmental variables into models helps assess how external conditions, such as temperature or soil composition, influence pipeline performance and safety.

Benefits of Using Machine Learning Approaches

The application of machine learning to predictive modeling and risk assessment in hydrogen pipelines confers multiple benefits as depict Fig. 9.5.

9.5 Failure Probability Estimation

Failure probability estimation in hydrogen pipelines is crucial for ensuring safety, reliability, and efficiency in the production and transport of hydrogen, particularly as this energy source gains traction as a clean alternative in the energy landscape. Recent advancements in machine learning (ML) methodologies have significantly enhanced

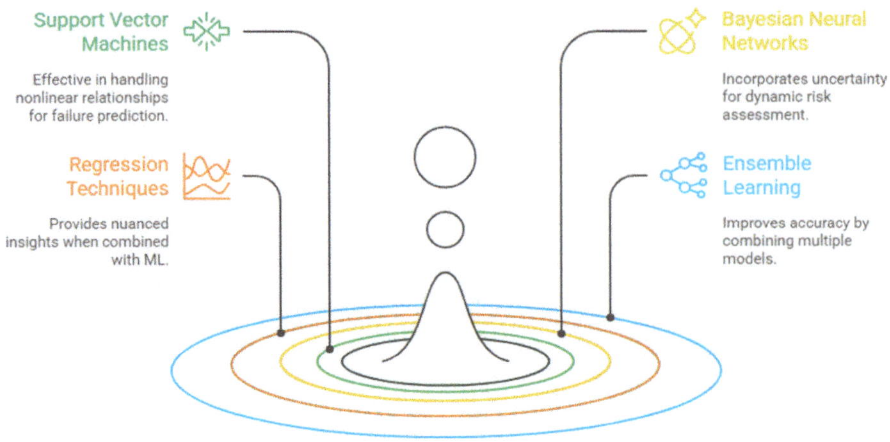

Fig. 9.6 Machine learning in failure probability estimation

the ability to estimate the likelihood of failures in pipeline operations, allowing for the development of predictive maintenance protocols and risk management strategies.

In the context of hydrogen pipelines, failure probability estimation helps operators anticipate the likelihood of various failure modes such as leaks, ruptures, or structural failures. Accurately predicting these failures allows for proactive measures to be taken, thereby minimizing potential hazards and reducing operational downtime. Furthermore, regulatory frameworks increasingly demand organizations to quantify the risks associated with their installations, making failure probability estimation an essential component of pipeline management.

9.5.1 Machine Learning Approaches for Estimating Failure Probability

Machine learning techniques have transformed the landscape of failure probability estimation by providing powerful tools to analyze and interpret complex datasets. Several fundamental approaches are employed in this domain a shown in Fig. 9.6.

9.5.2 Key Data Inputs

To effectively utilize machine learning for failure probability estimation in hydrogen pipelines, several key data inputs are required:

- **Operational Metrics**: Real-time data from sensors measuring pressure, temperature, flow rates, and other critical operational parameters provide essential context for machine learning models. The inclusion of this data helps models understand the normal operating conditions and identify deviations indicative of potential failures.

- **Historical Failure Data**: A comprehensive historical database of past incidents and failure events is central to training machine learning models. This data serves to establish patterns associated with previous failures, contributing to the model's predictive power.
- **Inspection and Maintenance Records**: Regular inspection results and maintenance logs help confirm the integrity of components and system performance. Data from these records can guide probability estimates by highlighting factors contributing to prior failures.

9.6 Visualization and Decision Support Tools

The integration of visual analytics allows operators to handle extensive datasets generated by IoT sensors, operational logs, and historical inspections more efficiently. For instance, the use of machine learning algorithms to identify patterns and anomalies related to pipeline integrity can be complemented by visualization techniques that present these findings in a user-friendly manner [17]. By transforming raw data into meaningful visual narratives, decision-makers can quickly grasp significant insights regarding pipeline performance, safety risks, and maintenance needs.

Dynamic dashboards are key components of visualization and decision support systems, offering real-time monitoring capabilities while allowing for exploratory data analysis. They can present various operational metrics, such as flow rates, pressure levels, and temperature readings, through intuitive graphical representations like line charts, heat maps, and bar graphs [18]. These visual tools enable operators to quickly assess the state of pipeline systems at a glance and respond promptly to any deviations that might indicate potential failures. Furthermore, interactive elements within these dashboards empower users to filter data based on specific criteria, facilitating targeted analyses that are relevant to their immediate operational context.

Advanced predictive models can be integrated into visual analytics platforms to forecast potential failures and assess risk probabilities associated with different operational scenarios. By utilizing predictive analytics, operators can simulate various conditions and visualize the corresponding outcomes [19]. This predictive capability is pivotal in understanding how changes in operational parameters or external influences, such as environmental conditions, may impact the likelihood of pipeline disruptions. By equipping decision-makers with these insights, organizations can prioritize maintenance efforts on high-risk segments and allocate resources more effectively.

The importance of explainability in decision-making processes also cannot be overstated. Visualization and decision support tools can help elucidate the underlying mechanisms of machine learning models, making their predictions more interpretable. For example, techniques that visualize feature importances or decision paths assist decision-makers in understanding why specific risks are forecasted and how certain operational parameters influence those predictions. By fostering greater trust in predictive models and their outputs, these tools encourage user engagement and facilitate collaborative problem-solving among stakeholders.

9.6.1 Dashboards and Alert Systems

Dashboards designed for hydrogen pipeline management integrate data from various sources, including sensor measurements and operational logs, into a cohesive visual interface. By employing advanced visual analytics, these dashboards transform complex and large datasets into user-friendly visual representations. For instance, dashboards might display visual indicators such as pressure trends and flow rates, allowing operators to quickly assess the pipeline system's state at a glance [20]. Instant access to crucial information is vital for making informed operational decisions, particularly in environments where rapid response times are essential for safety.

The capability of dashboards to provide real-time alerts based on predefined thresholds enhances operators' responsiveness to potential risks. For example, if a sudden drop in pressure or an abnormal increase in temperature is detected, the system can trigger an alert, notifying the relevant personnel to investigate the issue immediately [21]. Designed effectively, alert systems can improve operational safety by allowing for rapid responses to emergent situations, thus mitigating the risk of accidents that could have dire consequences. This proactive risk management approach is particularly critical in hydrogen pipeline management, where the consequences of leaks or failures can be severe.

The design and usability of dashboards significantly influence their effectiveness in monitoring and alerting. A user-centered design approach ensures that the dashboard caters to the specific needs of operators and decision-makers, promoting efficient interaction with the system and facilitating timely decision-making. Challenges in usability often hinder the adoption of dashboards; therefore, designing intuitive interfaces that present information clearly is vital for encouraging user engagement. User feedback should be incorporated throughout the design process to refine dashboard functionalities and enhance user satisfaction [22].

Dashboards can facilitate collaborative decision-making among various stakeholders involved in hydrogen pipeline operations. By providing a shared platform for visualizing data and insights, organizations can foster effective communication and enhance coordination among different functional teams, including engineering, operations, and safety personnel. This collaborative approach is essential in ensuring that all team members work toward centralized goals and respond appropriately to alerts generated by the system [23].

Despite the advantages of dashboards and alert systems, challenges related to data integration and security remain. The complexity of integrating data from various sources, including disparate sensor systems and databases, can hinder the reliability of displayed information. Additionally, safeguarding sensitive operational data against unauthorized access while providing necessary access to legitimate users is vital. Employing strong cybersecurity measures alongside secure authentication protocols is crucial to maintaining the integrity of dashboard systems [21].

9.6.2 Integration with Asset Management Platforms

Integration with asset management platforms represents a significant advancement in the operational efficiency and safety management of hydrogen pipelines. By connecting digital twin technologies with robust asset management frameworks, organizations can leverage real-time data, predictive analytics, and visualization tools to optimize the performance and reliability of their pipeline systems. This integration enables comprehensive oversight and informed decision-making, thus enhancing the sustainability and safety of hydrogen transport.

Asset management platforms, such as Enterprise Resource Planning (ERP) systems, provide organizations with the tools necessary for managing the entire lifecycle of their assets effectively. These platforms offer features for tracking the condition of pipeline components, scheduling maintenance, and managing expenditure on repairs and replacements. Successful integration of digital twin technology into these platforms enhances existing capabilities by feeding real-time operational data and predictive insights directly into asset management workflows. This functionality enables operators to maintain an up-to-date understanding of the health and performance of their pipeline systems, ensuring that appropriate resources are allocated where they are most needed.

One of the benefits of integrating digital twins with asset management platforms is the capability for predictive maintenance. By employing machine learning algorithms that analyze operational data, organizations can forecast when specific components of the pipeline are likely to fail based on historical performance data and current operating conditions [24]. Asset management platforms can utilize this predictive data to create targeted maintenance schedules that minimize downtime and associated costs, significantly enhancing asset utilization and long-term performance. Additionally, the incorporation of detailed inspection data—captured through digital twin technologies—provides a comprehensive view of asset conditions, allowing for more informed decision-making regarding repair scheduling and resource allocation.

The use of blockchain technology in conjunction with asset management platforms can further enhance the integrity and security of the data related to hydrogen pipelines. Blockchain integration enables secure, transparent record-keeping of asset usage, conditions, and maintenance history, thus facilitating trust among stakeholders and regulatory agencies. By leveraging decentralized ledger technology, organizations can ensure that asset data is immutable and verifiable, which is crucial for compliance and operational audits [25].

Despite these advantages, challenges remain in the successful integration of digital twin technologies with asset management platforms. Data interoperability is one such critical challenge, as diferrences in data formats and standards can impede effective communication between systems [26]. Organizations must prioritize developing robust APIs (Application Programming Interfaces) that can facilitate seamless data transfers between the various components involved in pipeline management. Additionally, ensuring that the integration does not compromise system security is essential, as asset management platforms must protect sensitive operational data from unauthorized access and cyber threats.

References

1. Vallée A (2023) Digital twin for healthcare systems. Front Digit Health 5:1253050
2. Alemde V (2025) Innovative process technologies: advancing efficiency and sustainability through optimization and control. Int J Res Publ Rev 6(2):1941–1955
3. Hussain M et al (2024) Application of artificial intelligence in the oil and gas industry. Engineering applications of artificial intelligence. Springer, pp 341–373
4. Iranshahi K et al (2025) Digital twins: recent advances and future directions in engineering fields. Intell Syst Appl 26:200516
5. Adekunle P et al (2023) Application of big data and internet of things in the built environment: a bibliometric review. In: Proceedings of the 31st annual conference of the international group for lean construction (IGLC31)
6. Saputra YM, Alfian G (2023) Privacy aware-based federated learning framework for data sharing protection of internet of things devices. Indones J Electr Eng Comput Sci 31(2):979–985
7. Quy VK et al (2022) IoT-enabled smart agriculture: architecture, applications, and challenges. Appl Sci 12(7):3396
8. Mukherjee S et al (2022) Leveraging big data analytics in 5G-enabled IoT and industrial IoT for the development of sustainable smart cities. Trans Emerg Telecommun Technol 33(12):e4618
9. Alsaig A et al (2019) Characterization and efficient management of big data in iot-driven smart city development. Sensors 19(11):2430
10. Na HS, Hwang J, Kim H (2023) Which attributes should be considered in regulating the internet of things? Evidence from conjoint analysis. SAGE Open 13(4):21582440231209810
11. Min M et al (2025) Hydrogen risk assessment studies: a review toward environmental sustainability. Energies 18(2):229
12. Vessel HH-P (2020) A digital twin for safety and risk. In: Designing for digital transformation. co-creating services with citizens and industry: 15th international conference on design science research in information systems and technology, DESRIST 2020, Kristiansand, Norway, December 2–4, 2020, proceedings. Springer Nature
13. Chen H et al (2023) Design and application of logical range framework based on digital twin. Appl Sci 13(11):6589
14. Vempati S, Nalini N (2024) Securing smart cities: a cybersecurity perspective on integrating IoT, AI, and machine learning for digital twin creation. J Electr Syst 20(3):1420–1429
15. Vanitha C et al (2023) Efficient qualitative risk assessment of pipelines using relative risk score based on machine learning. Sci Rep 13(1):14918
16. Zhang P, Qin G, Wang Y (2019) Risk assessment system for oil and gas pipelines laid in one ditch based on quantitative risk analysis. Energies 12(6):981

17. Wiczling P, Kamedulska A, Kubik Ł (2021) Application of Bayesian multilevel modeling in the quantitative structure–retention relationship studies of heterogeneous compounds. Anal Chem 93(18):6961–6971
18. Ooge J, Verbert K (2022) Visually explaining uncertain price predictions in agrifood: a user-centred case-study. Agriculture 12(7):1024
19. Bhavnani SK et al (2022) A framework for modeling and interpreting patient subgroups applied to hospital readmission: visual analytical approach. JMIR Med Inform 10(12):e37239
20. Odeshina A et al (2024) Business intelligence dashboard optimization model for real-time performance tracking and forecasting accuracy. Int J Soc Sci Except Res 3:334–342
21. Katapally TR, Ibrahim ST (2023) Digital health dashboards for decision-making to enable rapid responses during public health crises: replicable and scalable methodology. JMIR Res Protoc 12(1):e46810
22. Rahman MA, Alam MS, Mrida MSH (2025) How interactive dashboards improve managerial decision-making in operations management. Am J Adv Technol Eng Solut 1(01):122–146
23. Zakir HI et al (2024) Next-generation public health surveillance: extreme heat event prediction and monitoring system. Eur J Public Health 34(Supplement_3):ckae144.1045
24. Maletič D et al (2020) The link between asset risk management and maintenance performance: a study of industrial manufacturing companies. Qual Innov Prosper 24(3):50–69
25. Wang H et al (2024) Construction of enterprise asset management accounting system based on blockchain technology. Appl Math Nonlinear Sci 9(1):1–22
26. Nepal MP et al (2021) Towards an integrated approach to infrastructure damage assessment in the aftermath of natural hazards. Buildings 11(10):450

Chapter 10
Risk Identification and Characterization

This chapter provides a comprehensive overview of the methodologies and frameworks essential for identifying and characterizing risks associated with hydrogen pipelines. The chapter begins by examining hydrogen-specific pipeline risks, including physical, chemical, and operational hazards, as well as external and internal threats unique to hydrogen transport.

It then explores a range of hazard identification tools such as HAZOP, What-If Analysis, and Failure Modes and Effects Analysis (FMEA), along with the use of risk registers to systematically categorize and document identified hazards. The chapter delves deeper into FMEA, outlining common failure modes in hydrogen pipelines, their potential consequences, and methods for detection.

Risk prioritization techniques are discussed next, with an emphasis on developing risk matrices, establishing scoring criteria, setting thresholds, and defining organizational risk tolerance levels. Finally, the chapter presents a variety of risk assessment frameworks tailored for hydrogen infrastructure, including qualitative and quantitative methods such as QRA and probabilistic risk models, to support informed decision-making and enhance pipeline safety and reliability.

10.1 Understanding Hydrogen-Specific Pipeline Risks

Frameworks such as those presented by Khan et al. [1] demonstrate the significance of addressing risks within supply chain management, particularly amidst growing cybersecurity threats. Their proposed methodologies stress the importance of risk identification in enhancing resilience and operational continuity amidst unpredictable risks inherent in the modern supply chain landscape. This proactive stance towards risk assessment aligns with ongoing debates aimed at mitigating disruptions in critical infrastructure.

M. Hussain et al., *Hydrogen Pipeline Integrity*, Green Energy and Technology,
https://doi.org/10.1007/978-981-95-5609-0_10

The transportation of hydrogen through pipelines introduces a distinct set of challenges compared to conventional natural gas or oil systems. While hydrogen pipeline technology is not entirely new—industrial hydrogen networks have existed for decades—the scale, pressure regimes, and materials used in emerging hydrogen infrastructure demand renewed attention to hydrogen-specific risks. These risks arise from hydrogen's unique physical, chemical, and mechanical properties, which can influence both the integrity of the pipeline and the safety of surrounding environments.

10.1.1 Physical, Chemical, and Operational Hazards

The identification and characterization of physical, chemical, and operational hazards play a crucial role in risk management across various sectors including food safety, healthcare, and industrial operations. Understanding physical, chemical, and operational hazards is essential for effective risk management. Each type of hazard presents unique challenges that can impact safety, health, and operational efficiency. Identifying these hazards and implementing appropriate control measures helps reduce accidents, occupational diseases, and other adverse outcomes. Moreover, hydrogen's wide flammability range (4–75% in air) and low ignition energy increase the probability of ignition in the event of a leak, creating a more stringent safety environment for hydrogen pipeline operations. Additionally, hydrogen's buoyancy means that in open-air releases, leaks tend to disperse rapidly upward. While this can reduce the risk of prolonged ground-level explosions, it complicates detection and monitoring, as hydrogen flames are nearly invisible in daylight and its odorless nature precludes human sensing. Thus, hydrogen-specific detection and ventilation strategies are required to complement material integrity measures. The key characteristics, examples, and implications of these hazards are summarized in Table 10.1.

10.1.2 Leakage, Detection, and Monitoring Challenges

Hydrogen's small molecular size and low density make it inherently more prone to leakage than other gases. Even minor defects in seals, gaskets, or valve interfaces can result in persistent losses. The consequences of such leaks extend beyond safety—economic losses and environmental implications arise if large-scale hydrogen distribution systems operate inefficiently.

Traditional gas detection systems, often designed for methane or propane, are not sufficient for hydrogen. Hydrogen sensors must respond rapidly at low concentration levels and function reliably under variable pressure and temperature conditions. Optical sensors, catalytic bead detectors, and electrochemical sensors are being refined to meet these demands. Modern pipeline systems are increasingly

Table 10.1 Summary of physical, chemical, and operational hazards

Hazard type	Definition/ description	Key examples	Findings/implications
Physical hazards	Environmental and workplace factors that may cause harm to individuals or facilities	– Foreign bodies and environmental contaminants in food – Excessive noise, poor lighting, poor ergonomics	– Poor handling and inadequate conditions increase risks in food safety – Poor workplace conditions contribute to occupational diseases – Preventive measures and better workplace environments are essential
Chemical hazards	Harmful substances that cause health issues upon exposure	– Flammable solvents – Noxious fumes in healthcare – Toxicants in welding	– Awareness and training reduce exposure risks – Welders face combined risks from chemical and physical factors – Comprehensive risk assessments must consider interactions of hazards
Operational hazards	Risks from unsafe operations and workplace practices that affect safety and efficiency	– Improper handling of materials in construction – Working at heights – Ergonomic strain and disinfectant exposure in healthcare	– Rigorous safety protocols are needed in high-risk jobs – Continuous education and safety management systems reduce risks in healthcare – Unmanaged operational hazards cause accidents and low morale – Integrated management is needed to address infrastructure and human factors

integrating digital twins and continuous monitoring technologies, enabling predictive maintenance and early detection of anomalies in pressure, flow, or chemical composition.

10.1.3 Operational and Pressure Management Risks

Hydrogen's compressibility and low energy density per unit volume mean that pipelines must transport greater volumetric flow rates to deliver equivalent energy compared to natural gas. This often leads to higher operating pressures, which can intensify the effects of embrittlement and fatigue. Transient pressure events, such as surge waves or rapid decompression, also have more pronounced effects in hydrogen systems due to its high diffusivity and low viscosity.

Proper pressure management, including advanced valve control, surge suppression systems, and careful regulation of start-up and shutdown procedures, is vital. Operators must adopt hydrogen-specific modeling and simulation tools to predict flow dynamics and pressure transients accurately.

10.1.4 Safety Culture and Risk Mitigation Strategies

Understanding hydrogen-specific risks extends beyond engineering—organizational safety culture and regulatory frameworks play an equally vital role. Hydrogen pipeline design codes (such as ASME B31.12 and ISO 16111) provide guidance on material selection, testing protocols, and allowable stress limits, yet continuous improvement and adaptation are needed as real-world experience grows.

Risk mitigation should combine technical, operational, and systemic measures:

- **Technical**: Use of embrittlement-resistant materials, leak-tight fittings, and redundant detection systems.
- **Operational**: Rigorous maintenance schedules, hydrogen-specific training for personnel, and controlled pressure cycling.
- **Systemic**: Integration of probabilistic risk assessment (PRA) methods, regulatory oversight, and public transparency.

10.1.5 Toward Resilient Hydrogen Infrastructure

As global energy systems transition toward cleaner fuels, hydrogen's role in decarbonizing heavy industry, transportation, and power generation will expand. Ensuring the safe and reliable transport of hydrogen is fundamental to this transition. A deep understanding of hydrogen-specific pipeline risks enables engineers, policymakers, and operators to design resilient infrastructures that safeguard public safety while fostering innovation in the hydrogen economy.

10.1.6 External and Internal Threats

The identification and analysis of external and internal threats are fundamental to effective risk management in sectors such as national security, corporate operations, and community safety. External threats originate outside an organization or community, while internal threats arise from within. Understanding both types of threats allows for proactive measures that enhance resilience, operational stability, and overall security. The key characteristics, examples, and implications of external and internal threats are summarized in Table 10.2.

10.2 Hazard Identification Tools

Hazard identification is a critical step in risk management across industries, ensuring that potential threats to health, safety, and the environment are recognized and assessed. Various tools, both qualitative and quantitative, are used to identify hazards systematically. Recent advancements also integrate technology, such as machine learning and hybrid analytical approaches, to improve accuracy and efficiency. The key hazard identification tools, their characteristics, and applications are summarized in Table 10.3.

Table 10.2 Summary of external and internal threats

Threat type	Definition/ description	Key examples	Findings/implications
External threats	Risks originating outside an organization or community	– Natural disasters – Geopolitical tensions – Cyberattacks (e.g., SQL injection, CSRF) – Public health crises – External economic pressures	– Perception of threats varies across societal groups, influencing cohesion and polarization – Cybersecurity requires proactive defense measures – International conflicts and external pressures can affect domestic governance and internal security priorities
Internal threats	Risks arising from within an organization or community	– Mismanagement, corruption, internal dissent – Personnel-related issues – Insider data breaches – Internal divisions in governance (ethnic, political)	– Systemic social issues can create cycles of internal risk – Effective HR and personnel management are crucial in organizations – Insider threats in IT systems can cause financial/reputational damage – Internal political or community divisions can reduce overall security effectiveness

Table 10.3 Hazard identification tools

Tool type	Tool/Method	Description/Approach	Applications/Findings
Qualitative	HAZOP (Hazard and operability study)	Structured brainstorming to identify deviations from design intent	Effective in identifying potential system failures
	What-if analysis	Scenario-based technique to anticipate potential undesirable events	Flexible across domains; useful for early hazard recognition
	Preliminary hazard analysis (PHA)	High-level overview of risks based on existing knowledge	Useful in chemical process industries; prioritizes areas for detailed study
Quantitative	Bayesian networks	Statistical models analyzing interrelationships between factors	Enhances risk assessments, e.g., flood risk evaluation
	Fault tree analysis (FTA)	Top-down analysis of potential causes of unwanted events	Investigates fault relationships; informs safety improvements
	HIRA (Hazard identification and risk assessment)	Combines hazard identification with risk evaluation	Proactive approach in sectors like nanotechnology
Advanced/Hybrid	Machine learning/deep learning	Predictive modeling using AI, e.g., hyperspectral imaging	Improved accuracy in identifying solid hazardous chemicals
	Fuzzy logic + HAZOP	Combines traditional tools with fuzzy multi-attribute analysis	Enhances sensitivity and effectiveness in complex environments (e.g., gas facilities)

10.2.1 HAZOP, What-If Analysis, and FMEA

Hazard identification is a critical step in risk management across multiple industries, including manufacturing, healthcare, and process engineering. Among the widely used methodologies for hazard identification are Hazard and Operability Study (HAZOP), What-If Analysis, and Failure Modes and Effects Analysis (FMEA). This section provides a comprehensive discourse on these methodologies, exploring their frameworks, applications, strengths, and limitations.

The Hazard and Operability Study (HAZOP) methodology is a systematic and structured approach designed to identify potential hazards and operability issues within a process. Originating from the chemical industry in the 1960s, HAZOP has established itself as a cornerstone of process safety analyses. The method utilizes a team-based approach where multidisciplinary experts brainstorm potential deviations from the design intent of a process [2, 3]. Each deviation is assessed using defined guide words, such as "more," "less," "as well as," and "none," to stimulate discussion regarding how each deviation can lead to hazardous situations.

An example of this application can be found in a study conducted by Bargues et al. [4], which utilized HAZOP in the context of a fuel storage terminal. Their research underscored the effectiveness of HAZOP in not only identifying risks associated with fuel storage and handling but also in suggesting necessary operational adjustments and safeguards. HAZOP has proven invaluable in other sectors as well; for instance, Eltahan et al. [5] applied HAZOP in assessing risk in petroleum production units, demonstrating its versatility beyond traditional chemical applications.

What-If Analysis: An Alternative and Flexible Approach

The What-If Analysis tool offers a more flexible alternative for hazard identification compared to HAZOP. This methodology involves designing hypothetical scenarios to explore potential failures and their consequences. This informal brainstorming technique encourages creativity and out-of-the-box thinking about system failures that may not be immediately apparent in a structured approach like HAZOP.

What-If Analysis is particularly beneficial when quick assessments are necessary or when there is limited documentation on existing processes. As noted by Ramzan et al. [2], What-If Analysis can efficiently complement more rigorous analysis techniques, such as HAZOP and FMEA, by providing preliminary insights that can guide deeper investigations. This responsive approach to hazard identification has been effectively utilized in various industries, including healthcare, where rapid changes in protocols may necessitate a swift hazard evaluation.

Failure Modes and Effects Analysis (FMEA) complements HAZOP and What-If Analysis by focusing on potential failure modes within a system and evaluating their impact on process functionality and safety. FMEA is structured around identifying possible failure modes, their causes, effects, and the likelihood of their occurrence. FMEA is widely adopted across industries, including manufacturing, aerospace, and healthcare, for its systematic approach to risk assessment.

Integration and Synergy Among Methodologies

The combined use of HAZOP, What-If Analysis, and FMEA underscores a trending integrative approach in risk assessment methodologies. By leveraging the strengths of each approach, organizations can enhance hazard identification, risk evaluation, and mitigation strategies. For instance, the integration of HAZOP with FMEA has been demonstrated to provide comprehensive insights, ensuring that potential hazards are evaluated not only in isolation but in a systemic context.

10.2.2 Risk Registers and Categorization

Risk registers and categorization are essential components of effective risk management systems across various fields, including healthcare, finance, and industrial sectors. They provide a structured approach to identifying, assessing, and categorizing risks, allowing organizations to implement appropriate strategies for mitigation and response. The transportation and storage of hydrogen, particularly via pipelines, pose various risks that necessitate rigorous hazard identification and categorization processes. Utilizing risk registers is essential for systematically documenting and managing these risks, thereby ensuring compliance with safety regulations and minimizing potential hazards.

The implementation of risk registers allows for systematic tracking of risks over time, facilitating effective communication among stakeholders involved in hydrogen pipeline operations. Maintaining an updated risk register is crucial for enhancing operational safety and ensuring that emerging risks are promptly addressed. This dynamic tool serves as both a management and communication resource, fostering a culture of safety throughout the hydrogen supply chain.

Categorization of Risks in Hydrogen Pipelines

Given the unique characteristics of hydrogen, including its low ignition energy and tendency to permeate materials, categorizing risks associated with hydrogen pipelines is essential for effective management. Risk categorization typically involves classifying risks based on their nature, potential impacts, and likelihood of occurrence. In the hydrogen industry, common risk categories are shown in Fig. 10.1

Implementation of Risk Registers in the Hydrogen Industry

When implementing risk registers in the context of hydrogen pipelines, it is essential to involve stakeholders from various disciplines, including engineering, operations, safety, and regulatory compliance. Collaborative input can enhance the comprehensiveness of the risk register by integrating diverse perspectives on potential risks and effective mitigation strategies.

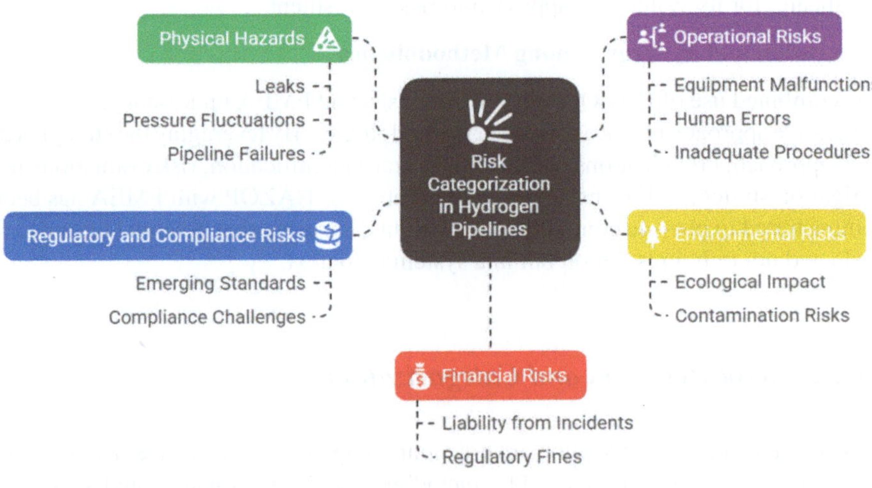

Fig. 10.1 Risk categorization in hydrogen pipelines

The establishment of a risk assessment framework is pivotal for categorizing and prioritizing risks in hydrogen pipeline operations. Utilizing quantitative and qualitative methodologies can aid in evaluating the likelihood and impact of identified risks. This assessment leads to informed decision-making regarding resource allocation for risk management initiatives, ensuring that the most significant risks are addressed first. Moreover, regular reviews and updates of the risk register are paramount in reflecting changes in operations, regulations, or emerging technologies within the hydrogen industry. This ongoing evaluation can enhance resilience by fostering adaptability to evolving safety standards and operational environments.

10.3 Failure Modes and Effects Analysis (FMEA)

Failure Modes and Effects Analysis (FMEA) is a structured and systematic approach utilized for identifying potential failure modes within a process or product and their impact on system performance. Particularly relevant in the hydrogen industry, FMEA assists in recognizing risks associated with hydrogen production, storage, and transportation, ensuring that safety and operational integrity are prioritized throughout the hydrogen supply chain.

FMEA Methodology

The FMEA process is initiated by assembling a multidisciplinary team that includes experts from various fields, such as engineering, safety, operations, and quality assurance. The team collaborates to identify all components, processes, and systems associated with hydrogen operations, followed by the identification of potential failure modes for each element. The FMEA procedure typically involves steps as Fig. 10.2.

In the hydrogen sector, FMEA has garnered attention for addressing the myriad challenges posed by hydrogen technologies. For example, Dang et al. [6] emphasize the application of FMEA in assessing the risks associated with hydrogen-powered aircraft systems, identifying critical failure modes that could compromise safety. Additionally, Felseghi et al. [7] explore the applicability of FMEA in evaluating hydrogen storage systems, examining potential failure modes related to material performance under hydrogen exposure.

Another significant advantage of FMEA is its flexibility and adaptability. It can be applied across various stages of the hydrogen supply chain, from production to storage to transportation, making it a valuable tool in different contexts. This versatility allows companies to scale their analyses according to their specific operational requirements.

Despite its strengths, FMEA is not without limitations. One of the primary challenges is the dependence on team expertise and experience. As Sotoodeh and Gudmestad [8] note, inexperienced teams might overlook critical failure modes or incorrectly assess their severity or occurrence ratings, leading to inadequate risk management strategies. This highlights the need for well-trained personnel in conducting effective FMEA analyses.

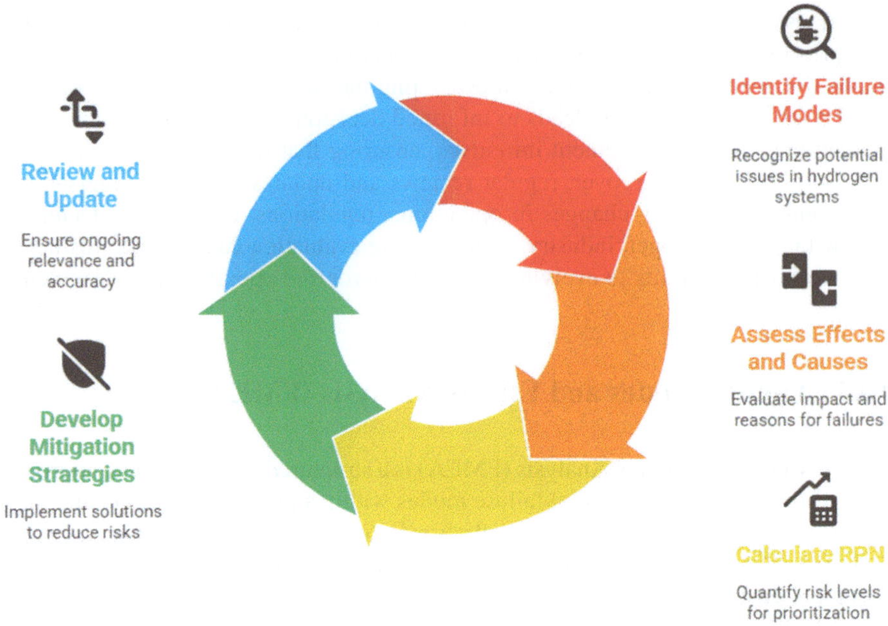

Fig. 10.2 FMEA process cycle

Executing FMEA can be resource-intensive, requiring significant time and effort to thoroughly investigate each component of complex systems. Organizations must balance the benefits of a thorough FMEA process with the resources available, making it critical to prioritize based on the context and severity of identified risks.

10.3.1 Typical Hydrogen Pipeline Failure Modes

In the transport of hydrogen through pipelines, understanding the various failure modes is crucial for preventing incidents and ensuring safety. Hydrogen pipelines have unique characteristics that differentiate their failure modes from those of traditional natural gas pipelines. Given hydrogen's low density and high diffusivity, its mechanisms of failure are critical to address. A few of them are shown in Fig. 10.3.

10.3.2 Consequences of Hydrogen Pipeline Failures

The consequences of failures in hydrogen pipelines can be severe, encompassing both safety and environmental issues. When hydrogen leaks occur, they can lead to dangerous situations, including fires and explosions, due to hydrogen's highly

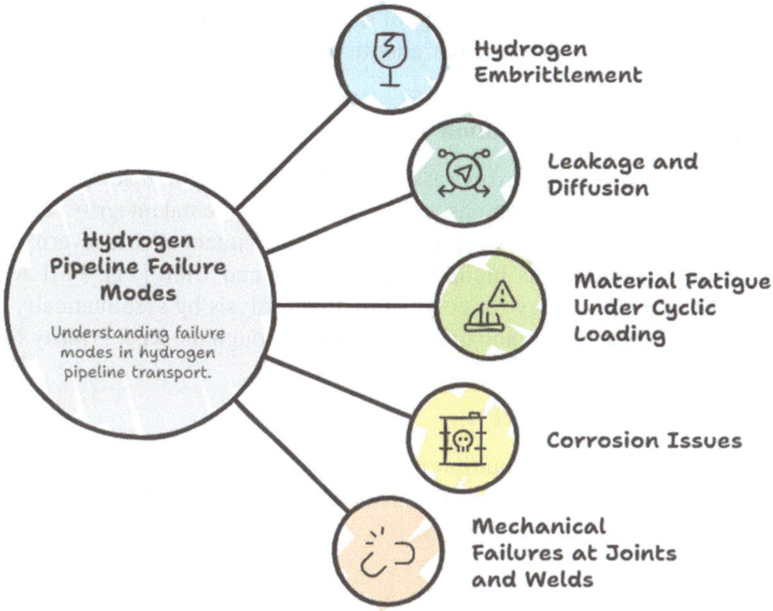

Fig. 10.3 Exploring hydrogen pipeline failure modes

flammable nature. As indicated by Russo et al. [9], the failure of a hydrogen pipeline poses significant threats to human life and can cause extensive damage to buildings in the vicinity. Hydrogen flames are nearly invisible, and their high diffusion rate can result in rapidly spreading gas clouds, posing challenges for both detection and containment.

The environmental consequences of hydrogen leaks can disrupt local ecosystems and potentially contribute to greenhouse gas emissions if not effectively managed, although hydrogen itself does not directly contribute to greenhouse gases. With the increased deployment of hydrogen as an energy carrier, understanding and mitigating such risks is vital for regulatory compliance and public safety. The increasing incidence of hydrogen-blended natural gas pipelines further complicates risk management, as discussed by Wang et al. [10], who analyze the potential cumulative effects of hydrogen and natural gas on pipeline integrity.

10.4 Risk Prioritization and Risk Matrix Development

Risk prioritization is a crucial aspect of risk management that determines the order in which risks should be addressed based on their potential impact and likelihood of occurrence. In the context of the hydrogen industry, particularly with hydrogen pipelines, effective prioritization is vital for ensuring safety and operational integrity.

This section discusses the methodology of risk prioritization, including the development of a risk matrix, with particular attention to the application of Failure Modes and Effects Analysis (FMEA).

Understanding Risk Prioritization

Risk prioritization processes involve assessing identified risks and determining which pose the greatest threat to operations, safety, and environmental integrity. This procedure generally includes two key components: the assessment of risk severity and the likelihood of occurrence. As highlighted by Testik and Unlu [11], FMEA serves as one effective methodology for conducting this analysis by systematically identifying potential failure modes and quantifying risk through the Risk Priority Number (RPN).

1. **Risk Priority Number (RPN)**

The RPN is calculated by multiplying three factors: the severity (S) of the failure mode, the likelihood of occurrence (O), and the detectability (D) of the failure. The formula can be represented as follows:

$$RPN = S \times O \times D$$

Higher RPN values indicate more critical failure modes that require immediate attention. For example, a failure mode with a severity of 9, an occurrence rating of 4, and a detection rating of 2 would yield an RPN of 72, suggesting a high priority for mitigation efforts.

Development of a Risk Matrix

A risk matrix is a visual tool that allows risk assessors to plot risks based on their severity and likelihood of occurrence, facilitating a clearer understanding of risk levels at a glance. The risk matrix typically consists of a two-dimensional grid where one axis represents the probability (likelihood of occurrence) and the other represents the consequence (severity of the risk).

2. **Framework for Risk Matrix Creation**

The development of a risk matrix involves several steps:

- **Defining Risk Categories**: The first step is to categorize risks according to their nature and potential breaches, such as physical hazards, operational risks, or environmental risks associated with pipelines. This categorization helps in systematically mapping risks pertinent to hydrogen transportation.
- **Establishing Severity and Likelihood Levels**: A clear scale for assessing severity (the consequences of failure) and likelihood (the probability of occurrence) should be established. This could be a simple scale, such as low, medium, and high, or a more detailed numerical scale from 1 to 5 or 1 to 10. This ensures consistency in risk assessments across the organization.

- **Plotting Risks on the Matrix**: Once risks are assessed based on the established criteria, they can be plotted onto the matrix. For instance, a risk categorized as having significant consequences (e.g., severe failure resulting in a gas leak explosion) and high likelihood (e.g., frequent operational stress on pipeline materials) would be placed in the high-risk zone of the matrix.

Integrating FMEA with Risk Assessment

FMEA can significantly enhance the risk prioritization process when integrated into risk matrix development. The incorporation of detection times into their FMEA processes, which directly affect risk evaluations. By including detection capabilities in the risk assessment, organizations can enhance their ability to intervene before failures occur.

Integrating fuzzy logic, as demonstrated by Deng and Jiang [12] in their study on FMEA, offers a more nuanced approach to risk evaluation by addressing uncertainties associated with human judgment and vague data. Using fuzzy inference systems in conjunction with traditional FMEA enhances the accuracy of evaluations and allows for more precise prioritization outcomes.

10.4.1 Scoring Criteria and Thresholds

In risk assessment, especially within the context of hydrogen pipeline safety, establishing scoring criteria and thresholds is essential for effectively prioritizing risks and making informed decisions. Scoring criteria define the method of evaluation for risks, while thresholds delineate the levels at which risks become unacceptable and necessitate intervention. This section delineates the scoring criteria commonly utilized in risk assessments, particularly in industries dealing with hazardous materials, along with the thresholds that guide decision-making processes.

Scoring Criteria

1. **Severity (S)**: The severity rating assesses the potential impact or consequence of a failure mode on safety, environment, and operations. It is typically characterized on a numerical scale where higher scores indicate more severe consequences. For hydrogen pipelines, severity could include categories such as:
    - **1 (Insignificant)**: No significant impact on operations; minor inconvenience.
    - **2 (Minor)**: Minor injuries, small leaks, or transient environmental impacts.
    - **3 (Moderate)**: Significant operational disruption or moderate injuries requiring first aid.
    - **4 (Major)**: Major injuries requiring hospitalization or significant environmental damage.
    - **5 (Catastrophic)**: Fatalities, major environmental disaster, or extensive infrastructure damage.

2. **Likelihood of Occurrence (O)**: This criterion evaluates the probability of a risk occurring. It is often assessed on a scale from low to high, with corresponding numerical assignments. For instance:
   - **1 (Rare)**: Unlikely to occur; less than a 5% chance.
   - **2 (Unlikely)**: Could occur at some time; 5–20% chance.
   - **3 (Possible)**: Might occur occasionally; 20–50% chance.
   - **4 (Likely)**: Will probably occur; 50–80% chance.
   - **5 (Almost Certain)**: Expected to occur in most circumstances; more than 80% chance.
3. **Detection (D)**: The detection rating evaluates the likelihood of detecting a failure mode before it results in a significant consequence. This aspect is crucial in risk analysis as it determines the effectiveness of monitoring and management systems.
   - **1 (Certain)**: Very likely to be detected before failure occurs.
   - **2 (Somewhat Likely)**: Likely to be detected with some monitoring efforts.
   - **3 (Moderately Likely)**: Detection is possible but uncertain.
   - **4 (Unlikely)**: Low chance of detection prior to failure.
   - **5 (Rarely Detected)**: Very difficult to detect until after significant consequences occur.

Thresholds for Action

After calculating the RPN for identified risks, it is essential to establish thresholds that dictate when action must be taken. These thresholds offer guidance on prioritizing interventions or improvements based on the assessed risk levels. Typical threshold levels may include:

- **RPN < 40 (Low Risk)**: Risks falling into this category may be acceptable with routine monitoring and do not warrant immediate action.
- **RPN 40–100 (Moderate Risk)**: Risks in this range should be closely monitored and may require consideration for mitigation measures. Organizations may choose to implement enhanced monitoring systems and preventive controls.
- **RPN > 100 (High Risk)**: Risks categorized as high risk require immediate attention and action. This might involve implementing corrective measures, redesigning processes, or initiating a management plan to reduce risk exposure.

10.4.2 Risk Tolerance Levels

In the risk assessment framework, particularly applicable to the hydrogen industry and the management of hydrogen pipelines, establishing risk tolerance levels is essential for guiding decision-making processes. Risk tolerance refers to the degree of variability in outcomes that an organization or individual is willing to accept while pursuing objectives. It is a critical component in the development of safety measures, regulatory compliance, and overall risk management strategies. This section outlines the concept of risk tolerance, its significance in assessing risks associated with hydrogen pipelines, and methodologies for establishing tolerance levels.

Risk tolerance can be defined as the willingness of decision-makers to accept the inherent uncertainties and potential negative outcomes associated with different actions. In contexts such as public health and safety, understanding risk tolerance is crucial for determining acceptable levels of risk exposure. As emphasized by Houtven et al. [13], risk tolerance is context-dependent and can vary significantly across individuals and groups, making it important to tailor risk management strategies accordingly.

Risk tolerance levels can influence stakeholder acceptance of risk management decisions, impacting the overall effectiveness of implemented strategies. For instance, Veazie et al. [14] indicate that factors such as regulatory focus can influence individual risk tolerance, which in turn affects their decision-making behavior. This variability highlights the importance of defining quantitative and qualitative measures of risk tolerance across different stakeholders involved in hydrogen pipeline operations.

Establishing Risk Tolerance Levels

Establishing clear risk tolerance levels involves a systematic approach to quantifying acceptable risks associated with hydrogen pipeline operations. The following steps are critical in this process:

1. **Stakeholder Engagement**: Engaging stakeholders—including regulatory bodies, operational personnel, and community representatives—helps gather diverse perspectives on acceptable risk levels. Participation from a wide range of stakeholders leads to more comprehensive assessments and promotes transparency in decision-making.
2. **Quantitative Measures**: Quantitative assessment of risk tolerance can involve statistical methods to determine thresholds for acceptable risk levels. For instance, metrics such as Value at Risk (VaR) can be applied to financial components of hydrogen projects.
3. **Utilization of Risk Matrices**: Implementing a risk matrix aids in visualizing where specific risk scenarios fall within acceptable boundaries. By categorizing risks based on their severity and likelihood, organizations can easily identify which risks are above or below their established tolerance levels.
4. **Benchmarking**: Organizations can benchmark against industry standards and best practices to help define appropriate risk tolerance levels. Drawing from literature and existing frameworks informs risk thresholds that have been validated in similar contexts.
5. **Scenario Analysis**: Engaging in scenario analysis helps organizations test the limits of their risk tolerance under various operational conditions. This practice is essential in the hydrogen industry, where the characteristics of hydrogen necessitate adaptive strategies to manage its risks effectively.

Implications for the Hydrogen Industry

In the context of hydrogen pipelines, risk tolerance levels must account for the unique properties of hydrogen, including its flammability and the potential for embrittlement in materials. Establishing appropriate risk tolerance levels is critical for ensuring worker safety, protecting the environment, and maintaining public trust in hydrogen transport infrastructure.

Research conducted by Jibril and Shaban [15] highlights that defining acceptable risk levels can facilitate informed decision-making in the management of construction and industrial risks, aligning closely with safety protocols relevant to the hydrogen industry. Moreover, while the concept of risk aversion, noted in some financial contexts, does inform safety assessments, it is essential to distinguish between individual risk perceptions and broader collective risk tolerance in infrastructure management.

10.5 Risk Assessment Frameworks for Hydrogen Pipelines

Risk assessment frameworks are essential for managing the complexities and inherent hazards associated with hydrogen pipelines. As the hydrogen industry evolves and expands, developing robust frameworks becomes increasingly critical, given the unique characteristics of hydrogen as a gas. Hydrogen's small molecular size and high diffusivity, combined with its flammability, necessitate rigorous risk evaluation methods to ensure safety.

A comprehensive risk assessment framework for hydrogen pipelines typically entails several stages, as depict Fig. 10.4, including risk identification, risk analysis, risk evaluation, and risk mitigation planning. Initial stages involve identifying potential hazards, which may include leakage, mechanical failure, and the risk of hydrogen embrittlement in pipeline materials. Following hazard identification, the risks are analyzed based on their potential consequences and the probabilities of occurrence.

The development of a risk matrix is a vital aspect of this framework, providing a visual representation of risks based on their severity and likelihood of occurrence. The matrix enables stakeholders to prioritize risks, facilitating targeted risk management efforts. One critical consideration in creating an effective risk matrix for hydrogen pipelines is the establishment of suitable scoring criteria to evaluate identified risks.

In forming risk matrices specifically for hydrogen pipelines, various studies have focused on developing criteria that account for the unique properties and threats associated with hydrogen transport. For instance, Gu et al. [16] propose that the severity of potential consequences, such as gas leaks or explosions, should be evaluated along with the likelihood of occurrence, emphasizing the importance of incorporating specific metrics reflecting the operational environment of hydrogen pipelines. However, the relevance of this study to hydrogen pipeline risk assessment is limited as it primarily discusses natural gas systems.

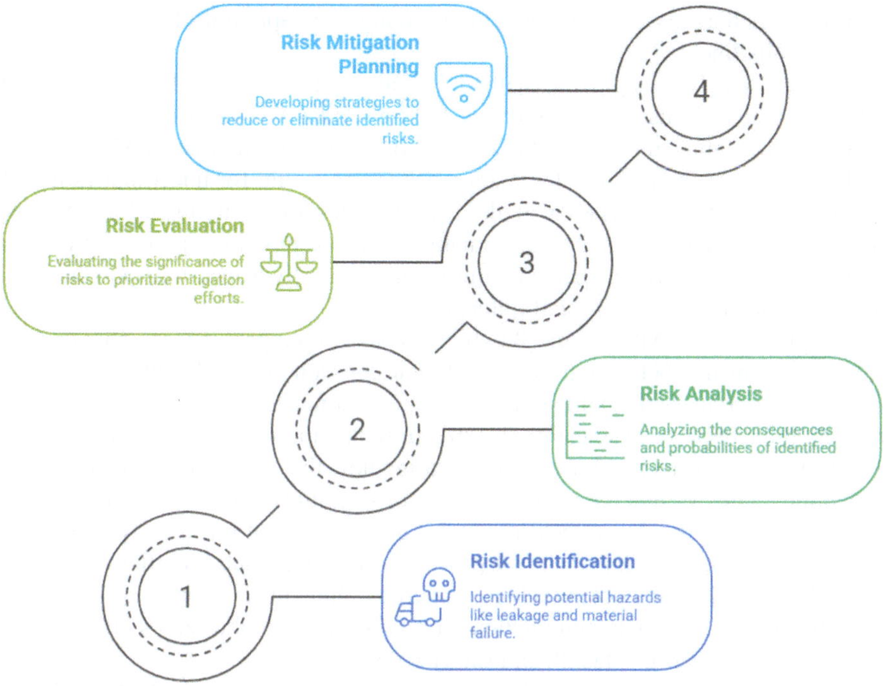

Fig. 10.4 Risk assessment framework for hydrogen pipelines

Once potential risks have been identified and quantified, risk tolerance levels play an essential role in determining which risks are acceptable and which require immediate intervention. Determining the organization's risk tolerance is vital to minimizing adverse consequences while enabling optimal operational performance. As detailed by Bęben and Steliga [17], clear guidelines regarding risk tolerance levels help organizations navigate the inherent uncertainties associated with pipeline transmission, including hydrogen, delineating acceptable and intolerable risk thresholds.

10.5.1 Hazard Identification and Risk Analysis Methods

One of the prominent methods used in risk assessment is the Hazard Identification and Risk Assessment (HIRA) process. This method is particularly well-suited for the hydrogen industry, as it facilitates the identification of potential hazards, assessment of risks, and implementation of control measures. Anis and Luthfan highlight [18] that HIRA effectively provides an organized approach to safety management by enabling practitioners to systematically evaluate workplace hazards in specific industries, such as plastic recycling, emphasizing its adaptability for application in hydrogen pipelines.

Another widely recognized method is Failure Modes and Effects Analysis (FMEA), which focuses on identifying failure modes within systems and evaluating their potential impacts. In the context of hydrogen pipelines, FMEA can be modified to incorporate fuzzy logic approaches to account for uncertainties in risk assessment. Research by Hassan et al. [19] illustrates how a modified FMEA using fuzzy rule bases can enhance hazard identification for pipelines, particularly in the petroleum industry, which shares commonalities with hydrogen transport in terms of risks associated with leaks and failures.

Complementing FMEA is the Bowtie analysis, which provides insights into the causal relationships between hazards and their consequences. This method emphasizes the importance of establishing barriers and controls to prevent incidents and mitigate their impacts. Alencar et al. [20] study the application of Bowtie analysis specifically for subsea pipelines, demonstrating how the technique can map out risk mitigation strategies that are applicable to hydrogen infrastructure as well.

The Job Safety Analysis (JSA) method is also significant for identifying hazards and assessing risks associated with job processes. This approach classifies work activities to better understand potential hazard sources. Djunaidi and Umami [21] validate the applicability of JSA in conjunction with HIRA and emphasize its effectiveness in assessing occupational health and safety risks.

Numerical simulations and modeling contribute significantly to better hazard identification. Hu et al. [22] emphasize the value of simulations in studying the dispersion of hydrogen in pipeline environments, allowing for the anticipation of potential hazards under various scenarios.

References

1. Khan S, Haleem A, Khan MI (2024) A risk assessment framework using neutrosophic theory for the halal supply chain under an uncertain environment. Arab Gulf J Sci Res 42(3):852–870
2. Ramzan N, Compart F, Witt W (2007) Methodology for the generation and evaluation of safety system alternatives based on extended Hazop. Process Safety Progress 26(1):35–42
3. Jabbari M et al (2021) Risk assessment of fire, explosion and release of toxic gas of Siri–Assalouyeh sour gas pipeline using fuzzy analytical hierarchy process. Heliyon 7(8)
4. Fuentes-Bargues JL et al (2017) Risk analysis of a fuel storage terminal using HAZOP and FTA. Int J Environ Res Public Health 14(7):705
5. Eltahan FM et al (2024) Applying a semi-quantitative risk assessment on petroleum production unit. Sci Rep 14(1):7603
6. Dang X et al (2025) Risk Assessment of hydrogen-powered aircraft: an integrated HAZOP and fuzzy dynamic bayesian network framework. Sensors 25(10):3075
7. Felseghi R-A et al (2019) Hydrogen fuel cell technology for the sustainable future of stationary applications. Energies 12(23):4593
8. Sotoodeh K, Gudmestad OT (2023) Valve design considerations in liquid hydrogen systems to prevent failure. Int J Interact Des Manuf (IJIDeM) 17(3):1429–1441
9. Russo P, De Marco A, Parisi F (2020) Assessment of the damage from hydrogen pipeline explosions on people and buildings. Energies 13(19):5051

10. Wang A et al (2021) Study on hydrogen permeation behavior of X80 steel under AC stray current interference. Anti-Corros Methods Mater 68(2):64–76
11. Testik OM, Unlu ET (2023) Fuzzy FMEA in risk assessment for test and calibration laboratories. Qual Reliab Eng Int 39(2):575–589
12. Deng X, Jiang W (2017) Fuzzy risk evaluation in failure mode and effects analysis using a D numbers based multi-sensor information fusion method. Sensors 17(9):2086
13. Van Houtven G et al (2011) Eliciting benefit–risk preferences and probability-weighted utility using choice-format conjoint analysis. Med Decis Making 31(3):469–480
14. Veazie PJ et al (2014) Regulatory focus affects physician risk tolerance. Health Psychol Res 2(2):1621
15. Jibril A, Shaban BA (2021) Risk management in construction projects in Somalia. Int J Adv Eng, Sci Appl 2(2):38–41
16. Gu S et al (2025) Optimal design of hydrogen-blended natural gas pipeline network considering separation systems. AIChE J 71(2):e18648
17. Bęben D, Steliga T (2023) Monitoring and preventing failures of transmission pipelines at oil and natural gas plants. Energies 16(18):6640
18. Anis M, Luthfan HA (2024) Evaluation of OHS practices based on work accident risk analysis using HIRA, FTA, and WISE methods (case study: plastic recycling business X). In: E3S web of conferences 517:15005. EDP Sciences
19. Hassan S et al (2022) Modified FMEA hazard identification for cross-country petroleum pipeline using fuzzy rule base and approximate reasoning. J Loss Prev Process Ind 74:104616
20. Alencar M et al (2023) Risk identification and bowtie analysis for risk management of subsea pipelines. In: 33rd European safety and reliability conference
21. Djunaidi M, Umami H (2024) Occupational health and safety analysis using job safety analysis and hazard identification risk assessment and risk control methods. In: E3S web of conferences 517:15003. EDP Sciences
22. Hu D et al (2024) Comprehensive review of hydrogen leakage in relation to fuel cell vehicles and hydrogen refueling stations: status, challenges, and future prospects. Energy Fuels 38(6):4803–4835

Chapter 11
Quantitative Risk Assessment (QRA)

This chapter provides a comprehensive overview of Quantitative Risk Assessment (QRA) as applied to hydrogen pipelines, emphasizing its role in ensuring operational safety and informed decision-making. The chapter begins with the fundamentals of QRA, outlining key methodologies and modeling approaches, along with essential data requirements and assumptions necessary for robust risk analysis. It then delves into probabilistic models for pipeline failures, highlighting the use of statistical failure data, relevant probability distributions, and advanced simulation techniques such as Monte Carlo and Bayesian models to characterize failure scenarios.

The chapter discusses risk metrics and decision-making criteria, focusing on frequency-consequence analysis and frameworks for risk acceptance and cost–benefit evaluation of mitigation measures. The final section explores the integration of QRA with integrity management practices, illustrating how QRA supports inspection and maintenance planning and facilitates effective risk communication to stakeholders. Collectively, the chapter presents QRA as a critical tool in managing the unique challenges of hydrogen pipeline systems, balancing safety, reliability, and economic considerations.

11.1 Fundamentals of QRA for Pipelines

To properly assess the risks related to pipelines, it is imperative to establish a comprehensive understanding of both qualitative and quantitative assessment methods. QRA integrates multiple analytical techniques, including probabilistic modeling and Bayesian networks, which help in transcending traditional evaluation formats [1]. These methodologies allow for the quantification of risks through detailed data analysis, enabling stakeholders to determine the likelihood of pipeline failures and the potential impacts thereof [2]. The effective employment of these methods is crucial,

M. Hussain et al., *Hydrogen Pipeline Integrity*, Green Energy and Technology,
https://doi.org/10.1007/978-981-95-5609-0_11

as pipelines are inherently vulnerable to various failures, including leaks and ruptures, which can have catastrophic consequences for public safety and the environment.

Contemporary QRA frameworks often utilize methodologies such as Fault Tree Analysis and Event Tree Analysis for systematic risk breakdown [3]. These analyses facilitate the identification and assessment of multiple risk scenarios, estimating both the probabilities of these events occurring and their potential consequences. For instance, researchers have applied these frameworks to evaluate the risks associated with urban gas pipelines, focusing on factors like population density and the structural integrity of pipelines. Such assessments provide critical insights into risk distribution and implications for infrastructure management strategies.

The reliability of QRA outputs can be further enhanced through real-time data integration, allowing for dynamic risk assessments that adapt to changes in conditions or operational contexts. This has become increasingly relevant, particularly in light of the rapid evolution of pipeline systems and technologies, which introduces new risks and uncertainties that traditional QRA methodologies may not fully account for [4].

The deployment of Advanced Quantitative Risk Analysis (AQRA) methodologies, which encompass sophisticated simulation techniques and data analytics, is also on the rise. This approach enables the evaluation of the interaction between severe weather events, geological conditions, and pipeline integrity [5]. Through these advanced assessments, better emergency response protocols can be formed, enhancing overall safety and preparedness in crisis scenarios.

The understanding and improvement of QRA practices are inherently linked to the need for a culturally embedded safety ethos within organizations. Cultivating a safety culture that prioritizes proactive risk management can substantially mitigate the risks associated with pipeline operations. Training and continuous education surrounding QRAs and risk management practices can empower stakeholders to make informed decisions that enhance pipeline safety.

11.1.1 Methodology and Modeling Approaches

One foundational methodology utilized within QRA paradigms is Fault Tree Analysis (FTA). This analytical tool evaluates the probability of a specific failure event, identified as the top event, by breaking it down into contributory basic events. The probability of each basic event can be calculated based on historical data or expert judgment, allowing for a comprehensive understanding of the pathways that lead to potential system failures [6]. Integrating FTA into pipeline risk assessments offers a clear visual representation of failure events and their interdependencies, thus facilitating better communication among stakeholders and decision-makers.

Event Tree Analysis (ETA) complements FTA by focusing on the consequences of a primary failure event. Following an initiating accident, ETA models the potential resulting scenarios and their probabilities, enabling a thorough evaluation of the

Table 11.1 Comparison of fault tree analysis (FTA) and event tree analysis (ETA) in pipeline risk assessment

Aspect	Fault tree analysis (FTA)	Event tree analysis (ETA)
Focus	Identifies **causes** of system failures	Explores **consequences** of initiating events
Approach	Deductive (top-down)	Inductive (forward-looking)
Starting point	Undesired system failure	Initiating accident or primary failure
Outcome	Provides insight into root causes and failure paths	Models possible scenarios and their probabilities
Integration benefit	When combined with ETA, gives a **holistic view** of causes and consequences	When combined with FTA, enables **comprehensive risk assessment** with downstream impacts

various consequences stemming from a single failure. Table 11.1 shows comparison of Fault Tree Analysis (FTA) and Event Tree Analysis (ETA) in Pipeline Risk Assessment. By combining FTA and ETA, pipeline operators can gain a holistic understanding of both the causes of failures and their downstream impacts. This approach also allows for the incorporation of real-time data, enhancing the robustness of the risk assessment.

QRA methodologies integrate Monte Carlo simulations to address uncertainties in risk assessments. This technique involves repeated random sampling to compute the probabilities of various outcomes, providing an empirical approach to estimating the risk associated with pipeline operations. Through the Monte Carlo method, assessors can analyze the impact of variability in key parameters, such as pressure, temperature, and material properties, on the likelihood and consequences of pipeline failure [7]. The ability to simulate numerous scenarios enhances the reliability of the results and supports effective decision-making strategies for mitigating identified risks.

The application of Geographic Information Systems (GIS) in conjunction with QRA provides another dimension to pipeline risk modeling. By spatially analyzing risk factors such as population density, environmental sensitivity, and proximity to infrastructure, GIS technology enables stakeholders to visualize and prioritize risks according to geographical considerations. This spatial dimension can significantly enhance emergency management and response planning, allowing for informed decision-making regarding pipeline operations and incident response strategies.

11.1.2 Data Requirements and Assumptions

The successful implementation of Quantitative Risk Assessment (QRA) for pipelines hinges on the rigorous collection and application of data, alongside clearly defined assumptions that guide the assessment methodologies. Data requirements in QRA pertain to quantitative parameters that characterize pipeline operations, environmental conditions, and historical failure incidents, while assumptions are the underlying foundations upon which the analysis is predicated.

Data regarding pipeline attributes, including material specifications, age, diameter, wall thickness, and operating pressure, form the backbone of any QRA [8]. The performance of models that predict the likelihood of pipeline failures—including the impact of environmental factors on structural integrity—depends crucially on the accuracy of such data. For instance, historical records of pipeline fractures and leaks, including failure rates and their causes, provide quantitative inputs that enhance the robustness of the risk models. This data often includes information derived from full-scale experimental studies, which serve both to validate predictive models and to develop new methodologies for risk assessments.

Geographical data plays an essential role in risk assessments. The integration of Geographic Information Systems (GIS) enables the spatial analysis of risks associated with pipeline routes, including factors such as population density, land use, seismic activities, and proximity to water bodies. By mapping these variables, QRA processes can prioritize pipeline segments that are at higher risk due to their environmental contexts. Spatial data fusion models further enhance this understanding by combining various types of information, such as geometric, temporal, and semantic characteristics, allowing for a more detailed risk characterization [9].

11.2 Probabilistic Models for Hydrogen Pipeline Failures

The failure of hydrogen pipelines can pose substantial risks to public safety and infrastructure due to the unique properties of hydrogen as a transported medium, including its high diffusivity, low ignition energy, and the potential for hydrogen embrittlement in pipeline materials. Consequently, a probabilistic modeling approach is critical to effectively assess the likelihood and consequences of hydrogen pipeline failures.

Probabilistic risk assessment (PRA) as shown in Fig. 11.1, provides a structured method for identifying potential failure modes and quantifying the associated risks. Various models, including Fault Tree Analysis (FTA) and Event Tree Analysis (ETA), are often employed within PRA to decompose complex systems and analyze the cascading effects of identified failures. For hydrogen pipelines, specific failure modes such as leakage, rupture, and explosion must be systematically evaluated due to the unique nature of hydrogen.

A multitude of factors influences the failure probabilities of hydrogen pipelines, including material properties, operational pressures, and environmental conditions. For example, Hydrogen-Induced Cracking (HIC) and Sulfide Stress Corrosion Cracking (SSCC) are significant corrosion mechanisms that can diminish the structural integrity of pipeline materials. These mechanisms necessitate the integration of material degradation models into probabilistic assessments. Moreover, studies indicate that accumulating hydrogen within pipeline systems can exacerbate risks

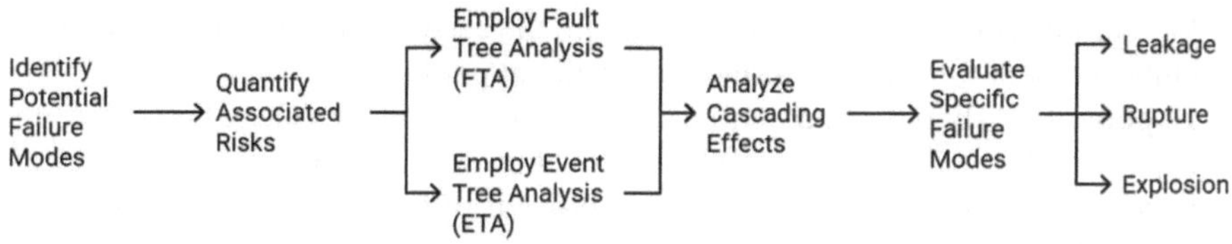

Fig. 11.1 Probabilistic risk assessment frameworks for hydrogen pipelines

associated with internal pressure changes, potentially leading to catastrophic failure if not properly managed [10].

Recent advancements incorporate machine learning techniques alongside traditional probabilistic methods to enhance predictive accuracy regarding pipeline failures. By utilizing Artificial Neural Networks (ANN) or Support Vector Machines (SVM), researchers can analyze large datasets related to historical failures, operational metrics, and material properties to derive predictive models for failure probabilities. These models can be continually updated with real-time operational data, providing a dynamic risk assessment tool.

Bayesian approaches have emerged as a robust method for updating failure probabilities as new information becomes available. These methods enable users to incorporate prior knowledge and continuously learn from operational experiences, particularly valuable in environments characterized by uncertainty and variability in pipeline integrity [11, 12]. Utilizing Bayesian networks facilitates the integration of qualitative assessments with quantitative data, yielding a comprehensive view of the risk landscape associated with hydrogen pipelines.

11.2.1 Statistical Failure Data and Distributions

Statistical failure data and distributions are vital components of probabilistic modeling for hydrogen pipeline failures. Understanding these elements allows engineers to predict the reliability and operational lifespan of hydrogen pipelines, which is particularly crucial given hydrogen's unique properties and the safety implications associated with its transport.

A variety of statistical distributions are employed to model failure rates in hydrogen pipelines. Among the most commonly used are the Weibull, Exponential, and Gamma distributions, each possessing unique characteristics that make them suitable for different applications in failure rate analysis.

- **Weibull Distribution**: This distribution is particularly powerful in failure analysis due to its flexibility in modeling different types of failure rates. With its scale and shape parameters, the Weibull distribution can represent increasing, constant, or decreasing failure rates, making it adaptable to various failure conditions of hydrogen pipelines. For instance, in the context of hydrogen transport, the

Weibull distribution can effectively capture the early failures related to hydrogen embrittlement followed by a stable operational period.

- **Exponential Distribution**: Often associated with memoryless processes, the exponential distribution is useful for modeling scenarios where the failure rate is constant over time. This simplicity allows it to be easily applied in contexts where detailed historical data is limited. Although hydrogen pipelines may not always exhibit constant failure rates due to varying operational pressures and conditions, the exponential distribution can serve as a preliminary model before more complex modeling is employed.
- **Gamma Distribution**: The gamma distribution provides further flexibility and can model the time until a certain number of failures occur. It can reflect systems where failures are not independent, which is relevant in the context of hydrogen pipelines experiencing concurrent stressors (e.g., environmental and operational stresses). The gamma distribution's shape parameter allows it to model the transition from lower to higher failure rates as pipelines age or as operational demands fluctuate.

One noteworthy concept in failure rate analysis is the bathtub curve, which describes the failure rate over a product's life cycle. Initially, products experience rapid failure rates (infant mortality phase), followed by a stable period, and then an increase in failures as products reach the end of their life [13]. This characteristic has been observed in hydrogen pipelines, especially considering the implications of hydrogen embrittlement, which can lead to unforeseen failures after prolonged exposure to high-pressure hydrogen environments.

11.2.2 Simulation Techniques: Monte Carlo and Bayesian Models

In the context of probabilistic modeling for hydrogen pipeline failures, simulation techniques such as Monte Carlo simulation and Bayesian models offer powerful tools for risk assessment and reliability analysis. These methodologies assist researchers and engineers in quantifying the uncertainties associated with hydrogen transport and predicting potential failure scenarios more effectively. Table 11.2 discusses the principles, applications, and advantages of simulation techniques as they pertain to hydrogen pipeline failures.

Table 11.2 Simulation techniques for hydrogen pipeline failures: principles, applications, and advantages

Technique	Principles	Applications in hydrogen pipelines	Advantages
Monte Carlo simulation (MCS)	Stochastic modeling using random sampling to assess uncertainty in input parameters	Evaluates probabilities of failure modes (leaks, ruptures). Reliability analysis of corroded pipelines. Models various distributions (Weibull, Normal) to characterize failure rates	Flexible; accommodates complex interactions; captures uncertainty; supports maintenance prioritization
Subset simulation	Advanced variant of MCS focusing on rare-event probability estimation. Uses progressive sampling from failure subsets	Estimation of low-probability but catastrophic failures in hydrogen pipelines	Reduces computational cost; efficient modeling of rare events; maintains accuracy
Bayesian models	Probabilistic framework incorporating prior knowledge, expert opinion, and real-time updates	Predicts corrosion rates; models dependencies among failure modes; updates probabilities as new data emerges	Dynamic; adaptive with new data; enables proactive risk management
Integration with machine learning (ML)	Combines data-driven ML models with probabilistic simulations (MCS/ Bayesian)	Predictive modeling of failure mechanisms; optimization of pipeline integrity management systems	Improves robustness; identifies hidden patterns; shifts management from reactive to proactive
Real-world applications and case studies	Application of simulation models to real hydrogen pipeline and material studies	Failure probability of natural gas pipelines converted for hydrogen; modeling hydrogen-induced cracking (HIC) in steels	Provides actionable insights; guides infrastructure upgrades; supports preventative design

11.3 Risk Metrics and Decision-Making Criteria

The development and implementation of effective risk metrics and decision-making criteria are vital for ensuring the safety and reliability of hydrogen pipelines. As the use of hydrogen as an energy carrier gains traction, particularly through the repurposing of existing natural gas pipelines, establishing comprehensive risk assessments is critical to guide infrastructure management decisions. Figure 11.2 explore various risk metrics, decision-making criteria, and its implications for hydrogen pipeline safety through statistical analysis and qualitative assessments, utilizing significant references from the literature.

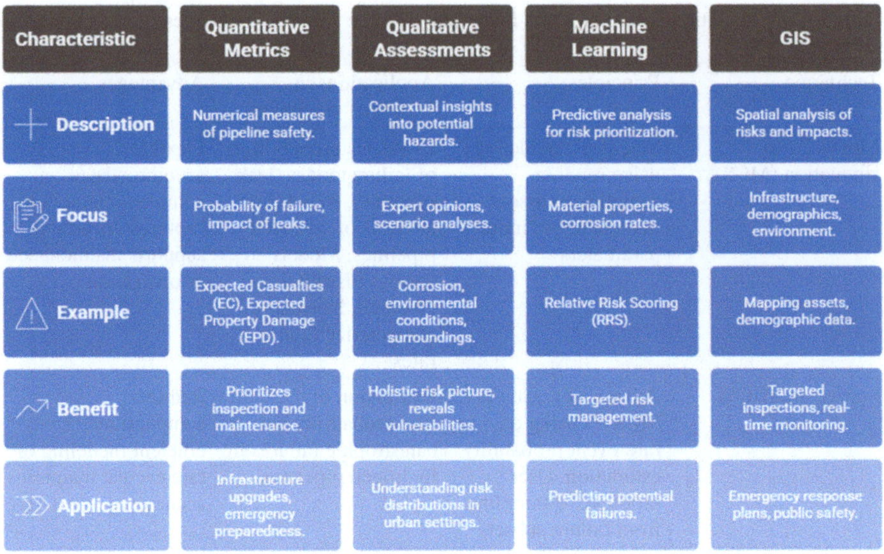

Fig. 11.2 Risk assessment methods for hydrogen pipelines

Parameters like corrosion, environmental conditions, and surroundings of the pipeline can be central to qualitative assessments. For instance, pipeline operators may consider demographic variables, building structures, and socio-economic factors to inform their understanding of risk distributions within urban settings [14]. These qualitative assessments highlight the intricacies of risk interactions and can drive action in pipeline management by revealing underlying vulnerable components that may not be apparent through numbers alone.

Establishing decision-making criteria based on risk metrics is essential for effective pipeline management. These criteria should consider the acceptable level of risk associated with pipeline operations and the necessary response actions when risks exceed predetermined thresholds. The development of risk acceptance criteria plays a key role in this process, as outlined by Zhang et al. [15], distinguishing between acceptable and unacceptable risk levels based on quantitative assessments of potential impacts.

Utilizing a structured decision-making approach that integrates quantitative and qualitative assessments helps pipeline operators navigate complex situations where multiple factors might impact risk levels. For example, criteria may involve thresholds set for the likelihood of incidents based on pipeline material integrity, operational practices, and environmental conditions. This "risk-based" approach ensures that resources are allocated efficiently to mitigate the most pressing risks [15].

11.3.1 Frequency and Consequence Analysis

Understanding the frequency and consequence analysis is integral for managing the risks associated with hydrogen pipelines. This analysis is crucial for decision-making processes, enabling effective risk mitigation strategies and ensuring safe hydrogen transport. Figure 11.3 shows Hydrogen Pipeline Risk Management Cycle.

Frequency and consequence analyses play complementary roles in the assessment of hydrogen pipeline risks. Frequency analysis focuses on estimating how often a failure event is likely to occur within a defined time frame, typically expressed in terms such as probability of failure or mean time between failures. This metric is particularly important for operational decision-making, as it enables pipeline operators to prioritize inspection schedules, maintenance programs, and resource allocation toward segments most vulnerable to failure. The accuracy of frequency estimates depends on the availability and quality of historical incident records, operational monitoring data, and environmental factors that can affect pipeline integrity.

Consequence analysis, by contrast, shifts the focus from likelihood to impact. It evaluates the severity of outcomes once a failure has occurred, considering dimensions such as human safety, environmental damage, and economic disruption. In the case of hydrogen pipelines, where flammability and potential for rapid dispersion elevate the stakes, consequence analysis provides insights into the spatial extent of damage zones, the vulnerability of nearby populations, and the potential for cascading effects on critical infrastructure. These insights are indispensable for emergency planning, regulatory compliance, and the design of mitigation strategies.

When applied together, frequency and consequence analyses allow for a structured, risk-based approach that balances how often failures are expected with how severe their outcomes may be. This dual perspective is essential for decision-making in hydrogen transport, as it ensures that both recurring, lower-impact events and rare but catastrophic failures are considered within a unified framework. A

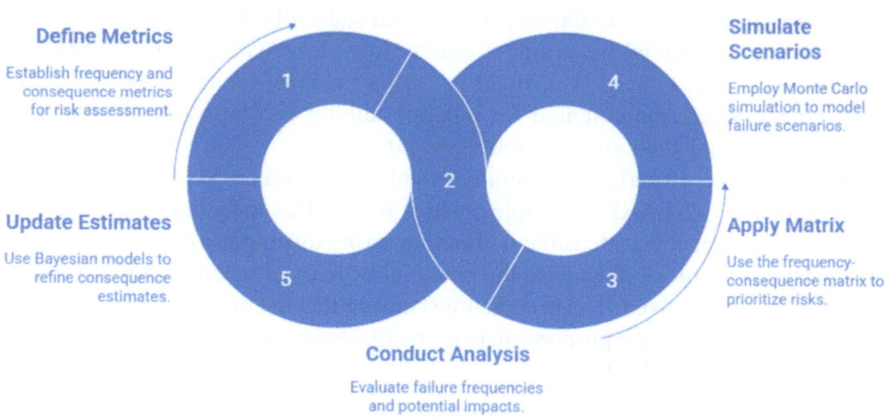

Fig. 11.3 Hydrogen pipeline risk management cycle

Table 11.3 Comparison of frequency versus consequence analysis in hydrogen pipeline risk assessment

Aspect	Frequency analysis	Consequence analysis
Definition	Estimates how often a failure may occur over a given time	Estimates the potential impacts if a failure occurs
Primary goal	Quantify likelihood of failures	Evaluate severity of outcomes
Typical metrics	Failure probability, mean time between failures (MTBF)	Fatality count, economic loss, environmental damage
Data sources	Historical incident data, inspection records, environmental factors	Leak size, population density, proximity to assets, weather conditions
Use in practice	Prioritize maintenance and inspection	Inform emergency planning, zoning, and mitigation

concise comparison of these two analytical perspectives is provided in Table 11.3, which highlights their definitions, goals, typical metrics, data sources, and practical applications.

11.3.2 Risk Acceptance and Mitigation Cost–Benefit

Risk acceptance and mitigation cost–benefit analysis are fundamental components in the decision-making process concerning hydrogen pipelines. As hydrogen infrastructure expands, establishing criteria for acceptable risks and understanding the cost implications of risk mitigation strategies becomes essential for managing public safety and compliance with regulatory standards.

1. **Defining Risk Acceptance**

   Risk acceptance refers to the level of risk that stakeholders (including operators, regulators, and the public) are willing to tolerate in the face of the potential for adverse consequences. This concept is critical in various sectors, including infrastructure management, where the potential for pipeline failures can have significant safety, environmental, and economic repercussions [16, 17].

   Risk acceptance criteria are generally established based on "As Low As Reasonably Practicable" (ALARP) principles, which dictate that risks must be minimized to levels that are as low as feasible without incurring disproportionate costs [18]. In this context, it is crucial to balance the potential benefits of risk mitigation activities against the costs involved. The process must ensure that the financial resources allocated to risk reduction are proportionate to the risk being managed, per the principle of risk proportionality [17].

2. **Cost-Benefit Analysis in Risk Mitigation**

Fig. 11.4 Risk acceptance and mitigation cost–benefit analysis

Cost-benefit analysis (CBA) is employed to evaluate the economic feasibility of implementing risk mitigation measures. By quantifying both the costs associated with preventive measures and the anticipated benefits from reduced risk exposure, organizations can make informed decisions on safety investments as shown in Fig. 11.4.

For hydrogen pipelines, the factors included in the CBA might comprise upfront costs for upgrading pipeline materials, implementing monitoring technologies, and operational costs for maintenance and inspections. Simultaneously, it is essential to estimate the potential financial impacts of pipeline failures, including damages from leaks or explosions, remediation costs, and liabilities associated with public safety. This quantifiable comparison helps stakeholders determine whether the benefits of safety investments justify the associated costs.

When assessing specific mitigation strategies for hydrogen pipelines, it is important to consider the type of technology employed, the pipeline context (urban vs. rural), and the specific failure modes being addressed. For hydrogen, measures may include upgrading pipeline materials to those resistant to hydrogen embrittlement and implementing advanced monitoring systems to enhance safety [19].

A methodology proposed by Sim et al. [17] emphasizes the need to conduct a thorough evaluation of potential mitigation strategies against both their short-term costs and long-term benefits. By employing a multifaceted approach that incorporates statistical failure data, cost analyses, and stakeholder input, operators can make well-founded decisions that enhance pipeline integrity and public safety.

11.4 Integrating QRA with Integrity Management

Integrating Quantitative Risk Assessment (QRA) with integrity management is a pivotal approach to ensuring the safety and reliability of hydrogen pipeline systems, as depict in Fig. 11.5. This integration not only focuses on assessing risks but also places emphasis on maintaining the integrity of pipeline assets throughout their operational lifetime. As hydrogen pipelines are increasingly recognized for their role in sustainable energy initiatives, implementing robust risk management practices is essential for mitigating potential hazards associated with their use.

1. **Understanding Integrity Management**

Integrity management refers to an organization's commitments and actions to ensure pipeline systems operate safely and efficiently over time. It encompasses a holistic view that combines regular inspection, monitoring, maintenance, and

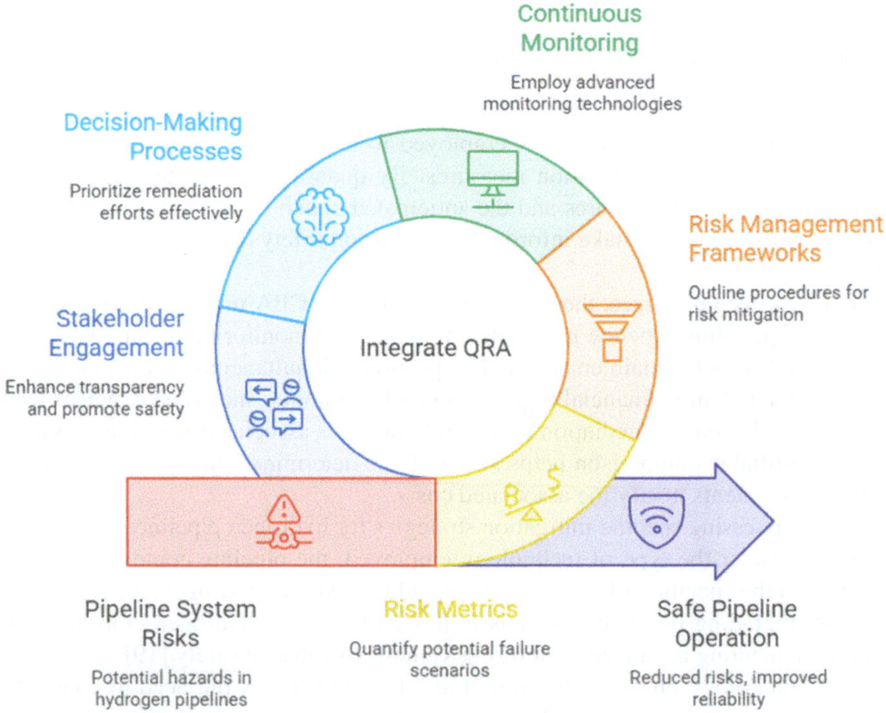

Fig. 11.5 Integrating QRA with integrity management

strategic decision-making aimed at prolonging the service life of pipeline assets and preventing failures. By integrating QRA, integrity management can effectively quantify and prioritize risks associated with hydrogen transport, thereby improving operational resilience.

2. **Risk Metrics for Integrity Management**

To incorporate QRA into integrity management, risk metrics must be established that quantify potential failure scenarios, estimate failure frequencies, and assess the corresponding consequences of those failures. These metrics provide the necessary data to inform decisions regarding maintenance and resource allocation.

Frequency and Consequence Metrics: Metrics such as failure frequency and consequence severity form the backbone of QRA in integrity management. By using these metrics, operators can identify high-risk segments of the pipeline that require immediate attention. This prioritization enhances the allocation of resources towards the most critical infrastructure components, maximizing the impact of maintenance efforts.

Life Cycle Cost Analysis: Life cycle cost metrics, which consider all costs associated with a pipeline from inception to decommissioning, can be integrated into QRA frameworks. This enables stakeholders to identify the most cost-effective strategies for maintaining pipeline integrity over the long term. A thorough understanding of these costs facilitates decision-making about whether to invest in preventive measures or to accept certain risks based on their economic implications.

3. **Implementing Risk Management Frameworks**

The integration of QRA into integrity management often necessitates the development of comprehensive risk management frameworks, see Fig. 11.6. These frameworks should outline procedures for risk identification, assessment, and mitigation that align with organizational goals. Key components include below:

- **Continuous Monitoring and Inspection**: Employing advanced technologies such as remote sensing and smart sensors allows for continuous monitoring of pipeline integrity. By integrating real-time data with QRA, operators can identify potential risks promptly and take corrective action.
- **Decision-Making Processes**: Informed decision-making is central to effective risk management. By using risk metrics, organizations can prioritize remediation efforts and allocate budgetary resources based on the anticipated benefits and risks. This structured approach aids in avoiding unnecessary expenditures and ensures a focus on the most critical integrity challenges.
- **Stakeholder Engagement**: Engaging stakeholders—including regulatory bodies, local communities, and industry partners—in the risk assessment process enhances transparency and promotes a culture of safety and trust. This engagement can lead to more refined risk acceptance thresholds that reflect both operational realities and societal expectations.

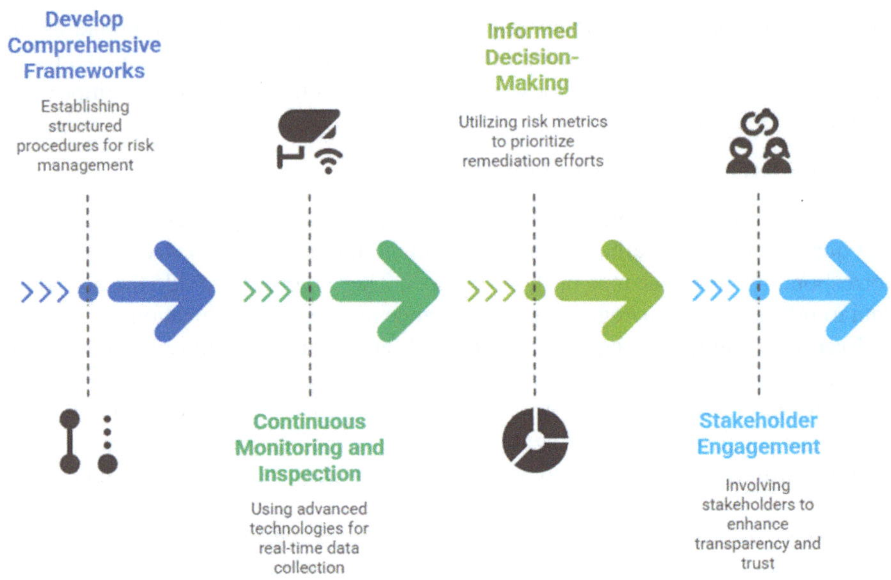

Fig. 11.6 Implementing risk management frameworks

11.4.1 Use in Inspection and Maintenance Planning

Integrating Quantitative Risk Assessment (QRA) into the inspection and maintenance planning of hydrogen pipelines is essential for managing integrity and safety effectively. Figure 11.7 shows Optimizing Hydrogen Pipeline Maintenance.

1. **Risk-Based Inspection and Maintenance Planning**

Risk-Based Inspection (RBI) is an established methodology that aligns inspection and maintenance activities with the identified risks associated with specific pipeline segments. By targeting resources toward high-risk areas, RBI enhances the efficiency of maintenance operations while ensuring safety. According to Ratnayake [20], traditional planning methods relied heavily on prescriptive practices; however, RBI allows for a more dynamic strategy that utilizes risk analysis data to prioritize inspections based on the likelihood of failure and the potential consequences. This adaptability is especially relevant in the context of hydrogen pipelines, where operational challenges can significantly influence failure rates.

2. **Cost-Optimal Inspection Approaches**

Determining the optimal frequency and scope of inspections is a critical element of effective maintenance planning. Akinsanya et al. [21] highlighted the vital role that time variability and uncertainty play in the cost-effective design of inspection schedules. Their findings emphasize the necessity of rational tools to achieve a balance between the costs of inspections and the benefits gained from mitigating potential

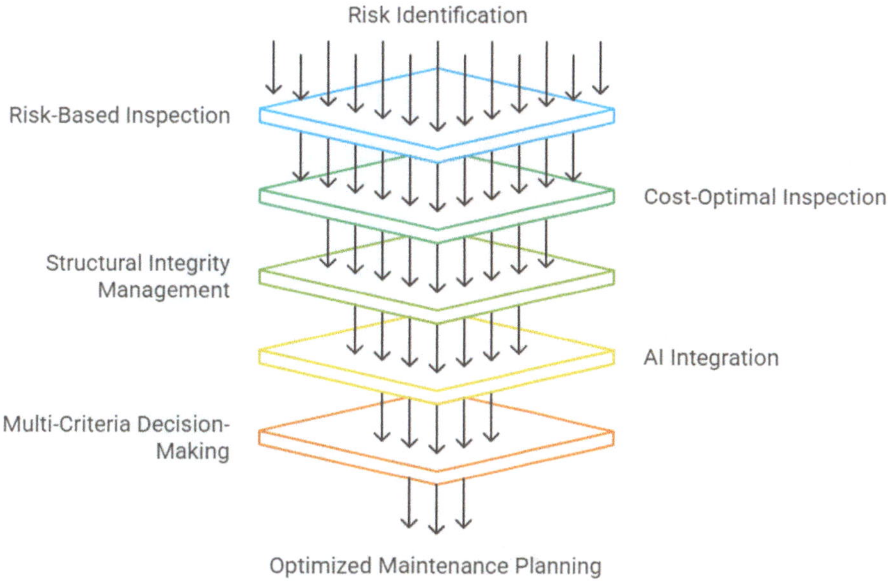

Fig. 11.7 Optimizing hydrogen pipeline maintenance

risks. For hydrogen pipelines, where material degradation may occur due to hydrogen embrittlement, integrating cost analyses of inspections and maintenance planning informs decisions that are both economically viable and focused on operational safety.

3. **Structural Integrity Management Frameworks**

The implementation of structural integrity management frameworks, as discussed by Li and Zou [22], provides a systematic approach to planning inspections and maintenance for hydrogen pipelines. Their research outlines the need for inspection frameworks that consider both historical data and the probabilistic modeling of failure risks. Incorporating such frameworks into maintenance planning allows operators to establish comprehensive inspection strategies that address expected degradation patterns over the life cycle of the pipeline. A Structural Integrity Management Cycle is shown in Fig. 11.8.

The integration of artificial intelligence with RBI, as explored by Akinsanya et al. [21], enhances the predictive capabilities of inspection planning, allowing for adjustments based on real-time data and evolving operational conditions. This approach leads to adaptive maintenance strategies that ensure continuous safety without incurring prohibitive costs.

4. **Multi-Criteria Decision-Making (MCDM)**

Integrating MCDM approaches into QRA for hydrogen pipelines can further refine inspection and maintenance decision-making processes. By evaluating multiple

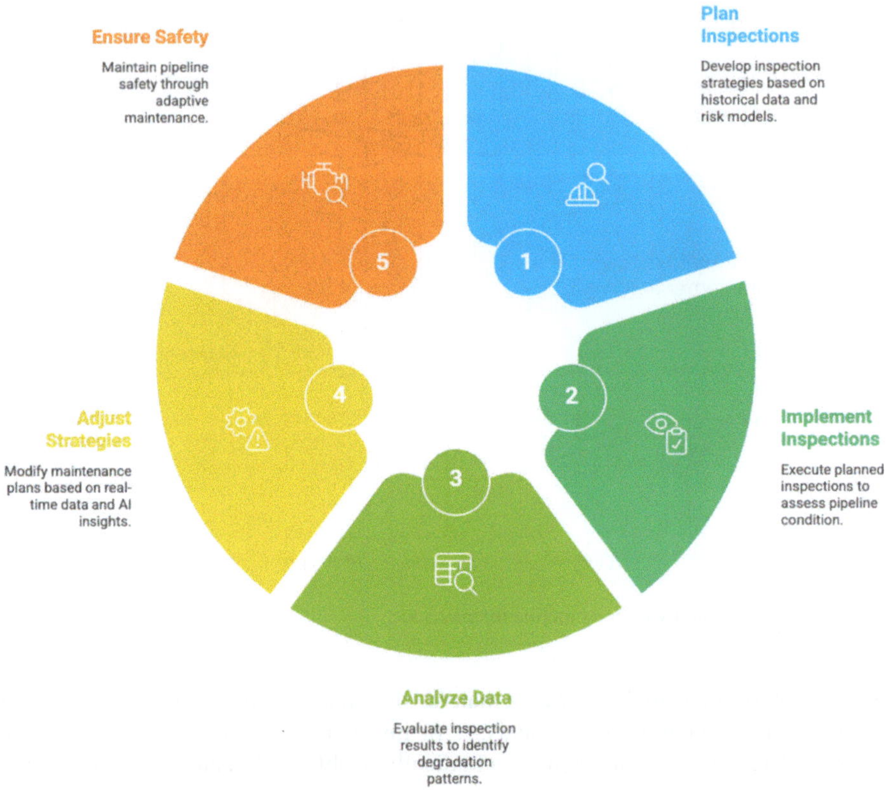

Fig. 11.8 Structural integrity management cycle

criteria—such as risk, cost, resource availability, and operational impact—stakeholders can prioritize inspection plans that unify safety and cost-effectiveness. For instance, Lelo et al. [23] emphasized the importance of proportional hazard modeling within risk-based inspection methodologies, allowing decision-makers to analyze the relationship between risk parameters and maintenance actions.

Implementing frameworks that utilize MCDM allows for systematic balancing of trade-offs and more informed resource allocations. This aligns well with current industry trends toward leveraging predictive analytics to optimize monitoring and maintenance strategies based on dynamic operational conditions.

11.4.2 Communication to Stakeholders

Effective communication with stakeholders is crucial in managing risks associated with hydrogen pipelines and integrating Quantitative Risk Assessment (QRA) into integrity management practices. Stakeholders—including regulatory bodies, local communities, industry partners, and the general public—must be informed and engaged in the decision-making process surrounding hydrogen transportation infrastructure. This section explores strategies for communicating risk assessments, the importance of transparent dialogue, and techniques for fostering stakeholder engagement.

1. **Importance of Stakeholder Communication**

The integration of QRA into risk management frameworks necessitates that stakeholders are informed about potential risks, mitigation strategies, and the rationale behind decisions regarding pipeline operations. Effective communication can build trust and enhance cooperation among parties involved. Conversely, poor communication may lead to misunderstandings, resistance to projects, and diminished public confidence. As the public discourse around hydrogen energy becomes increasingly relevant, addressing stakeholder concerns is essential for developing and maintaining acceptance.

2. **Tailored Communication Strategies**

    1. **Identifying Stakeholder Groups**: The first step in stakeholder communication is identifying key stakeholders that may be affected by or have an interest in hydrogen pipeline operations. These may include:

        - Regulatory authorities tasked with ensuring safety and compliance.
        - Environmental organizations concerned about potential ecological impacts.
        - Local communities living near pipeline routes.
        - Industry partners involved in the construction, operation, and maintenance of hydrogen pipelines.

    2. **Customized Messaging**: Tailoring messages to resonate with different audience groups is paramount. Regulatory agencies might require detailed technical information and risk assessments that align with safety regulations, while local communities may prefer simplified explanations focusing on safety and environmental impacts. Adopting varied approaches to information delivery can bridge the gap between technical language and public understanding, thereby facilitating the effective communication of critical safety information.

3. **Using Visual Tools**

The use of visuals, such as infographics or maps, can significantly enhance the clarity of communications related to hydrogen pipeline risks. Tools like Geographic Information Systems (GIS) can provide visual representations of pipeline routes, potential risk zones, and safety measures in place. Such visual aids facilitate understanding by transforming complex data into accessible and digestible formats.

4. **Engaging Stakeholders Through Dialogue**

1 **Regular Meetings and Workshops**: Hosting informational sessions, workshops, and community meetings allows for open discussions about hydrogen pipeline operations and associated risks. These forums provide stakeholders with opportunities to express their concerns, ask questions, and engage directly with experts—fostering collaboration and transparency. It should be emphasized that the dialogue built on trust and transparency will facilitate a culture of safety in energy operations.

2 **Feedback Mechanisms**: Establishing feedback mechanisms enables stakeholders to provide input on risk assessments and management strategies. Surveys, public forums, and online platforms for discussion can be leveraged to gather insights and refine communication strategies based on community feedback. This level of engagement builds public support and can enhance the legitimacy of hydrogen pipeline initiatives.

5. **Regulatory Compliance and Reporting**

Compliance with regulatory expectations is essential in stakeholder communication. Regular public reports on risk assessments, pipeline inspections, and safety incidents can demonstrate transparency and accountability. Compliance with standards set forth by authorities such as the United States Department of Transportation (DOT) reinforces a company's commitment to safety, allowing stakeholders to monitor operational practices effectively.

6. **Leveraging Technology for Communication**

Modern communication technologies can enhance engagement with stakeholders. Utilizing social media platforms, websites, and mobile applications to disseminate information about hydrogen pipelines allows for real-time updates and broadens access to crucial safety information. Employing digital platforms can improve public outreach efforts, ultimately contributing to a more informed and engaged citizenry.

7. **Crisis Communication Planning**

In the event of an incident involving a hydrogen pipeline, having a robust crisis communication plan is essential. Stakeholders must receive timely and accurate information to maintain trust and mitigate public concerns. Protocols should be established for disseminating relevant information, addressing community responses, and outlining safety steps in resonant and empathetic language.

References

1. Wang X, Duan Q (2019) Improved AHP–TOPSIS model for the comprehensive risk evaluation of oil and gas pipelines. Pet Sci 16(6):1479–1492
2. Jiang F, Dong S (2021) Risk-based integrity model for offshore pipelines subjected to impact loads from falling objects. Proc Inst Mech Eng, Part M: J Eng MaritE Environ 235(2):623–641
3. Qin G et al (2022) An information entropy-based risk assessment method for multiple-media gathering pipelines. J Infrastruct Preserv Resil 3(1):19

4. Dawotola AW, Van Gelder P, Vrijling J (2012) Design for acceptable risk in transportation pipelines. Int J Risk Assess Manag 16(1–3):112–127
5. Sarvanis GC, Karamanos SA (2017) Analytical model for the strain analysis of continuous buried pipelines in geohazard areas. Eng Struct 152:57–69
6. Mouli-Castillo J et al (2021) A quantitative risk assessment of a domestic property connected to a hydrogen distribution network. Int J Hydrogen Energy 46(29):16217–16231
7. Lis Y et al (2012) Comparisons of food and drug administration and european medicines agency risk management implementation for recent pharmaceutical approvals: report of the international society for pharmacoeconomics and outcomes research risk benefit management working group. Value in Health 15(8):1108–1118
8. Acton MR et al (2000) A full scale experimental study of fires following the rupture of natural gas transmission pipelines. In: International pipeline conference. American society of mechanical engineers
9. Asha LN et al (2023) A quantitative approach of measuring sustainability risk in pipeline infrastructure systems. Sustainability 15(19):14229
10. Cerniauskas S et al (2020) Options of natural gas pipeline reassignment for hydrogen: cost assessment for a Germany case study. Int J Hydrogen Energy 45(21):12095–12107
11. Sulaiman NSA et al (2022) Integration of Bayesian network with fuzzy analytical hierarchy process for determining the pipeline conditions. Process Saf Prog 41:S187–S196
12. Li C et al (2023) Dynamic risk assessment of oil and gas pipeline failure based on DBN model. In: Second international conference on applied statistics, computational mathematics, and software engineering (ASCMSE 2023). SPIE
13. Mahmoudi E, Jafari AA (2017) The compound class of linear failure rate-power series distributions: model, properties, and applications. Commun Stat-Simul Comput 46(2):1414–1440
14. Rahimi F et al (2024) Temporal dynamics of urban gas pipeline risks. Sci Rep 14(1):5509
15. Zhang P, Qin G, Wang Y (2019) Risk assessment system for oil and gas pipelines laid in one ditch based on quantitative risk analysis. Energies 12(6):981
16. Liu P, Yang R, Xu Z (2019) How safe is safe enough for self-driving vehicles? Risk Anal 39(2):315–325
17. Sim KB, Lee ML, Wong SY (2022) A review of landslide acceptable risk and tolerable risk. Geoenvironmental Disasters 9(1):3
18. Maselli G et al (2020) Estimation of risk levels for building construction projects. In: International conference on computational science and its applications. Springer
19. Roche CA et al (2019) Chemoprevention acceptance and adherence in women with high-risk breast lesions. Breast J 25(2):190–195
20. Ratnayake RC (2012) Challenges in inspection planning for maintenance of static mechanical equipment on ageing oil and gas production plants: the state of the art. In: International conference on offshore mechanics and arctic engineering. American society of mechanical engineers
21. Akinsanya AO et al (2020) Cost-optimal planning of inspections and maintenance of production tubings subject to scale deterioration. In: International conference on offshore mechanics and arctic engineering. American society of mechanical engineers
22. Li L, Zou G (2024) A system-level reliability growth model for efficient inspection planning of offshore wind farms. J Mar Sci Eng 12(7):1140
23. Lelo NA, Heyns PS, Wannenburg J (2023) Development of an approach to incorporate proportional hazard modelling into a risk-based inspection methodology. J Qual Maint Eng 29(1):265–285

Chapter 12
Mitigation Strategies and Emergency Response

This chapter delves into the comprehensive approaches used to mitigate risks associated with pipeline systems and to enhance organizational preparedness for emergency scenarios. This chapter is structured around four key pillars: preventive mitigation strategies, repair and rehabilitation techniques, emergency response planning, and training and preparedness. Each section provides both theoretical frameworks and practical applications aimed at improving pipeline integrity, safety, and resilience.

The first section, Preventive Mitigation Strategies, examines proactive measures designed to reduce the likelihood of pipeline failures. It covers design and material controls, emphasizing the selection of corrosion-resistant materials, adherence to engineering standards, and incorporation of fail-safe features during the design phase. It also highlights the importance of operational limits and maintenance practices, focusing on pressure and flow monitoring, inspection intervals, and predictive maintenance to identify and address potential issues before they escalate.

In the second section, Repair and Rehabilitation Techniques, the chapter outlines methods for restoring pipeline integrity after damage or deterioration. This includes mechanical repairs and composite wraps, which offer fast, cost-effective solutions for localized defects, and pipeline replacement and upgrades, which are necessary when structural integrity is compromised or when compliance with updated regulatory standards is required. Case studies and performance data are used to illustrate the effectiveness and limitations of each technique.

The third section, Emergency Response Planning, underscores the importance of having a structured and responsive plan in place to address incidents such as leaks, ruptures, or explosions. The chapter discusses leak and rupture detection and isolation technologies, including SCADA systems, pressure sensors, and automated shut-off valves, which enable rapid identification and containment of failures. Additionally, it stresses the value of coordination with local authorities and emergency services, detailing communication protocols, joint response exercises, and mutual aid agreements to ensure a swift and unified response.

M. Hussain et al., *Hydrogen Pipeline Integrity*, Green Energy and Technology,
https://doi.org/10.1007/978-981-95-5609-0_12

The final section, Training and Preparedness, emphasizes human factors in pipeline safety. It covers operator training programs, designed to instill a deep understanding of pipeline systems, emergency protocols, and hazard recognition. The use of simulation is also explored, highlighting its role in scenario-based training, decision-making under pressure, and reinforcing response readiness through realistic, repeatable exercises.

12.1 Preventive Mitigation Strategies

One of the most critical preventive mitigation strategies for hydrogen pipelines is the implementation of robust infrastructure safety measures. According to Lin et al. [1], comprehensive models can assess the potential impact radius of hydrogen pipelines based on jet fire radiation, thus informing safe operational practices and emergency preparedness planning. Effective monitoring mechanisms can be integrated with pipeline infrastructure to detect leaks early and prevent catastrophic failures. Skryabina et al. [2] emphasize the necessity of major incident plans that provide staff with clear operational frameworks to act swiftly and accurately during emergencies, which can reduce the level of stress associated with a major incident. Such frameworks enable quick responses, thereby mitigating the consequences related to incidents in environments with hydrogen infrastructure.

Effective risk assessment methodologies should also be adapted specifically to hydrogen pipelines. Skryabina et al. [2] discuss the importance of examining incident response capabilities in historical contexts, citing significant events like Hurricane Katrina as learning points for future planning. This empirical approach provides insights into how similar methodologies can be utilized to understand and mitigate the risks associated with hydrogen pipeline emergencies. The strategies observed in historical contexts highlight the pressing need for municipalities to implement tailored incident command systems (ICS) that incorporate the unique aspects of hydrogen as a combustible material.

Public engagement and community education also play pivotal roles in mitigating risks associated with hydrogen pipelines. The importance of public health emergency planning that adapts to evolving incident dynamics; through community engagement, preparedness can be improved substantially [3]. Proactive communication campaigns can educate communities on the nature of hydrogen leaks and provide guidelines on safety measures they should observe if an incident occurs. By raising awareness, communities become part of the mitigation effort, rather than passive bystanders.

Another integral aspect of preventive mitigation strategies involves regulatory compliance and incorporation of new technologies. The integration of current technological advancements with emergency management plans can significantly improve preparedness levels during unforeseen events [4]. Digital tools capable of real-time monitoring and data analysis enhance risk management strategies, leading to more effective emergency responses. By integrating data-driven insights into emergency plans, responders can better anticipate incidents before they materialize—a conceptual shift from traditional reactive approaches to a proactive framework.

Emergency management systems must adapt these approaches with an emphasis on cross-agency collaboration. The interdependencies of agencies involved in emergency management are highlighted by Wang and Wei [5], who discuss the need for comprehensive coordination concerning incident management within urban contexts. This calls for establishing a unified command structure that integrates input from various stakeholders—including safety regulators, emergency responders, and local communities—to ensure a holistic and coherent approach to managing hydrogen pipeline emergencies.

The application of advanced analytical methods such as machine learning in predictive analysis can contribute significantly to preventive strategies. Research by Mukhopadhyay et al. [6] emphasizes the efficiency of online decision-theoretic approaches in predicting incident likelihood and enhancing resource allocation in emergency response. These computational methods enable emergency services to anticipate high-risk scenarios and prepare accordingly, thereby minimizing potential harm associated with hydrogen pipelines.

12.1.1 Design and Material Controls

The successful implementation of hydrogen pipelines hinges on meticulous design and material controls tailored to mitigate the unique risks associated with hydrogen as an energy carrier. These considerations are paramount due to hydrogen's distinct physical and chemical properties, which can lead to challenges such as hydrogen embrittlement, leakage, and material degradation, Fig. 12.1 shows some of the strategies which are explained briefly in below section.

1. ***Material Selection for Hydrogen Pipelines***

The selection of appropriate materials is fundamental in the design of hydrogen pipelines. According to Chen et al. [7], ongoing research and development aimed at establishing standards for hydrogen pipeline infrastructure in China emphasize the priority of selecting materials resistant to hydrogen's adverse effects, which stem primarily from embrittlement phenomena. For instance, Maruschak et al. [8] provide insights into how the degradation of steel materials under in-service conditions can inform the assessment of damage in gas pipelines, highlighting that understanding how materials behave over time is crucial. Moreover, studies indicate that non-metallic composite pipelines, such as reinforced thermoplastic composite pipes (RTPs), provide a promising alternative, as they exhibit increased resistance to hydrogen effects compared to traditional metallic materials [9].

Hydrogen embrittlement (HE) is a critical consideration in material design. Pipeline steels, particularly high-strength variants, experience significant degradation in mechanical properties when exposed to hydrogen due to interactions at the

Fig. 12.1 Ensuring safety and reliability of hydrogen pipelines

atomic level [10, 11]. Shin et al. [10] clarify that this degradation can lead to premature failures in service, emphasizing the urgent need for suitable material choices that account for these risks.

2. ***Advanced Protective Coatings***

To mitigate the effects of hydrogen exposure, the use of coatings has been proposed as a protective strategy. Coating solutions can enhance the lifespan of steel pipelines by providing a barrier to hydrogen diffusion. Khwaja and Paul [12] emphasize that implementing exterior and interior coatings can significantly reduce damage associated with hydrogen ingress. Similarly, Byrne et al. [13] note that polyethylene coatings have demonstrated effectiveness in minimizing hydrogen embrittlement in existing pipeline systems.

3. ***Monitoring and Maintenance Strategies***

Regular monitoring and maintenance of hydrogen pipelines are indispensable for ensuring safety and efficiency. Technologies for real-time leak detection, such as hybrid systems employing fiber optic sensors, have shown promise in enhancing the reliability of hydrogen transport networks. Continuous monitoring of hydrogen concentration and pressure, as emphasized by Xu et al. [14], plays a pivotal role in preventing accidents and maintaining operational reliability under variable conditions associated with hydrogen blending.

4. ***Design Considerations for Pressure Variations***

Design controls must also consider the pressure dynamics associated with hydrogen transport. Being the lightest element, hydrogen requires careful management to avoid excessive pressure loss and maintain safe operational limits. The combination of computational fluid dynamics (CFD) modeling and real operational data can lead to optimized pipeline designs that accommodate the unique pressures associated with hydrogen transportation [15]. Ban et al. [16] illustrate the need to evaluate pressure fluctuations in hydrogen-blended natural gas pipelines and their implications for pipeline integrity under various operational scenarios.

Tools like deep learning models for predictive analysis of mixing uniformity represent important advancements that can enhance hydrogen transport systems by optimizing flow dynamics within pipelines. This approach can aid engineers in designing pipeline structures that minimize turbulence and maximize efficiency during hydrogen transport.

5. ***Structural Integrity and End-of-Life Considerations***

Beyond the operational phase, end-of-life considerations for hydrogen pipelines require strategic planning. Understanding the residual life of pipelines subjected to hydrogen service is crucial for safe decommissioning and replacement procedures. Research has shown that aging pipelines may develop flaws that are exacerbated by hydrogen presence, necessitating thorough evaluations to assess their structural integrity [17].

Adaptive management strategies that incorporate periodic assessments of material integrity can help ensure that the transition to hydrogen transport does not compromise public safety or lead to environmental hazards. For instance, robust risk modeling regarding hydrogen-enriched natural gas pipelines can inform operational decisions and decommissioning timelines, thereby enhancing overall safety frameworks [18].

12.1.2 Operational Limits and Maintenance Practices

Operational limits and maintenance practices are critical in ensuring the safety, reliability, and efficiency of hydrogen pipeline systems. Given the unique properties of hydrogen and the associated risks, such as hydrogen embrittlement and leakage, adhering to stringent operational parameters and establishing meticulous maintenance protocols are crucial for minimizing hazards, which will help to move from reactive to proactive maintenance as shown in Fig. 12.2.

1. Establishing Operational Limits

Operational limits for hydrogen pipelines are primarily dictated by the material properties of the pipeline, the properties of hydrogen, and regulatory standards. Hydrogen volume fraction and pipeline operating pressure must be meticulously controlled to mitigate risks associated with hydrogen embrittlement in steel pipelines. It is generally recommended that the hydrogen content in blended natural gas

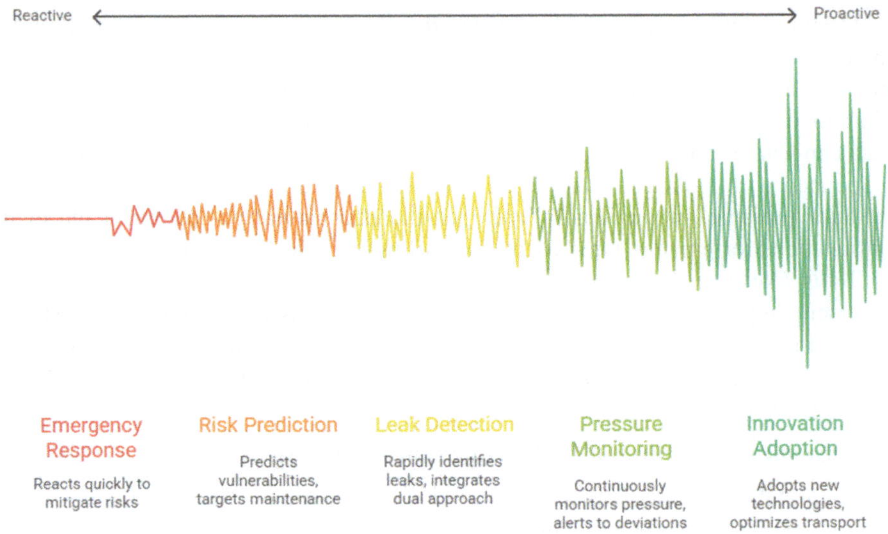

Fig. 12.2 Hydrogen pipeline maintenance ranges from reactive to proactive

pipelines remain below 20% to avoid compromising structural integrity. Exceeding this threshold can lead to premature failures, necessitating strict monitoring and adherence to set operational parameters [19].

2. Maintenance Practices

Regular maintenance is paramount in safeguarding hydrogen pipeline networks. Rasty et al. [20] emphasize that effective maintenance strategies should focus on preventive measures, including scheduled inspections to detect signs of corrosion and wear stemming from hydrogen exposure. With the potential for hydrogen embrittlement, pipeline steels, particularly those with higher strength, require more frequent assessments as their susceptibility to hydrogen damage increases. Periodic maintenance checks should also include evaluation of cathodic protection systems, which, if overly aggressive, can exacerbate embrittlement effects.

3. Risk Assessment Methodologies

Incorporating thorough risk assessment methodologies is essential for effective pipeline maintenance. Li et al. [21] state that systematic risk prediction and quantitative risk assessment must incorporate factors specific to hydrogen transport to prepare for potential incidents. Techniques such as fault tree analysis and failure mode effects analysis can assist in identifying vulnerabilities within the pipeline system that could lead to hydrogen leakages or catastrophic failures. Moreover, Xu et al. [14] argue that simulations and modeling of hydrogen flow within pipelines can provide insights into how hydrogen blending ratios affect pipe integrity under varying conditions.

4. Emergency Preparedness

Emergency preparedness is a vital component of maintenance practices within hydrogen pipeline systems. Proper response protocols must be established, which include comprehensive training for on-site personnel and clear communication channels for reporting incidents. Establishing robust emergency response procedures ensures that safety protocols are systematically followed in the event of a leak or other emergency scenarios, facilitating quick actions to mitigate risks associated with hydrogen exposure.

12.2 Repair and Rehabilitation Techniques

The integrity of hydrogen pipelines is challenged by leaks, embrittlement, and corrosion, necessitating advanced repair and rehabilitation methods. Table 12.1 outlines modern approaches, emphasizing their mechanisms, advantages, and applicability to hydrogen infrastructure.

12.2.1 Pipeline Replacement and Upgrades

The increasing adoption of hydrogen as an energy carrier necessitates the implementation of robust pipeline systems able to transport this low-molecular-weight gas safely and efficiently. As the existing infrastructures struggle to meet the

Table 12.1 Repair and rehabilitation techniques for hydrogen pipelines

Technique	Mechanism	Advantages	Applicability	References
Composite repair	FRP/CFRP wraps or bonded patches	High tensile strength, resists hydrogen effects, minimal service disruption	Structural defects, high-pressure pipelines	[22, 23]
Clamp repair	External clamps for localized damage	Quick installation, maintains flow, versatile in subsea use	Corrosion, perforations, deformations	[24]
Trenchless rehabilitation	Polymer grouting, non-excavation methods	Cost-effective, minimal surface disruption, faster completion	Urban buried pipelines, leak sealing	[25]
Welding and mechanical	Direct welding, mechanical repair methods	Strong, permanent solution; allows structural changes	Severe damage, structural alterations	[26]
Monitoring and assessment	Smart sensors, ultrasonic and electromagnetic inspections	Real-time monitoring, detects hidden defects, ensures repair reliability	Post-repair verification, long-term monitoring	[12, 27]

demands posed by hydrogen transport, pipeline replacement and upgrades become indispensable.

1. ***Rationale for Pipeline Replacement***

The need for pipeline replacement primarily arises from several factors, including the aging of existing infrastructure, the risk of material degradation due to hydrogen exposure, and the inadequacies of aged pipelines to handle the specific demands of hydrogen transport. The transition to hydrogen energy necessitates the retirement of older infrastructures that were primarily designed to transport natural gas, as these pipelines may be susceptible to risks including hydrogen embrittlement and leakage. Furthermore, pipeline failure incidents, such as those documented in the U.S. Pipeline and Hazardous Materials Safety Administration (PHMSA) reports, underscore the safety imperatives that drive the push for replacements. Maintaining obsolete pipelines can sometimes elevate the risks of leaks or catastrophic failures, with potential environmental and economic repercussions significantly outweighing the costs associated with replacing them [1].

2. ***Considerations for Upgrading Existing Infrastructure***

When upgrading existing pipelines to meet the demands of transporting hydrogen, see Fig. 12.3, several technical and regulatory considerations come into play.

a ***Material Compatibility***

Researchers emphasize the importance of selecting materials that demonstrate resistance to hydrogen-induced failures. Pipeline steels can experience substantial degradation when exposed to significant hydrogen concentrations [2]. Therefore, upgrading involves utilizing materials that can withstand the specific mechanical stresses associated with hydrogen, including changes in pressure, temperature, and the potential for embrittlement.

b. ***Regulatory Compliance***

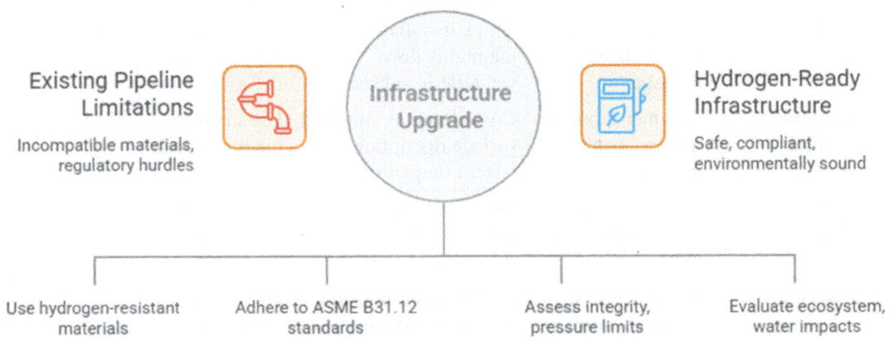

Fig. 12.3 Upgrading pipelines for hydrogen transport

Strict regulatory frameworks guide the upgrade process to ensure safety and environmental compliance. The American Society of Mechanical Engineers (ASME) has developed standards, like ASME B31.12, that provide guidance on the design, construction, and operation of hydrogen piping systems. These standards ensure that upgrades meet safety protocols while remaining economically viable [28].

c. ***Hydrogen Blending and Storage***

With the existing natural gas infrastructure many times adapting pipelines for hydrogen blending or storage, substratum information must be reevaluated. Upgrading existing facilities to accommodate hydrogen blends necessitates reassessment of pipeline integrity and operational pressure limits, as the physical properties of hydrogen may expose existing weaknesses [29]. Evaluating system capacity and performance under differentiated operational scenarios becomes critical.

d. ***Environmental Impact***

Environmental assessments are integral to the replacement and upgrade process. Evaluating potential environmental impacts associated with pipeline installation or replacement—including effects on local ecosystems, water resources, and surrounding communities—is mandated in many jurisdictions. Advanced technologies such as geographic information systems (GIS) can aid in performing environmental impact assessments accurately [3].

3. ***Innovative Solutions and Technologies***

The implementation of innovative technologies can enhance the efficiency and safety of pipeline replacement and upgrades:

- **Innovative Materials**

The development of novel lightweight, corrosion-resistant materials, such as advanced polymers and composites, has the potential to revolutionize pipeline construction and replacement. These materials offer improved durability in hydrogen service and significantly reduce transport costs due to their lower weight. Research by Holder, et al. [4] emphasizes the advancements in applicable thermoplastic materials that provide robust protection while exhibiting excellent hydrogen permeability properties.

- **Smart Pipeline Monitoring Technologies**

Upgraded infrastructures may incorporate smart monitoring technologies that provide real-time data on operational conditions. These technologies utilize a combination of sensors, machine learning, and predictive analytics to monitor pipeline integrity actively. The implementation of these systems can extend the effective lifecycle of pipelines, allowing for timely intervention before significant failures occur [6].

- **Hybrid Replacement Strategies**

The hybrid approach of replacing only sections of the pipeline promotes cost-effectiveness and minimizes construction impacts. By targeting specific high-risk areas for full replacement while upgrading remaining sections with composite wraps or advanced coatings, utilities can ensure compliance with safety standards while managing costs effectively [30].

- **Trenchless Technology**

Employing trenchless technology for pipeline replacement minimizes surface disruption and reduces repair costs associated with excavation. This technique utilizes specialized equipment to install new pipelines without extensive digging, significantly lowering the environmental impact. Its effective use in urban areas is critical, where space is constrained, and excavation risks can lead to severe public disruption [30].

12.3 Emergency Response Planning

Emergency response planning is a critical component of disaster management, aimed at ensuring efficiency and effectiveness in responding to emergencies, particularly in scenarios involving natural disasters. Given the unpredictable nature of such events and their potential catastrophic consequences, well-structured emergency response plans are indispensable. This section examines various facets of emergency response planning, focusing on the need for coordination, communication, training, and the incorporation of new technologies.

1. ***Need for Coordination Among Various Stakeholders***

The complexity of disaster situations necessitates collaborative planning across multiple sectors and organizations. The works of Huang and Pai [31] highlight the importance of understanding the roles of different stakeholders, including governments, emergency services, and public organizations, in fostering suitable adaptive responses to disasters. Failure to effectively coordinate disaster response efforts can lead to fragmented efforts, resulting in inefficient resource utilization and prolonged recovery timelines.

2. ***Communication Strategies***

Effective communication is fundamental to emergency response planning. Goniewicz et al. [32] highlight that information dissemination regarding emergency procedures, risks, and safety measures significantly affects the readiness of healthcare professionals in disaster scenarios. Therefore, establishing robust communication channels before disasters strike is essential to ensure that parties involved understand their roles and responsibilities.

Risk communication strategies must be tailored to different audiences. Different stakeholders possess varying levels of knowledge and available information, creating the need for targeted communication efforts that consider these disparities. The research by Huang and Pai [31] illustrates how critical information must flow seamlessly between authorities and the public for effective adaptive behavior in emergencies.

3. ***Training and Preparedness***

Training is a cornerstone of effective emergency response planning. Baek and Han [33] advocate for practical training exercises that allow personnel from diverse sectors, including fire services and health centers, to enhance their responsive capabilities in times of crisis. Joint emergency exercises can improve coordination skills and provide valuable experience in dealing with diverse types of disasters.

Palinkas et al. [34] further emphasize that ongoing education and training initiatives are critical for community-based organizations (CBOs) to sustain their preparedness levels, particularly in light of unforeseen challenges such as pandemics. Engagement strategies focusing on lived experiences during past disasters can also shape future preparedness efforts, reinforcing the efficacy and relevance of training programs.

4. ***Incorporation of Technology***

Advancements in technology are transforming emergency response efforts. The use of Geographic Information Systems (GIS) and remote sensing technologies can support disaster preparedness by providing accurate real-time data during emergencies. Furthermore, big data analytics can aid in identifying patterns and making informed decisions during crises, thereby improving resource allocation and response strategies [35].

12.4 Training and Preparedness

Training and preparedness play a critical role in emergency management, particularly when it comes to effectively responding to crises such as natural disasters or public health emergencies. By providing first responders, healthcare professionals, and local authorities with the necessary skills and knowledge, communities can enhance their resilience and capacity to manage unexpected events.

1. ***Importance of Training in Emergency Response***

Training programs equip individuals with the essential skills and knowledge necessary for efficient emergency response. Programs focused on specialized topics, such as pediatric emergency care and trauma management, provide healthcare professionals with the ability to address urgent medical needs that arise in crises. For instance, Yaprak and Alıncak [36] conducted a study that demonstrated the positive impact of a year-long pediatric emergency medicine training program for international medical graduates, emphasizing the importance of comprehensive training to enhance service delivery during emergencies.

2. ***Multi-Disciplinary Training Approaches***

The training of first responders should encompass multi-disciplinary approaches, promoting collaboration between different emergency services and healthcare professionals. For example, the integration of emergency medical dispatcher training has been identified as an effective strategy for enhancing pre-hospital care delivery in resource-limited settings [37]. This collaborative training fosters inter-agency communication and coordination, which are critical during emergencies.

Innovative training programs that combine practical exercises with theory contribute to improved response capabilities. Simulation-based training, as highlighted by Bredmose et al. [38], enables healthcare providers and emergency personnel to practice their skills in high-stakes scenarios and develop decision-making skills under pressure. Such real-world simulations strengthen both individual and team performance, ultimately leading to better patient outcomes during emergencies.

3. ***Building Community Preparedness***

Community engagement in emergency preparedness training is essential for fostering an informed and resilient population. Training community members in first aid, CPR, and emergency response protocols can significantly enhance resilience during natural disasters or public health crises. For instance, Hossain et al. [39] highlighted the importance of training community-based responders in managing drowning casualties in rural areas, demonstrating the importance of localized preparedness efforts.

Training initiatives should not only target professionals but also empower ordinary citizens with life-saving skills and knowledge. Engaging in community preparedness programs helps establish a culture of emergency readiness, where individuals are motivated to actively participate in emergency response efforts, thereby enhancing overall community resilience.

12.4.1 Operator Training Programs

Operator training programs are essential for preparing emergency responders and other personnel to effectively manage crises associated with hazardous materials, including hydrogen transport systems. These training programs focus on equipping operators with specialized skills, knowledge, and preparedness strategies necessary for effective emergency response.

1. ***Core Components of Operator Training Programs***

Successful operator training programs often incorporate several core components:

a. **Hazard Recognition and Risk Assessment**

Training should start with educating operators on identifying potential hazards associated with the operation of hydrogen pipelines. Understanding the risks linked to hydrogen as a low-molecular-weight, flammable gas is critical. Naser and Saleem

[40] emphasize that knowledge of emergency and disaster management can empower health professionals to navigate complex situations effectively. Workers need to be equipped with skills that allow them to assess risks accurately in real-time scenarios.

b. **Emergency Response Protocols**

Developing clear emergency response protocols is imperative, and these protocols should detail the steps operators must take when responding to incidents, including leaks, ruptures, or fires. While the cited reference by Phiri et al. [41] discusses perceptions of occupational hazards, it does not directly apply to emergency protocols in hydrogen transport systems.

References

1. Lin Y et al (2024) A model for assessing the potential impact radius of hydrogen pipelines based on jet fire radiation. Fire 7(2):38
2. Skryabina EA et al (2020) The role of emergency preparedness exercises in the response to a mass casualty terrorist incident: a mixed methods study. Int J Disaster Risk Reduct 46:101503
3. Freedman AM et al (2013) Addressing the gap between public health emergency planning and incident response: lessons learned from the 2009 H1N1 outbreak in San Diego County. Disaster Health 1(1):13–20
4. Holder N et al (2017) Principles of mental health intervention for survivors of major disasters. Psychiatr Ann 47(3):124–127
5. Wang J, Wei R (2023) Study on urban resilience based on the analysis of supply guarantee facilities during epidemic closure—a case study of Shanghai in 2022. Open J Civ Eng 13(1):58–82
6. Mukhopadhyay A et al (2019) An online decision-theoretic pipeline for responder dispatch. In: Proceedings of the 10th ACM/IEEE international conference on cyber-physical systems
7. Chen X et al (2024) Research on standards and standard system of hydrogen pipeline in China. In: E3S web of conferences 520:04016. EDP sciences
8. Maruschak P et al (2014) Influence of in-service degradation on strain localization in steel of main gas pipelines. In: AIP conference proceedings. American Institute of Physics
9. Zhang X et al (2024) Molecular simulation study on the hydrogen permeation behavior and mechanism of common polymers. Polymers 16(7):953
10. Shin S-H et al (2024) EffEct of Microstructural constituEnts on HydrogEn EMbrittlEMEnt rEsistancE of aPi X60, X70, and X80 PiPElinE stEEls. Arch Metall Mater 69
11. Cai L et al (2022) Experimental investigation on the hydrogen embrittlement characteristics and mechanism of natural gas-hydrogen transportation pipeline steels. Mater Res Express 9(4):046512
12. Khwaja SA, Paul S (2022) Inspection of coated hydrogen transportation pipelines. Appl Sci 12(19):9503
13. Byrne N et al (2023) Influence of hydrogen on vintage polyethylene pipes: slow crack growth performance and material properties. Int J Energy Res 2023(1):6056999
14. Xu W et al (2024) Simulation study on hydrogen concentration distribution in hydrogen blended natural gas transportation pipeline. PLoS ONE 19(12):e0314453
15. Bu F et al (2024) Analysis of leakage and diffusion characteristics and hazard range determination of buried hydrogen-blended natural gas pipeline based on CFD. ACS Omega 9(37):39202–39218

16. Ban J et al (2024) Study for hydrogen migration characteristics in the elbow of a hydrogen-doped natural gas pipeline under normal transport and shutdown conditions. ACS Omega 9(48):47621–47636
17. Sapuzhak Y, Soviak I (2023) Assessment of the residual lifetime of a defective pipeline at different hydrogen concentrations in the metal. In: Proceedings of the international young scientists conference on materials science and surface engineering, pp 204–207. Karpenko Physico-Mechanical Institute of NAS of Ukraine
18. Yang K et al (2024) Risk modelling of hydrogen-enriched natural gas on pipelines and gas-electric coupled systems. IET Energy Syst Integr 6(3):253–267
19. Li J, Xie B, Gong L (2024) Numerical research on leakage characteristics of pure hydrogen/hydrogen-blended natural gas in medium-and low-pressure buried pipelines. Energies 17(12):2951
20. Rasty J, Parker O, Mills M (2022) Forensic engineering investigation of factors contributing to the explosion of an international natural gas pipeline. J Natl Acad Forensic Eng 39(2)
21. Li J, Song F, Zhang X (2024) A review on hazards and risks to pipeline operation under transporting hydrogen energy and hydrogen-mixed natural gas. Sci Technol Energy Transit 79:9
22. Zainal N et al (2018) Tensile properties of epoxy grout incorporating graphene nanoplatelets for pipeline repair. In: MATEC web of conferences. EDP Sciences
23. Chen J et al (2021) Finite element analysis of composite repair for damaged steel pipeline. Coatings 11(3):301
24. Zhao B et al (2023) Design of enhanced pipeline repair clamp. Material strength and applied mechanics. IOS Press, pp 143–149
25. Gao D et al (2012) Taking Fangcun district of Guangzhou as an example to discuss the new joint repair technology of water distribution network. Appl Mech Mater 226:2328–2334
26. Shan X et al (2024) A Methodology to determine the maximum allowable repair time for critical units of natural gas pipeline systems using gas supply reliability theory. Energy Proceedings 43(4)
27. Wang Y et al (2024) A novel leakage sensing system of hydrogen transportation pipeline based on hybrid UWFBG array. In: Advanced sensor systems and applications XIV. SPIE
28. Chen R et al (2010) An empirical examination of IT-enabled emergency response: the cases of Hurricane Katrina and Hurricane Rita. Commun Assoc Inf Syst 26(1):8
29. Barilo N, Hamilton J, Weiner SC (2017) First responder training: supporting commercialization of hydrogen and fuel cell technologies. Int J Hydrog Energy 42(11):7536–7541
30. Shubayr N (2025) Evaluating nurses' psychological and operational preparedness for mass-casualty events in Saudi Arabia. Int Nurs Rev 72(1):e70002
31. Huang K-H, Pai J-T (2019) A study of disaster risk communication and adaptive behaviour based on rail station protection. Int Rev Spat Plan Sustain Dev 7(3):4–16
32. Goniewicz K et al (2020) The impact of experience, length of service, and workplace preparedness in physicians' readiness in the response to disasters. J Clin Med 9(10):3328
33. Baek S, Han S (2021) Factors influencing emergency medical competencies of health centers and fire stations in areas that are vulnerable to earthquakes. Clin Exp Emerg Med 8(3):192
34. Palinkas LA et al (2021) A rapid assessment of disaster preparedness needs and resources during the COVID-19 pandemic. Int J Environ Res Public Health 18(2):425
35. Majemite MT et al (2024) Evaluating the role of big data in US disaster mitigation and response: a geological and business perspective. Eng Sci Technol J 5(2):338–357
36. Yaprak R, Alıncak F (2023) Evaluation of in-service training needs of coaches working in the provincial directorate of youth and sports (Gaziantep Province sample). Eğitim ve Yeni Yaklaşımlar Dergisi 6(2):367–382
37. Jacobson CL et al (2021) Emergency medical dispatcher training as a strategy to improve pre-hospital care in low-and middle-income countries: the case study of Nepal. Int J Emerg Med 14(1):28
38. Bredmose PP et al (2021) National Implementation of in situ simulation-based training in helicopter emergency medical services: a multicenter study. Air Med J 40(4):205–210

39. Hossain MJ et al (2020) Impact of community-based first responder development for the management of drowning casualties in rural areas of Bangladesh. Afr J Emerg Med 10(4):219–223
40. Naser WN, Saleem HB (2018) Emergency and disaster management training; knowledge and attitude of Yemeni health professionals-a cross-sectional study. BMC Emerg Med 18(1):23
41. Phiri A et al (2024) Assessment of workers' perception of occupational hazards at Nampundwe mine in Zambia. medRxiv, 2024.11. 26.24317988

Chapter 13
Repair and Rehabilitation Techniques

This chapter provides a comprehensive exploration of contemporary repair and rehabilitation techniques applicable to infrastructure and pipeline systems, emphasizing decision-making criteria, practical methodologies, and post-repair validation processes. The chapter begins with a critical examination of the factors influencing repair decisions, including a systematic assessment of defect severity and the balancing of cost implications with operational downtime. This foundational analysis guides the selection of appropriate repair interventions.

The core mechanical repair methods are detailed, highlighting traditional and innovative approaches such as clamps, sleeves, and welding techniques that restore structural integrity with minimal disruption. The chapter further advances into composite repair technologies, showcasing their advantages in terms of durability, flexibility, and reduced environmental impact.

In addressing long-term solutions, the rehabilitation and upgrading section discusses pipeline relining and replacement strategies, integrating cutting-edge materials and engineering approaches designed to extend asset life and improve performance. The utilization of advanced materials, including fiber-reinforced polymers and other novel composites, is presented as a transformative trend in rehabilitation practices.

Concluding the chapter is a thorough overview of inspection and validation procedures essential for ensuring repair efficacy and safety compliance. Post-repair testing protocols are outlined, emphasizing non-destructive evaluation techniques and performance verification. The documentation and approval process is also discussed, underscoring the importance of regulatory adherence and quality assurance in the rehabilitation workflow.

Overall, this chapter serves as a vital resource for engineers, maintenance professionals, and decision-makers involved in the repair and rehabilitation of critical infrastructure, offering both theoretical insights and practical guidance to optimize asset management and operational resilience.

M. Hussain et al., *Hydrogen Pipeline Integrity*, Green Energy and Technology,
https://doi.org/10.1007/978-981-95-5609-0_13

Overall, this chapter serves as a vital resource for engineers, maintenance professionals, and decision-makers involved in the repair and rehabilitation of critical infrastructure, offering both theoretical insights and practical guidance to optimize asset management and operational resilience.

13.1 Criteria for Repair Decisions

Fundamentally, the evaluation of repair criteria involves understanding the pipeline's failure modes and the mechanisms that lead to these failures. Various studies highlight the criticality of failure mode analysis as a foundational step in decision-making for pipeline maintenance. For instance, Pietrucha-Urbanik Škerlič et al. [1] demonstrate that different segments within a pipeline system exhibit varying failure rates, emphasizing the need for tailored repair strategies based on specific operational pressure points within the pipeline. The review also reflects the importance of statistical evaluation in predicting and addressing pipeline failure patterns, thus underscoring the necessity for empirical data-driven approaches in establishing repair criteria.

In addition to the deterministic analyses, probabilistic methodologies provide a rich framework for repair decision-making. For example, the work of Frangopol et al. [2] discusses the application of Poisson distribution models in assessing pipeline failures, which can guide repair decision-making under earthquake conditions. This showcases that repair criteria should be flexible and capable of adapting to external stressors that could exacerbate existing vulnerabilities within the pipeline network.

Corrosion presents a significant challenge in the domain of hydrogen pipelines, necessitating robust criteria for assessing integrity loss and determining repair methodologies. The analysis conducted by Kim et al. [3], elucidates various corrosion mechanisms, advocating for rigorous integrity management protocols that can proactively mitigate corrosion's damaging effects. The categorization of metal loss and the establishment of corrective measures, can enhance the efficacy of repair strategies for corroded pipeline sections, thereby extending operational longevity.

Identifying repair determinants requires a multidimensional approach that comprises mechanical properties, historical performance data, and environmental considerations. The research presented by Choi et al. [4] describes how dent-weld interaction can significantly inform repair decisions. This interaction impacts the thresholds for acceptability and subsequently influences the choice of repair methods, reflecting the necessity for an interdisciplinary approach combining mechanical engineering and material science in the repair decision rationale.

Repair methodologies often require validation to ensure that they withstand operational pressures and environmental influences. For instance, recent studies into composite repair systems, particularly in offshore applications [5], indicate that careful assessment and criteria establishment for these methodologies can yield significant benefits in terms of material performance and repair efficacy.

In assessing the cost implications of repair methodologies, the selection criteria should also integrate economic analyses to evaluate the long-term viability of repair strategies. Insights from research on pipeline repair prioritization such as that by Udechukwu et al. [6] highlight the importance of an expert judgment-based prioritization framework that can discern necessary repairs based on economic and functional criteria.

The analysis of failure risk factors, such as pipeline dents due to mechanical impacts or stresses, emphasizes the need to establish clear and systematic repair criteria [7]. Identifying the mechanical implications of defects through the evaluation of operational pressure and strain responses can help in formulating effective repair strategies that mitigate risk while preserving pipeline integrity. The role of technology in supporting repair decision-making cannot be overlooked. Advanced diagnostic techniques, such as Ground Penetrating Radar (GPR) and integrated imaging systems, as explored by Gibson and Rioja [8], enable a more nuanced understanding of pipeline conditions. Consequently, the integration of these technologies into repair planning processes can enhance the precision of condition assessments, making it easier to prioritize repairs.

13.1.1 Assessment of Defect Severity

Assessment of defect severity in hydrogen pipelines is a crucial component that influences repair decisions. By evaluating the impact of various types of defects, such as corrosion, cracks, and coating flaws, pipeline operators can determine appropriate maintenance actions, ensuring safety and integrity throughout the lifespan of the infrastructure.

Corrosion defects are one of the most prevalent and concerning issues faced by hydrogen pipelines. Colindres et al. [9] provide significant insights into how the depth and shape of a corrosion defect influence the failure pressure of pipelines. Their work highlights that deeper defects are more likely to lead to failure compared to longer, but shallower defects. This aligns with results from Naamani et al. [10], who employed finite element analysis (FEA) to assess internal and external corrosion defects on pipelines, reinforcing the necessity of understanding defect geometry in pressure capacity evaluations.

The application of advanced detection techniques such as Direct Current Voltage Gradient (DCVG) surveys can play a pivotal role in assessing coating defect sizes. Anes-Arteche et al. [11] discuss the effectiveness of DCVG in locating and estimating the severity of coating defects. Although the technique excels in locational accuracy, operational challenges remain in quantifying the exact size of the defects, underscoring the need for combined assessment techniques. Engaging with probabilistic and deterministic methodologies further enhances the reliability of defect severity assessments. The work of Verstraete et al. [12] supports the critical evaluation of pipeline girth weld defects under varying stress conditions, necessitating a defined relationship between loading conditions and defect characteristics for precise assessments. A semi-deterministic approach offers more tailored risk evaluations, as presented by Seghier et al. [13], which simultaneously incorporated probabilistic risk assessments for better estimation of defect impacts.

The categorization of defects based on their potential danger is another vital consideration discussed in the work by Bushinskaya and Timashev [14]. Their graphical approach allows operators to make informed maintenance decisions based on a defect's characteristics and its criticality to structural performance. This prioritization is critical in environments where rapid maintenance interventions are required to avert failures. Moreover, the severity assessment must also take into account external factors affecting pipeline integrity. The study by Chen et al. [15] on external corrosion defect growth illustrates how operational conditions—including internal pressure and environmental factors—can significantly influence failure risk. Management strategies should, therefore, include considerations of environmental impacts on corrosion rates and defect propagation to aid in preventative actions.

13.1.2 Cost and Downtime Considerations

Assessing cost and downtime in the repair of hydrogen pipelines is crucial for optimizing maintenance strategies while ensuring safety and operational efficiency. The economic impact of repairs can be significant, influencing not only the immediate fiscal considerations of pipeline operators but also broader implications for the supply chain and energy distribution, see Fig. 13.1.

Understanding these factors entails a multifaceted analysis, covering direct repair costs, indirect costs due to downtime, and key decision-making aspects to devise effective repair strategies.

Fig. 13.1 Hydrogen pipeline repair: costly downtime challenges

Direct Repair Costs

Direct repair costs encompass materials, labor, and equipment expenses incurred during maintenance interventions. Research indicates that labor constitutes a substantial portion of repair expenditures, with skilled labor demands rising due to increasing complexity in pipeline systems [16]. Detailed analyses of repair costs often incorporate specific methodologies such as Activity-Based Costing (ABC), which allocates costs more accurately among various maintenance activities. This methodology allows better identification of costly elements in repair operations, as demonstrated by Frangopol et al. [2], emphasizing how utilizing comprehensive costing strategies helps in budgetary planning and forecasting.

The choice of materials for repairs can significantly impact costs and performance. The evolving nature of repair technologies, such as composite wraps and advanced welding techniques, presents trade-offs between upfront costs and long-term durability. Evidence indicates that opting for higher immediate expenditures concerning advanced materials can yield substantial long-term savings by reducing downtime and enhancing the lifespan of repair solutions. For example, composite materials have demonstrated superior mechanical properties under hydrogen service, which may justify the initial investment through eventual operational efficiency.

Indirect Costs Due to Downtime

While direct repair costs are critical, indirect costs associated with downtime during repairs pose significant challenges for pipeline operators. Downtime in hydrogen pipelines can lead to lost revenue and customer dissatisfaction, particularly in industries reliant on consistent hydrogen supply, such as fuel cells and ammonia production. Studies published by Solla et al. [5] illustrate how quantifying lost production during repair activities can guide strategic downtime management efforts.

The potential economic impact of downtime can be assessed through various methodologies, including loss of revenue analysis. This analysis correlates directly to the type of operation affected by repair activities, as certain sectors may experience more pronounced financial fallout. For instance, a study by Udechukwu et al. [6] notes that prolonged downtime in hydrogen distribution systems not only hinders operational flow but also places strain on supply chains, thereby amplifying market volatility during outages.

In addressing downtime, pipeline operators may position themselves to streamline repair processes through advanced planning and risk mitigation measures. Utilizing predictive analytics to identify potential outages may result in more proactive maintenance schedules, minimizing unplanned downtimes. Additionally, implementing continuous monitoring and sensor technologies in pipeline systems allows for timely intervention, which is evidenced by the findings of [7] that quantify reductions in emergency repairs.

Financial Modeling and Decision-Making Strategies

Financial modeling plays a critical role in evaluating total cost implications of repair interventions. Utilizing models such as Net Present Value (NPV) or Internal Rate of

Return (IRR) can assist decision-makers in valuing repair proposals against operational risks and expected future cash flows [8]. For example, employing NPV in budgeting repair costs allows stakeholders to balance near-term expenses with long-term benefits, systematically allocating resources towards the most impactful interventions.

Leveraging for duration trade-offs also supports decision-making surrounding repairs. Operators may conduct cost–benefit analyses that balance rapid repairs against higher costs versus slower repairs allowing a more economically feasible approach while ensuring that pipeline integrity remains uncompromised. The association of maintenance with downtime through a risk-based framework has been notably explored by Colindres et al. [9]. Their research highlights how adopting risk-informed management strategies improves financial forecasting and ultimately supports better operational stability.

13.2 Mechanical Repair Methods

Table 13.1 presents a comparative overview of mechanical repair methods for hydrogen pipelines, emphasizing their technical principles, benefits, and inherent limitations. Composite material systems, particularly fiber-reinforced polymer (FRP) wraps, offer lightweight, corrosion-resistant reinforcement for diverse defect types, though their long-term performance under hydrogen service remains under investigation. Mechanical clamping methods provide rapid, non-intrusive solutions for localized deterioration, whereas welding-based techniques enable permanent restoration but require stringent control of metallurgical effects and embrittlement risks. Hybrid repair approaches demonstrate potential for addressing multifaceted defects through combined methodologies. Furthermore, the integration of advanced diagnostic and analytical tools, such as non-destructive evaluation (NDE) and finite element analysis (FEA), enhances the precision and reliability of repair interventions. Collectively, these methods constitute a comprehensive framework for maintaining pipeline integrity under the demanding conditions of hydrogen transport.

The selection of the appropriate mechanical repair method for hydrogen pipelines depends on various factors, including the type and severity of the defect, the pipeline's operating conditions, and the available resources and expertise. In some cases, a combination of repair techniques may be employed to address complex or multifaceted issues, as demonstrated by the hybrid repair approach discussed earlier [17].

The integration of advanced technologies, such as non-destructive evaluation (NDE) techniques and finite element analysis (FEA), can enhance the effectiveness of mechanical repair strategies. NDE methods, including ultrasonic testing, magnetic flux leakage, and ground-penetrating radar, can provide detailed information about the pipeline's condition, enabling more targeted and efficient repair interventions [9]. FEA, on the other hand, can be used to model the mechanical behavior of the repaired pipeline, optimizing the repair design and ensuring its suitability for the operational environment [11, 18].

Table 13.1 Mechanical repair methods

Repair method	Description	Advantages	Limitations/ considerations
Composite materials (FRP wraps/patches)	Use of fiber-reinforced polymer (FRP) wraps or patches to reinforce damaged pipeline sections	– Conforms to complex geometries – Corrosion resistant – High strength-to-weight ratio – Effective for corrosion, cracks, dents	Long-term durability and performance under hydrogen exposure still under evaluation
Mechanical clamping (clamps/sleeves)	Installation of metallic clamps or sleeves around damaged pipeline sections	– Restores structural integrity – Avoids hot work – Quick to install – Suitable for localized defects	May not be effective for large or widespread defects
Welding-based repairs (buildup, fillet welded patches)	Deposition of additional material to restore wall thickness and strength	– Permanent structural restoration – Widely used in conventional pipeline repair	– Risk of heat-affected zones – Requires skilled personnel and specialized equipment – Hydrogen embrittlement risks
Hybrid repair techniques	Combination of composite bonding and mechanical interventions (e.g., hole drilling + patching)	– Addresses complex defects – Provides multi -layered reinforcement	More complex implementation; may require advanced design validation
Advanced support tools (NDE & FEA)	Non-destructive evaluation (ultrasonic, MFL, GPR) and finite element analysis to guide repair design	– Enables accurate defect detection – Optimizes repair strategy – Reduces risk of failure	Requires advanced technology, expertise, and computational resources

13.2.1 Clamps, Sleeves, and Welding Repairs

The mechanical repair methods involving clamps, sleeves, and welding as shown in Fig. 13.2, are vital for maintaining the integrity and operational efficiency of hydrogen pipelines. As infrastructures age and experience wear, these repair techniques serve as essential solutions to mitigate leaks, restore structural integrity, and extend the lifespan of pipeline systems.

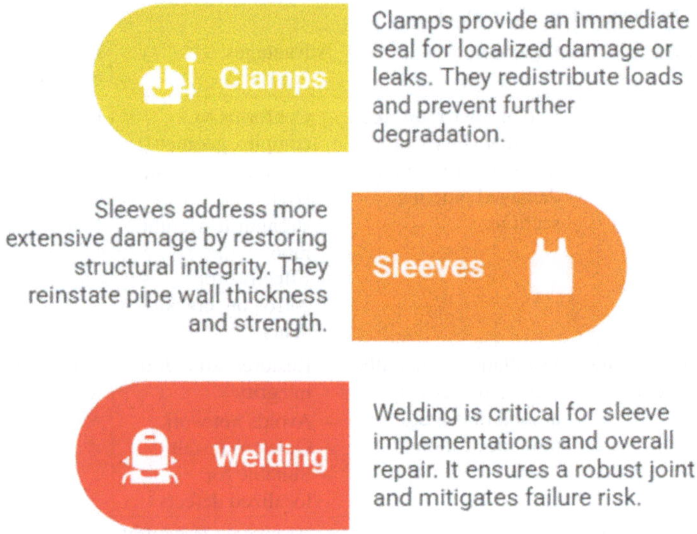

Fig. 13.2 Pipeline repair methods

The primary function of a repair clamp is to provide an immediate, effective means of sealing leaks caused by corrosion, mechanical damage, or deterioration. Modern clamp designs ensure a robust fit over the damaged section, effectively redistributing loads while preventing further degradation. Zhao et al. [19] emphasize that clamp repair technology is particularly applicable in the energy sector for addressing leakage due to mechanical damage or corrosion while enabling quick installation without extensive downtime.

Sleeves are another crucial mechanical repair option for pipelines, particularly suited for addressing more extensive damage or defects. The repair sleeve method involves fitting a sleeve over the damaged section of a pipeline to restore its structural integrity. This method can effectively reinstate the pipe wall thickness and strength, which is critical in maintaining the pipeline's operational pressure capabilities.

Welding plays a pivotal role in sleeve installations. Studies have shown that the quality of the weld between the sleeve and the parent material impacts the overall effectiveness of the repair. Zhang et al. [20] investigate the effects of fillet weld size and sleeve material strength on the residual stress distribution in welded joints. Their findings indicate that optimizing weld parameters can enhance structural safety and extend the lifespan of the repair.

The technical aspects of welding repairs, including pre-weld preparation, post-weld inspection, and monitoring, are critical components leading to successful repair outcomes. Consequently, numerical simulations such as those discussed by Alian et al. [21] have become increasingly relevant, enabling a thorough understanding of the transient thermal fields and stress distributions developed during the welding of sleeve repairs. The insights gained from such simulations facilitate the optimization of welding parameters to improve joint integrity and long-term performance.

In a recent study, Deng et al. [22] evaluated the performance of grouted sleeve connections under tensile loads, highlighting their application in high-stress environments common in hydrogen pipelines. Their work underscores the importance of understanding the mechanical properties of both the sleeve and welded joint, as they directly impact the overall repair efficacy.

13.2.2 Composite Repair Technologies

Composite repair technologies as shown in Table 13.2, represent a critical advancement in the rehabilitation of hydrogen pipeline systems, offering lightweight, corrosion-resistant, and mechanically robust solutions for structural reinforcement. By leveraging materials such as fiber-reinforced polymers (FRPs), adhesives, and thermoplastic composites, these technologies restore pipeline integrity while minimizing downtime and operational disruptions. Advances in bonding methods, patch optimization, and durability testing have further established composites as reliable alternatives to traditional repair strategies, aligning with the growing need for resilient infrastructure in hydrogen transport networks.

13.3 Rehabilitation and Upgrading

Rehabilitation and upgrading of hydrogen pipelines are fundamental processes aimed at enhancing the safety, reliability, and efficiency of hydrogen transport systems. These processes involve the use of modern materials and technologies, as shown in Fig. 13.3, to restore pipeline integrity and upgrade existing infrastructure to meet contemporary operational standards and environmental demands.

1. ***Importance of Rehabilitation and Upgrading***

Rehabilitation of hydrogen pipelines is necessitated by factors such as material degradation, corrosion, and changing operational requirements. Aging infrastructure can lead to increased maintenance costs, reduced operational efficiency, and heightened safety risks [23]. As such, rehabilitation strategies not only address existing defects but also incorporate modern practices and materials to extend the service life of hydrogen pipelines and minimize potential failures.

The rationale behind upgrading existing systems is multifaceted. As highlighted by Ivanov [23], the application of advanced composite materials in various industries demonstrates their efficacy in reconditioning infrastructure. The integration of these materials into pipeline systems significantly enhances strength, durability, and resistance to harsh operational environments typical of hydrogen transport.

Table 13.2 Composite repair technologies for hydrogen pipelines

Repair approach	Description/key features	Advantages	Limitations/ considerations
Fiber-reinforced polymer (FRP) repairs	Use of CFRP and other FRPs to reinforce defective sections	– High strength-to-weight ratio – Corrosion resistance – Effective load distribution	Long-term hydrogen compatibility requires further validation
Adhesive bonding	Use of adhesives to bond composite materials to pipeline surfaces	– Uniform load transfer – Reduces stress concentrations – Avoids secondary stresses from fasteners	Surface preparation critical; adhesive durability under hydrogen exposure must be confirmed
Fusion bonding techniques	Melting thermoplastic composites to create cohesive repair interfaces	– Simplified process – Reduced surface prep – Faster repairs, reliable joints	Limited industrial adoption; process control required
Patch repair optimization	Design and configuration of composite patches to optimize stress distribution	– Improves repair strength – Tailors load-bearing capacity – Enhances durability	Patch geometry must be carefully designed; may require advanced analysis
Performance and durability enhancements	Advanced bonded patches and stress-transfer improvements	– Extends service life- High adaptability – Strong resistance to corrosion and degradation	Long-term monitoring required in hydrogen environments

2. ***Composite Materials in Pipeline Rehabilitation***

Composite materials, particularly fiber-reinforced polymers (FRPs), have garnered significant attention in pipeline rehabilitation due to their favorable mechanical properties and lightweight nature. These materials provide excellent tensile strength, corrosion resistance, and adaptability to various environmental conditions, which are critical for maintaining hydrogen pipeline integrity. Rajak et al. [24] indicate that composites reinforced with synthetic or natural fibers are crucial in responding to the increasing demands for lightweight and high-strength materials in industrial applications.

Research shows that composite materials can be applied in various configurations, including wraps and patches, which provide strategic reinforcement to damaged sections of pipelines. Their application allows for in-situ repairs that minimize disruption and downtime throughout the rehabilitation process. The effectiveness of these repairs has been documented through case studies demonstrating improved operational lifespans and safety margins of repaired pipelines [25].

3. ***Advanced Joining Techniques***

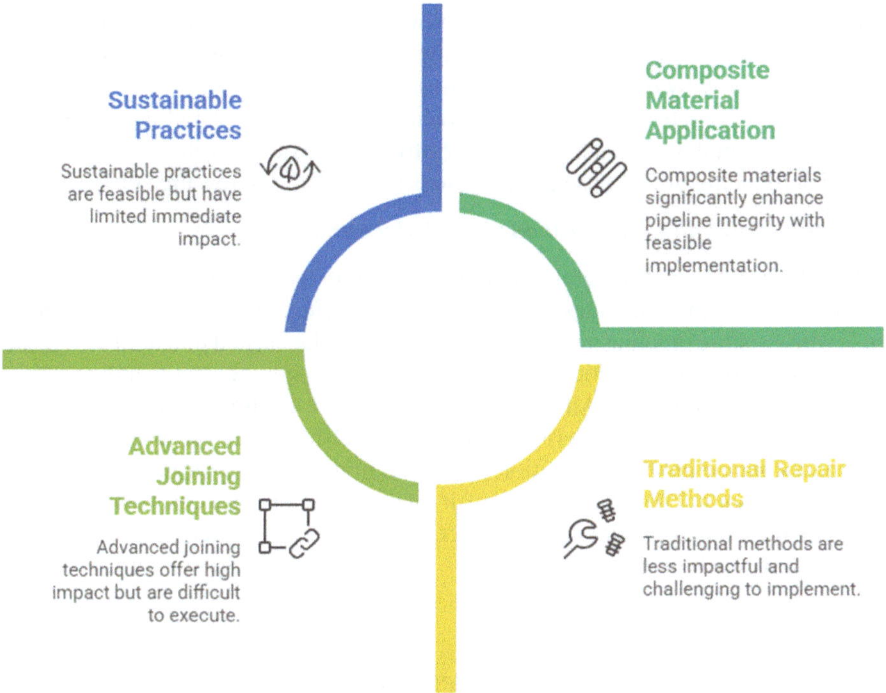

Fig. 13.3 Prioritizing rehabilitation and upgrading strategies for hydrogen pipelines

Upgrading hydrogen pipelines may necessitate innovative joining techniques. The use of thermoplastic composites, coupled with advanced joining methods, has been explored extensively. Ku et al. [26] discuss how microwave-assisted joining processes can enhance the bonding of thermoplastic composites, leading to stronger and more reliable connections. This technology can significantly synergize with the rehabilitation process, providing efficient and rapid joining solutions that enable quick repairs and upgrades.

Advanced joint designs, such as scarf joints and overlap joints, further enhance the integrity of composite repairs. The optimal design can significantly reduce stress concentrations, promoting better load distribution across the pipeline. This is particularly vital for hydrogen pipelines, where pressure fluctuations may result in increased fatigue stress along joint areas [27].

4. ***Sustainable Practices in Rehabilitation***

Sustainability factors play an increasingly crucial role in the rehabilitation and upgrading of hydrogen pipelines. The development and application of composite materials derived from renewable resources, as discussed by Oliver et al. [28] highlight the industry's commitment to environmental sustainability. Utilizing natural fibers for reinforcing composites in rehabilitation not only reduces the carbon footprint associated with traditional composite production but also contributes to the circular economy by repurposing waste materials.

The implementation of sustainable practices in pipeline rehabilitation enhances the environmental profile of hydrogen infrastructure and aligns with global initiatives aimed at reducing greenhouse gas emissions and promoting resource efficiency.

5. ***Challenges and Considerations in Rehabilitation***

While the potentials of rehabilitation and upgrading using composite materials are significant, certain challenges must be addressed. The compatibility of new materials with existing pipeline systems, regulatory compliance, and potential unforeseen operational stresses are critical factors to consider during the design and execution of rehabilitation projects. Advancements in structure-health monitoring technologies can mitigate these concerns by providing real-time data on pipeline integrity and performance post-rehabilitation [29]. Additionally, proper training and certification of personnel involved in the repair and upgrade process ensure adherence to best practices and regulatory frameworks, further ensuring safety and reliability in hydrogen pipeline operations.

13.3.1 Pipeline Relining and Replacement Options

Pipeline rehabilitation is essential for ensuring the safety and efficiency of hydrogen transport, with relining and replacement serving as two key strategies. Relining, including techniques such as Cured-in-Place Pipe (CIPP) and composite material applications, offers cost-effective, minimally disruptive solutions that extend pipeline life and improve resistance to corrosion. In contrast, replacement via traditional open-cut trenching or modern trenchless methods like horizontal directional drilling (HDD) is necessary when pipelines are beyond repair, with advanced composites further enhancing durability. Both approaches involve trade-offs between cost, long-term reliability, and environmental impacts, highlighting the importance of balancing economic and ecological considerations in infrastructure renewal (Fig. 13.4).

Pipeline relining is an increasingly popular option for rehabilitating aging infrastructure without the need for extensive excavation. This trenchless technology involves the insertion of a new pipe or a lining material into the existing pipeline, effectively sealing defects and restoring structural integrity while minimizing disruption to the surrounding environment [30].

One widely used relining method is the Cured-in-Place Pipe (CIPP) technique. This method utilizes a resin-impregnated flexible tube that is inserted into the damaged pipeline and then cured to form a new pipe within the existing structure. CIPP has been shown to be particularly advantageous for reducing costs and minimizing downtime, as noted by Kobayashi et al. [31]. The effectiveness of CIPP is further demonstrated by studies indicating that it can extend the life of aging pipelines for several decades, ensuring continued reliability in service. While relining is often

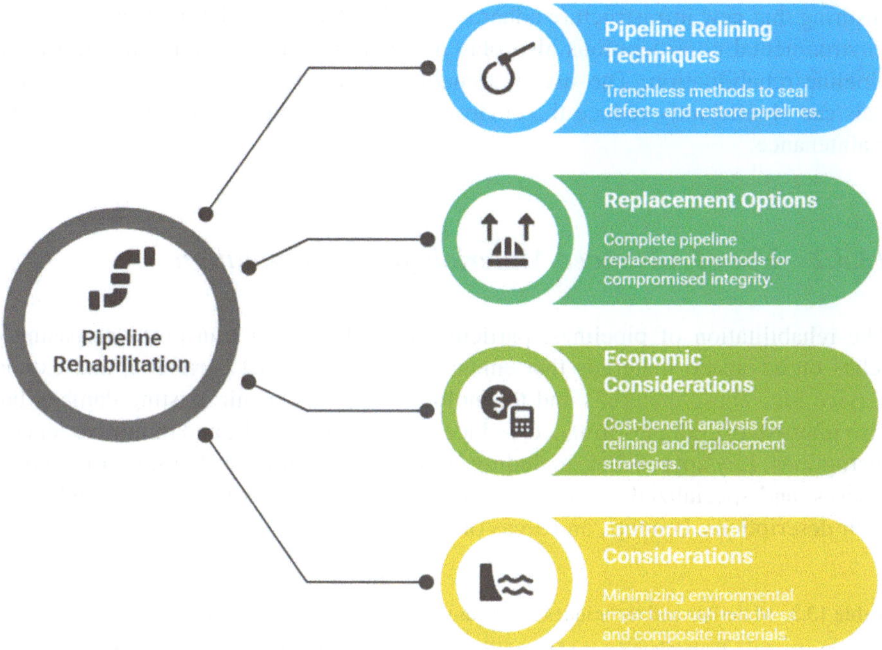

Fig. 13.4 Strategies for pipeline rehabilitation

preferred due to its efficiency and minimal disruption, complete pipeline replacement may be unavoidable under specific circumstances—especially when the integrity of existing infrastructure is compromised beyond repair. Replacement options vary greatly depending on project requirements, environmental factors, and regulatory standards.

Traditional open-cut trenching techniques have served as the conventional method for pipeline replacement, allowing for complete removal of damaged segments and installation of new pipes. However, this method can be both time-consuming and disruptive, particularly in urban areas or environmentally sensitive regions [32]. In addition, the restoration of surface areas after excavation adds to the overall project cost and timeline, presenting a challenge to pipeline operators.

The advent of trenchless technologies has opened new avenues for pipeline replacement. Horizontal directional drilling (HDD) represents a significant advancement in this domain, allowing for the installation of replacement pipelines underground without extensive surface disruption. This method is particularly advantageous for crossing waterways or sensitive ecological areas, as highlighted by McIntosh et al. [33]. HDD has demonstrated effectiveness in various applications, including replacing deteriorating water mains and gas pipelines.

Both relining and replacement strategies present various economic implications for pipeline operators. While relining may offer a lower immediate cost and faster implementation, replacement options can provide long-term cost benefits by ensuring that new infrastructure adheres to updated safety and efficiency standards. Environmental considerations also play a critical role in decision-making around pipeline rehabilitation. The use of trenchless technologies and composite materials can significantly reduce the environmental footprint associated with pipeline maintenance.

13.3.2 Use of Advanced Materials for Rehabilitation

The rehabilitation of pipelines, particularly for hydrogen transport, increasingly relies on advanced materials that enhance durability, resist corrosion, and extend service life. These materials and technologies not only repair existing damage but also improve overall performance, reduce maintenance needs, and minimize service disruptions. Key approaches, including composites, relining systems, reinforcement sleeves, and specialized coatings, are summarized in Table 13.3, which highlights their descriptions, benefits, and areas of application.

Table 13.3 Materials and techniques for sustainable pipeline rehabilitation

Category	Technology/ material	Description	Advantages	Application focus
Composites	FRPs (fiber-reinforced polymers)	Lightweight, high-strength composite wraps with customizable properties	Corrosion-resistant, hydrogen-embrittlement resistant, adaptable, long service life	Hydrogen pipelines, high-pressure systems
Relining Systems	CIPP (cured-in-place pipe)	Resin-impregnated flexible liner inserted and cured inside existing pipelines	No excavation, seamless lining, durable under seismic stress, minimal disruption	Urban pipelines, aging water/gas networks
Reinforcement	Grouted steel and composite sleeves	External sleeves filled with grout to reinforce pipeline walls	Restores strength, protects from external loads, handles fluctuating pressures	Damaged sections of hydrogen and oil/gas pipelines
Protective barriers	Epoxy grouts and specialized coatings	High-performance bonding materials and moisture-resistant coatings (e.g., superhydrophobic)	Strong adhesion, superior anti-corrosion, reduced maintenance, sustainable	Harsh environments, corrosion-prone zones

13.4 Inspection and Validation After Repair

Following the repair of hydrogen pipelines, thorough inspection and validation processes are critical to ensure that the rehabilitation methods employed have restored integrity and safety. These processes utilize a variety of non-destructive testing techniques and monitoring technologies to verify that the repaired sections meet operational standards and do not compromise safety. Figure 13.5 represents a comprehensive pipeline inspection framework applied after hydrogen pipeline repairs. Following rehabilitation, ensuring the integrity and safety of repaired sections is critical. The framework integrates multiple methods, including in-line inspection (ILI) technologies, such as magnetic flux leakage and intelligent PIG tools enhanced with machine learning, to accurately detect and classify defects. Complementary non-destructive testing (NDT) techniques, including ultrasonic, radiographic, and eddy current testing, provide detailed evaluation of welds and joints. Strategic inspection planning, guided by risk-based approaches, prioritizes high-risk areas while optimizing resources and minimizing operational interruptions. Validation of ILI data through direct inspections ensures accuracy and continuous improvement in defect characterization. Additionally, emerging technologies such as robotics, automated inspection systems, and AI-driven analytics enhance both the safety and precision of inspections, enabling a proactive and adaptive approach to post-repair pipeline management.

1. ***In-Line Inspection Technologies***

In-line inspection (ILI) is a widely adopted method for assessing the integrity of pipelines after repairs. This technique typically involves the use of a pipeline inspection gauge (PIG), which is propelled through the pipeline to collect data related to defects or anomalies [34]. These gauges are equipped with various sensors, including magnetic, acoustic, and optical sensors, which provide comprehensive data regarding the structural condition of the pipeline [35].

Research indicates that ILI is effective for identifying areas susceptible to defects. For instance, magnetic flux leakage (MFL) technology can detect wall thinning, cracks, and other anomalies, thereby providing critical insights into the health of the pipeline post-repair [36]. Importantly, integrating advanced data analytics into ILI systems enhances the interpretation of collected data and enables more accurate assessments of pipeline integrity.

An example of this integration is found in the work by Liu et al. [37], which presents an intelligent in-line inspection tool driven by the medium in the pipeline, utilizing machine learning to analyze inspection data, thereby improving defect detection and classification. These improvements are crucial for validating the effectiveness of repairs and making informed decisions for ongoing maintenance.

2. ***Visual and Non-Destructive Testing (NDT)***

In conjunction with ILI, visual inspection and various non-destructive testing (NDT) techniques play a vital role in validating repairs. Techniques such as ultrasonic testing

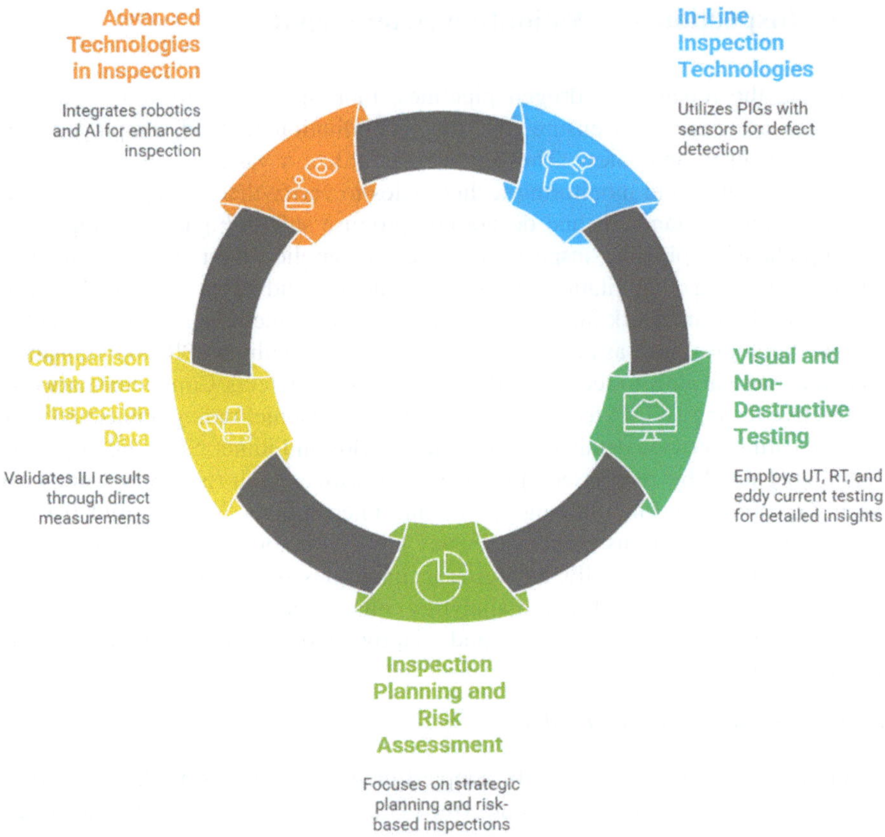

Fig. 13.5 Comprehensive pipeline inspection framework

(UT), radiographic testing (RT), and eddy current testing provide detailed insights into pipeline welds and joints, which are often critical failure points. For example, ultrasonic NDT enables the detection of internal defects that may not be visible from external inspections. The effectiveness of UT during post-repair inspections has been extensively addressed in literature, demonstrating its role in confirming the soundness of repaired joints and identifying critical defects that could lead to failure.

Duan's [38] work highlights the role of digital radiographic testing (DRT) in providing data on the condition of pressure pipeline systems. The ability to visualize the internal condition of pipelines using advanced imaging techniques enhances the reliability of inspection outcomes post-repair.

3. ***Inspection Planning and Risk Assessment***

Developing an efficient inspection plan is essential for managing interruptions and ensuring that all repair validations are comprehensive and methodical. Research by Wang et al. [39] emphasizes careful planning that incorporates factors such as the condition of previously repaired sections, potential environmental hazards, and regulatory guidelines. This strategic approach enables operators to prioritize inspection efforts based on risk assessments and optimize resource allocation.

The concept of risk-based inspections (RBI) has become increasingly prevalent. RBI frameworks allow for focusing inspection efforts on high-risk areas of pipelines, ensuring that the most critical segments are evaluated thoroughly after repairs. These practices contribute to a proactive maintenance culture, prioritizing safety and efficiency.

4. ***Comparison with Direct Inspection Data***

Validation of in-line inspection results often requires comparison with direct inspection data obtained from localized examinations. For example, Caleyo et al. [39] suggest that excavating specific pipeline sections to validate ILI data against direct measurements is a common practice. This step confirms the accuracy of remote inspections and provides invaluable insights into defect characterization and severity.

The validation process involves correlating the type and size of identified defects from ILI data with discrepancies found during direct inspections. Such comparisons foster continuous improvement in inspection methodologies, enhancing the precision and reliability of data obtained during ILI procedures.

5. ***Advanced Technologies in Inspection***

Emerging technologies such as robotics and automated inspection systems enhance the effectiveness and safety of pipeline inspections after repairs. These technologies enable inspections in environments that are otherwise difficult or dangerous for human operators. For example, the development of robots dedicated to pipeline inspection can perform inspections autonomously and effectively identify defects in real-time.

Recent advances in artificial intelligence and machine learning further support the automation of data analysis and defect recognition processes. Systems leveraging these technologies can significantly enhance decision-making regarding maintenance and create a more fluid and responsive pipeline management system.

13.4.1 Post-Repair Testing Requirements

Following the repair of hydrogen pipelines, a comprehensive set of post-repair testing requirements is essential to ensure the integrity, safety, and long-term performance of the rehabilitated infrastructure. These testing procedures validate the effectiveness of the repair methods employed and provide critical data to guide future maintenance strategies.

1. ***Pressure Testing***

One of the primary post-repair testing requirements is pressure testing, which involves subjecting the repaired pipeline section to controlled pressure levels to assess its structural integrity and leak-tightness. This testing is typically conducted in accordance with industry standards and regulatory guidelines, such as ASME B31.12 for hydrogen pipelines.

Pressure testing can take various forms, including hydrostatic testing, where the pipeline is filled with water and pressurized, or pneumatic testing, where compressed air or an inert gas is used. The choice of testing medium depends on factors such as pipeline material, operational conditions, and environmental considerations. Research has shown that these pressure tests can effectively identify defects or weaknesses in the repaired pipeline, allowing for further remediation before the system is returned to service.

2. ***Non-Destructive Evaluation (NDE)***

Non-destructive evaluation techniques play a crucial role in post-repair testing, providing detailed information about the condition of the repaired pipeline without compromising its structural integrity. These techniques include, but are not limited to, ultrasonic testing (UT), magnetic particle inspection (MPI), and eddy current testing (ECT).

UT, for instance, can be used to detect and characterize defects within the pipeline wall, such as cracks, corrosion, and weld imperfections. Studies have demonstrated the effectiveness of UT in validating the quality of repaired pipeline sections, ensuring that the repair methods have adequately restored the structural integrity. Similarly, MPI and ECT can be employed to assess the condition of the pipeline's surface and near-surface regions, identifying potential defects that could compromise the long-term performance of the repair.

3. ***Leak Detection and Monitoring***

Leak detection and monitoring are essential components of post-repair testing, as they ensure that the repaired pipeline section is free from leaks and can maintain its integrity under operational conditions. This testing may involve the use of advanced technologies, such as fiber optic sensors, acoustic emission monitoring, or tracer gas detection.

Research has shown that the integration of these leak detection systems with repair validation processes can provide real-time data on the pipeline's condition, enabling proactive maintenance and early intervention in the event of any emerging issues. This approach enhances the overall reliability and safety of the rehabilitated hydrogen pipeline infrastructure.

4. ***Corrosion Monitoring***

Given the susceptibility of pipelines to corrosion, especially in the context of hydrogen transport, post-repair testing must include comprehensive corrosion monitoring. This may involve the installation of corrosion monitoring probes, electrochemical measurements, or the use of advanced inspection techniques, such as magnetic flux leakage (MFL) or guided wave ultrasonic testing (GWUT).

By establishing a baseline for the repaired pipeline's corrosion condition, operators can develop targeted maintenance strategies and monitor the long-term performance of the repair. Research has demonstrated the importance of integrating corrosion monitoring into post-repair testing protocols to ensure the longevity and reliability of the rehabilitated infrastructure.

13.4.2 Documentation and Approval Process

The documentation and approval process for post-repair validation of hydrogen pipelines is a critical component in ensuring the integrity and safety of the rehabilitated infrastructure. This comprehensive process involves the systematic recording of repair activities, the analysis of test results, and the formal approval by relevant authorities and stakeholders. By adhering to a robust documentation and approval framework, pipeline operators can demonstrate compliance with regulatory requirements, facilitate informed decision-making, and maintain the long-term reliability of the hydrogen transport system.

1. ***Repair Documentation***

   The documentation of the repair process begins with the detailed recording of all activities undertaken during the rehabilitation of the pipeline. This includes, but is not limited to, the following:

   1. Condition assessment reports: Comprehensive documentation of the pre-repair pipeline condition, including the identification and characterization of defects.
   2. Repair methodology: A detailed description of the repair techniques employed, including the materials used, the installation process, and any modifications to the existing pipeline infrastructure.
   3. Quality control records: Documentation of all quality control measures taken during the repair process, such as material testing, welding inspections, and dimensional checks.
   4. Post-repair testing results: Comprehensive documentation of the various post-repair testing procedures, including pressure testing, non-destructive evaluation, leak detection, and corrosion monitoring.
   5. Photographic and video evidence: Visual documentation of the repair process and the final condition of the rehabilitated pipeline section.

This comprehensive documentation serves as a valuable reference for future maintenance activities, provides evidence of compliance with regulatory requirements, and supports the decision-making process for pipeline operators.

2. ***Data Analysis and Reporting***

   The analysis of the post-repair testing data is a crucial step in the documentation and approval process. Pipeline operators must carefully review the results of pressure tests, non-destructive evaluations, leak detection, and corrosion monitoring to ensure that the repaired section meets or exceeds the required performance standards.

The analysis of this data should be presented in the form of detailed reports, which may include the following elements:

1. Comparison of pre-repair and post-repair conditions: Highlighting the improvements achieved through the rehabilitation process.
2. Identification of any remaining or newly detected defects: Providing a clear understanding of the pipeline's current condition and any areas requiring further attention.
3. Recommendations for future maintenance: Based on the analysis of the test results, recommendations for ongoing monitoring, preventive maintenance, or additional repairs may be provided.
4. Compliance with regulatory requirements: Demonstrating that the repaired pipeline section meets all applicable safety, environmental, and industry standards.

These reports serve as the foundation for the approval process and provide a comprehensive record of the rehabilitation efforts.

3. ***Approval Process***

The approval process for post-repair validation involves the review and acceptance of the repair documentation and test results by relevant authorities and stakeholders. This may include the following:

1. Internal approval: Review and sign-off by the pipeline operator's engineering and operations teams, ensuring that the repair meets the company's standards and operational requirements.
2. Regulatory approval: Submission of the repair documentation and test results to the appropriate regulatory agencies, such as the Department of Transportation (DOT) or the Pipeline and Hazardous Materials Safety Administration (PHMSA), for review and approval.
3. Third-party validation: Engagement of independent, third-party inspectors or engineering firms to review the repair process and validate the test results, providing an additional layer of assurance.
4. Stakeholder approval: Consultation with relevant stakeholders, such as local communities, environmental organizations, or emergency response agencies, to address any concerns or considerations related to the repaired pipeline section.

The approval process ensures that the rehabilitated pipeline section meets all necessary safety, environmental, and operational requirements before being returned to service, thereby safeguarding the integrity of the hydrogen transport system.

4.***Ongoing Monitoring and Maintenance***

The documentation and approval process does not end with the completion of the repair and the initial validation. Pipeline operators must establish a comprehensive monitoring and maintenance program to ensure the long-term performance and reliability of the rehabilitated infrastructure.

This may include the implementation of continuous monitoring systems, regular inspections, and the development of predictive maintenance strategies based on the analysis of the repair documentation and test results. By maintaining a robust monitoring and maintenance program, pipeline operators can proactively address any emerging issues and ensure the sustained safety and efficiency of the hydrogen transport system.

References

1. Škerlič S, Sokolovskij E, Erčulj V (2020) Maintenance of heavy trucks: an international study on truck drivers. Eksploatacja i Niezawodność 22(3):493–500
2. Frangopol DM, Sabatino S, Soliman M (2015) Maintenance and safety of deteriorating systems: a life-cycle perspective. In: Proceedings of the second international conference on performance-based and life-cycle structural engineering (PLSE 2015), 48–57
3. Kim C et al (2024) Spall repair patch health monitoring system using BIM and IoT. Buildings 14(6):1589
4. Choi H, Lee J, Kim J (2022) Economical inspection methods assisted by unmanned aerial vehicle for bridges in Korea. Sens Mater 34(12):4717–4736
5. Solla M, Pérez-Gracia V, Fontul S (2021) A review of GPR application on transport infrastructures: troubleshooting and best practices. Remote Sensing 13(4):672
6. Udechukwu IM et al (2024) Maintenance culture and socio economic development in Enugu State Nigeria. J Policy Dev Stud 15(1):174–188
7. Kethamukkala K, Liu Y (2023) Information fusion and data augmentation for risk-based maintenance optimization of hydrogen gas pipelines. In: 15th annual conference of the prognostics and health management society, PHM 2023. 2023. Prognostics and Health Management Society
8. Gibson J, Rioja F (2017) Public infrastructure maintenance and the distribution of wealth. Econ Inq 55(1):175–186
9. Capula Colindres S, et al (2020) Effects of depth in external and internal corrosion defects on failure pressure predictions of oil and gas pipelines using finite element models. Adv Struct Eng **23**(14):3128–3139
10. Al Naamani H et al (2024) Numerical prediction with finite element analysis (FEA) of burst pressure in pipelines with interacting internal & external corrosion defects. Eng Res Exp 6(4):045585
11. Anes-Arteche F et al (2017) Challenges in the application of DCVG-survey to predict coating defect size on pipelines. Mater Corros 68(3):329–337
12. Verstraete M et al (2015) Single-specimen evaluation of tearing resistance in SENT testing. Eng Fract Mech 148:324–336
13. Ben Seghier MEA, et al (2018) Structural reliability of corroded pipeline using the so-called Separable Monte Carlo method. J Strain Anal Eng Des 53(8):730–737
14. Bushinskaya A, Timashev S (2018) Predictive maintenance of pipelines with different types of defects. Russ J Construct Sci Technol 4(1):25–33
15. Chen J, et al (2019) A study on the safety factor for corrosion assessment of oil and gas pipeline through in-line inspection. Key Engineering Materials 795:233–238
16. Gianninia L, et al (2024) Towards cost effective inspection strategies for hydrogen pipelines: current challenges and potential solutions. In: The 34th European safety and reliability conference at, Kraków, Poland
17. Yang Y, Xie H (2021) Determination of optimal MR&R strategy and inspection intervals to support infrastructure maintenance decision making. Sustainability 13(5):2664
18. Lambrescu I, Minescu M, Diniță A (2019) Implementing of 3D scanning techniques in the analytical and numerical assessment of pipelines with volumetric surface defects. Revista de Chimie (Rev. Chim.) 70(12):4138–4144

19. Zhao B et al (2023) Design of enhanced pipeline repair clamp. Material strength and applied mechanics. IOS Press, pp 143–149
20. Zhang H et al (2021) Effects of fillet weld size and sleeve material strength on the residual stress distribution and structural safety while implementing the new sleeve repair process. Materials 14(23):7463
21. Alian AR, Shazly M, Megahed MM (2013) Finite element simulation of in-service sleeve repair welding of gas pipelines. Appl Mech Mater 313:957–961
22. Deng P et al (2023) Finite element analysis of corrosion tubular T-joint repaired with grouted clamp. Adv Civil Eng 2023(1):6634023
23. Ivanov VA (2020) Reconditioning of worn process equipment using composite materials. Int J Emerg Trends Eng Res 8(6):2635–2642
24. Rajak DK et al (2019) Fiber-reinforced polymer composites: manufacturing, properties, and applications. Polymers 11(10):1667
25. Koumoulos EP et al (2019) Research and development in carbon fibers and advanced high-performance composites supply chain in Europe: a roadmap for challenges and the industrial uptake. J Compos Sci 3(3):86
26. Ku HS, Lee KF, Li CW (2003) Thermal analysis of joining thermoplastic composites using microwaves. HKIE Trans 10(1):14–20
27. Machado MVF et al (2025) Micromechanics for polymer matrix laminated composites: a literature review of fundamental models, advances and a trend analysis for future researches. Observ Econ Latinoam 23(5):e10103–e10103
28. Oliver B et al (2019) Natural-fiber-reinforced polymer composites for automotive parts manufacturing. Key Eng Mater 793:9–16
29. Ćoralić A, et al (2023) Testing of mechanical properties of polymer PA6–30% glass fibres. In: IOP conference series: materials science and engineering. IOP Publishing
30. Wang J, Wang C, Xin Z (2024) Study on the morphologic and flow state of polyacrylonitrile particles in a microchannel reactor. Ind Eng Chem Res 63(11):4991–4999
31. Kermanshachi S, Cobanoglu MM, Damnjanovic I (2017) An optimal preventive maintenance model for natural gas transmission pipelines. In: Pipelines 2017. pp 517–526
32. Man JP et al (2025) Development of an innovative pipeline with fusion, digital planning, and three-dimensional printing to improve mitral valve interventional care. Echocardiography 42(5):e70184
33. McIntosh R, Littlestar G, Ekelund A (2014) Using HPIR class composite pipeline systems to overcome the challenges of rehabilitating or replacing a pipeline across a navigable waterway and environmentally sensitive wetlands. In: International pipeline conference. American Society of Mechanical Engineers
34. Nguyen H-H, Park J-H, Jeong H-Y (2023) A simultaneous pipe-attribute and PIG-Pose estimation (SPPE) using 3-D point cloud in compressible gas pipelines. Sensors 23(3):1196
35. Li R et al (2023) Research on internal shape anomaly inspection technology for pipeline girth welds based on alternating excitation detection. Sensors 23(17):7519
36. Feng Q et al (2016) Literature review: theory and application of in-line inspection technologies for oil and gas pipeline girth weld defection. Sensors 17(1):50
37. Liu S, Wang H, Li R (2022) Attention module magnetic flux leakage linked deep residual network for pipeline in-line inspection. Sensors 22(6):2230
38. Duan Z, et al (2025) Influence of medium temperature on digital radiographic parameters during online inspection of pressure piping systems. In: Fifth international conference on telecommunications, optics, and computer science (TOCS 2024). SPIE
39. Wang Y, Su C, Xie M (2024) Optimizing inspection plan for corroded pipeline with considering imperfect maintenance. Proc Inst Mech Eng Part O J Risk Reliab 238(2):417–428

Chapter 14
Emerging Technologies and Innovations

This chapter explores the forefront of technological advancements and innovations shaping the future of materials science, inspection methodologies, and digital transformation in pipeline integrity management. The chapter begins with a comprehensive review of advances in materials science, highlighting the development of hydrogen-resistant alloys designed to enhance durability and safety in corrosive environments. It further examines the evolution of smart coatings and self-healing materials, emphasizing their potential to significantly reduce maintenance costs and extend asset lifespan.

The discussion progresses to next-generation inspection and monitoring techniques, focusing on the integration of robotics and drones to enable more efficient, accurate, and safe pipeline assessments. Complementing these physical inspection tools, the chapter delves into AI-driven data analytics, showcasing how machine learning algorithms and predictive models transform raw inspection data into actionable insights, improving decision-making processes.

In addressing digital transformation, the chapter underscores the role of blockchain technology in ensuring data integrity and traceability across complex pipeline networks. It also evaluates the impact of cloud computing and edge analytics, which facilitate real-time data processing and enhance responsiveness in integrity management systems.

Finally, the chapter outlines future research directions, identifying key challenges and opportunities that lie ahead in adopting these emerging technologies. It advocates for collaborative industry initiatives to accelerate innovation, promote standardization, and foster cross-sector partnerships essential for advancing pipeline safety and sustainability. Through this multidimensional analysis, this chapter provides a forward-looking perspective on how emerging technologies and innovations will redefine pipeline integrity management in the coming decades.

M. Hussain et al., *Hydrogen Pipeline Integrity*, Green Energy and Technology,
https://doi.org/10.1007/978-981-95-5609-0_14

14.1 Advances in Materials Science

The accelerating transition to a hydrogen economy hinges on finding efficient and durable materials that can enhance the production, storage, and transportation of hydrogen. This transition is driven by the urgent need to reduce carbon emissions and improve energy security. Recent innovations in materials science are central to addressing the challenges associated with hydrogen energy systems, particularly in terms of storage and pipeline integrity. This section explores these advances, focusing on developments related to hydrogen storage materials, pipeline construction materials, and strategies to mitigate hydrogen embrittlement.

One key area of advancement is the development of nanostructured materials for hydrogen storage. Nanomaterials, such as carbon nanotubes and graphene, have demonstrated significant potential in improving the structural integrity and durability of hydrogen storage solutions [1, 2]. These materials enhance the performance of hydrogen storage tanks and pipelines, addressing crucial challenges such as hydrogen embrittlement, which affects the long-term reliability of metal components under hydrogen exposure. Research indicates that incorporating nanomaterials can lead to significant improvements in the storage capacity and efficiency of hydrogen systems [1, 3]. Such enhancements facilitate the safe storage and transport of hydrogen, essential for a reliable hydrogen supply chain.

In addition to nano-engineered materials, the exploration of metal–organic frameworks (MOFs), zeolite imidazole frameworks (ZIFs), and covalent organic frameworks (COFs) has emerged as an innovative approach for hydrogen storage [3]. These reticular materials exhibit high porosity and tailorability, allowing for effective hydrogen adsorption and storage at varied pressures and temperatures. The combination of these advanced materials with state-of-the-art engineering practices can lead to the development of hybrid systems that integrate hydrogen production, storage, and utilization, furthering the efficiency of hydrogen energy systems.

Another pressing issue in hydrogen energy applications is the phenomenon of hydrogen embrittlement, a process that compromises the mechanical properties of metals when exposed to hydrogen [4, 5]. Recent efforts to develop polymeric coatings and composite materials aim to alleviate the risks of embrittlement in pipes and storage tanks [4]. Polymeric coatings serve as effective barriers, reducing hydrogen permeation into metal substrates and protecting them from degradation. Moreover, advancements in high-strength steels and specialized welding techniques enhance the resilience of structural materials, allowing them to better withstand the aggressive conditions presented by hydrogen service environments [5, 6].

The compatibility of existing pipeline materials with hydrogen is another critical area of research. Switching from natural gas to blended hydrogen poses significant challenges as hydrogen's unique properties—including its small molecular size and high diffusivity—can noticeably exacerbate material degradation processes [7]. Evaluating the performance of traditional materials like polyethylene and steel under hydrogen-rich environments is essential to maintaining pipeline integrity [8]. Investigations into the fatigue resistance and slow crack growth of these materials under hydrogen exposure reveal pathways to enhance their performance and longevity in renewable energy applications [9].

Materials engineering is thus pivotal in overcoming the barriers faced by hydrogen energy systems. As advancements continue, the focus remains on developing innovative materials that can effectively manage the challenges associated with hydrogen, including improved storage capabilities and enhanced resistance to embrittlement. The evolution of hydrogen energy systems is increasingly intertwined with multidisciplinary collaboration among chemists, materials scientists, and engineers to harness sustainable energy technologies effectively [10, 11].

14.1.1 Hydrogen-Resistant Alloys

The development of hydrogen-resistant alloys (see Fig. 14.1) is crucial for enhancing the performance and safety of hydrogen-related applications, including pipelines, storage tanks, and various energy systems. This section discusses recent advances in hydrogen-resistant alloys, emphasizing their composition, microstructure, and mechanical properties.

One key approach to improving HE resistance in structural steels, such as the widely used 12% chromium martensitic steels, involves alloying with elements that can trap hydrogen and prevent its detrimental impact on mechanical properties. For instance, the addition of niobium and molybdenum can significantly enhance the hydrogen resistance of steels by forming carbides that serve as hydrogen traps [12]. Studies indicate that this mechanism not only reduces hydrogen diffusion rates but also improves the overall mechanical performance of the alloy under hydrogen exposure. Consequently, advanced heat treatments and alloy designs are being implemented to optimize these alloying effects.

Research indicates that the microstructural characteristics of alloys greatly influence their resistance to hydrogen embrittlement. For instance, fine-grained microstructures exhibit higher resistance to hydrogen degradation than coarser structures, as grain boundaries can act as barriers to hydrogen diffusion [13]. Recent studies on high-strength pipeline steels, such as those used in hydrogen transportation, have shown that the presence of acicular ferrite and bainitic structures can significantly improve their performance in hydrogen environments [14]. These microstructural features not only enhance strength but also mitigate the risk of embrittlement by reducing hydrogen ingress.

Looking into specific alloys, 316L stainless steel is regarded for its excellent corrosion resistance and mechanical properties, making it a popular choice for hydrogen applications [15]. Recent investigations have revealed that modifications in its microstructure, for instance, through controlled weld procedures can further enhance its performance by minimizing the effects of hydrogen charging that compromise mechanical integrity. Additionally, the interplay between austenitic transformations and the alloy's resistance properties illustrates the complexities involved in developing effective hydrogen-resistant materials [16].

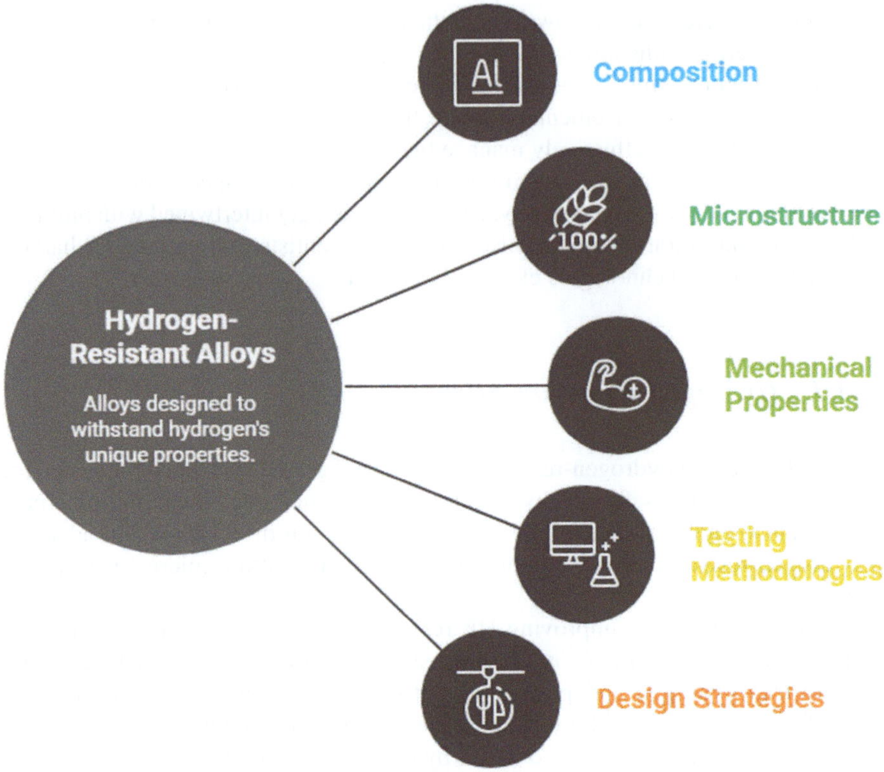

Fig. 14.1 Exploring hydrogen-resistant alloys

The design of novel materials, such as high-nitrogen stainless steels, is gaining prominence due to their superior mechanical properties and inherent resistance to HE [17]. These materials reformulate the traditional perspectives on alloy design, demonstrating that high nitrogen content can bolster both strength and ductility while simultaneously mitigating hydrogen uptake. Experimental data suggest that the combination of alloy composition and controlled processing conditions can yield materials that perform effectively under hydrogen exposure, propelling advancements in hydrogen transport technologies.

Advanced testing methodologies, including electrochemical hydrogen charging experiments and hydrogen diffusion measurements, are essential in evaluating the HE resistance of different alloys. According to research, techniques such as slow strain rate testing (SSRT) and the use of microcantilever beams enable precise assessments of how various alloy compositions behave under hydrogen-rich environments [18, 19]. Such methodologies facilitate the development of predictive criteria for material selection that prioritize the prevention of HE.

Importantly, the knowledge gained from experimental work and theoretical modeling must converge to inform the design of alloys capable of withstanding the unique challenges posed by hydrogen. Interdisciplinary collaboration between materials scientists, mechanical engineers, and chemists is vital in crafting a comprehensive approach to hydrogen-resistant alloys, ensuring that theoretical advancements translate into practical applications for industries from energy to transportation.

14.1.2 Smart Coatings and Self-Healing Materials

The advancement of smart coatings and self-healing materials has garnered significant attention in the context of improving the resilience and longevity of structures within various applications, notably in hydrogen environments. Smart coatings not only provide protective barriers against environmental stresses but also possess the ability to autonomously repair damage incurred due to external influences. This capability is crucial in hydrogen applications where infrastructure materials are susceptible to hydrogen embrittlement and corrosion.

A noteworthy category of smart coatings is those designed with self-healing properties. For example, Zhang and Xiao [20] have demonstrated a silicone polyurea waterproof coating capable of autonomously healing scratches and minor damages. The material's chemical formulation aids in quickly restoring its structural integrity, demonstrating its applicability in environments where exposure to hydrogen could induce material fatigue. Such materials can significantly extend the service life of protective coatings, offering a dual function of both resilience against environmental penetration and remedial capabilities post-damage.

Similarly, Li et al. [21] have reported on a self-healing superhydrophobic coating featuring a disulfide-bonded polyurethane structure. Their experimental results indicated that scratches on the surfaces could heal within hours at room temperature, underlining the practicality of such coatings in maintaining surface functionality over extended durations. The incorporation of responsive polymers that can react to mechanical damage enhances the utility of coatings in critical applications, suggesting a vital step in combating the deterioration caused by hydrogen-related wear.

The concept of smart coatings extends beyond mere protection and self-repair, as highlighted by Zhang et al. [22], who explored active corrosion protection mechanisms within their innovative coatings. By integrating layered double hydroxide structures into a cerium-modified matrix, the smart coating was able to respond to corrosion stimuli and heal itself when subjected to minor abrasions. This dynamic response not only mitigates corrosion but also facilitates material recovery, thus extending the overall lifetime of components operating in hydrogen-rich environments.

The use of carbon nanomaterials within coating formulations has also shown promise for corrosion protection and structural enhancements. Singh et al. [23] reported on a microwave-assisted bio-vitrimer framework incorporating reduced graphene oxide (rGO) that can self-heal upon damage, effectively providing a robust barrier against corrosion. The ability of these smart coatings to dynamically modify their properties based on environmental interactions positions them as innovative solutions in modern material science, particularly relevant for hydrogen applications.

A fascinating aspect of self-healing technology is the utilization of microcapsule systems to deliver healing agents autonomously upon damage. For instance, Ni et al. [24] developed a smart self-healing coating that incorporates microcontainers filled with bioactive agents capable of mitigating corrosion and biofouling, responding to surface damage by releasing these agents. Such systems ensure ongoing surface protection that adapts to usage conditions and wear, reinforcing the durability of hydrogen infrastructure.

Notably, the development of smart coatings with enhanced adaptability to stimuli is gaining traction. Research by Hong et al. [25] discussed high-entropy alloy coatings that could dynamically respond to hydrogen exposure, effectively mitigating embrittlement through controlled structural transitions. Consequently, such coatings can aim to pre-emptively thwart harmful effects by manipulating their properties based on environmental changes.

The methodologies for creating such advanced coatings vary, but emerging trends favor the use of nanostructures as fundamental components due to their superior mechanical and reactive properties. Incorporating nanofillers can significantly enhance the mechanical performance and resilience of coatings. For instance, Wu et al. [26] explored a nanofluid that responds to environmental stimuli while providing self-healing properties, indicating a new frontier in adaptive coatings technology.

Focusing on their application in dynamic environments, materials science continues to evolve with techniques like atomic layer deposition, providing precisely controlled thickness and uniformity of smart coatings for various substrates [27]. This refinement in manufacturing processes is essential to meet the specifications required for infrastructures subjected to hydrogen, ensuring long-lasting performance and reliability.

14.2 Next-Generation Inspection and Monitoring

Modern inspection techniques harness AI and machine learning to automate the identification of defects. Research has indicated that using machine learning algorithms facilitates real-time defect detection and classification in concrete structures, which is pivotal for maintaining structural integrity [28]. Through image analysis, these systems can minimize human error during inspections, increase efficiency, and reduce costs associated with manual inspections. For instance, convolutional neural networks (CNNs) have been successfully employed in image processing to improve the detection speeds of concrete classifying defects, thus revolutionizing civil infrastructure monitoring.

The use of UAV technology has transformed traditional inspection methods, providing access to challenging locations while ensuring safety and efficiency. UAVs equipped with high-resolution cameras and LiDAR sensors are increasingly deployed for detailed structural assessments, such as monitoring power transmission lines and wind turbine blades [29, 30]. This approach minimizes risks to human inspectors and enables the collection of high-dimensional data that can be analyzed for rapid identification of deteriorations or malfunctions. UAV-mounted systems have shown effectiveness in facilitating inspections in large and complex infrastructures, ensuring that potential issues are identified early and remedial actions can be implemented swiftly.

LiDAR technology has emerged as a game changer in transportation infrastructure monitoring. Research has documented that LiDAR enables automatic damage detection with millimeter accuracy by processing point clouds, depicting intricate structural features in three dimensions [31]. This capability allows engineers to precisely document and analyze surface conditions that would be difficult to assess via conventional visual inspection methods. Furthermore, the integration of augmented reality (AR) with LiDAR applications has been identified as a promising direction for future developments, allowing dynamic visualizations to support remote inspections and decision-making processes.

The role of data management systems is paramount in this landscape. The integration of Building Information Modeling (BIM) with inspection technologies has streamlined the process of managing inspection data and structural asset information [31]. BIM frameworks enable the visualization and analysis of collected data, facilitating clearer insights into structural conditions and aiding maintenance planning. As the construction industry increasingly adopts Industry 4.0 principles, the synergy between inspection data and digital twins promises improved operational efficiencies through enhanced information sharing and decision-making mechanisms [32].

14.2.1 Robotics and Drones for Inspection

The advent of drones and robotic systems represents a significant leap in inspection methodologies across various industries, particularly in civil engineering, infrastructure maintenance, and environmental monitoring. Drones, also known as unmanned aerial vehicles (UAVs), equipped with advanced sensors and imaging technologies, have proven to be invaluable tools for performing efficient, accurate, and safe inspections in challenging and hazardous environments.

One of the primary advantages of employing drones for inspection is their ability to access hard-to-reach areas. Suthar et al. [33] present innovative developments in robotic drone arms that can extend the capabilities of UAVs, allowing them to perform complex inspections on civil structures, thus improving the quality and thoroughness of assessments. This functionality is particularly beneficial in scenarios where human inspectors might face dangerous conditions, such as inspecting high-rise buildings, bridges, or towers.

The integration of machine learning and artificial intelligence with drone technology has improved data collection and analysis processes. This synergy enables real-time processing of inspection data, facilitating quicker decision-making based on unprecedented levels of detail collected during the inspection process [34]. By utilizing advanced algorithms, drones can autonomously identify defects, such as cracks or corrosion, thereby enhancing predictive maintenance strategies in various infrastructures, including power lines and industrial facilities [35].

The case studies conducted by various researchers further emphasize the effectiveness of drones in monitoring specific industrial applications, such as wind turbine blade inspections or power line assessments. For instance, drone-based inspection methods drastically reduce the need for manual inspections, mitigating the risks associated with climbing towers or performing aerial inspections in precarious settings [36]. The employment of UAVs for these purposes has been shown to reduce inspection times while providing high-resolution imagery for more accurate assessments, thus underscoring the potential of drones to enhance operational efficiencies across multiple sectors.

Zhong et al. [37] provide a systematic review of the use of drones for roofing inspections, highlighting their potential to enhance the building inspection process through aerial photography and imaging analysis. By capturing comprehensive 3D data of roof surfaces, drones can significantly expedite the identification of issues, allowing for timely maintenance that helps extend the lifespan of roofing materials and reduces long-term costs.

14.2.2 AI-Driven Data Analytics

AI-driven analytics provides a data-centric approach to resource allocation in inspections, emphasizing efficiency by focusing on high-risk areas. Zhou et al. [38] detail a sliding window-based machine-learning framework that enables regulatory agencies to optimize their inspection resources by prioritizing interventions at high-risk enterprises, thereby reducing environmental violations. This data-driven strategy boosts the effectiveness of inspections by directing resources where they are most needed, ultimately supporting sustainability initiatives and ensuring compliance with environmental regulations, see Fig. 14.2.

Advancements in deep learning methodologies have improved the accuracy of inspections and permitted the automation of complex visual assessments. Jenssen and Roverso [39] highlight the use of UAVs integrated with deep learning frameworks to conduct intelligent inspections of power line components, emphasizing the efficiency and safety of autonomous inspections. The combination of drone technology with AI not only accelerates the inspection process but also increases its accuracy by minimizing human error and fatigue factors.

AI algorithms enhance quality control and defect detection in manufacturing processes. Yu et al. [40] present an algorithm that integrates the YOLO (You Only Look Once) object detection framework with an attention mechanism, allowing for efficient and accurate defect detection in manufacturing settings. This approach showcases how machine learning can adaptively improve operational workflows by decreasing reliance on manual inspections and enhancing quality assurance measures.

Fig. 14.2 AI-driven inspection applications

Predictive maintenance frameworks facilitated by AI have proven advantageous in prioritizing inspections, as highlighted by Yin et al. [41], their work shows that online machine learning methods achieve accuracy comparable to traditional offline methods while demonstrating faster classifier training, thereby enhancing maintenance strategies. By effectively analyzing sensor data in real-time, organizations can proactively address potential issues before they escalate, which ultimately contributes to improved operational reliability.

The challenges of integrating machine learning into existing inspection protocols remain significant. Ensuring the interpretability and transparency of AI models while minimizing biases in data analysis continues to be a key focus for researchers and practitioners alike. Continued efforts to establish best practices and standardized frameworks will be crucial for the successful adoption of AI-driven analytics in inspection processes.

14.3 Digital Transformation in Pipeline Integrity

One of the notable advancements in pipeline integrity management is the application of machine learning techniques for predictive maintenance and risk assessment. Emerging studies, such as those by Yin [41], emphasize the importance of predictive and optimization techniques in monitoring pipeline systems, specifically focusing on leak detection and spill response strategies, refer to Fig. 14.3. Predictive analytics allows operators to anticipate failures and address vulnerabilities before they lead to significant incidents, thereby safeguarding both the environment and economic interests.

The integration of intelligent feature recognition methods, as demonstrated by Fan and Feng, [42] enhances the assessment capabilities of pipeline integrity. By utilizing advanced algorithms for defect detection, organizations can identify abnormalities such as bending strain or displacement in natural gas pipelines, enabling timely interventions and maintenance. This proactive approach is crucial as a pipeline leak can lead not only to environmental damage but also to significant economic losses due to production disruptions, underscoring the necessity of advanced monitoring systems.

The deployment of digital twin technology represents another considerable advance in the digital transformation of pipeline management. This approach involves creating virtual representations of physical assets, which can be continuously updated with real-time data. Digital twins allow operators to monitor pipeline conditions, simulate performance under various scenarios, and analyze the effects of modifications or environmental factors. The use of such technologies promises to optimize the management of infrastructure investments by providing insights into equipment performance and lifespan.

The shift towards integrated digital platforms facilitates seamless communication and data sharing across various stakeholders. As proposed by Massel and Massel [43], the development of interconnected systems fosters collaboration and enhances decision-making processes. Through integrated digital platforms, operators can access a cohesive data ecosystem, allowing for comprehensive analysis and effective communication regarding pipeline integrity.

AI-driven data analytics, as highlighted in various studies, enhances the capacity to manage and analyze vast amounts of data collected from sensors and monitoring

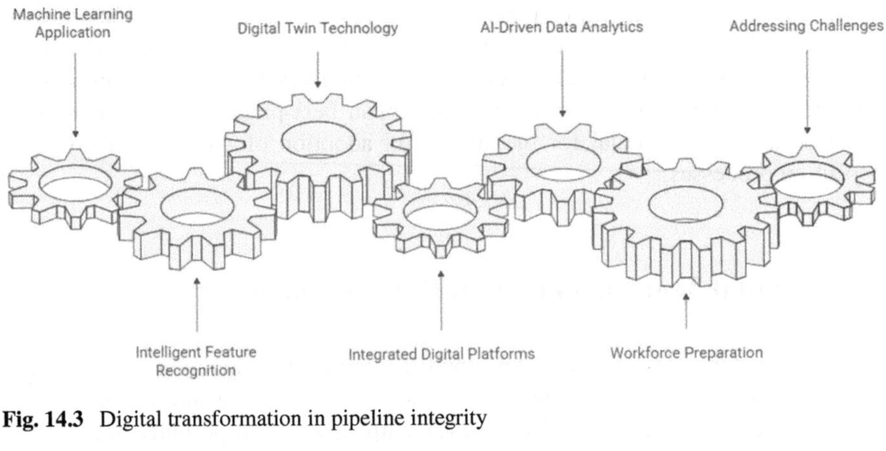

Fig. 14.3 Digital transformation in pipeline integrity

systems. The ability to process this information efficiently enables companies to derive actionable insights, which are critical for maintaining pipeline integrity. With the rising significance of the Internet of Things (IoT) in infrastructure management, companies are increasingly utilizing IoT solutions to collect real-time data, thereby improving operational oversight.

The preparation of the workforce for this digital transformation is essential. Organizations must focus on digital literacy and provide training for employees to effectively utilize these advanced technologies. The human element in adopting digital transformation cannot be overstated, as skilled personnel are needed to interpret complex data outputs and make informed decisions based on analytics.

Despite the significant strides made in digital transformation for pipeline integrity, challenges remain. The complexity of data integration, the need for interoperability among various systems, and concerns regarding cybersecurity are critical issues that organizations must address. Ensuring that data from diverse sources is harmonized and accessible is paramount for the successful implementation of comprehensive integrity management solutions.

14.3.1 Blockchain for Data Integrity

Blockchain technology represents a transformative approach to ensuring data integrity across various applications, particularly within infrastructure and pipeline management. By providing a decentralized ledger that is immutable and secure, blockchain enhances the ability to maintain accurate records while preventing unauthorized alterations, making it a valuable tool for organizations focused on data integrity. This section explores the implementation of blockchain technology for ensuring data integrity in pipeline management and related fields.

At its core, blockchain operates as a distributed ledger technology that utilizes cryptographic principles to maintain data integrity. As detailed by Wibowo and Christian [44], the presence of blockchain technology mitigates doubts surrounding data authenticity, particularly in the context of audit data integrity. The built-in characteristics of blockchain—such as transparency, permanence, and verifiability—render it an excellent solution for assuring the integrity of data pertaining to pipelines and infrastructure.

In the context of pipeline integrity, the application of blockchain can enhance the monitoring of materials and products along the supply chain. For instance, Pooja [45] highlights how blockchain can facilitate better data integrity by ensuring that all transactions related to materials are securely recorded in a tamper-proof environment. This capability is particularly critical in the context of regulatory compliance, where stakeholders need to demonstrate that all materials used in pipeline construction or maintenance have been sourced and handled according to specified standards.

The synergy between blockchain and Internet of Things (IoT) technologies further enhances data integrity management. Berko et al. [46] describe how IoT networks, when supplemented with blockchain technology, improve data security and transparency while enabling robust data integrity mechanisms. The combination allows for continuous monitoring of pipeline conditions and immediate recording of any irregularities in real-time, ensuring an accurate historical record of the pipeline's operational status.

Despite the promises of blockchain in maintaining data integrity, challenges related to scalability, energy consumption, and integration with existing systems persist. It is essential for stakeholders to collaborate in developing standardized protocols that ensure consistency in blockchain applications across various domains. The potential for blockchain to facilitate seamless interoperability between different systems can lead to significant enhancements in reliability and efficiency, particularly in managing complex infrastructures like pipelines.

14.3.2 Cloud Computing and Edge Analytics

One of the primary benefits of combining cloud computing and edge analytics is the ability to process and analyze vast amounts of data closer to the source of generation, which reduces latency and bandwidth usage. Singh et al. [47] emphasize that edge computing complements cloud services by providing real-time data processing capabilities at locations where data is generated, ultimately improving operational responsiveness in various applications, including pipeline monitoring. This capability is particularly crucial in scenarios where timely decision-making is essential for maintaining asset integrity and preventing failures.

The challenges associated with large-scale data transmission to centralized clouds are addressed effectively through edge computing. As noted by Huang et al. [48], edge nodes are better equipped to manage tasks with low computational complexity, allowing for rapid local processing of essential data in the context of IoT applications. This architecture not only minimizes communication overhead but also enhances the speed and efficiency of data analytics, facilitating more agile response times in pipeline monitoring scenarios.

In the context of pipeline operations, sensors deployed throughout the infrastructure can generate vast amounts of data. Edge analytics allows these sensors to perform preliminary data processing, filtering, and analysis locally, and only the most relevant information is sent to the cloud for further analysis. This design minimizes latency and ensures that critical data insights are raised immediately, as underscored by Shahra et al. [49], who demonstrate the benefits of optimized data processing through edge computing techniques.

The deployment of machine learning algorithms at the edge has further propelled the capabilities of these systems. Liu et al. [50] discuss how distributed deep learning models can process IoT data directly at the edge, ensuring timely insights and predictions. This approach enables organizations to utilize real-time data for decision-making, optimizing pipeline operation processes while minimizing the likelihood of failures.

The implementation of cloud and edge computing also introduces challenges, such as managing the security and privacy of data processed at the edge. As suggested by Costa and Beko [51], various measures must be deployed to safeguard data against unauthorized access during transmission and processing. Organizations should adopt comprehensive security frameworks that ensure data integrity and comply with regulatory requirements while harnessing the benefits of edge analytics.

References

1. Shaker LM, Al-Amiery AA, Al-Azzawi WK (2024) Nanomaterials: paving the way for the hydrogen energy frontier. Discover nano 19(1):3
2. Alasali F, et al (2024) A review of hydrogen production and storage materials for efficient integrated hydrogen energy systems. Energy Sci Eng 12(5):1934–1968
3. Alabdulhadi RA, et al (2025) Potential use of reticular materials (MOFs, ZIFs, and COFs) for hydrogen storage. ACS Appl Energy Mater 8(3):1397–1413
4. Kapuscinsky N, et al (2024) Polymeric coatings for preventing hydrogen embrittlement in industrial storage and transmission systems. ACS Appl Eng Mater 2(11):2488–2503
5. Cai L, et al (2022) Experimental investigation on the hydrogen embrittlement characteristics and mechanism of natural gas-hydrogen transportation pipeline steels. Mater Res Exp 9(4):046512
6. Cairney J, et al (2022) The effect of hydrogen on the deformation of pearlite in steels. Preprint
7. Ghomashchi R (2023) Green energy revolution and substitution of hydrocarbons with hydrogen: distribution network infrastructure materials. Energies 16(24):8020
8. Byrne N, et al (2023) Influence of hydrogen on vintage polyethylene pipes: slow crack growth performance and material properties. Int J Energy Res 2023(1):6056999
9. Ahad MT, et al (2023) An overview of challenges for the future of hydrogen. Materials 16(20):6680
10. Kut P, Pietrucha-Urbanik K, Zeleňáková M (2024) Assessing the role of hydrogen in sustainable energy futures: a comprehensive bibliometric analysis of research and international collaborations in energy and environmental engineering. Energies 17(8):1862
11. Fan Z (2024) The role of hydrogen in achieving sustainable energy systems: challenges and opportunities. Highlights Sci Eng Technol 116:237–240
12. Si Y, et al (2022) Hydrogen embrittlement and microstructure characterization of 1500 MPa martensitic steel. Steel Res Int 93(10):2200295
13. Li Y, et al (2021) Hydrogen-assisted brittle fracture behavior of low alloy 30CrMo steel based on the combination of experimental and numerical analyses. Materials 14(13):3711
14. Gou J, et al (2023) Hydrogen-induced cracking in CGHAZ of welded X80 steel under tension load. Metals 13(7):1325
15. Hwang B-K, et al (2025) Notch sensitivity of hydrogen-charged 316L stainless steel: experimental insights into mechanical degradation and fracture mechanics. Materials 18(6):1274
16. Kashkarov EB, et al (2015) The formation of stable hydrogen impermeable TiN-based coatings on zirconium alloy Zr1% Nb. In: IOP conference series: materials science and engineering 81:012017. IOP Publishing
17. Balyts' kyi O, et al (2015) Specific features of the fracture of hydrogenated high-nitrogen manganese steels under conditions of rolling friction. Mater Sci 50(4):604–611
18. Lee H, et al (2016) The chemical deposition method for the decoration of palladium particles on carbon nanofibers with rapid conductivity changes. Nanomaterials 6(12):226
19. Yin C, et al (2020) Hydrogen concentration distribution in 2.25 Cr-1Mo-0.25 V steel under the electrochemical hydrogen charging and its influence on the mechanical properties. Materials 13(10):2263

20. Zhang X, Xiao Z (2023) An autonomously self-healing silicone polyurea waterproof coating for combustible cartridge cases. Propellants, Explos, Pyrotech 48(2):e202200239
21. Li C, et al (2022) Near-infrared responsive smart superhydrophobic coating with self-healing and robustness enhanced by disulfide-bonded polyurethane. ACS Appl Mater Interfaces 14(40):45988–46000
22. Zhang G, et al (2018) Active corrosion protection by a smart coating based on a MgAl-layered double hydroxide on a cerium-modified plasma electrolytic oxidation coating on Mg alloy AZ31. Corros Sci 139:370–382
23. Singh P, et al (2024) Microwave-assisted self-healable biovitrimer/rGO framework for anticorrosion applications. ACS Appl Mater Interfaces 16(40):54693–54705
24. Ni X, et al (2021) Design of a smart self-healing coating with multiple-responsive superhydrophobicity and its application in antibiofouling and antibacterial abilities. ACS Appl Mater Interfaces 13(48):57864–57879
25. Hong Z, et al (2022) Hydrogen isotope permeation behavior of AlCrFeTiNb, AlCrMoNbZr and AlCrFeMoTi high-entropy alloys coatings. Coatings 12(2):171
26. Wu J, et al (2024) A super-adhesive 2D diamond smart nanofluid with self-healing properties and multifunctional applications. ACS Appl Mater Interfaces 16(31):41435–41449
27. Prasadam VP, et al (2019) Atomic layer deposition of vanadium oxides: process and application review. Mater Today Chem 12:396–423
28. Karimzadeh A, Shoghli O (2020) Predictive analytics for roadway maintenance: a review of current models, challenges, and opportunities. Civil Eng J 6(3):602–625
29. Zhang N, et al (2025) Three-dimensional reconstruction of power transmission lines using UAV oblique photography and LiDAR point clouds. In: Third international conference on geographic information and remote sensing technology (GIRST 2024). SPIE 13551
30. Peng H, et al (2023) Edf-yolov5: an improved algorithm for power transmission line defect detection based on yolov5. Electronics 13(1):148
31. Manalo JRD, et al (2024) LiDAR health monitoring of transport infrastructure: automatic damage detection using classification of point clouds. In: Earth resources and environmental remote sensing/GIS applications XV. SPIE 13197
32. Hussain M, Zhang T, Seema M (2023) Adoption of big data analytics for energy pipeline condition assessment-a systematic review. Int J Press Vessels Pip 206:105061
33. Suthar B, et al (2023) Robotic drone arm for civil structures inspection: challenges and future directions. In: E3S web of conferences 430:1192. EDP Sciences
34. Sadhin AH, et al (2024) YOLO: a competitive analysis of modern object detection algorithms for road defects detection using drone images. Baghdad Sci J 21(6):24
35. Kolios A (2024) Assessing risks for the use of drones for wind turbine inspections. J Phys Conf Ser 2767:032030. IOP Publishing
36. Shafiee M, et al (2021) Unmanned aerial drones for inspection of offshore wind turbines: a mission-critical failure analysis. Robotics 10(1):26
37. Zhong W, et al (2025) The adoption of UAVs for enhancing safety in construction industry: a systematic literature review. Intell Infrast Const 1(1):3
38. Zhou Q, et al (2023) Sliding window-based machine learning for environmental inspection resource allocation. Environ Sci Technol 57(44):16743–16754
39. Jenssen R, Roverso D (2019) Intelligent monitoring and inspection of power line components powered by UAVs and deep learning. IEEE Power Energy Technol Syst J 6(1):11–21
40. Yu L, et al (2022) An efficient yolo algorithm with an attention mechanism for vision-based defect inspection deployed on FPGA. Micromachines 13(7):1058
41. Yin Y, et al (2023) Industrial product quality analysis based on online machine learning. Sensors 23(19):8167
42. Fan Y, Feng XX (2023) Research on integrity Management of long distance pipeline. In: E3S web of conferences 385:03011. EDP Sciences
43. Massel LV, Massel AG (2019) Digital transformation of Russia energy sector: methods and intelligent technologies of scientific substantiation of strategic decisions. In: EPJ web of conferences 217:01011. EDP Sciences

44. Wibowo T, Christian Y (2021) Usage of blockchain to ensure audit data integrity. Equity 24(47), 10.34209
45. Pooja P, Chikhale MM, Dhir S (2025) Uncovering the strategic potential of blockchain technology adoption: a systematic literature review. Strateg Chang 34(2):151–180
46. Berko LO (2025) Advanced supply chain analytics: leveraging digital twins, IoT and blockchain for resilient, data-driven business operations. World J Adv Res Rev 25(2):1777–1799
47. Singh R, Kovacs J, Kiss T (2022) To offload or not? an analysis of big data offloading strategies from edge to cloud. In: 2022 IEEE world AI IoT congress (AIIoT). IEEE
48. Huang J, et al (2024) Construction and research on cloud-edge collaborative power measurement and security model. EAI Endors Trans Energy Web 11(1)
49. Shahra EQ, et al (2024) Intelligent edge-cloud framework for water quality monitoring in water distribution system. Water 16(2):196
50. Liu D, et al (2019) A survey on secure data analytics in edge computing. IEEE Internet Things J 6(3):4946–4967
51. Costa PA, Beko M (2019) Dependable and secure voting mechanism in edge computing. Fut Internet 11(12):262

Chapter 15
Policy, Economics, and Investment Outlook

This chapter delves into the critical interplay between policy frameworks, economic factors, and investment considerations that collectively shape the development and expansion of hydrogen infrastructure. The chapter begins by exploring the regulatory landscape, highlighting key international and regional policies that underpin hydrogen deployment, as well as essential safety and environmental regulations designed to ensure sustainable and secure operations. It then examines the economic drivers and market dynamics influencing hydrogen projects, focusing on cost structures, funding models, and the role of incentives and subsidies in accelerating market adoption. The discussion advances to identify the spectrum of investment risks—including technical, operational, and market-related challenges—and presents risk mitigation strategies through insurance and financial instruments tailored to the unique demands of the hydrogen sector. Finally, the chapter offers strategic recommendations for investors and operators, emphasizing best practices for due diligence, comprehensive risk assessment, and the importance of long-term planning aligned with sustainability goals. Through this integrated perspective, the chapter provides valuable insights to policymakers, investors, and industry stakeholders seeking to navigate the complex yet promising landscape of hydrogen infrastructure investment.

15.1 Regulatory Frameworks Supporting Hydrogen Infrastructure

The development of regulatory frameworks supporting hydrogen infrastructure is crucial for facilitating the transition toward a hydrogen economy. As nations and regions worldwide engage in this transition, it becomes evident that specific policy initiatives are necessary to promote hydrogen production, storage, and utilization sustainably. This multifaceted approach is essential not only for addressing

M. Hussain et al., *Hydrogen Pipeline Integrity*, Green Energy and Technology,
https://doi.org/10.1007/978-981-95-5609-0_15

climate change but also for bolstering energy security and enhancing industrial competitiveness.

The European Union (EU) has taken a leading position in establishing regulatory frameworks that support the hydrogen economy. Specifically, the EU recognizes clean hydrogen as a key component of its climate strategy, energy security, and technological leadership. The EU is developing comprehensive policies that encompass supply-side incentives and binding demand-side targets to stimulate domestic production and avoid external dependencies [1]. Additionally, the EU aims to create a Single Hydrogen Market, designed to enhance market integration and promote investment in hydrogen technologies [2]. Such regulatory frameworks are integral to ensuring that hydrogen plays a significant role in the EU's energy transition, aligning economic activities with climate goals.

Moreover, countries like Germany and the Netherlands have articulated their hydrogen strategies, which hinge on government support mechanisms, technological advancements, and international collaborations. Behrendt emphasizes that the future of industrial hydrogen will largely depend on effective regulations that facilitate renewable resource utilization and public acceptance, particularly when deploying hydrogen technologies for industrial applications [3]. The Dutch government's hybrid approach combines regulatory obligations and financial subsidies aimed at fostering both low-carbon hydrogen production and the utilization of hydrogen derived from natural gas with carbon capture and storage (CCS). These initiatives are essential for creating an efficient, scalable hydrogen value chain.

In Asia, countries such as Japan and South Korea are also making significant strides in hydrogen policy. Japan's government has implemented the "Basic Hydrogen Strategy," which emphasizes reducing hydrogen costs and increasing production capabilities by 2030 [4]. This strategy aligns with Japan's broader goals of establishing a hydrogen-powered society and contributing to global emissions reduction efforts. Similarly, South Korea's policies are driving hydrogen technology development, highlighting the importance of regulatory frameworks that encourage the construction of hydrogen refueling stations and storage infrastructure [5]. The swift advancements in these countries illustrate how regulatory clarity can catalyze hydrogen adoption within transportation and energy sectors.

To optimize hydrogen production and storage on a global scale, strategic policy initiatives must be implemented. Akinsooto et al. [2] stress the importance of enhancing hydrogen production from renewable sources, such as electrolysis powered by renewable energy. Policies that streamline processes for producing hydrogen sustainably can address challenges related to cost and reliability, facilitating its integration into existing energy systems. The necessity of continuous government support for hydrogen infrastructure was echoed in research identifying barriers such as high production costs and technological gaps in storage and vehicle integration. Addressing these barriers through well-designed regulatory frameworks will be pivotal for maximizing hydrogen's potential in the energy mix.

International collaboration plays a significant role in shaping effective regulatory frameworks. The experiences and practices across different countries can inform and improve domestic policies. For example, the comparative analysis of hydrogen policies between China and Russia showcases varying approaches and regulatory environments that impact their respective hydrogen economies [6]. Scholars argue that such comparisons enable nations to identify best practices and relevant policy patterns, aiding their own strategic planning. Consequently, enhancing cooperation on hydrogen deployment can yield substantial benefits in terms of technology transfer, market access, and knowledge sharing.

Investment incentives and financing mechanisms are key components of regulatory frameworks that support hydrogen infrastructure. Governments need to explore innovative financing solutions to lower the financial barriers associated with hydrogen projects. Initiatives such as public–private partnerships can share risks and promote resource-sharing among private sector entities and governmental institutions [7]. Establishing clear financial incentives can stimulate investments in research and development, as well as infrastructure projects essential for hydrogen integration into existing energy systems.

As countries navigate the complexities of establishing hydrogen frameworks, the importance of aligning economic and environmental objectives is paramount. Policies that incentivize green hydrogen production can significantly contribute to emission reductions while promoting local economic growth. International bodies and regional alliances can provide crucial support in harmonizing regulations across different jurisdictions, facilitating trade, and optimizing technology deployment [8]. Furthermore, as nations commit to multi-faceted strategies to transition towards a hydrogen economy, regulatory frameworks must remain adaptable to embrace the rapid pace of technological change and evolving market conditions.

15.1.1 International and Regional Policies

The development of hydrogen policies worldwide reflects a combination of national priorities, regional cooperation, and global sustainability goals. Different countries and regions adopt varying strategies—ranging from decentralized experimentation and technological innovation to collaborative frameworks and integration with sustainable development objectives. Table 15.1 summarizes key international and regional hydrogen policies, highlighting their approaches, strategic focuses, and long-term goals.

International and regional policies are crucial for shaping the hydrogen economy. The ongoing dialogues between countries that leverage lessons learned from local experimentation and technological innovations, while considering the socio-economic dynamics of each region, will ultimately determine hydrogen's role in the global energy landscape moving forward.

Table 15.1 International and regional hydrogen policies

Region/country	Policy approach	Key focus areas	Notable insights/ references
China	Decentralized regulatory framework with national oversight	Local experimentation, regional tailoring, innovation	Encourages local solutions while aligning with national hydrogen strategies [9]
United States	Regional hydrogen hubs with national coordination	Competition for resources, scalability, innovation	Regional competition fosters growth and innovation in hydrogen projects [9]
Japan	Strong government-led strategy with heavy R&D investment	Electrolysis technologies, renewables integration, long-term hydrogen economy	Strategic investments aligned with renewable policies [10]
European Union	Coordinated framework among member states with national variations	Joint investments, regulatory clarity, carbon neutrality goals	Collaboration across stakeholders (gov., industry, academia) [11]
Germany (EU leader)	Trailblazer in hydrogen ecosystem	Policy clarity, cross-sectoral collaboration	Strong policy and stakeholder engagement [11]
Southern Africa	Integration of hydrogen with SDGs via Water-Energy Nexus	Renewable energy utilization, energy and water security, green economy	Aligns hydrogen with sustainable development and job creation [12]
Australia	Integrated into national energy and climate policies	Hydrogen in renewable mix, export potential, solar and wind resources	Aims to be global hydrogen leader [13]
United Arab Emirates (UAE)	Integration into existing energy systems	Renewable-coupled hydrogen, efficiency, low-carbon strategy	National strategy positions UAE as global hydrogen player [14]
EU–Sub-Saharan Africa Collaboration	Cross-regional partnerships	Knowledge transfer, investment, bridging resource and tech gaps	Strengthening global hydrogen cooperation [15]

15.1.2 Safety and Environmental Regulations

Safety regulations pertaining to hydrogen production and usage must address the unique characteristics of hydrogen. Being a highly flammable gas, hydrogen presents specific hazards during production, storage, and transport. Key materials and designs must be employed to prevent leaks, explosions, and embrittlement, especially in pipelines. For instance, Revinova et al. [16] assert that the storage and transportation methods for hydrogen must consider its potential to cause embrittlement in various materials, particularly metals commonly used in pipeline construction. Careful selection of materials, alongside adherence to safety standards, is vital in reducing risks associated with hydrogen being transported at high pressures.

Life Cycle Assessment (LCA) serves as a valuable tool for evaluating the environmental impacts associated with hydrogen technologies across their entire life cycle, from production to end-use, as shown in Fig. 15.1. This comprehensive approach allows stakeholders to identify potential environmental footprints and areas for improvement. For instance, Hamed et al. [17] highlight the importance of LCA in assessing the environmental implications of both blue and green hydrogen production processes. By taking into account factors such as greenhouse gas emissions, energy consumption, and waste generation throughout the hydrogen value chain, LCA provides essential insights into the sustainability of various hydrogen production route options.

Transportation regulations surrounding hydrogen must be well-defined to ensure safety during movement from production sites to end users. Lasocki [18] noted that regulations governing the transport of hydrogen through pipelines differ greatly from those for conventional fossil fuels. They must account for the high pressures utilized in hydrogen gas transport and the need for sufficient safety technology to prevent leaks. The European Committee for Standardization has begun developing standard protocols that address these unique transportation challenges while prioritizing safety, which aligns with the emerging regulatory needs in the industry.

Collaboration among governments, industry stakeholders, and the scientific community is critical in shaping effective safety and environmental regulations. As different entities contribute their expertise, comprehensive frameworks can be established that account for various aspects of hydrogen technologies. A strategic partnership between public and private sectors can facilitate knowledge sharing and

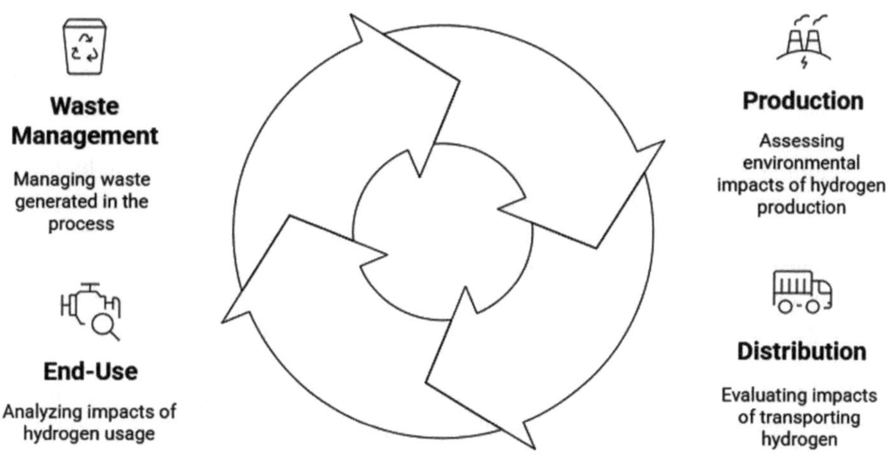

Fig. 15.1 Life cycle assessment of hydrogen technologies

collaborative problem-solving, thereby fostering innovation and leading to more effective regulatory strategies [19].

15.2 Economic Drivers and Market Dynamics

A primary economic driver for hydrogen adoption is the decreasing cost of renewable energy sources, particularly solar and wind power, which significantly impact hydrogen production costs. As highlighted by Jalil-Vega and Hawkes [20], retrofitting existing gas networks to accommodate hydrogen is a cost-effective approach for heat decarbonization, provided that hydrogen retail prices remain competitive. This aligns with Walsh et al. [13], who emphasize that the economics of hydrogen projects are intrinsically linked to geospatial factors such as proximity to transportation infrastructure and energy sources. When renewable energy generation becomes cheaper and more available, the economic framework supporting green hydrogen becomes more attractive.

Investment patterns play a significant role in shaping the hydrogen economy. Fazioli and Pantaleone [21] observe that substantial public investment is required to develop hydrogen infrastructure and technologies. They note that local and national financial resources primarily drive the hydrogen sector, emphasizing the essential role of government policy in facilitating these investments. The importance of public funding is also discussed by Dorel et al. [22], who indicate that government incentives, grants, tax exemptions, and financing measures are necessary to enhance the competitiveness of hydrogen technologies and support research and infrastructure.

The socio-economic impact of hydrogen infrastructure investment has been emphasized in emerging markets. Judijanto et al. [23] note that the transition to clean energy, including hydrogen, positively influences household socioeconomic development, thus demonstrating a broader economic benefit beyond just energy applications. This perspective is relevant in assessing the multifaceted impact of hydrogen investments on local economies, showcasing that the hydrogen sector can deliver substantial benefits, particularly in rural or underdeveloped areas.

Regional dynamics and policy frameworks significantly influence the hydrogen market. Rezk et al. [24] highlight that renewable energy targets and carbon reduction commitments act as crucial drivers for deploying green hydrogen technologies, particularly in regions with strong political will and investment strategies. Additionally, cross-border hydrogen trade agreements, as mentioned by Sadik-Zada [25], facilitate international cooperations by creating new markets and supply chains that can attract investments and enhance technology transfer.

Building a robust hydrogen economy requires the integration of stakeholder perspectives and the consideration of public perceptions. Research by González-Ruíz et al. [26] suggests that effective communication strategies and stakeholder engagement are necessary to build trust and public acceptance of hydrogen technologies. The social acceptance of hydrogen as a clean energy solution is essential for successful market penetration and the establishment of necessary infrastructure.

15.2.1 Cost Structures and Funding Models

The cost structures for hydrogen projects are shaped by several factors, including production methods, infrastructure requirements, and market dynamics. Hydrogen can be produced via various methods, with electrolysis powered by renewable energy sources being the most favorable in terms of sustainability [27]. The integration of intermittent renewable sources into hydrogen production presents economic efficiencies through the coupling of hydrogen generation with energy storage systems. This not only reduces costs but also ensures a consistent supply of hydrogen, which is vital for sectors relying on this energy carrier.

The overall cost of hydrogen production significantly depends on the initial capital investment required for technology and infrastructure. For instance, large-scale production facilities such as those utilizing steam methane reforming (SMR) or electrolysis incur high upfront costs related to equipment, installation, and maintenance. The variability in production costs affects hydrogen pricing in the market, and as these costs decrease through technological advancements, the competitiveness of hydrogen as an energy source improves markedly. Reports suggest that with technological improvements and economies of scale, the cost of renewable hydrogen could potentially drop below fossil fuel prices in the coming years.

Funding models for hydrogen projects must consider diverse financial instruments and strategies to mitigate the financial risks associated with high capital expenditures. Public funding plays a crucial role in hydrogen project financing, especially in the early stages of development. Various governments have initiated support mechanisms—including grants, subsidies, and tax incentives—to stimulate investment in hydrogen infrastructure. For example, the European Union's dedication to becoming a climate-neutral economy by 2050 has prompted substantial public investments in green hydrogen production facilities and R&D initiatives [1]. This public funding complements private investments, as private sector stakeholders are often risk-averse and may require assurance of sustainable returns on their investments.

Partnerships between public and private sectors can enhance the funding landscape for hydrogen projects. Collaborative frameworks allow for shared investment risks and foster innovation through collective expertise and resources. Examples of successful public–private partnerships include financing models developed for large infrastructure projects, which facilitate knowledge transfer while minimizing individual financial burdens on stakeholders.

The involvement of international financial institutions (IFIs) and development banks can significantly aid in funding hydrogen projects, particularly in developing economies. IFIs can provide concessional financing or guarantees to encourage private sector investments, thereby bridging the financing gap prevalent in many regions. Their involvement is crucial in regions with limited local capital markets or higher perceived risks, which can deter potential investments in hydrogen infrastructure.

15.2.2 *Incentives and Subsidies for Hydrogen Projects*

Incentives and subsidies are key mechanisms accelerating the hydrogen economy by reducing costs, stimulating innovation, and encouraging investment. They not only support early-stage projects but also shape long-term market dynamics, enabling integration with renewable resources and advancing decarbonization goals. The Table 15.2 outlines the main types of incentives, their impacts, challenges, and examples from different regions.

Table 15.2 Incentives and subsidies for hydrogen projects

Category	Key aspects	Examples/cases	Challenges and considerations
Financial incentives	Grants, subsidies, tax credits; reduce LCOH; boost early-stage projects	US Inflation Reduction act—tax credits; production subsidies for green hydrogen	Market dependency on subsidies; ensuring cost competitiveness
Production incentives (pathway-specific)	Targeted policies for diverse hydrogen production methods	Incentives for by-product hydrogen from industrial processes	Balancing incentives across pathways; avoiding over-dependence
Policy frameworks and stability	Cohesive frameworks aligning subsidies, infrastructure, and renewables	Long-term regulatory stability to attract investment	Need for predictable, integrated policies across markets
Multi-stakeholder partnerships	Combining government, private sector, academia for hydrogen adoption	Aviation hydrogen projects with financial and regulatory backing	Aligning diverse interests; managing infrastructure cost
Market barriers and challenges	"Chicken-and-egg" dilemma: low demand versus infrastructure gaps	Australia—incentives to boost local demand	Coordinating supply–demand growth; timing issues
International cooperation and competition	Incentives to attract foreign investment and partnerships	Morocco—customs and tax exemptions for green hydrogen	Balancing local benefits with global competition
Integration with renewables	Linking hydrogen production with solar/wind for synergy	Techno-economic potential for hybrid energy-hydrogen projects	Requires further evidence and analysis
Future prospects and adaptations	Continuous adjustment of incentives to evolving market	Cost assessments to refine support; transitional incentives for emerging tech	Ensuring incentives remain agile and support innovation

15.3 Investment Risks and Risk Mitigation

Investment risks associated with hydrogen projects arise from a multitude of factors, including market volatility, technological uncertainty, regulatory fluctuations, and geopolitical aspects and a few of them are shown in Fig. 15.2. To navigate this complex landscape, effective risk mitigation strategies are essential for ensuring the successful execution of hydrogen infrastructure and technology investments.

Investment risks in hydrogen projects can be classified into several categories, including economic, technological, environmental, regulatory, and market risks. Karplus et al. [28] identify economic risks as a primary concern, notably the potential for stranded capital if projects fail to achieve financial viability.

Effective risk mitigation begins with a thorough risk analysis framework that identifies, assesses, and prioritizes risks. The Monte Carlo simulation method has gained traction as an analytical tool for understanding the range of potential outcomes and their probabilities in investment decisions. This method can incorporate various risk factors and uncertainties, providing insights into scenarios that may impact the project's profitability and feasibility [29]. By utilizing simulation techniques, project managers can visualize risk profiles and make informed decisions regarding resource allocation and contingency planning.

To counterbalance investment risks, various financial instruments can be employed, including insurance products, public–private partnerships (PPPs), and government subsidies. For instance, insurance policies that specifically cover technology obsolescence or unexpected operational failures can protect investors from incurring high losses [30]. These financial products can be designed to address the unique challenges of hydrogen projects, thus providing security and encouraging investment.

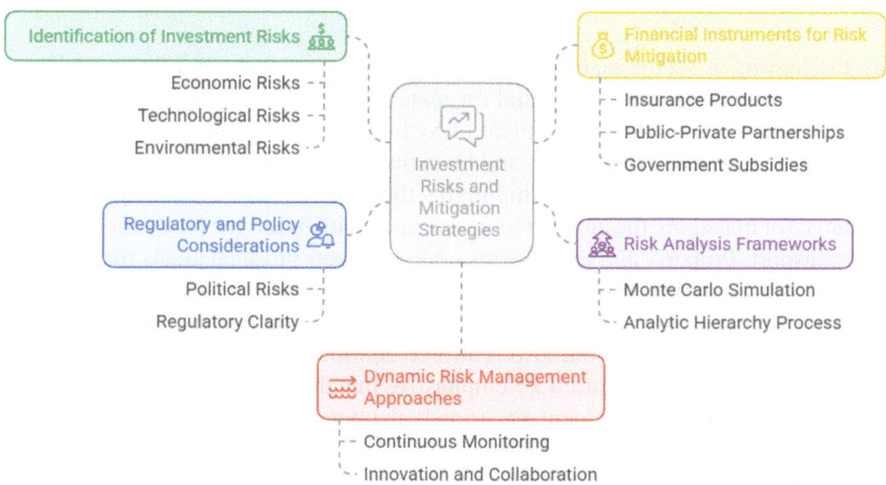

Fig. 15.2 Investment risks and mitigation strategies in hydrogen projects

The regulatory environment significantly influences investment risk in hydrogen projects. Chen et al. [31] indicate that political risks, especially when investing in overseas infrastructure projects, can deter foreign direct investment due to concerns over policy stability and regulatory changes. Governments can mitigate these risks by establishing clear, stable, and supportive policy frameworks that provide confidence to investors. Financial mechanisms—such as tax credits, grants, or feed-in tariffs—can encourage investment in hydrogen technologies while minimizing perceived regulatory risks.

Dynamic risk management strategies can enhance resilience against investment risks by adapting to changing market conditions and technological advancements. Continuous monitoring and evaluation of project performance allow stakeholders to identify emerging risks early and modify strategies accordingly. Research by Ginzburg and Ryzhkova [32] highlights the importance of real-time risk assessments in managing construction project risks, suggesting that feedback mechanisms can be beneficial in navigating investment uncertainties.

15.3.1 Technical, Operational, and Market Risks

The hydrogen sector faces multidimensional risks—technical, operational, and market-related—that influence project viability, costs, and investor confidence. Understanding these risks and applying mitigation strategies is essential for stakeholders. Some of the risks are discussed in Table 15.3.

15.3.2 Insurance and Financial Instruments

As the hydrogen sector matures, various insurance products and financial instruments become increasingly essential for managing risks, securing investments, and facilitating the successful deployment of hydrogen technologies. Figure 15.3 illustrates the critical role of insurance and financial instruments in supporting hydrogen projects as the sector matures. It highlights that specialized insurance products are essential for managing the unique risks associated with hydrogen production, storage, and transport. Property and casualty insurance protects physical assets from damage or loss, while liability insurance safeguards developers against potential environmental and operational claims. By providing financial guarantees, insurers not only mitigate investor concerns but also reinforce confidence in the safe deployment of hydrogen technologies. Figure 15.3 emphasizes that these insurance mechanisms are fundamental to risk management, ensuring both operational security and stakeholder reassurance in hydrogen initiatives.

Figure 15.3 also depicts the complementary role of financial instruments and policy support in facilitating hydrogen investments. Green bonds, for example, provide a mechanism for raising capital while attracting environmentally conscious

Table 15.3 Hydrogen project risk matrix

Risk category	Specific risks	Potential impacts	Mitigation strategies
Technical risks	– Technology failures in electrolysis/fuel cells – Integration issues with intermittent renewables – Delays in R&D and technology adoption	– Production delays – Increased capital and operational costs – Reduced project feasibility	– Use proven technologies and robust engineering designs – Continuous R&D to enhance efficiency – Comprehensive technical feasibility assessments
Operational risks	– Machinery breakdowns – Supply chain disruptions – Insufficient workforce skills	– Downtime and operational inefficiencies – Higher operational costs – Safety and quality issues	– Predictive maintenance and IoT-based monitoring – Lean management principles – Workforce training and capacity building
Market risks	– Demand fluctuations – Competition from alternative energy technologies – Policy and subsidy changes	– Stranded assets – Reduced revenue streams – Project uncompetitiveness	– Diversify hydrogen applications (transport, industry, energy storage) – Explore international markets and trade opportunities – Collaborate via consortia for market intelligence
Cross-cutting risk mitigation	– Combined effects of technical, operational, and market risks	– Unanticipated financial losses – Strategic misalignment	– Implement robust risk management frameworks (identification, assessment, response) – Scenario planning for future uncertainties – Hedging via financial instruments – Secure contractual agreements with off-takers/suppliers – Analytical modeling (AHP + Monte Carlo simulations)

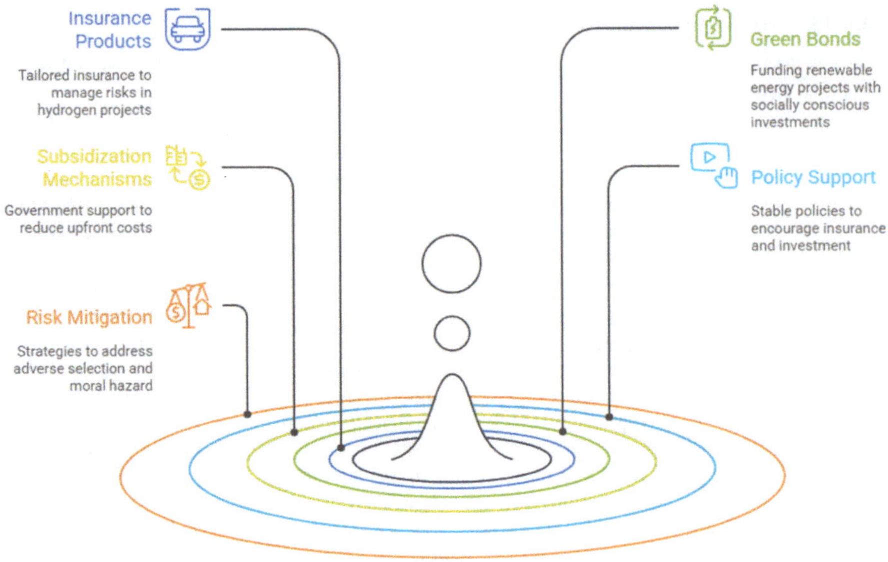

Fig. 15.3 Financial strategies for hydrogen projects

investors, spreading financial risk across institutions. Subsidies and government incentives further reduce the upfront and operational costs of hydrogen projects, improving competitiveness against conventional energy sources. The effectiveness of these instruments is strongly linked to stable policy frameworks, which enhance market confidence and encourage insurance uptake. Additionally, Fig. 15.3 addresses challenges such as adverse selection and moral hazard, showing that risk-adjusted premiums, strict underwriting, and transparent monitoring are necessary to maintain market stability and promote responsible project management in the hydrogen sector.

15.4 Strategic Recommendations for Investors and Operators

For investors and operators in the hydrogen sector, long-term project success depends on proactive strategies that balance risk management, innovation, financial resilience, and sustainability. Table 15.4 summarizes eight key strategic actions—ranging from risk assessments to ESG integration—that can guide stakeholders in navigating the evolving hydrogen economy.

Table 15.4 Strategic recommendations for hydrogen investors and operators

Strategic action	Focus/key actions	Benefits
Conduct rigorous risk assessments	Use Monte Carlo simulations, AHP, and continuous risk monitoring	Improves project feasibility, early identification of risks, tailored mitigation
Foster innovation through collaboration	Build partnerships with tech developers, academia, and governments	Accelerates commercialization, enhances R&D efficiency, shares best practices
Pursue diversified investment strategies	Diversify across technologies, geographies, and applications (transport, industry, storage)	Reduces exposure to volatility, increases resilience and returns
Leverage financial instruments and insurance	Utilize green bonds, PPPs, and insurance for downtime/supply chain risks	Enhances financial viability, safeguards investments
Engage with regulatory frameworks	Align with policies, incentives, and engage regulators early	Facilitates approvals, improves funding access, anticipates policy shifts
Invest in skills development and capacity building	Training programs, workforce upskilling, culture of safety and innovation	Boosts efficiency, reduces operational risks, strengthens resilience
Monitor and adapt to market trends	Track competitor actions, emerging tech, consumer demand, and investor sentiment	Improves decision-making, strengthens competitive positioning
Focus on sustainable practices and ESG factors	Integrate ESG in strategy; adopt sustainable operational practices	Enhances investor attractiveness, mitigates climate risk, supports long-term performance

15.4.1 Long-Term Planning and Sustainability

Figure 15.4 on Strategic Pillars for the Hydrogen Economy highlights the essential components required to ensure long-term planning and sustainability in the sector. At its core, the framework emphasizes aligning projects with global sustainability agendas, particularly the United Nations Sustainable Development Goals (SDGs). By integrating principles of clean energy, climate action, and community development, hydrogen initiatives can strengthen their market positioning while attracting support from regulators and investors. The figure also illustrates the importance of embedding lifecycle analysis into project planning, ensuring that environmental impacts are measured across every stage of hydrogen production and distribution. This approach not only addresses sustainability risks but also guides continuous improvement and innovation in the industry.

Another key dimension shown in the figure is the integration of financial and environmental performance, underscoring the need to balance profitability with

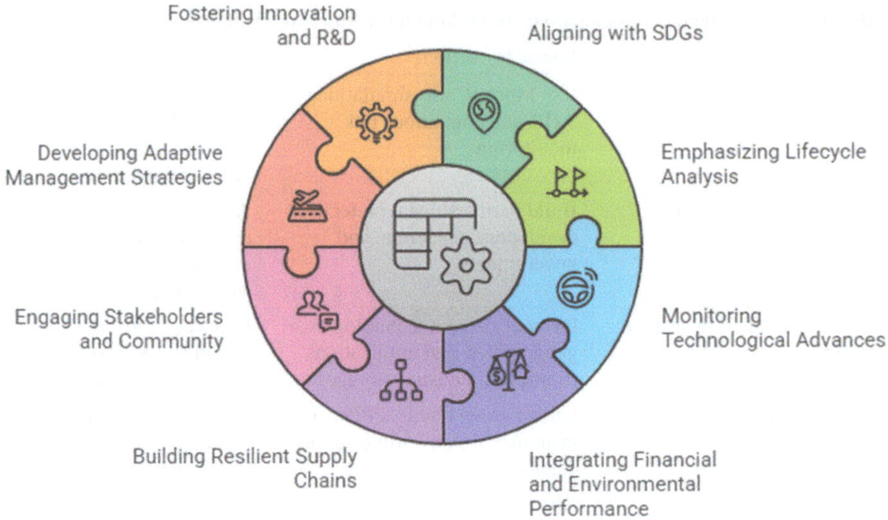

Fig. 15.4 Strategic pillars for hydrogen economy

sustainability metrics. The pillars also reflect the dynamic nature of technological progress, supply chain resilience, and stakeholder engagement. Monitoring innovations, building robust logistics networks, and fostering transparent community relationships are crucial for creating adaptable and trusted hydrogen ecosystems. Furthermore, the figure highlights adaptive management strategies and sustained investments in research and development (R&D), which equip the sector to navigate uncertainty and remain competitive. Together, these interconnected sections provide a comprehensive roadmap for advancing a resilient and future-ready hydrogen economy.

References

1. Zabanova Y (2024) The EU in the global hydrogen race: bringing together climate action, energy security, and industrial policy. In: The geopolitics of hydrogen: European strategies in global perspective00, vol 1. Springer Nature Switzerland, Cham, pp 15–47
2. Akinsooto O, Ogundipe OB, Ikemba S (2024) Strategic policy initiatives for optimizing hydrogen production and storage in sustainable energy systems. Int J Front Res Rev 2(2):001–021
3. Behrendt F (2025) The future of industrial hydrogen: renewable sources and applications for the next 15 years. Clean Energy 9(1):3–8. Oxford University Press UK
4. Ohira E (2018) Japan's current policy and activity toward realizing a hydrogen based society. In: Electrochemical society meeting abstracts MA2018-02:1635. The Electrochemical Society, Inc.
5. Shin J-E (2022) Hydrogen technology development and policy status by value chain in South Korea. Energies 15(23):8983

6. Roucham B, Zaghdoud O (2025) Mapping green hydrogen and renewable energy research in extended BRICS (Brazil, Russia, India, China, South Africa and Others): a bibliometric approach with a future agenda. Hydrogen 6(2):33
7. Fan Z (2024) The role of hydrogen in achieving sustainable energy systems: challenges and opportunities. Highlights Sci Eng Technol 116:237–240
8. El Ghammad O, et al (2025) Opportunities and challenges for a green hydrogen-based economy. In: Obstacles facing hydrogen green systems and green energy. pp 283–300
9. Gong X, Quitzow R, Boute A (2024) Developing China's hydrogen economy: national regulation through local experimentation. Trans Environ Law 13(2):337–367
10. Chaube A et al (2020) The role of hydrogen in achieving long term Japanese energy system goals. Energies 13(17):4539
11. Tholen L et al (2021) The green hydrogen puzzle: towards a german policy framework for industry. Sustainability 13(22):12626
12. Mabhaudhi T et al (2016) Southern Africa's water–energy nexus: towards regional integration and development. Water 8(6):235
13. Walsh SD et al (2021) Evaluating the economic fairways for hydrogen production in Australia. Int J Hydrogen Energy 46(73):35985–35996
14. Ibrahim MD, Binofai FA, Mohamad MO (2022) Transition to low-carbon hydrogen energy system in the UAE: sector efficiency and hydrogen energy production efficiency analysis. Energies 15(18):6663
15. Ballo A et al (2022) Law and policy review on green hydrogen potential in ECOWAS countries. Energies 15(7):2304
16. Revinova S et al (2024) Hydrogen in energy transition: the problem of economic efficiency, environmental safety, and technological readiness of transportation and storage. Resources 13(7):92
17. Hamed AM, et al (2023) A review on blue and green hydrogen production process and their life cycle assessments. In: IOP conference series: earth and environmental science. IOP Publishing
18. Lasocki J (2018) Ammonia and conventional engine fuels: comparative environmental impact assessment. In: E3S web of conferences 44:00091. EDP Sciences
19. Yazdi M et al (2023) Enabling safe and sustainable hydrogen mobility: circular economy-driven management of hydrogen vehicle safety. Processes 11(9):2730
20. Jalil-Vega FA, Hawkes AD (2018) Spatially resolved optimization for studying the role of hydrogen for heat decarbonization pathways. ACS Sustain Chem Eng 6(5):5835–5842
21. Fazioli R, Pantaleone F (2021) Macroeconomic factors influencing public policy strategies for blue and green hydrogen. Energies 14(23):7938
22. Dorel S et al (2024) Green hydrogen, a solution for replacing fossil fuels to reduce CO_2 emissions. Processes 12(8):1651
23. Judijanto L, Ilham, Vandika AY (2024) The effect of clean energy technology infrastructure development on regional economic growth in Indonesia. West science nature and technology 2(3):164–171
24. Rezk MRA et al (2023) Future scenarios of green hydrogen in the MENA countries: the case of Egypt. Insights Into Reg Dev 5:92–114
25. Sadik-Zada ER (2021) Political economy of green hydrogen rollout: a global perspective. Sustainability 13(23):13464
26. González-Ruiz JD et al (2023) Green bonds for renewable energy in Latin America and the caribbean. Energy J 44(5):45–66
27. Li X et al (2023) Latest approaches on green hydrogen as a potential source of renewable energy towards sustainable energy: spotlighting of recent innovations, challenges, and future insights. Fuel 334:126684
28. Karplus VJ et al (2025) Risks in the design of regional hydrogen hub systems: a review and commentary. Risk Anal 45(3):581–599
29. Fabianová J et al (2023) A comprehensive methodology for investment project assessment based on Monte Carlo simulation. Appl Sci 13(10):6103

30. Zhu L et al (2020) Analysis of strategic directions in sustainable hydrogen investment decisions. Sustainability 12(11):4581
31. Chen H, Wan A, Peng B (2025) Configuration path identification of investment risk in C hina's overseas energy projects: an exploration based on LDA and fsQCA. Environ Prog Sustain Energy 44(2):e14549
32. Ginzburg AV, Ryzhkova AI (2018) Assessment of construction project «Pure» risks. Materials science forum 931:1245–1248. Trans Tech Publ

Chapter 16
Mitigation Strategies and Future Outlook

This chapter presents a comprehensive overview of mitigation strategies and emerging trends that are essential to ensuring the safety, integrity, and long-term viability of hydrogen pipeline infrastructure. The chapter opens with a focused examination of technologies aimed at preserving pipeline integrity, detailing the application of advanced protective coatings and linings, the adaptation of cathodic protection systems to hydrogen-specific environments, and innovative repair and rehabilitation methods designed to extend asset life while maintaining operational safety.

Subsequently, the chapter addresses hydrogen safety and emergency response, outlining industry-standard safety protocols and best practices that mitigate risks during handling and transport. It further explores structured incident response frameworks and mitigation plans that ensure rapid and effective action in the event of pipeline leaks or failures.

Looking toward the future, the chapter identifies key trends and challenges facing hydrogen infrastructure development. It investigates recent advances in materials science and inspection technologies that enhance monitoring and predictive maintenance capabilities. Additionally, it discusses the integration of hydrogen pipelines with renewable energy systems, emphasizing their role in energy transition strategies. The chapter concludes by analyzing policy, economic, and market forces that will shape future investments and innovation in the hydrogen sector. This forward-looking perspective offers critical insights for engineers, policymakers, and investors aiming to build a resilient and future-ready hydrogen infrastructure network.

16.1 Mitigation Technologies for Pipeline Integrity

Mitigation technologies for pipeline integrity, especially in the context of hydrogen transportation, play a crucial role in ensuring the safe and reliable delivery of hydrogen as a part of contemporary energy systems. The high risks associated with

M. Hussain et al., *Hydrogen Pipeline Integrity*, Green Energy and Technology,
https://doi.org/10.1007/978-981-95-5609-0_16

pipeline operation necessitate an integrated approach to integrity management that utilizes advanced technologies for monitoring, assessment, and proactive intervention. Each aspect of pipeline integrity from design to operational monitoring must be treated with equal attention to validate safety, reliability, and environmental responsibility.

One pivotal aspect of enhancing the integrity of hydrogen pipelines is the application of reliability engineering concepts. Traditional pipeline design and operation standards primarily focus on failure prevention but often lack integration with robust reliability practices. Reliability engineering tools should be employed throughout the pipeline's lifecycle, from Design Failure Mode and Effects Analysis (DFMEA) through to Reliability-Centered Maintenance (RCM) practices, thereby ensuring comprehensive integrity management [1]. This integration fosters a culture where potential failure modes can be anticipated and mitigated before they lead to significant issues.

Operational practices must adapt to the unique challenges posed by hydrogen as a transport medium, particularly due to its propensity for inducing material degradation, such as embrittlement. The analysis of hydrogen gas within existing natural gas pipelines has been conducted using geographic information systems (GIS) to optimize flow management and operational safety [2]. GIS allows the mapping of pipelines, capturing terrain data that can significantly enhance the risk management processes and emergency response strategies. By combining GIS data with real-time operational metrics, operators can develop a comprehensive understanding of pipeline dynamics under various conditions.

In terms of monitoring technologies, much progress has been made in non-destructive testing (NDT) techniques specifically designed for hydrogen pipelines. Tools such as Magnetic Flux Leakage (MFL) and Ultrasonic Testing (UT) are now employed to detect and mitigate potential leaks or material weaknesses before catastrophic failures occur [3]. The adoption of advanced NDT not only minimizes risks associated with leaks but also supports the overall safety and reliability of hydrogen transportation systems.

Recent advancements in machine learning and artificial intelligence provide powerful frameworks for pipeline integrity management. Predictive models developed using machine learning techniques can analyze vast amounts of operational and historical data to identify patterns that precede failures [4]. This predictive capability allows for condition-based maintenance strategies, optimizing resource allocation and extending the operational lifespan of the pipelines [5]. By integrating these intelligent systems, operators can respond swiftly to emerging risks and enhance the overall safety of hydrogen transportation networks.

The integration of data from multiple sources into a unified management system represents another significant step forward in ensuring pipeline integrity. Multi-source data fusion allows for a cohesive view of various integrity indicators, effectively informing decision-making processes regarding pipeline operation and maintenance. This includes assessments of corrosion rates, stress levels, and material degradation metrics, all of which are crucial when considering the unique properties of hydrogen and its potential impact on pipeline integrity.

Economic considerations play a notable role in the adoption of mitigation technologies for pipeline integrity. The integration of hydrogen into existing natural gas infrastructure must be economically viable to encourage investment and expansion [6]. Cost–benefit analyses that factor in both capital and operational expenditures alongside potential risk mitigation outcomes are essential for justifying technology deployment, particularly in regions transitioning to hydrogen economies.

16.1.1 Protective Coatings and Linings

The application of protective coatings and linings in hydrogen pipelines is critical for ensuring the integrity and safety of these infrastructures, see Fig. 16.1. As hydrogen is recognized for its potential to revolutionize energy systems, the unique challenges associated with its transportation under pressure necessitate the development and implementation of advanced protective measures.

First and foremost, the use of specialized coatings plays a vital role in preventing hydrogen permeation and protecting steel pipelines from corrosive environments. MXene coatings have shown promise as effective barriers against hydrogen diffusion due to their nano-structured properties that create tortuous paths hindering the movement of hydrogen ions [7]. This approach not only mitigates corrosion but also enhances the mechanical integrity of pipeline steels, making them more resistant to the corrosive effects of a hydrogen atmosphere.

Coatings designed for high-performance applications must also address the challenges posed by the electrochemical behavior of pipeline materials. For instance,

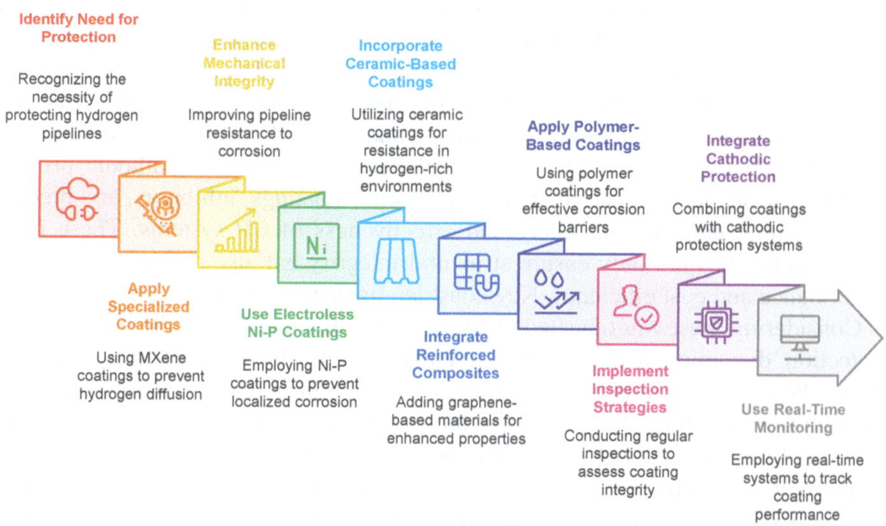

Fig. 16.1 Protective coatings and linings for hydrogen pipelines

electroless nickel-phosphorus (Ni–P) coatings have been studied for their effectiveness in preventing localized corrosion [8]. The creation of uniform and defect-free coatings reduces potential sites for corrosion initiation and extends the operational lifespan of pipelines, particularly in high-stress environments.

Polymer-based coatings have emerged as a practical solution for providing an effective barrier against corrosion. The incorporation of functionalized polymers, such as fusion-bonded epoxy composites, enhances adhesion properties and impermeability to water and ionic contaminants [9]. Studies demonstrate that abrupt transitions in temperature and corrosive media significantly affect the longevity and integrity of pipelines; thus, protective coatings are essential for managing these dynamic operational conditions effectively.

Research suggests that coatings should be complemented with real-time monitoring systems to track changes in their integrity and performance. Intelligent systems that utilize machine learning and predictive analytics improve the efficiency of maintaining these protective measures. For example, corrosion prediction models enhance decision-making regarding maintenance schedules by assessing possible breaches in the coating and the electrochemical conditions surrounding pipelines [10].

16.1.2 Cathodic Protection in Hydrogen Environments

Cathodic protection (CP) is a key method used to safeguard metals from corrosion by applying a negative electrical charge to the surface, which reduces electrochemical reactions. The two main approaches are sacrificial anodes and impressed current systems. However, in hydrogen-rich environments, CP poses unique challenges, particularly the risk of overprotection, which can lead to excessive hydrogen evolution. This condition not only diminishes the effectiveness of protection but also increases susceptibility to hydrogen embrittlement and stress corrosion cracking. Maintaining the balance between corrosion prevention and minimizing hydrogen damage requires precise monitoring, control, and material-specific considerations.

Recent developments, such as modulated impressed current cathodic protection (ICCP), advanced material choices, protective coatings, inhibitors, and predictive modeling, enhance the safety and effectiveness of CP systems. These integrated approaches not only ensure structural integrity but also optimize long-term performance and cost efficiency. Key considerations are summarized in Table 16.1.

Considering these multifaceted challenges, a holistic understanding of cathodic protection dynamics within hydrogen environments must incorporate not only electrochemical reactions but also material science principles. The role of added inhibitors or materials designed to reduce hydrogen uptake presents remarkable promises for mitigating risks associated with cathodic protection systems [11, 12]. Furthermore, coatings that enhance performance can be deployed in conjunction with cathodic protection to provide a dual layer of defense against corrosion and hydrogen damage.

Table 16.1 Key aspects of cathodic protection in hydrogen environments

Aspect	Details	Practical implications
Principle of CP	Applying negative charge to metal surface to reduce corrosion reactions	Extends service life of pipelines, offshore structures, and storage tanks
Types of CP systems	Sacrificial anodes, impressed current systems	Choice depends on scale, cost, and environmental conditions
Risk in hydrogen environments	Overprotection causes excessive hydrogen evolution, leading to embrittlement and cracking	Requires careful monitoring of potential levels to avoid structural failures
Advancements	Modulated ICCP adjusts current in real-time, reducing hydrogen risks	Enhances system efficiency and prevents overprotection damage
Material considerations	Anode choice (Al, Zn) and steel type influence hydrogen uptake and embrittlement risk	Selecting suitable alloys reduces risk of failure in high-strength steels
Complementary measures	Use of inhibitors and coatings to reduce hydrogen absorption	Provides dual protection, lowering maintenance costs and extending lifespan
Modeling and simulation	Predictive algorithms simulate CP under varying conditions (temperature, stress, pH)	Helps optimize CP design before implementation, saving cost and reducing trial-and-error

To optimize the overall effectiveness of cathodic protection in hydrogen environments, ongoing research must focus on developing numerical modeling techniques that can predict the performance of CP systems under varying conditions, including temperature, pH, and stress states [13]. Implementing advanced modeling algorithms allows for the simulation of cathodic protection scenarios, including the interaction with environmental variables that influence hydrogen solubility and embrittlement susceptibility [14].

16.1.3 Innovative Repair and Rehabilitation Methods

The maintenance of pipelines is a critical challenge, especially as aging infrastructures face degradation from corrosion, fluctuating pressures, and accidental impacts. To address these issues, innovative repair and rehabilitation methods have been developed, see Fig. 16.2, focusing on strengthening pipeline integrity, extending service life, and minimizing operational disruptions. These methods broadly include the application of composite materials, trenchless repair technologies, advanced monitoring techniques, and rigorous evaluation approaches. Together, they represent a shift from reactive to proactive maintenance, enabling safer and more sustainable pipeline operations.

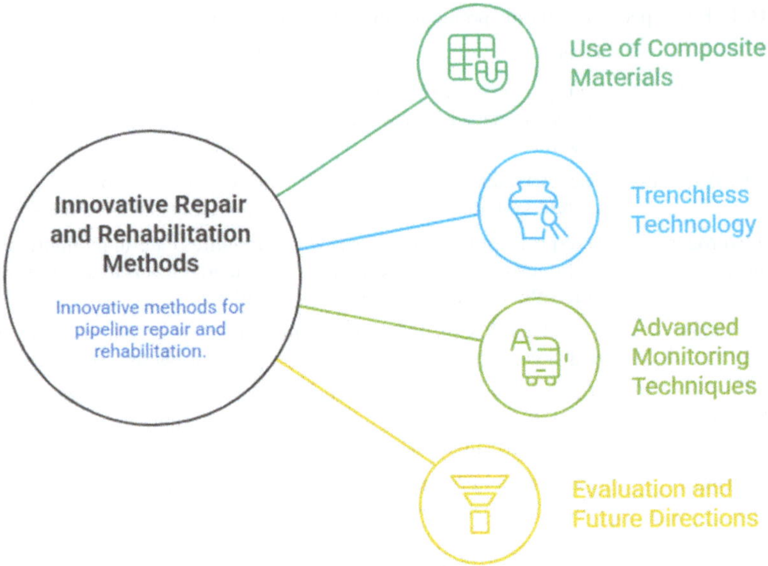

Fig. 16.2 Innovative pipeline repair and rehabilitation methods

Use of Composite Materials in Pipeline Repair

Composite wraps and fiber-reinforced polymer materials offer lightweight, strong, and corrosion-resistant solutions for repairing cracked or corroded pipelines. By improving load transfer and reducing localized stress, they extend pipeline service life. Finite element methods are often used to optimize wrap design for various operating conditions [15]. Studies show that geometry and material selection influence repair effectiveness, particularly in handling through-wall cracks and high-pressure conditions. These composites also perform well in aggressive environments, such as hydrogen transport systems.

Trenchless Technology and Its Advantages

Trenchless methods, such as cured-in-place pipe (CIPP) lining, provide non-invasive rehabilitation options that avoid large-scale excavation. These techniques reduce downtime, environmental disruption, and repair costs. Recent developments in polymer grouting further allow rapid sealing of leaks and restoration of structural support, making them valuable for hydrogen pipelines and other sensitive applications [16].

Advanced Monitoring Techniques

Modern repairs are increasingly supported by advanced sensors and data-driven monitoring. Fiber Bragg grating sensors detect localized defects in composite-repaired sections, while machine learning algorithms analyze real-time and historical data to predict failures and optimize maintenance schedules [17]. This integration enhances reliability and supports proactive intervention strategies.

16.2 Hydrogen Safety and Emergency Response

Hydrogen safety and emergency response is a critical area of focus as hydrogen technologies evolve and expand into various applications, including transportation, industrial processes, and energy systems. Effective safety protocols and responsive strategies are paramount to mitigate risks associated with hydrogen's flammability and explosiveness. Figure 16.3 synthesizes contemporary insights on safety training, regulatory frameworks, and emergency response strategies to optimize the management of hydrogen-related incidents.

One of the primary elements of ensuring safety in hydrogen environments is the implementation of comprehensive safety training for emergency responders. Training programs should equip first responders with essential knowledge regarding hydrogen's unique hazards. Such training can encompass not just the characteristics of hydrogen but also safe handling strategies, incident management, and public

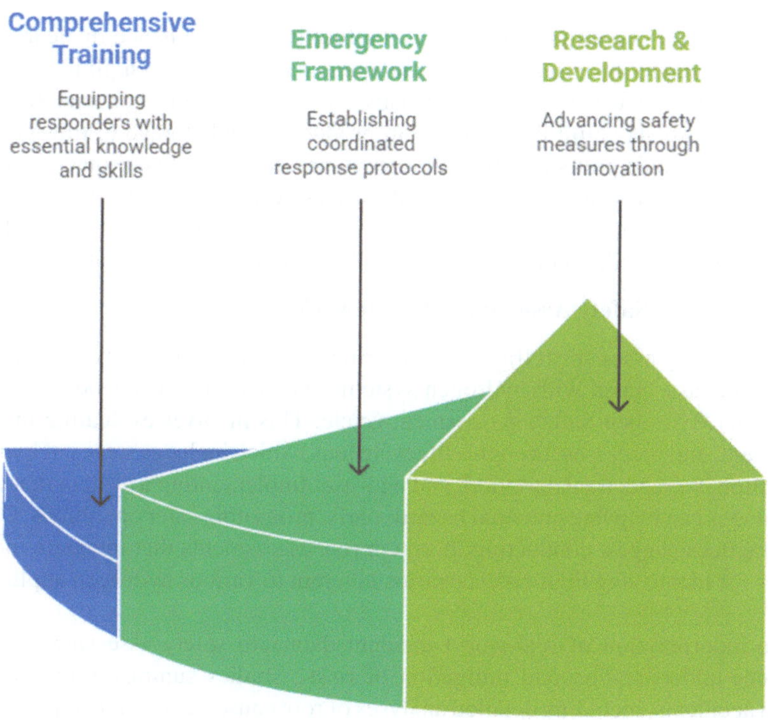

Fig. 16.3 Enhancing hydrogen safety

safety communications during emergencies [18]. The importance of effective training is well-supported in the literature, as it directly influences responders' performance and confidence during real incidents.

Hydrogen emergencies require well-defined response frameworks that ensure coordinated efforts among various agencies. A systematic approach, inclusive of risk assessment and the development of Standard Operating Procedures (SOPs), is crucial in enhancing preparedness and mitigating negative outcomes associated with hydrogen incidents [19]. Existing frameworks can be improved by integrating lessons learned from other industries that manage flammable gases, such as natural gas.

Continued research into the technical and operational safety measures associated with hydrogen is necessary to inform emergency response practices. The development of novel technologies for hydrogen detection and leak monitoring can significantly improve the safety of hydrogen infrastructure and response initiatives [20]. Understanding hydrogen's diffusion and combustion properties will facilitate the formulation of more effective incident response strategies, ensuring first responders are prepared for various scenarios.

16.2.1 Safety Protocols and Best Practices

Hydrogen safety is a critical concern as the fuel gains prominence in clean energy systems. Owing to its unique physical and chemical properties—high flammability, rapid diffusivity, and low molecular density—hydrogen requires specialized safety measures across its entire lifecycle. From production and storage to transportation and end-use, robust protocols are necessary to prevent accidents, protect personnel, and maintain public trust. Table 16.2 synthesizes safety protocols, best practices, and regulatory frameworks, drawing on research, industry standards, and technological innovations to provide a consolidated guide for safe hydrogen utilization.

Comprehensive Safety Assessment Framework

A holistic safety assessment framework is critical to identifying, analyzing, and mitigating risks associated with hydrogen systems. The authors of this book presented (Fig. 16.4) Hydrogen Safety Assessment Cycle. This involves evaluating facilities, equipment, and processes through a lifecycle lens, which includes stages of hydrogen production, storage, transportation, and end-use. Implementing a system that covers these stages can help flag potential hazards early, promoting safer operations. Current best practices suggest conducting thorough risk assessments that integrate methodologies for identifying high-risk scenarios inherent to various hydrogen applications [21].

The incorporation of real-world incident data into safety assessments greatly enhances understanding and mitigation of risks. Studies summarizing hydrogen-related accidents, including detailed analyses of root causes, can guide improvements in operational protocols and safety measures [21]. These learnings should actively

Table 16.2 Safety protocols and best practices in hydrogen utilization

Focus area	Key practices/guidelines
Comprehensive safety assessment framework	Lifecycle risk evaluation of production, storage, transport, and end-use; incorporation of real-world incident data; application of advanced risk identification methodologies
Storage and transportation safety	Adherence to NFPA and international standards; strict inspection and maintenance schedules; use of composite/high-strength materials to reduce leak and rupture risks
Emergency response protocols	Leak detection and management; evacuation planning; responder training with simulations; community communication strategies; public awareness initiatives
Technological innovations	Real-time leak detection systems; computational fluid dynamics (CFD) for dispersion modeling; smart storage systems with nanomaterials and composites
Regulatory frameworks and standards	Development of international and national safety standards; continuous updates based on research and industry input; stakeholder engagement for policy refinement

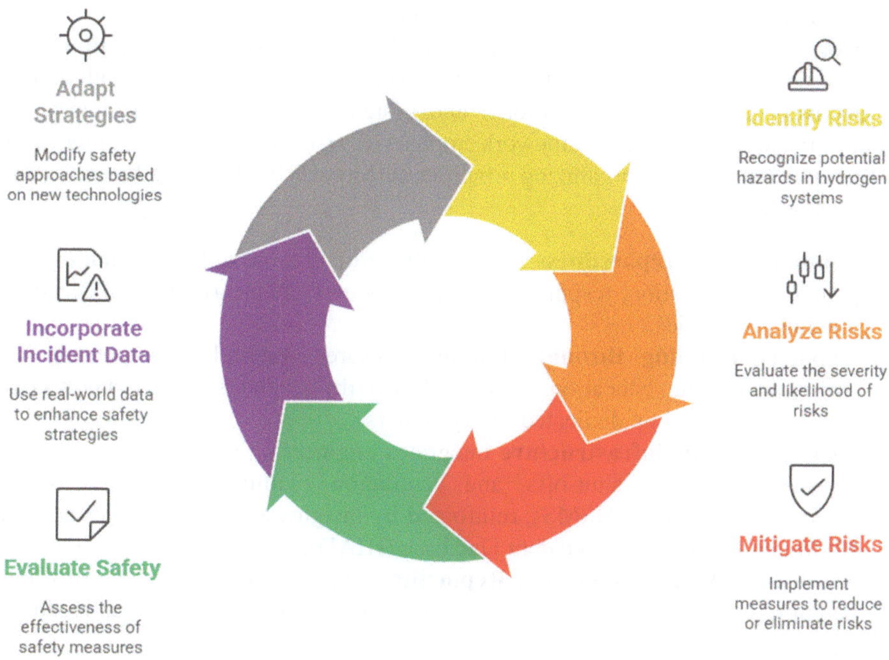

Fig. 16.4 Hydrogen safety assessment cycle

inform the development of new safety strategies that adapt dynamically to evolving hydrogen technologies and applications.

16.2.2 Incident Response and Mitigation Plans

Effective incident response and mitigation plans are crucial for addressing the unique risks associated with hydrogen due to its flammable nature and potential for explosive reactions. As industries increasingly adopt hydrogen technologies, it is imperative to establish protocols that not only prepare emergency responders for potential incidents but also outline proactive measures to mitigate risks before incidents occur. Table 16.3 synthesizes the core dimensions of effective incident response and mitigation plans for hydrogen safety. It highlights the interrelated thematic areas—ranging from comprehensive planning and responder training to technological innovations and regulatory compliance—that collectively underpin organizational resilience in managing hydrogen-related risks. Each dimension is supported by empirical evidence, industry standards, and case studies, thereby illustrating the necessity of adopting a multi-layered and integrated approach to safety management. This structured presentation enables a systematic understanding of how proactive measures, continuous learning, and collaborative governance contribute to minimizing the risks associated with hydrogen technologies.

Conceptual Framework: Hydrogen Incident Response and Mitigation

The conceptual framework (Fig. 16.5) illustrates six interdependent pillars that collectively strengthen organizational and systemic resilience against hydrogen-related risks. At its core, the framework emphasizes *Hydrogen Incident Response and Mitigation* as the central organizing principle, surrounded by six mutually reinforcing dimensions.

- **Foundation of Preparedness** provides the structural basis through multi-phase planning (preparation, response, recovery, review) and clearly defined decision-making hierarchies.
- **Capacity Building through Training** ensures responder competence via hydrogen-specific education, scenario-based drills, and sustained knowledge transfer facilitated by dedicated safety centers.
- **Risk Mitigation Infrastructure** integrates engineering safeguards—including sensors, emergency shut-offs, and ventilation—within a Hydrogen Safety Management System (HSMS), reinforced by insights from case studies and the Hydrogen Incident and Accident Database (HIAD).
- **Knowledge Management and Reporting** highlights the importance of transparent reporting systems, centralized data repositories, and continuous feedback loops to refine safety practices.
- **Technological Enablement** underscores the role of innovations such as real-time monitoring, GIS-based situational awareness, and predictive simulations in enhancing emergency response capacity.

Table 16.3 Key components of hydrogen incident response and mitigation plans

Thematic area	Key elements
Comprehensive incident response plans	– Multi-phase approach (preparation, response, recovery, review) – Clearly defined roles and responsibilities – Rapid decision-making mechanisms
Training and preparedness	– Hydrogen-specific first responder training – Scenario-based exercises and simulations – Regular updates aligned with technological advances – Hydrogen safety centers for dissemination
Mitigation strategies for hydrogen risks	– Leak detection systems and emergency shut-offs – Ventilation and facility design – Regular inspection and maintenance – Hydrogen Safety Management System (HSMS) implementation
Incident reporting and data management	– Centralized reporting systems – Documentation of near misses and incidents – Continuous improvement through lessons learned – Integration with Hydrogen Incident and Accident Database (HIAD)
Technological innovations	– Real-time monitoring and sensor networks – GIS-enabled situational awareness – Simulation models for diffusion and combustion – Investment in predictive safety infrastructure
Regulatory compliance and collaboration	– Standardized regulatory guidelines – Inter-agency and industry collaboration – Community engagement and trust-building – Dissemination of best practices

- **Governance and Collaboration** calls for robust regulatory frameworks, multi-stakeholder partnerships, and active community engagement to foster trust and harmonize safety practices across the hydrogen ecosystem.

Figure 16.5 demonstrates that hydrogen safety requires not only robust technical safeguards but also institutional learning, cross-sectoral collaboration, and proactive governance. By linking these six pillars to the central mission of incident response and mitigation, the framework provides a holistic guide for both industry practitioners and policymakers seeking to manage the evolving challenges of hydrogen adoption.

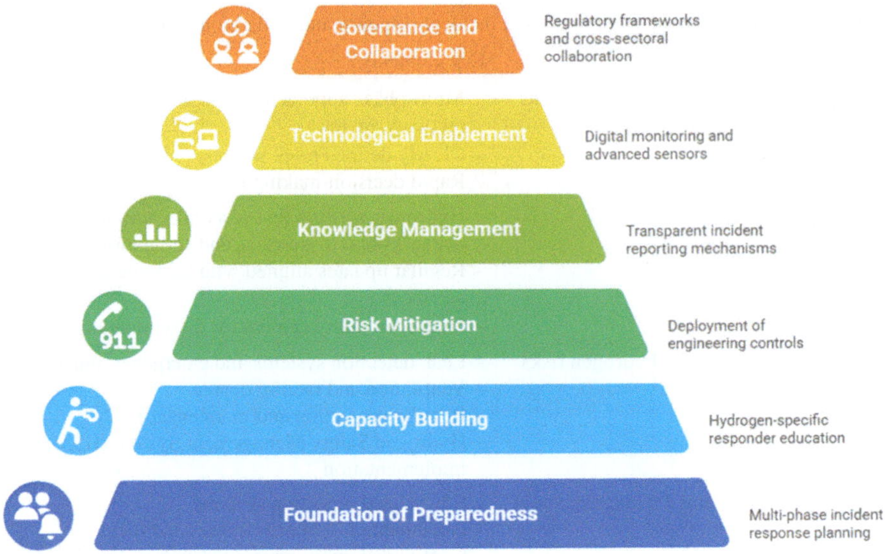

Fig. 16.5 Hydrogen incident response framework

16.3 Future Trends and Challenges in Hydrogen Pipeline Infrastructure

One significant trend is the repurposing of existing natural gas pipelines to accommodate hydrogen transport. This approach allows for a more cost-effective and efficient transition by utilizing established infrastructure, thereby reducing the need for extensive new construction while minimizing initial capital investments [22]. Existing pipeline networks can initially transport hydrogen-methane blends, requiring only gradual modifications to facilitate higher concentrations of hydrogen in the future.

Technological innovations are paving the way for enhanced safety and efficiency in hydrogen deployment. Continuous advancements in materials science are addressing hydrogen embrittlement—the degradation of metals caused by hydrogen absorption—by focusing on the development of hydrogen-compatible materials and coatings [23]. Future infrastructure projects will likely prioritize these innovations to ensure the resilience of pipelines against the unique properties of hydrogen.

Another emerging trend is the integration of smart technologies for monitoring and managing pipeline operations. The application of machine learning and Internet of Things (IoT) solutions is expected to enhance the integrity management of hydrogen pipelines, allowing for real-time monitoring of pressure, temperature, and flow rates. These technologies are vital for predicting and preventing failures, thereby ensuring a safer operational environment.

1. ***Challenges in Hydrogen Pipeline Infrastructure***

Despite the promising trends, several challenges hinder the advancement of hydrogen pipeline infrastructure. A primary concern is the economic feasibility of retrofitting existing pipelines to meet hydrogen's distinct characteristics, which differ significantly from natural gas [24]. The associated costs of modifying physical infrastructure, ensuring material compatibility, and implementing safety measures can be substantial, particularly for older pipelines lacking in-line monitoring systems.

Public perception and acceptance of hydrogen as a viable energy carrier pose their own set of challenges. Much of the general public lacks familiarity with hydrogen technologies, leading to apprehensions about safety and environmental impacts. Addressing these concerns through education and transparent communication strategies is vital for gaining public support for hydrogen infrastructure projects [25].

2. ***Environmental and Safety Considerations***

Environmental sustainability remains a paramount consideration in the development of hydrogen pipeline infrastructure. The adoption of best practices that evaluate the lifecycle emissions associated with hydrogen production, storage, and transportation is essential to ensuring that hydrogen contributes meaningfully to carbon reduction targets [26]. Infrastructure projects must integrate environmental assessments to identify potential risks to ecosystems and ensure compliance with sustainability goals.

Safety considerations, particularly concerning the flammability and explosive nature of hydrogen, must govern the design and operation of pipeline networks. The design of new distribution systems needs to prioritize safety mechanisms such as robust leak detection, pressure management, and emergency shutoff capabilities to prevent incidents [27]. Moreover, continuous monitoring and regular maintenance routines should be integrated into operational protocols to identify potential vulnerabilities before they escalate into incidents.

3. ***Future Prospects and Strategic Recommendations***

   Looking ahead, strategic recommendations for advancing hydrogen pipeline infrastructure include below with visuals in Fig. 16.6.

   1. **Investment in R&D**: Increased funding for research into advanced materials and technologies that improve the safety and efficiency of hydrogen transport should be prioritized. This encompasses the development of enhanced coatings, monitoring systems, and hydrogen-compatible materials.
   2. **Collaboration among Stakeholders**: Engaging multiple stakeholders, including government, industry players, and communities, will help align efforts towards decentralized hydrogen infrastructure, ensuring that plans reflect the diverse needs and expectations of all parties involved.
   3. **Building Public Trust**: Developing outreach initiatives that educate the public on hydrogen safety, benefits, and potential applications will help alleviate fears and foster community acceptance. Effective communication strategies will be crucial in demystifying hydrogen technologies and their role within the broader energy landscape.

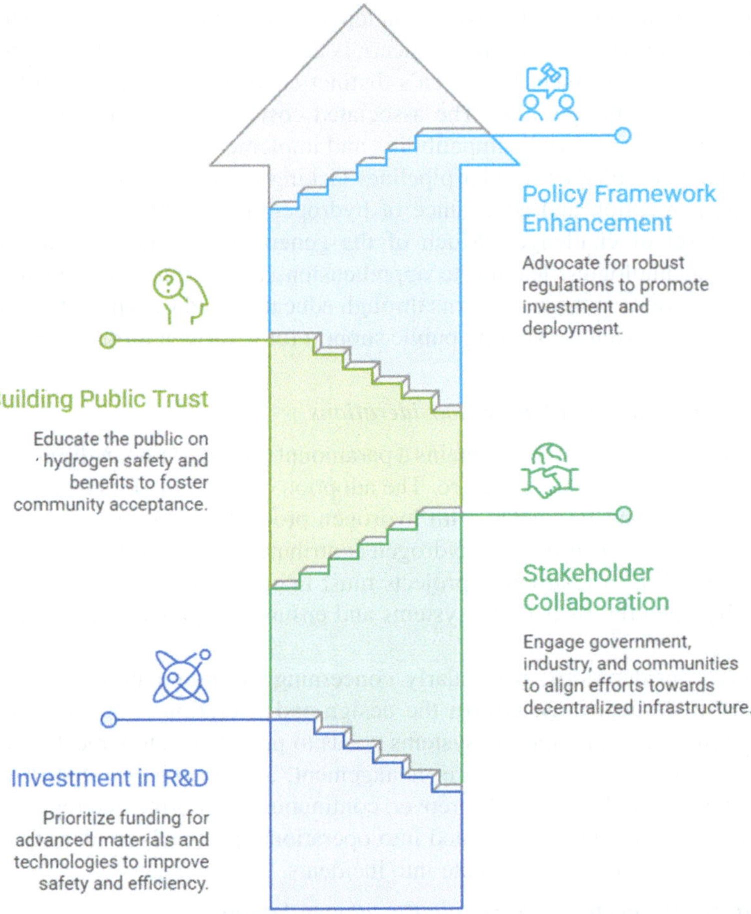

Fig. 16.6 Advancing hydrogen infrastructure

4. **Policy Framework Enhancement**: Advocating for a robust regulatory framework that encompasses safety, environmental, and operational protocols specific to hydrogen infrastructure is essential for promoting investment and deployment.

16.3.1 Advances in Materials and Inspection Technologies

As hydrogen adoption accelerates, the development of advanced materials and inspection technologies is critical for ensuring the safety and integrity of hydrogen pipeline infrastructure. This section discusses the latest trends in material science and innovations in inspection methodologies that are pivotal in addressing the unique challenges posed by hydrogen transportation, emphasizing hydrogen embrittlement, compatibility issues, and the need for reliable monitoring systems.

1. ***Advanced Materials for Hydrogen Pipelines***

One of the foremost trends in engineering hydrogen pipelines is the exploration of new materials that can withstand hydrogen's permeation and embrittlement effects. Recent literature highlights polymeric coatings and composite materials as promising solutions. Yuan et al. discuss various materials, including polymers, metals, ceramics, and composites, while emphasizing the need for evaluating hydrogen barrier performance and compatibility with pipeline activities [28]. The development of high-performance coatings can significantly enhance the longevity of pipeline materials by preventing hydrogen infiltration and reinforcing structural integrity.

Research indicates that advanced pipelines made from hydrogen-resistant alloys, such as nickel and chromium-based alloys, have shown superior resistance to hydrogen embrittlement compared to conventional materials). Innovations in composite materials that incorporate nanotechnology are also emerging, offering enhanced mechanical properties and resistance to chemical degradation under hydrogen exposure. The ability of these materials to maintain performance in high-pressure environments positions them as vital candidates for future hydrogen infrastructure [29].

2. ***Inspection Technologies for Hydrogen Pipelines***

Effective inspection technologies are fundamental for maintaining the safety and integrity of hydrogen pipelines. The adoption of advanced inspection methods, including In-Line Inspection (ILI) technologies such as Magnetic Flux Leakage (MFL), is particularly important. Inspections using MFL tools must account for hydrogen embrittlement, as traditional inspection materials may be vulnerable under hydrogen-rich environments. The ongoing development of ILI tools specifically designed for hydrogen service reflects the industry's commitment to preserving pipeline integrity [30].

The integration of smart monitoring systems that utilize fiber-optic sensors has shown promise in detecting leaks and monitoring pipeline conditions in real-time. These sensors can be embedded within the pipeline material and provide continuous data regarding pressure and temperature fluctuations, helping to identify potential failures before they escalate into serious incidents. As highlighted in the literature, computerized predictive algorithms that integrate IoT technology can significantly enhance the monitoring capabilities of hydrogen infrastructures, leading to more proactive maintenance strategies [31].

3. ***Lifecycle and Compatibility Assessments***

Conducting lifecycle assessments of pipelines, especially those being transitioned from natural gas to hydrogen service, is crucial for understanding long-term performance and sustainability. Khaing and Yin [32] emphasize the importance of lifecycle management approaches that account for materials, environmental impacts, and economic considerations. Such assessments are essential for identifying materials that not only meet safety standards but also minimize long-term maintenance costs.

Compatibility assessments for existing pipeline materials must focus on their performance under various hydrogen concentrations. For example, the blending of hydrogen with natural gas presents distinct challenges that necessitate thorough evaluations of how different ratios impact pipeline integrity. Understanding these interactions helps inform standards and best practices for transitioning existing pipelines to accommodate hydrogen transportation more safely.

16.3.2 Integration with Renewable Energy Systems

The integration of hydrogen pipeline infrastructure with renewable energy systems represents a transformative opportunity in the energy sector, facilitating the transition to decarbonized energy solutions. As renewable energy production, particularly from sources like wind and solar, becomes more prominent, addressing the intermittency of these sources through hydrogen production and storage becomes increasingly relevant.

(a) **Advances in Hydrogen Production from Renewables**

Recent advancements in low-cost hydrogen production methods demonstrate significant potential for coupling hydrogen production with renewable energy systems. Thermochemical cycles utilize solar or biomass energy to drive hydrogen production, reducing reliance on grid electricity and minimizing the environmental footprint [33]. The development of these innovative techniques enhances the economic viability of hydrogen production, especially when paired with renewable energy's variable output.

The Power-to-X (PtX) approach has emerged as a critical strategy for integrating green hydrogen into the energy mix. This concept refers to the conversion of excess renewable energy into hydrogen and subsequently into other energy carriers or chemicals, contributing to sector coupling [34]. The utilization of green hydrogen in this context facilitates energy storage and helps alleviate surplus renewable energy, which is particularly critical during periods of high production and low demand.

(b) **Hydrogen Storage and Transportation Synergies**

Hydrogen energy storage plays a key role in mitigating challenges associated with renewable energy intermittency. By utilizing hydrogen as an energy storage medium, excess energy generated from renewables can be converted and stored, allowing for more reliable energy dispatch when demand peaks. Research highlights the effectiveness of integrating hydrogen storage systems with renewable generation to ensure system flexibility and resilience, offering improved operational outcomes [35]. Moreover, blending hydrogen with natural gas in pipeline networks optimizes existing infrastructure and enhances the decarbonization of the gas sector. Hydrogen-enriched natural gas (HCNG) is increasingly recognized as a practical transitional solution, enabling greater hydrogen utilization without the need for immediate comprehensive infrastructure overhauls for pure hydrogen transport [36]. Infrastructure adaptations should consider the storage, transportation, and blending of hydrogen with other fuels to optimize existing resources while facilitating the transition to greener alternatives.

(c) **Regulatory and Economic Considerations**

The trajectory toward integrating hydrogen with the renewable energy landscape is fraught with regulatory and economic challenges. Governments worldwide must establish comprehensive frameworks that support the development of hydrogen infrastructure while ensuring safety and compliance with energy standards. Streamlined regulations can facilitate investment in hydrogen technologies, making them more economically feasible and attractive to stakeholders.

Investments should focus on long-term strategic planning for hydrogen infrastructure that incorporates flexibility to adapt to future energy demands and technological advancements. Hydrogen production technologies, such as electrolysis powered by renewable energy sources, require supportive policies that promote cleaner alternatives while considering operational costs and efficiency. Understanding national and regional contexts will also help tailor strategies that align with specific renewable energy potentials.

(d) Collaborative Approaches and the Role of Industry

Collaboration among industry players, academia, and policymakers is essential to maximize the benefits of hydrogen integration within renewable systems. Stakeholders must work together to share best practices, build capabilities, and promote research initiatives aimed at identifying optimal hydrogen production methods, storage solutions, and transportation logistics [37]. Engaging local communities and stakeholders in developing hydrogen projects fosters transparency and public trust, which are crucial for the successful implementation of hydrogen technologies. Furthermore, pilot projects that demonstrate the feasibility and benefits of hydrogen integration into existing energy systems serve as valuable learning opportunities for refining strategies and promoting best practices. Successful integrations should be documented and analyzed to inform future initiatives and create scalable models for broader applications.

16.3.3 Policy, Economics, and Market Drivers

The advancement of hydrogen as a viable energy carrier hinges on the interplay of policy frameworks, market dynamics, and economic considerations. As countries work toward reducing greenhouse gas emissions and transitioning to clean energy, hydrogen offers significant opportunities for decarbonization across various sectors. This section discusses the critical policy initiatives, economic factors influencing market development, and the roles of various stakeholders in shaping the hydrogen economy.

(1) **Policy Frameworks and Support Mechanisms**

Robust policy frameworks are essential for promoting hydrogen technologies and facilitating their integration into existing energy systems. Governments worldwide are increasingly enacting policies that support hydrogen production, distribution, and end-use applications. These policies vary from direct financial incentives, such as subsidies and tax credits, to long-term strategies that outline national hydrogen roadmaps. For instance, the European Union has introduced Hydrogen Strategies that encourage research, deployment, and infrastructure investments to catalyze hydrogen market development.

An effective policy framework must also facilitate the establishment of standards and safety regulations specific to hydrogen. Current regulations are largely derived from natural gas protocols, necessitating adaptations to address hydrogen's unique properties. Stakeholders must collaborate to develop comprehensive standards that ensure safety and reliability while promoting innovation in hydrogen technologies.

(2) **Economic Drivers and Market Viability**

The economic viability of hydrogen production and utilization is influenced by multiple factors, including production costs, availability of renewable electricity, and market demand. The Levelized Cost of Hydrogen (LCOH)—which reflects the total cost of producing hydrogen over its lifespan—remains a critical metric for assessing the economic feasibility of hydrogen projects. Producing hydrogen through renewable energy sources, such as electrolysis powered by solar or wind energy, is gaining traction due to its potential for low carbon emissions [37, 38].

The hydrogen economy will benefit from economies of scale as production technologies become more mature and widespread. Investigating large-scale hydrogen production methods such as biomass gasification and steam methane reforming with carbon capture demonstrates potential pathways for more competitive hydrogen pricing. The transition from pilot projects to commercial-scale operations will require significant investment, highlighting the need for public–private partnerships that leverage diverse financing sources.

(3) **Market Dynamics and Global Competitiveness**

The rapid evolution of the hydrogen market is reshaping global energy landscapes. Countries rich in renewable resources, such as Australia and regions within the European Union, are vying to lead in hydrogen production and export. This competition creates opportunities for technology transfer, innovation, and investment among nations, but it also raises concerns about energy security and dependency, particularly as renewable hydrogen production scales up.

Moreover, as countries target net-zero emissions by mid-century, the role of hydrogen in international energy trade is expected to expand significantly. Hydrogen is positioned as a key export commodity that can enhance energy security while contributing to emissions reductions domestically and abroad. Regulatory clarity and trade agreements will be necessary to facilitate these international hydrogen markets, ensuring standardization and mutual recognition of safety protocols [39].

(4) **Investment and Infrastructure Development**

Investment in hydrogen infrastructure is pivotal for realizing its market potential. The deployment of hydrogen pipelines, storage facilities, and refueling stations requires substantial capital expenditures. Various studies indicate that public funding, alongside private investments, is necessary to underwrite these infrastructure projects, particularly given the capital-intensive nature of hydrogen facilities [40, 41]. Countries with supportive policies and investment incentives may exhibit more robust hydrogen infrastructure development, attracting both domestic and international investments.

Innovative funding mechanisms, such as green bonds and transition financing, can attract capital for hydrogen projects by linking investments to environmental impacts and sustainability outcomes. These financing models support stakeholders across the supply chain, from production to end-use, ensuring that the economic viability of hydrogen is linked to broader sustainability goals [42].

References

1. Omoya OA, Papadopoulou KA, Lou E (2019) Reliability engineering application to pipeline design. Int J Qual Reliabil Manag 36(9):1644–1662
2. Liu J et al (2021) Analysis of hydrogen gas injection at various compositions in an existing natural gas pipeline. Front Energy Res 9:685079
3. Khwaja SA, Paul S (2022) Inspection of coated hydrogen transportation pipelines. Appl Sci 12(19):9503
4. Amadhe FO, Anjorin RO, Uwoghiren FO (2024) Advancements in machine learning for pipeline integrity management: a comprehensive review of predictive and optimization techniques. Cogn J Multidiscipl Stud 4(11):129–138
5. Mahmoodzadeh Z et al (2020) Condition-based maintenance with reinforcement learning for dry gas pipeline subject to internal corrosion. Sensors 20(19):5708
6. Cerniauskas S et al (2020) Options of natural gas pipeline reassignment for hydrogen: cost assessment for a Germany case study. Int J Hydrogen Energy 45(21):12095–12107
7. Shi K et al (2021) MXene coatings: novel hydrogen permeation barriers for pipe steels. Nanomaterials 11(10):2737
8. Sun C et al (2019) Insights into the interfacial process in electroless Ni–P coating on supercritical CO_2 transport pipeline as relevant to carbon capture and storage. ACS Appl Mater Interfaces 11(17):16243–16251
9. Khare A, Vishwakarma M, Ahmed S (2019) Combating hydrogen embrittlement with graphene based coatings. Int J Adv Res Eng Technol 10:234–251
10. Deyab M et al (2018) Exploring corrosion protection properties of alkyd@ lanthanide bisphthalocyanine nanocomposite coatings. RSC Adv 8(4):1909–1916
11. Nyrkova L (2020) Stress-corrosion cracking of pipe steel under complex influence of factors. Eng Fail Anal 116:104757
12. Hussain M et al (2021) Application of big data analytics to energy pipeline corrosion management. Corros Manag 2021:28–29
13. Husby H (2025) The effect of CRA oxides on hydrogen permeation under cathodic protection conditions. In: Conference 2025. Association for materials protection and performance.

14. Chang W, et al (2013) Effect of cathodic polarization potential on hydrogen induced stress cracking of duplex stainless steel. In: NACE CORROSION. 2013. NACE
15. Bouadjra BB, Abdelkader M (2018) Optimization of the geometrical parameters of bonded composite wrap for repairing cracked pipelines. Fract Struct Integ 12(46):102–112
16. Amori KE, Hussain MN, Hilal HB (2018) Experimental investigation of pipeline in-service welding process. J Petrol Res Stud 8(1):18–28
17. Rjeb A, et al (2025) Fiber Bragg grating sensors for detecting localized metal loss in composite-sleeved pipelines. In: Optical sensing and precision metrology. SPIE
18. Barilo N, Hamilton J, Weiner SC (2017) First responder training: Supporting commercialization of hydrogen and fuel cell technologies. Int J Hydrogen Energy 42(11):7536–7541
19. Stalker L et al (2022) Communicating leakage risk in the hydrogen economy: lessons already learned from geoenergy industries. Front Energy Res 10:869264
20. Genovese M, Blekhman D, Fragiacomo P (2024) An exploration of safety measures in hydrogen refueling stations: delving into hydrogen equipment and technical performance. Hydrogen 5(1):102–122
21. Simonetto M, Pascoe J-A, Sharpanskykh A (2025) Preliminary safety assessment of a liquid hydrogen storage system for commercial aviation. Safety 11(1):27
22. Abbas AJ et al (2024) Transitioning to a hydrogen economy: exploring the viability of adapting natural gas pipelines for hydrogen transport through a case study on compression vs looping. Gases 4(2):74–96
23. Ghomashchi R (2023) Green energy revolution and substitution of hydrocarbons with hydrogen: distribution network infrastructure materials. Energies 16(24):8020
24. Xie Z et al (2024) A review of hydrogen storage and transportation: progresses and challenges. Energies 17(16):4070
25. Lemieux K, et al (2025) Unusual encounters in medical health physics and nuclear medicine: learning from the unexpected. Health Phys 129(5):351–358
26. Madžarević AR et al (2020) The Fuzzy–AHP synthesis model for energy security assessment of the Serbian natural gas sector. Symmetry 12(6):908
27. Javaheri V (2023) Steel pipeline for the hydrogen storage and delivery: metallurgical viewpoint for finnish ecosystem. Fut Technol 2(1):58–61
28. Li Y, et al (2024) Gap analysis of coating and liner for hydrogen pipeline. In: International pipeline conference. American Society of Mechanical Engineers
29. Hao G, et al (2024) Current status and challenges in the development of hydrogen transmission pipeline technology. In: E3S web of conferences 598:02008. EDP Sciences
30. Morris RD, Barker T (2021) Hydrogen pipeline in-line inspection case study. In: AMPP corrosion 2021. AMPP
31. Vijayakumar V, Jenn A, Fulton L (2021) Low carbon scenario analysis of a hydrogen-based energy transition for on-road transportation in California. Energies 14(21):7163
32. Khaing MM, Yin S (2025) Lifecycle management of hydrogen pipelines: design, maintenance, and rehabilitation strategies for Canada's clean energy transition. Energies 18(2):240
33. Sebastian S, Wijewardane S, Srinivasan S (2023) Recent advances in hydrogen production, storage, and fuel cell technologies with an emphasis on inventions, innovations, and commercialization. Solar Compass 8:100065
34. Cholewa T et al (2022) Process intensification strategies for power-to-X technologies. ChemEngineering 6(1):13
35. García-Miguel PLC et al (2024) Optimal operation and market integration of a hybrid farm with green hydrogen and energy storage: a stochastic approach considering wind and electricity price uncertainties. Sustainability 16(7):2856
36. Marino C, et al (2012) Energetic, economic and environmental sustainability of integrated techniques for energy production in buildings using hydrogen as storage system. RE&PQJ 1(10):1240–1244
37. He Y, et al (2024) Optimization of an SOC green hydrogen production storage and transportation system based on electricity-heat-gas multi-energy coupling. Preprints.

38. Agyekum EB et al (2022) A critical review of renewable hydrogen production methods: factors affecting their scale-up and its role in future energy generation. Membranes 12(2):173
39. Cashel J et al (2025) Chemical bonds containing hydrogen: choices for hydrogen carriers and catalysts. Angew Chem Int Ed 64(21):e202423661
40. Ismail ME (2020) Prevalence of COVID-19 pandemic: a paradigm shift to hydrogen economy. Preprints.
41. Pawłowski A, Żelazna A, Żak J (2023) Is the polish solar-to-hydrogen pathway green? A carbon footprint of AEM electrolysis hydrogen based on an LCA. Energies 16(9):3702
42. Fredershausen S et al (2021) Towards an understanding of hydrogen supply chains: a structured literature review regarding sustainability evaluation. Sustainability 13(21):11652

MIX
Papier aus verantwortungsvollen Quellen
Paper from responsible sources
FSC® C105338
FSC
www.fsc.org

If you have any concerns about our products,
you can contact us on
ProductSafety@springernature.com

In case Publisher is established outside the EU,
the EU authorized representative is:
Springer Nature Customer Service Center GmbH
Europaplatz 3, 69115 Heidelberg, Germany

Printed by Libri Plureos GmbH
in Hamburg, Germany